Mindful of Famine

Harvard University
Center for the Study of World Religions

Religions of the World

Editor: Lawrence E. Sullivan

Cambridge, Massachusetts

Mindful of Famine

Religious Climatology
of the
Warao Indians

Johannes Wilbert

Distributed by Harvard University Press
for the
Harvard University Center for the Study of World Religions

Copyright © 1996 The President and Fellows of Harvard College

All rights reserved
Printed in the United States of America

Publication of this volume was made possible in part by the David Rockefeller Center for Latin American Studies, Harvard University.

Library of Congress Cataloging-in-Publication Data

Mindful of famine : religious climatology of the Warao Indians / Johannes Wilbert.
    p.   cm. — (Religions of the world)
  Includes bibliographical references and index.
  ISBN 0-945454-10-4 (hardcover : alk. paper).
  ISBN 0-945454-11-2 (pbk. : alk. paper)
    1. Warao Indians—Religion. 2. Warao Indians—Rites and ceremonies. 3. Warao Indians—Folklore. 4. Man—Influence of environment—Venezuela—Orinoco River Delta. 5. Weather forecasting—Venezuela—Orinoco River Delta—Folklore. 6. Orinoco River Delta (Venezuela)—Religious life and customs. 7. Orinoco River Delta (Venezuela)—Climate. 8. Orinoco River Delta (Venezuela)—Social conditions. I. Wilbert, Johannes. II. Series.
F2319.2.W3M55 1996
299'.88—dc20   96-32031
                                                                CIP

To the memory of
George Peter Murdock

Foreword

Warao storytellers begin and end the day by narrating dramatic episodes of life-bearing myth at dawn and dusk, when the human community lives at the edge of darkness and light. Johannes Wilbert has listened attentively for over forty years. He has learned the wisdom tradition that allows the Warao to live on the edge: between the Orinoco River and the tidal swamps of its delta; between the dry seasons and the drenched weather that soaks their homeland twice each year; between the contact that acculturates colonial patterns and the isolation that fosters cultural survival; between ecstatic expansion of knowledge by healing shamans and chronic affliction of disease; between communal feast and community famine.

At one point in chapter three, Wilbert recounts calamities that struck the Winikina-Warao community during his first stay with them in 1954. Rains were particularly intense and prolonged; the interim dry season was cut even shorter by the early onset of the second rains. Sorely afflicted and short of food, people suffered physically from bodily afflictions and socially from mounting tensions. Death of the young and able-bodied was the surest symptom that the well-being of the community was unraveling. Wilbert details this disintegration in a moving memorial to the death of Juan, the nineteen-year-old son of the ranking priest-shaman (*wishiratu*) in the subtribe where Wilbert was hosted. Juan had contracted pulmonary tuberculosis months before while working as a wage laborer in the rice fields of Criollos.

Clearly, the young Wilbert was deeply touched by Juan's suffering and death during this first experience with the Warao. In the midst of the *nahanamu* festival held at a neighboring settlement in September, Juan could no longer join in the festivities. Wilbert and the young man's father eased Juan into Wilbert's canoe. Traveling through the cold night, Wilbert brought him on his last journey home. At the time Wilbert also began to suffer an acute strep infection, fever, and headache. He tells us that his own affliction brought Juan's to mind. He gave the dying man his woolen blanket. A bond was formed between the two young men.

In the weeks-long efforts to save him, every mental and moral resource was mobilized: myth, diagnostic techniques, medicine, weather lore, and ritual. There were open debates over the best advice to take and dramatic outbursts of emotion over the failure to save him. Though Juan succumbed, the community dealt with the tragedy of his loss and prevailed. Impressed by the creativity, precision, and abundance of the cultural resources with which the Warao face recurrent physical and social calamity, Wilbert has spent a professional lifetime learning to understand the sources of Warao culture.

From his first experience forward, Wilbert has learned from the Warao to be ever "mindful of famine." In *Mindful of Famine*, he examines how the Warao situate a flourishing human life within the changing weather patterns and precarious ecological systems of their world as well as within the shifting tides of sickness and death which inundate all human communities. He outlines the "weather religion" that is the basis for Warao culture; and he explains the history of beliefs, the operation of practices, and their relationship to one another in a coherent worldview that has responded dramatically to changes over time. At the center of meteorological and social systems are the lives of individual human beings—like Juan, his mother, his father, and his caregivers—with their sufferings, successes, and losses. Wilbert especially acknowledges his debt to key Warao figures like Antonio Lorenzano, Jaime Zapata, and Cesáreo Soto. Through the broad sweep of Wilbert's analysis of systems and history, one never loses sight of the fact that individuals are the seats of wisdom.

Why are the myths and ritual practices life-bearing? Because they bring the human community into fruitful relationship with material resources and the dynamic powers that transform one material form of life into another. The Warao draw life from the world around them. They insert themselves into the fruitful swirl of their ecology at the points where key transformations occur—where one form of life passes into another. Through their knowledge of the metamorphoses that underlie their world, they insinuate their lives into the powers of the rains, the winds, the forest, and the soil. The life-sustaining efficacy of food production, cooking, art, basketry, canoe-making, medicine, chant, dance, and house construction are all predicated on the knowledge of the key transformations that these underlying powers effect. Above all, the practices of weather religion and magic reflect keen knowledge of the creative principle at work in metamorphosis.

Wilbert demonstrates how the *namonina a re* ("transformation stories") comprise an ecological mythology, "a blueprint of interrelationships between humans and their environment which reveals a treasure of adaptive wisdom" invaluable for the preservation of Warao lifeways.

These fantastic accounts reveal relationships that exist among unlikely partners: specific plants, birds, animals, and spirits. They provide the mythic prehistory of current-day forms, illustrating how a particular microenvironment came into existence through a chain of metamorphic events which forever linked together the fate of raw materials, weather patterns, and the particular flora and fauna of a biotope.

Through the *namonina a re* themselves, human life also becomes implicated in the microenvironmental process. That is, human knowledge is efficaciously generated in the telling of the tales. By emplotting the interrelationships, the transformation stories allow human flourishing to graft itself into the environment precisely at the point of the life-giving transformations. On the basis of the wisdom embedded in the stories, ancestral knowledge is transmitted to the present generation, fertile powers are passed from the torrential waters and pollinating winds to the sago flour that feeds human life, and life-threatening foreign pestilences from the four quarters are confronted in the central arena of curing rituals.

One great transformation reflected in Warao weather religion is the upheaval of colonialism. Wilbert argues that intense and prolonged contact with European culture provoked a reformation in Warao thought and practice. In facing the threat of recurrent famine, the Warao absorbed cultural elements from European as well as other Native American cultures and synthesized them into a new meteorological paradigm within a coherent religious cosmology. With a detective's care, Wilbert sifts through the historical evidence of contact with Spanish, Arawak, and Carib cultures to build his case.

This is a new reading of Warao culture. Never before have the constraints of missionization, colonial encroachment, and slave raiding on the Warao been so carefully chronicled. Wilbert takes pains to show how the Warao made their way creatively through the "narrow passages" left open for cultural survival. He traces the effects of contact and constraints on Warao songs, narratives, ritual, and economic practices.

One might say that Wilbert's talents as a fieldworker and interpreter and his dedication and steadfastness to the task over four decades have resulted in the creation of an extraordinary "transformation story" in its own right. In order to get his story straight, Wilbert too is led to recognize unlikely juxtapositions and fantastic relationships. Above all, in Wilbert's narrative one finds the surprising coexistence of features from diverse meteorological paradigms, some from missionary scientists or colonials and others from neighboring tribes. From enemies and from allies the Warao have drawn elements from diverse worldviews and shuffled them together to form distinctly new understandings. Wilbert also achieves unlikely combinations, bringing together his research in cultural history, field anthropology, ecological studies, meteorology, comparative mythology, and the history of missions.

Wilbert introduces us to the pantheon of powers who govern the elements, the directions, and the forces that affect life through the weather. Above all, he conveys to us the knowledge and perspective of the two principal managers of weather: the rainmaker and the windmaker. The rainmaker is a shaman patronized by Tuyuna, the thunderbird of the trade winds that drive the monsoons from the south. Rainmakers are usually mature men whose means are sufficient to underwrite the instruction and initiation they must undergo. Though meek in demeanor, rainmakers invoke the powers of their double, the shrill sun bittern, to call forth thunderstorms that destroy life. The windmaker need undergo no ritual initiation. He is an instrumentalist, a practiced virtuoso on the *isimoi*, a sacred trumpet (more exactly, a clarinet). The windmaker imitates the mating sounds of his double, the heron. In doing so he invokes Hia, the Wind Father of the northern trade winds. Channelled through the transforming trumpet, the windmaker's breath becomes a creative cosmic wind that induces the sago deity to sustain life. Even the great ancestral gods at the cardinal directions depend on the windmaker's breath for life. These two ritual meteorological experts play key roles in surplus food procurement and storage. Through depictions of their dreams, activities, and education, Wilbert helps us understand the psychology of these two important cultural actors, as well as their place in the community and their knowledge of the material and social universe they affect.

Wilbert shows us how the myriad beliefs and practices that the Warao have preserved, created, or borrowed throughout history are woven together into coherent patterns. He offers evidence for postulating a close parallel relationship between the structures of the pantheon, guilds, initiatory brotherhoods, patterns of authority, and ritual designs of the Spanish and the Warao. Above all, the order and beauty of these complex orchestrations of difference come clearest in the great ritual moments. The recurrent sounding of the sacred trumpet during the sago harvest ritual, for instance, punctuates the rhythms of the days-long festival. The processions of ranked participants, the arrangements of offerings and foods, the careful regard for stylized sounds and silence, the ritual distributions, the underlying mythologies, and overarching theologies of the

Foreword

festival show how the Warao have compelled the diverse clouds of history into a manifest ritual order recognizably their own. Through their weather lore and their religious practice of it, they have inserted themselves at the creative center, between life-threatening calamities and life-sustaining transformations. Though ever mindful of famine and disaster, they have strived for much more than a life of bare survival without ornament, and achieved a lustrous religious life, rich with creative embellishments.

I am grateful to Johannes Wilbert for bringing this volume to the "Religions of the World" series, which publishes multiple disciplinary approaches to the full range of religious expressions: in art, medicine, law, literature, music, literature, liturgy, economy, and cosmological sciences. I wish to acknowledge with gratitude support from the David Rockefeller Center for Latin American Studies and its director John Coatsworth. Special thanks go to Kathryn Dodgson for her editorship of this volume and her management of publications at the Harvard University Center for the Study of World Religions.

Lawrence E. Sullivan, Director
Harvard University Center
for the Study of World Religions

Contents

List of Illustrations
Preface

Chapter 1	Land and Weather	3
	The Land	3
	The Weather	8
Chapter 2	Narrow Passages	23
	Pre-Columbian Invaders	23
	Warrior Cannibals	25
	Slave Raiders	27
	Colonial Missionaries	29
	Old World Pestilence	40
	Forced Labor and Servitude	45
	Postcolonial Missions	46
	Contemporary Survivors	50
Chapter 3	Warao Weather Lore	71
	Polluting Rain	71
	The Rainmaker	93
	Dying in the Rain	115
	Pollinating Wind	130
	The Windmaker	146
Chapter 4	South American Weather Lore	161
	Weather Practitioners	164
	Blowing against the Wind	167
	Chanting to the Rain	174
	Dancing away the Clouds	176
	Combative Responses	180
	Homeopathic Magic	190
	Rulers of the Elements	199
	South American Heritage	222

Chapter 5	Recasting Weather Religion	225
	Colonial Pattern	225
	The Warao Analogue	235
	Colonial Pattern and Warao Analogue	241
	Syncretistic Renewal	243
Chapter 6	Mindful of Famine	249
	Hunger's Dragging Loincloth	250
	Natural Cause of Food Uncertainty	251
	Anger and Fear	252
	Anticipatory Preventive	255

Appendix 261
Glossary of Warao Words 273
Bibliography 277
Index 325

Illustrations

Figures

Fig. 1.1.	Average annual distribution of rainfall for various sections of the Orinoco Delta and Guyana. Annual totals in mm. (Drawing by Amalie Orme)	10
Fig. 1.2.	Annual distribution of rainfall for five regions of Warao habitat (Orinoco Delta and Guyana). Ordinate values in mm/100, annual totals in mm. Venezuelan data based on period 1971–80. (Drawing by Amalie Orme)	11
Fig. 1.3.	Mean monthly and mean annual rainfall (mm), 1970–80, for the Winikina; annual availability of moriche sago and fruit, San José de Yaruara. (Drawing by Amalie Orme)	15
Fig. 1.4.	The sea and land breezes. (Drawing by Chase Langford)	16
Fig. 1.5.	Northern Hadley cell. (Drawing by Amalie Orme)	18
Fig. 1.6.	Orinoco regimen at Ciudad Bolívar: monthly mean levels, maxima, and minima at monthly intervals. (After Marrero 1964, 122; drawing by Amalie Orme)	20
Fig. 2.1.	Warao ethnopathology and epidemic disease. (Drawing by Noel Diaz)	62
Fig. 3.1.	The eight Lords of Rain and their stations. (Drawing by Noel Diaz)	74
Fig. 3.2.	Wind rose, Güiria, Gulf of Paria, Wind data for period 1951–70. (Drawing by Noel Diaz)	77
Fig. 3.3.	Dueling combat shield. (Drawing by Helga Adibi)	131

Fig. 3.4.	Moriche sago hoe. (Drawing by Helga Adibi)	140
Fig. 3.5.	Temple with enclosed upper compartment, where sacred paraphernalia are kept, and lower compartment (shown half-open), where the sago container is stored. (Drawing by José Luis Ulibarrena)	145
Fig. 3.6.	Cross section of the sacred trumpet. (Drawing by Helga Adibi)	148
Fig. 3.7.	The sacred trumpet. (Drawing by Helga Adibi)	148
Fig. 3.8.	Festively decorated sacred trumpet. (Drawing by Helga Adibi)	150
Fig. 3.9.	Deer-bone flute. (Drawing by Helga Adibi)	152
Fig. 3.10.	Daunona images. (Drawing by Helga Adibi)	156
Fig. 3.11.	Tuba-shaped carrying basket formerly used to transport human bones. (Drawing by Helga Adibi)	159
Fig. 4.1.	Bororo meteor conjuring. (Von den Steinen 1894, plate 30)	173
Fig. 4.2.	Selknam weather ceremony. (Gusinde 1931, fig. 88)	183
Fig. 4.3a, b.	Carajá devices of rain magic. (Krause 1911:33, figs. 182a, b)	189
Fig. 4.4.	Inca rain ceremony. (Pompa de Ayala 1936)	195
Fig. 4.5.	Shipaya fish demon, Master of Lightning. (Nimuendajú 1919–20)	204

Plates

Plate 2.1.	Demonstrating ancient method of fish gorge angling. Live bait is tied to end of fishing line on rod. Small backwater fish bite and are flipped into basket before they can let go of bait. Gorge works less well in rivers with larger species of fish and was replaced by iron fishhook. (Photograph Johannes Wilbert)	53
Plate 2.2.	River fishing required adoption of iron-tipped composite harpoon. Bait is held dangling from stick, close to water's surface, while harpoon is held on the ready. (Courtesy Lucy Millowitsch)	54

List of Illustrations xvii

Plate 2.3.	Sago flat cakes being baked, using bottom of traded casserole-type iron pot, in camp of provisional rectangular huts built to celebrate sago festival (1954). (Photograph Johannes Wilbert)	55
Plate 2.4.	Woman removing taro roots, brought home from garden, from folded-leaf basket. Taro and horticulture are relatively recent acquisitions of the Warao, introducing global culture change. Weather shamanism becomes obsolete because of this change in food economy. (Courtesy Peter T. Furst)	56
Plate 2.5.	River frontage village of pile dwellings housing semi-sedentary endogamous band. Three or four such villages constitute an endogamous subtribe of 200 to 300 people. Political leadership of villages and subtribes is more accentuated than in nonagricultural times. (Courtesy Peter T. Furst)	58
Plate 2.6.	Interior view of large pile dwelling sheltering three nuclear families of uxorilocal extended family. Houses like this belong to wife of founder couple. Observance of avoidance taboo vis-à-vis in-laws of either sex requires interpersonal communication to flow from the male founder through his wife and his daughters to their husbands. (Courtesy Peter T. Furst)	59
Plate 2.7.	Mealtime for women and children in kitchen house. Men eat in separate group. (Photograph Johannes Wilbert)	60
Plate 2.8.	Nuclear polygynous family returning from the garden. Dugout canoes of all sizes below 12 meters are used for daily chores. Canoes 12 meters and over, once used for overseas trading, are built by shamanic craftsmen in complex ritual procedure. (Courtesy Lucy Millowitsch)	61

Plate 2.9. Shaman curing woman through massaging and magical blowing of ailing body part. Pathogens are sucked out and blown away to remote part of forest. Despite access to Western health facilities, Warao shamanism continues to be fully functional; with increased mobility due to outboard motors, however, Warao now frequently consult Western health personnel. (Courtesy P. J. Ziegenaus) 64

Plate 2.10. Preparatory to sago festival, player of sacred trumpet leads men in a counter-clockwise circle dance. Woman has entered circle where she jumps up and down with locked feet, fixing gaze on sacred central pole. On other side of pole, partner steps sideways, swinging sacred rattle. Sago rite connects living with dead and propitiates "Grandfather" deities to protect the children from dying during rainy season. (Courtesy Sociedad de Ciencias Naturales La Salle, Caracas) 65

Plate 2.11. Early morning during sago festival (1954). Three baskets containing sago offering stand in middle of dancing platform constructed of moriche bark strips. Sets of large and small sacred trumpets and rattles rest near the central pole. Large "rattle of ruffled feathers" is sacrosanct instrument used on festive occasions. (Photograph Johannes Wilbert) 66

Plate 2.12. Primary and secondary burials of priest-shamans are miniature houses with walls of palm fronds lacking doors or windows. (Photograph Johannes Wilbert) 67

Plate 3.1. Sun bittern. Warao Thunderbird of the Netherworld. Father of Southern Trade Winds and Master of Solstitial Rains, Sun Bittern is the ally of the rain shaman. (Painting by Walter Arp. Arp 1980:133. Courtesy Fundación La Salle de Ciencias Naturales, Caracas) 84

List of Illustrations xix

Plate 3.2.	Rebuking a rainstorm. Warao rain shaman sitting on edge of pile dwelling, blowing against coming storm. (Courtesy Sociedad de Ciencias Naturales La Salle, Caracas)	95
Plate 3.3.	Juan's primary burial made from hollowed-out tree. Coffin is wrapped in temiche palm fronds and covered with layer of clay. Clay cover serves as trap for sorcerer, who is believed to visit grave of victim to suck blood from corpse. (Photograph Johannes Wilbert)	128
Plate 3.4.	Ritual shield fight. (Courtesy Sociedad de Ciencias Naturales La Salle, Caracas)	133
Plate 3.5.	Moriche palm (*Mauritia flexuosa*). "Tree of Life" of Warao and centerpiece of weather shamanism. (Photograph Johannes Wilbert)	138
Plate 3.6.	Man using moriche hoe to chop pith of moriche palm, while woman kneads pith to leach out sago. (Courtesy P. J. Ziegenaus)	140
Plate 3.7.	Women collecting chopped pith of moriche palm. (Courtesy Peter T. Furst)	142
Plate 4.1.	Selknam weather ceremony (Gusinde 1931, plate 37, photo 91). (Courtesy Anthropos Institut)	181
Plate 4.2.	Selknam weather ceremony (Gusinde 1931, plate 37, photo 92). (Courtesy Anthropos Institut)	182
Plate 4.3.	Tapirapé thunder ceremony. Shaman in nicotine trance challenges Thunder. (Courtesy Charles Wagley)	188

Maps

Map 1.1.	The Orinoco Delta and its major drainage canals (*caños*). (Drawing by Noel Diaz)	4
Map 1.2.	Warao settlement distribution (1932–34). Based on aerial photography. (Drawing by Amalie Orme, based on original draft by Douglas L. Holker)	6

Map 1.3. Annual distribution of rainfall in five regions of the Warao habitat (Orinoco Delta and Guyana). Ordinate values in mm/100, annual totals in mm. Delta data are based on the period 1971–80. (Drawing by Chase Langford)   12

Map 2.1. Principal traffic routes of Caribs in northern South America. (After Civrieux 1976:8bis; drawing by Chase Langford)   38

Map 4.1. Comparative South American weather lore. (Drawing by Chase Langford)   162

Map A.1. Colonial missions of Cumaná and Guayana. (Based on Carrocera 1968[1]:404–5 and Nectario María 1924; Drawing by Chase Langford)   263

Tables

Table 1.1.	Annual distribution of rainfall for five regions of Warao habitat (Orinoco Delta and West-Coastal Fringe of Guyana)	12
Table 3.1.	Warao Lords of Rain, their ranks, and locations	76
Table 3.2.	Relationship of rain lord ranking and wind condition	77
Table 5.1.	Colonial pattern and Warao analogue	241
Table A.1.	Warao only missions (Cumaná)	264
Table A.2.	Mixed Warao missions (Cumaná)	266
Table A.3.	Warao only missions (Guayana)	268
Table A.4.	Mixed Warao missions (Guayana)	268
Table A.5.	Warao settlements outside the Cumaná and Guayana missions	270

Preface

On a 1975 visit to the Orinoco Delta in Venezuela, I learned that the Warao Indians adhere to a complex form of weather religion centered on their rain shaman and their player of the sacred trumpet. Although I had earlier known about both practitioners and had then gathered a substantial body of ethnographic information on them, it was not until my visit in the 1970s that I fully realized the importance of these offices to Warao religion and the significance of their role in converting a climatologically adverse region into a habitat viable for human occupation. In this study, against the background of general weather lore, I describe the two religious practitioners whose offices serve to disarm the elements.

The rainmaker, holder of the first office, is magically empowered by the purported relationship between his practice and the climatically conditioned natural production of palm sago, traditionally the Warao's staple food. He also channels the anger generated by environmental stress and food deprivation away from animosity and violence into goodwill and congenial comportment. By fomenting a highly valued spirit of cooperation and altruistic demeanor among the members of his group, he seeks to prevent cultural disruption and social disintegration, attendant upon the famine syndrome and likely to aggravate seasonal hunger and to precipitate starvation.

The second officeholder, the player of the sacred trumpet, is a windmaker. Serving the guardian spirit of the instrument, he is in charge of the ritual production of palm sago, the substance that vitalizes the ancestral spirits, guarantees health and longevity for his people, and, most practical, provides the essential emergency rations in times of want.

The offices of rainmaker and windmaker complement and reinforce each other. To the Warao the two specialists were so important that human survival in the Orinoco Delta came to depend upon the successful implementation, year after year, of the mandates assigned to them.

Throughout their protracted residence on the threshold of the South American continent, the Warao have repeatedly been exposed to existential dangers. Some of the most threatening incidents (see chapter 2) demonstrate the extent to which the Orinoco Delta has functioned as a sanctuary for its beleaguered residents. Furthermore, accounts of such perilous events reveal the challenges these threats have posed to adaptive development and human survival in a marginal land. Negotiating such hurdles meant more than fire walks that, though terrifying and even scarring, would nevertheless have left the people and their culture essentially unchanged. Instead, the trials along the Warao's historic path emerge as what Hill (1988, 7) calls "narrow historical passages," which the Warao, like other contemporary small-scale societies, have successfully cleared, but not without experiencing their culture-modifying power. Absorbing such external forces by means of internally operative buffers of stability and by passing them through a number of sociocultural filters, Warao culture assimilated these outside impulses, repeatedly recreating itself in the process (Ortner 1984, 158–59). Scrutiny of some of the more treacherous cataracts of Warao history revealed the colonial frontier in general and the colonial missions in particular as dynamic agents of change that have left their imprint on Warao life. Together with other unsettling pre- and postcontact traumas, such untoward experiences have become fixtures of the people's historical consciousness and are reflected in their traditional lore, including their weather religion.

My description of the extreme weather conditions in the Orinoco Delta (see chapter 1) makes it clear that, rather than on passive endurance, adaptation to the deltaic environment depended on the ability of its inhabitants to create appropriate coping mechanisms to loosen the weather's grip on their existence. One such mechanism was the development of a religious climatology and a body of ritual practices designed, in part, to give humans manipulative power over weather denizens and other supernaturals. A large portion of this book (chapter 3) is dedicated to describing this strategy. A second coping mechanism was to borrow, from the ethnically pluralistic and multicultural colonial frontier, certain concepts and practices that enabled the Warao to stave off hunger and starvation. Consequently, some aspects of Warao weather religion have a non-Warao indigenous derivation, whereas others reveal either a European origin or a mixture of both indigenous and European.

In chapter 4 of this book I present a comprehensive, albeit not exhaustive, survey of South American climatological lore. My primary objective here is to place Warao weather religion into a continental context and to root its autochthonous components in a New World matrix of traditional beliefs. My secondary objective is to isolate the foreign elements of Warao weather religion and expose them as cultural borrowings. Rather than consider uncharacteristic traits as possibly local inventions, I chose to search for Mesoamerican and North American, as well as Asian, African, and European, parallels. I included Asia because sizable contingents of indentured laborers had been brought from India, China, and Indonesia to the Guianas, where they came into contact with refugee Warao living in the colonies. An inquiry into West African cultures seemed to be indicated because of the presence of African slaves and Bush Negroes in regions adjacent to areas of Warao occupation. The inclusion of Europe was appropriate because of the influence the colonial frontier might have exerted on Warao weather practices. To be sure, ethnologists (including myself) have heretofore practically ignored the potential effect of frontier life on Warao culture. Because of their isolation in the Orinoco Delta, it has usually been assumed that the Warao were only negligibly affected by events in colonial times. Even the presence, ever since 1925, of Capuchin missionaries in the Orinoco Delta has been deemed too recent to have had any significant impact on Warao religion.

The comparative search revealed that present-day Warao weather lore did indeed borrow mythological, linguistic, and economic elements from Arawak and Carib mission Indians (see chapter 5). But earlier allusions to a possible Mesoamerican origin of certain features of the Warao rain-gods complex (Wilbert 1993, 234) have proven too tangential to answer the central question concerning the etiologies of foreign elements in Warao weather religion. Together with interesting similarities that exist between weather beliefs and practices of the Warao and the Juracán complex of ancient and contemporary Maya, they appear, rather, to reflect the existence of a common substratum underlying cultures native to the West Indies and the Caribbean rim (Preuss 1986). The comparative discussion of South American weather lore hints at mythological relationships between American and Asian thunderbird motifs. And the examination of early Asiatic and European guilds, for example, has yielded important insights into the Spanish colonial institutions of brotherhoods and gremios of professional craftsmen (shipwrights) and musicians (e.g., player of the sacred trumpet) among the Warao. African cultural comparisons have failed to produce significant results. In the end, it was only after brushing aside the preconceived notion of the Warao's supposedly hermetic isolation in the tribal zone of eastern Venezuela that it became possible to answer more concretely the etiological query of their unconventional weather practices and beliefs. The results of this revisionary probe (chapter 2 and appendix) should dispel any doubts that European (i.e., Spanish)-Warao exchange was demographically significant, historically protracted, and culturally intensive enough—particularly in the late eighteenth and the early nineteenth centuries—to have exercised a powerful and lasting acculturative influence on Warao society.

The separation, for analytical purposes, of South American from European cultural elements in Warao weather religion, in addition to a comprehensive exposition of autochthonous lore, required close examination of Spanish mission culture in colonial times. This analysis permitted the identification of non-American elements of Warao weather religion as assimilated traits of European derivation (chapter 5). It is my hypothesis, then, that the adoption of cultural elements from other Native Americans, Spaniards, and Criollos of the colonial frontier has provoked a reformation of Warao religious climatology, sharply enhancing its function as an adaptive coping mechanism and improving the Warao's chances of survival in the atmospheric conditions of their homeland. More specifically, survival required the Warao to overcome the menace of seasonal hunger and recurrent famine owing to the exigencies of the weather in the Orinoco Delta (see chapter 6). In this sense, Warao weather religion exemplifies an effective means of hunger control, which, through the promotion of appropriate adaptive behavior, neutralizes the psychological and sociocultural symptoms of the famine syndrome. The present study seeks to acknowledge this remarkable accomplishment of human adaptability and to demonstrate, by way of connecting the scattered particulars of traditional weather lore into a single whole, the cohering paradigm of Warao ethnometeorology.

As most of my field data were collected from the Warao of the central Orinoco Delta, much of what is said here about rain shamans and rain lords or about players of sacred trumpets and sago rituals pertains primarily to the Winikina and by extension to the Arawabisi and the Mariusa subgroups of that region with whom the Winikina are interrelated. Thus, although I refer broadly in this book to weather-associated beliefs and practices of the Warao in general, it remains uncertain as to what extent this knowledge can be extended to the society as a whole. With regard to the general mythological background of the study, however, my longtime native field assistant, the late Cesáreo Soto, collected weather-related narratives from several subgroups of southeastern Warao. Some of this material as well as myths collected by other investigators was included in this study to gain a broader Warao perspective. I have taken sections of my manuscript back to Waraoland in order to discuss both content and exposition with my principal Winikina informant, the late Jaime Zapata, who was both rain shaman and sacred trumpet player, and with knowledgeable men from the middle Arawabisi and from the Nabasanuka. Much of my understanding of Warao culture grew out of focused conversations with Antonio Lorenzano, headman of a Winikina settlement and wise interpreter of his native traditions.

Library research on South American weather lore was conducted by myself and by then doctoral students Diane Adams, Sylvia Balzano, and Gabriele Kohpahl, of the UCLA Anthropology Department. We consulted 1,473 sources in the UCLA Research Library, off-campus libraries via interlibrary loan services, and the Human Relations Area Files. The probe yielded useful weather lore on 128 groups of South American Indians. The diligence, ethnographic expertise, and linguistic capability of the three student researchers are herewith recognized and gratefully acknowledged.

Finally, I acknowledge my indebtedness to the late Dr. Gerardo Reichel-Dolmatoff, longtime friend and colleague, for many extended conversations on Warao weather lore and for his comments on parts of the manuscript. Dr. George L. Siscoe of the UCLA Department of Atmospheric Sciences introduced me to the wonders of his discipline. Through conversations, library assistance, and exposure to faculty and students, he furthered my research in a most effective way. Dr. José Luis Méndez-Arocha, Caracas, made a special effort to produce the climatological data of the Orinoco Delta; Colonel Jesús René Ortega Hernandez, Chief of Meteorological Services, Ministry of Defense, Maracay, Venezuela, kindly confirmed the correctness of the wind rose data in the *Atlas de Venezuela*; Dr. Thomas R. Howell and Dr. James Northern of the UCLA Biology Department fielded many questions about the relevant avifauna mentioned in the study. Helpful as always, Director Edwin C. Krupp of the Griffith Observatory, Los Angeles, had the kindness to calculate for my benefit the timetables of the courses of certain constellations over the Orinoco Delta. Thanks are due also to an anonymous reader for constructive criticism of the original manuscript and for many helpful suggestions. Jill Silton researched some aspects of the climatological conditions related to Warao weather shamanism and provided the computer graphics of precipitation curves. Nina Moss and Sujata Duggal-Landon kindly assisted with the word-processing chores of the first draft. I am deeply indebted to Grace H. Stimson for editing the manuscript with professional skill and keenness of perception. A special word of appreciation and respect is due Kathryn Dodgson, the Center for the Study of World Religion's editor and director of production. Her high level of expertise has greatly enhanced the editorial quality and professional design of the book.

I am grateful to the Capuchin missionaries who offered me their friendship and logistic support. Work in the Orinoco Delta would have been much more difficult without their help. Throughout most of my professional career I have been fortunate in having the active support and intellectual inspiration of the late Dr. Franklin D. Murphy, former Chancellor of the University of California, Los Angeles. No words can adequately express my respect for and my appreciation of this generous benefactor of the humanities and the social sciences. Financial support for fieldwork and library research was generously provided by the Ahmanson Foundation.

This book is dedicated to the memory of former Yale professor George Peter Murdock who encouraged me to study the Warao and who supported my application for a grant from the Wenner-Gren Foundation to conduct my initial fieldwork in the Orinoco Delta. For this and for his teaching and guidance during the formative years of my career, I feel lastingly indebted to this towering scholar.

To all my Indian and non-Indian collaborators and supporters, I express my heartfelt thanks.

Los Angeles, summer 1995

Mindful of Famine

Chapter One

Land and Weather

The Land

Contemporary Indian societies of South America are often concentrated in regions difficult to reach or unattractive to potential intruders. In Venezuela, environments such as arid lands, rugged mountains, jungles, and mangrove swamps have served as refuges for a number of aboriginal populations, especially along the country's borders. In those areas the Indians have weathered the demographic and cultural upheaval that has marked the postconquest era. And although the turbulence has not left the refugees entirely unscathed, neither has it led to their physical extinction or to their cultural demise.

The seclusion provided by natural barriers was not the only factor guaranteeing the continuance of indigenous life. Equally crucial for survival were the strategies adopted by the Indians to maximize the limited resources in their retreats and to adapt on a continuing basis to internal and external pressures of culture change. Most of the approximately twenty-seven tribal groups in Venezuela, enjoying the dual advantage of relative seclusion and adaptation, have overcome the odds against physical and/or cultural extinction. One such group is the Warao of eastern Venezuela who, numbering approximately 29,000, constitute the second-largest Indian society in that country. The overwhelming majority of Warao live in the state of Delta Amacuro and in the delta proper. Several thousand inhabit the surrounding states of Bolívar, Monagas, and Sucre as well as the coastland of Guyana (Butt 1965, 75; Edwards and Charette 1980, 4). In earlier times the tribal territory extended into Surinam, but there the Warao have now become extinct (Kloos 1972, 348). Thus, the Orinoco Delta (lat. 8°30'–10°N, long. 60°40'–62°30'W), having sheltered its repeatedly beleaguered inhabitants in a natural sanctuary, is the nuclear homeland of the Warao.

One natural feature of the Orinoco Delta which has ensured seclusion for its inhabitants in premodern times is the labyrinthine character of its river system (map 1.1). Bounded on the south by the Rio Grande and on the west by the Manamo River, the delta is a fan-shaped area of alluvial deposits measuring approximately 23,700 square kilometers (Heinen and Caballero Arias 1992, 6). The Manamo branches off the main river (Rio Grande) at Barrancas, the apex (5.2 m) of the triangle. Barrancas is about 270 kilometers up

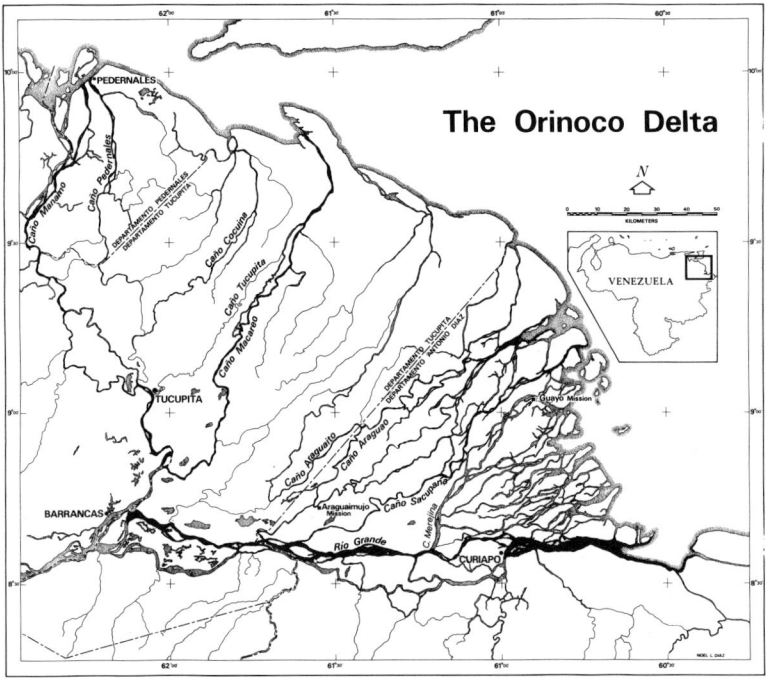

MAP 1.1
The Orinoco Delta and its major drainage canals (*caños*).
(Drawing by Noel Diaz)

the Rio Grande from the Atlantic Ocean and approximately 240 kilometers up the Manamo from the Caribbean Sea. The water of the Orinoco is carried through the delta by the Rio Grande and through nine so-called *caños*, which include the Manamo.

Navigating the major branches in and out of the delta requires no unusual skills, but in the maze of crisscrossing streams connecting the distributaries, an uninitiated intruder may easily go astray. The web of waterways becomes especially complex in the coastal belt, where one's geographic orientation is further challenged by the twice-daily tidal shifts in the currents of all the streams. The interconnecting waterways partition the alluvial plain of the delta into a scattering of irregularly sized islands, flat near the coast but saucerlike, with raised rims and sunken centers, farther inland. The Warao have traditionally made their homes on these low-lying islands of the lower delta, where "low-lying" means inundated land and waterlogged soil (map 1.2).[1] The swamps were thus a second natural safety feature that has offered sanctuary to the Warao by discouraging intruders.

The Geographic Zones

A closer look at the geography of the Orinoco Delta reveals the character of its natural barriers and identifies other impediments facing uninitiated interlopers.

The littoral zone:—Within the delta's lower region are two subparallel belts, the littoral zone and the intermediate zone (map 1.2). The former, closer to the 275-kilometer-long coastal arch, is permanently flooded by tidal water and excessive rainfall. As many of the swamp streams that drain this littoral strip (10 to 30 km wide) are not connected with the upland rivers, they carry rich humic acids. These so-called blackwater streams, which are devoid of mineralogenous matter, flow over a peaty and clayey base unrestrained by insular levees. The upper layer in the coastal zone consists of soft, humid clay (30 to 50 cm thick) which makes

---

[1] A "blind spot" in the southwestern sector of the map due to incomplete photographic documentation does not affect the argument of general settlement distribution proposed in the study.

walking across the swamp difficult and exhausting, even for natives. The elongated, low sand ridges running subparallel to or diverging from the coastline do, however, make the traverse easier. These sandy hummocks, or cheniers, covered with shrubby vegetation, offer a dry resting place not only to humans crossing the mud flats but also to land animals in search of higher ground.

The delta's complicated water system and its swamps are complemented by a third natural feature that has provided protection from invasion: the impenetrable mangrove belts that stabilize the coastline and encircle the islands exposed to strong tidal influences. Thus the islands behind the mangrove bulwark either are covered entirely by 20-meter-high mixed swamp forest, as in the south-

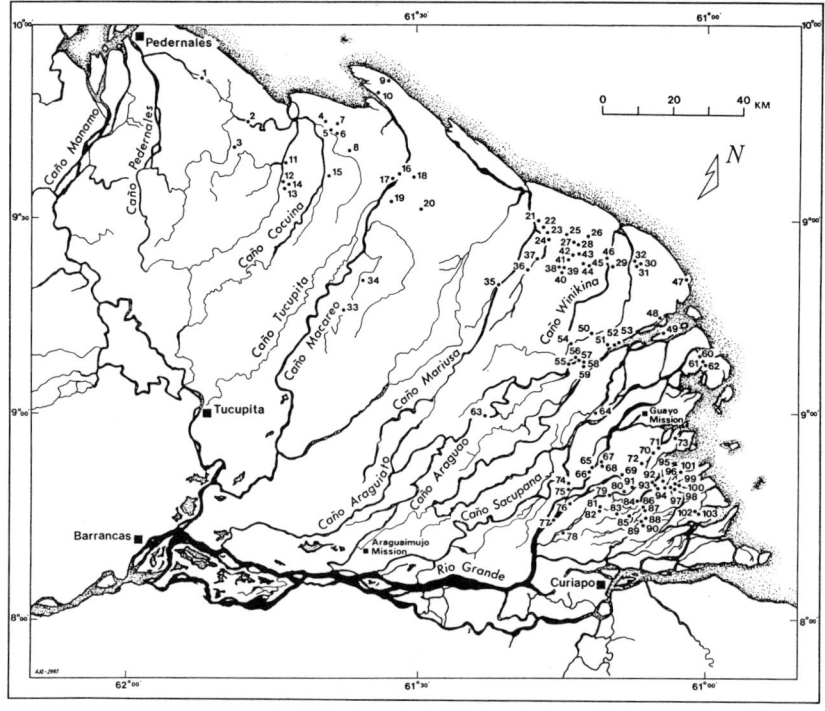

MAP 1.2
Warao settlement distribution (1932–34). Based on aerial photography. (Drawing by Amalie Orme, based on original draft by Douglas L. Holker)

eastern delta, or have several concentric bands of trees such as *sangrito* (*Pterocarpus officinalis*) and *paramanzillo* (*Symphonia globulifera*) with plank roots and superficial rooting. Most important for humans frequenting the littoral zone are clusters of moriche (*Mauritia flexuosa*) and temiche *(Manicaria saccifera)* palms growing on the islands. They are significant as sources of both food and critical raw materials.

The intermediate zone:—Inland from the littoral zone is the 40- to 80-kilometer-wide intermediate zone, which is also subject to tidal action (map 1.2). Although never permanently inundated by the sea, the area does suffer seasonal flooding, especially along its southern and western borders. Natural levees protect the middle courses of major drainage rivers, such as the Macareo, the Araguao, and the Sacupana, but levee building is minimal and irregular in this region. Penetration of the intermediate zone on foot is also impeded by low-lying, featureless, and frequently peaty and clayey marshes and backswamps. Bucare (*Erythrina glauca*) forests, palm swamps, and herbaceous swamps flourish on the island plains. Palm swamps support an open, bushlike vegetation and palm groves of moriche, temiche, and manaca (*Euterpe* sp.) in their permanently waterlogged soil. Herbaceous swamplands are even less inviting to the uninitiated than palm groves, as the soil of humic clay and very soft peat is quasi-permanently inundated. The vegetation, including ferns, sedges, shrubs, stunted trees, moriche palms, and floating grasses, is sparsely distributed.

The prelittoral zone:—Farther inland from the intermediate zone is the roughly triangular prelittoral zone of the upper delta (map 1.2). Completely fluvial, it is more easily accessible by river transport than the lower delta. Its Orinoco-connected distributaries, carrying suspended sediments, are known as brown water rivers. They are bordered by sand levees 3 to 4 meters high. Beyond the levees is a stretch of sandy loam 100 to 200 meters wide. Farther away from the rivers, the loam becomes silty, grading into clay, peaty clay, and, in the backswamps, into peat. Circumventing the permanently inundated lowest parts of the backswamps would not be altogether impossible for an intruder. Seasonally, however, the backwater swamps and the soil of the entire zone, except for levee crests, are almost completely covered by floodwater in regional deluges. During the primary dry season of the year, stretches of clay along the outer margins of the levees remain dry, giving them the appearance of 10- to 20-kilometer-wide floodplains. Point bars are frequently seen in the prelittoral zone, and oxbow lakes and silted-up channels are common throughout the levee system. Now the area is almost completely denuded of forest, but originally the levees were covered by rain forest, and the 15-meter-high bucare forests on the backswamps were interspersed with stands of moriche and manaca palms with heavy undergrowth (Müller 1956, 1959, 4–6; van Andel 1956, 1967; van Andel and Sachs 1964, 44–45; Vila 1960, 355–56; Voorde 1962; Wilbert 1979, 129–33).

The Weather

The Seasons

The annual mean temperature in the Orinoco Delta, lying well within the tropics, reaches a high of twenty-six degrees centigrade. Its diurnal temperature range is above the yearly average,[2] and its annual temperature range is less than five degrees centigrade. The seasons in the delta are therefore determined, not by small variations in annual temperature, but on the basis of rainfall, which fluctuates throughout the year (Snow 1976, 295–96, 322).

Orinoco Delta seasons are caused by the meandering, northward and southward, of the equatorial trough. The centerline of this broad and relatively low-pressure belt between the subtropical highs of the hemisphere is known as the intertropical convergence zone. The presence of the equatorial trough over the delta causes a wet season; its absence produces a dry season. In its northernmost position, the centerline of the equatorial trough lies at about twelve degrees north latitude, remaining in close proximity to the delta and allowing the southern trades only limited access to Waraoland. In contrast, the southernmost overland position of the intertropical convergence zone may dip below the Amazon, although the mean annual position of the centerline is at about five degrees north latitude, the so-called meteorological equator (Huschke 1959). In any event, the distance

---

[2] The yearly average is the difference between the mean temperatures of the warmest and coldest months.

of the southern center trough from the delta is longer than that of the northern centerline. Thus the northern trades retain a stronger hold on the Orinoco Delta than do their southern counterparts.

At the time of the vernal equinox, from mid-January to April, the centerline of the equatorial trough is in its southern position, south of the delta. During these months the Warao experience their primary (long and intense) dry season.[3] Following the path of the zenithal sun, the trough moves northward to pass Warao territory—for the first time—at the summer solstice, thereby giving rise to the primary (long and intense) wet season of the year.

At the time of the autumnal equinox, from mid-August to October, the centerline of the equatorial trough reaches its northern position, north of the delta. During these months the Warao experience a secondary (shorter and less intense) dry season. When the trough eventually follows the sun southward again, it passes Warao territory—for the second time—at the winter solstice and causes the secondary (shorter and less intense) wet season of the year.

Thus the Warao habitat, including the Orinoco Delta (except for its northwesternmost corner) and the coastal fringe of adjacent Guyana, is subject to a wet marine climate characterized by four seasons of equinoctial dry weather and solstitial rains (fig. 1.1). The primary dry season lasts from mid-January to mid-April (Winikina, Curiapo), or to the end of April (Araguaito) in the delta, and from mid-August through November in Guyana. The primary wet season, centered in June, lasts from mid-April to mid-August on the coast and from May to mid-August inland. The secondary dry season in the southeastern, central, and southwestern delta lasts from mid-August through October and from February through mid-April in Guyana. The secondary wet season in the central, southeastern, and southwestern delta includes the months of November, December, and part of January; in west coastal Guyana it spans the months of December and January.

---

[3] For the inversion of the primary and secondary dry seasons on the west coast of Guyana, see below.

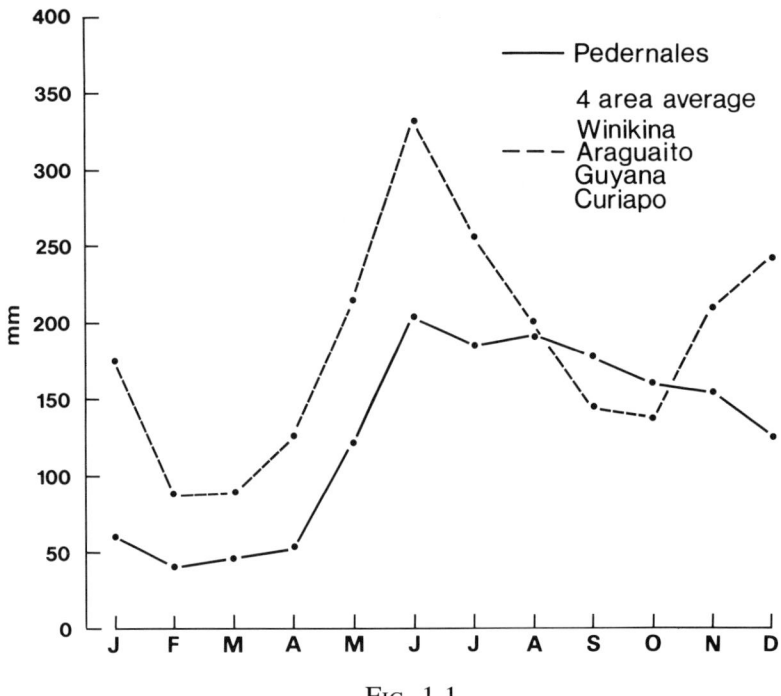

FIG. 1.1
Average annual distribution of rainfall for various sections of the Orinoco Delta and Guyana. Annual totals in mm. (Drawing by Amalie Orme)

Distribution of Rainfall

The mean annual rainfall in the southeastern, eastern, and central distribution sectors (Guyana, Curiapo, Winikina) is between 3,000 and 2,000 millimeters; in the western sectors (Araguaito, Pedernales) it is between 2,000 and 1,500 millimeters. Thus, within Warao territory the maximum rainfall decreases from east to west, in both total and monthly figures[4] (fig. 1.2).

[4] As pointed out by Heinen and Ruddle (1974, 123–24), the sporadic and short-range meteorological data available for the Orinoco Delta are insufficient to permit a valid statistical analysis of the rainfall pattern. The data given here are based on documents the author obtained through the cooperation of Dr. José Luis Méndez-Arocha from the Ministerio de Ambiente y Recursos Naturales Renovables, Dirección de Hidrología, División de Secretaría Técnica, Venezuela.

Land and Weather

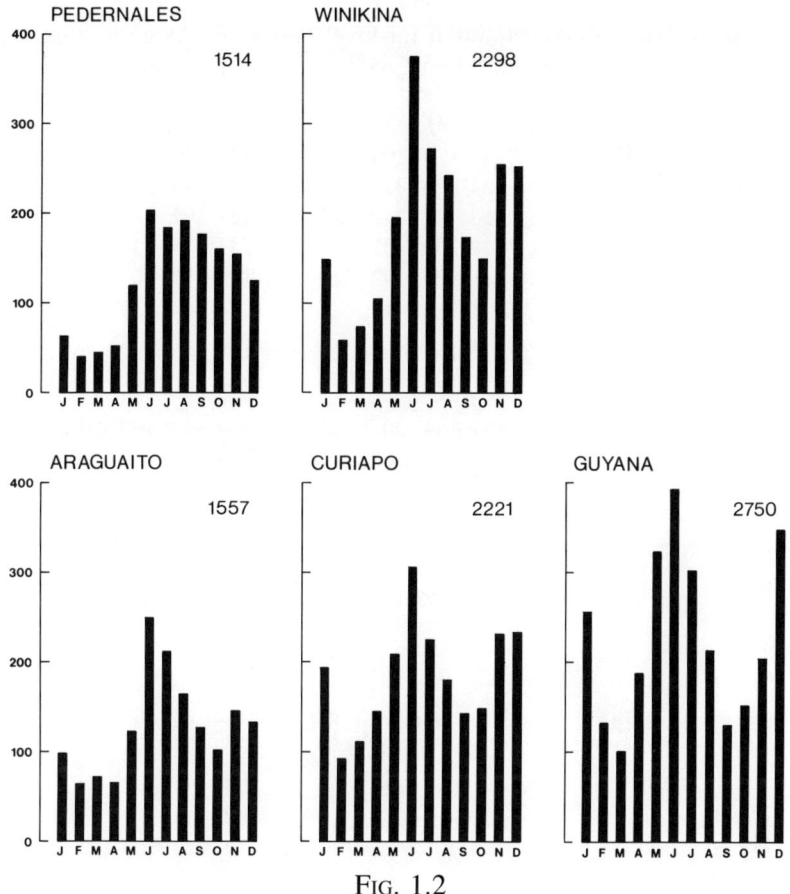

Fig. 1.2
Annual distribution of rainfall for five regions of Warao habitat (Orinoco Delta and Guyana). Ordinate values in mm/100, annual totals in mm. Venezuelan data based on period 1971–80. (Drawing by Amalie Orme)

To gain an overview of the annual distribution of rainfall for various regions of the Warao habitat, statistical data were collected from five weather stations, rather strategically located on the western coastal fringe of Guyana, and at Curiapo, Winikina, Araguaito, and Pedernales. Table 1.1 lists the month-to-month rain totals for each of the five stations, together with monthly and annual aggregate averages.

TABLE 1.1
Annual Distribution of Rainfall for Five Regions of Warao Habitat
(Orinoco Delta and West-Coastal Fringe of Guyana)

Regions	J	F	M	A	M	J	J	A	S	O	N	D	Totals
Pedernales	63	40	46	52	120	203	183	191	177	160	154	125	1514
Winikina	149	59	73	104	196	375	272	241	173	149	255	252	2298
Araguaito	99	63	71	66	122	249	211	165	128	102	147	134	1557
Curiapo	194	92	111	147	209	307	225	180	143	149	231	233	2221
Guyana W-CST Fringe	256	132	100	188	324	392	312	212	130	152	204	348	2750
Four Delta Reg. Aver.	126	63	75	92	162	283	223	194	155	140	197	186	1896
Delta/Guyana W-CST Fringe Aver.	152	77	80	111	194	305	241	198	150	142	198	218	2066

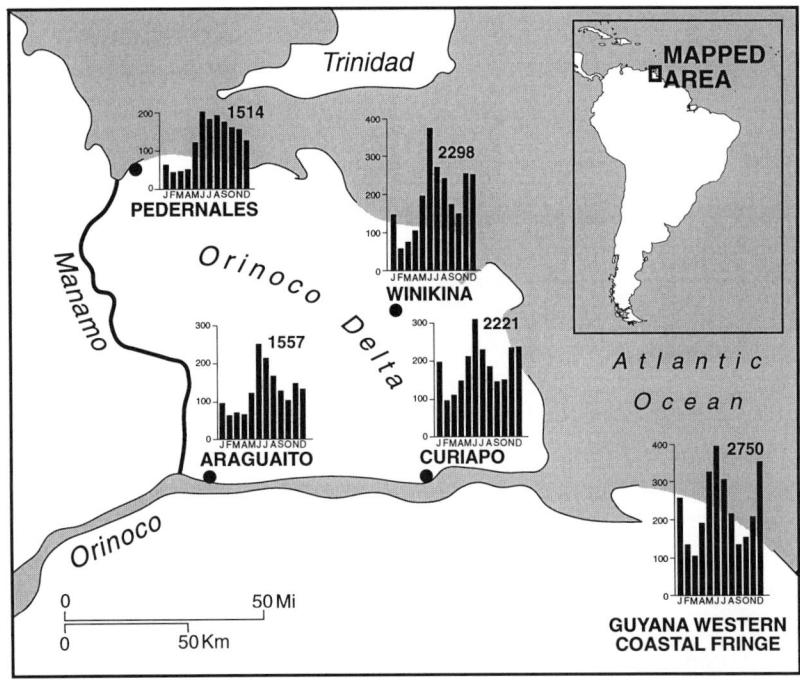

MAP 1.3
Annual distribution of rainfall in five regions of the Warao habitat (Orinoco Delta and Guyana). Ordinate values in mm/100, annual totals in mm. Delta data are based on the period 1971–80. (Drawing by Chase Langford)

Map 1.3, clarifying this somewhat confusing situation, demonstrates, despite some monthly shifts, the overall similarity of the rainfall patterns in the sectors of Guyana, Curiapo, Winikina, and Araguaito and the difference from the pattern in Pedernales. In that sector the weather profile for the first half of the year conforms roughly to the profile in the rest of Warao territory. Pedernales, however, does not have a secondary dry season; instead it seems to have a two-season cycle reminiscent of the Orinoco basin in central Venezuela (Marrero 1964, 177, fig. 197; Snow 1976, 295).

Precipitation, Seasonal Hunger, and Famine

Weather diseases and environmental stress attributable to climatic inclemency are gravely detrimental factors in the Warao Indians' struggle for survival. The main reason, though, for the existentialist importance of prevailing weather conditions in the Orinoco Delta is the interrelationship of the levels of precipitation, seasonal hunger, and recurrent famine.

Traditionally, Warao economy was based on moriche-palm sago. Fluctuations from abundance to scarcity of sago and other moriche food staples, however, are tied to the alternation of dry and wet seasons. During the equinoctial dry seasons, moriche sago and fruit are available, or even plentiful, whereas during the solstitial wet seasons they range from scarce to unavailable, causing seasonal hunger. In preagricultural times, as Heinen and Ruddle explain (1974, 120), "this seasonality led to pronounced scarcity during certain months of the year and to outright famines every four to five years."

Furthermore, during the primary rainy season continuous rainfall, at times lasting ten or more hours, is a frequent occurrence. Instead of these weak, slow-moving, disturbances, however, "the bulk of precipitation in this region falls in the form of brief, violent downpours, generally accompanied by thunder" (Heinen and Ruddle 1974, 124). These fast-moving storms affect only small areas (i.e., a few square kilometers) at a time; they are typically short-lived, sporadic, and random in their western trajectory across the delta. Whereas the slow-moving disturbances, affecting large tracts of land, may trigger moriche inflorescence over thousands of square kilometers, the fast-moving, more localized storms may cause moriche palms to flower only in the restricted area of a grove belonging to a single band or subtribe.

It is of special significance that regional and local rains not only produce the florescence of moriche palms, either throughout the delta or in restricted areas, but that they also simultaneously, apparently because of the flowering, cause the stem starch to disappear or to "fall into the roots," as the Warao would say. Regional rains and the corresponding moriche flowering may thus create a shortage of sago over a large area. Local storms and florescence may create a food crisis for only one particular band. In this event the affected group suffers want while their immediate neighbors enjoy plenty, a phenomenon more commonly associated with regions of widely varying ecosystems (de Garine and Harrison 1988; McCann 1987; Pottier 1986).

Moriche palms in the upper delta usually start blossoming in May, with the onset of the shower activity that precedes the primary rainy season. In the lower delta the blooming of moriche is delayed for several weeks. Apparently all the male palms blossom simultaneously, thus running out of sago at the same time. Female palms blossom in a more staggered fashion, allowing extension of the sago season (Heinen and Ruddle 1974, 123).

Figure 1.3 shows the interrelationship between the annual distribution—in Winikina territory—of rainfall and the concomitant fluctuations in the supply of moriche sago and fruit. Precipitation levels throughout the year clearly bear an inverse relationship to the abundance of moriche staples: the higher the rainfall the lower the provisions, and vice versa. During the principal dry season sago is abundant; after the vernal equinox, in April and May, some green fruit may appear on palms that flowered because of the rains of the preceding secondary wet season, in December. To a certain degree this fruiting may at times extend the availability of sago into the first part of the long wet season. As a general rule, however, the primary rainy season is the time of scarcity, as both sago and fruit are essentially lacking. During the secondary dry season sago again becomes available on a medium level of supply and fruit is plentiful.

Finally, during the secondary wet season moriche production diminishes once again, and both sago and fruit are scarce. Recognition of this interrelationship between precipitation and natural sago production is key to understanding the crux of Warao rain-shamanism; that is, he who is believed to control the rain in morichals is held to govern hunger and starvation.

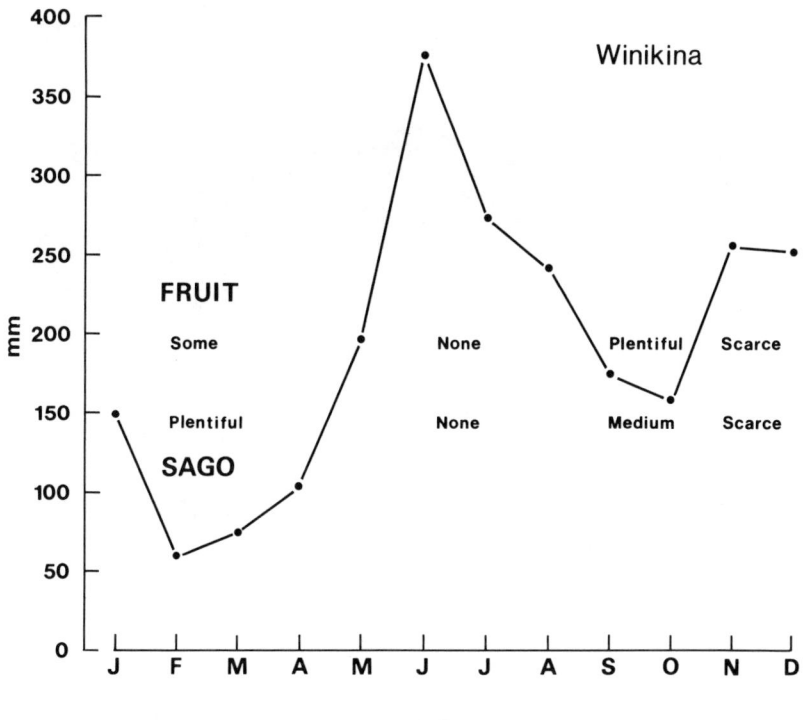

Fig. 1.3

Mean monthly and mean annual rainfall (mm), 1970–80, for the Winikina; annual availability of moriche sago and fruit, San José de Yaruara. (Drawing by Amalie Orme)

Sea and Land Breezes

As noted earlier, the Warao favor a 60-kilometer-wide band of the littoral and the lower intermediate zones of the Orinoco Delta for settlement and exploitation (map 1.2). Thus, most of the occupied tribal territory feels the influence of the small-scale convection system of sea and land breezes (fig. 1.4).

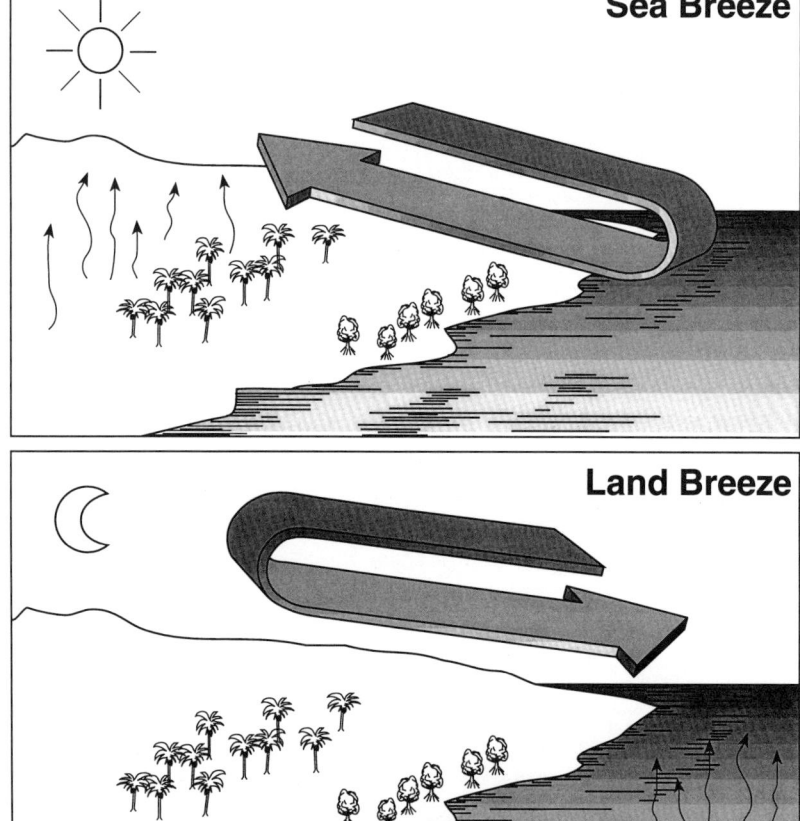

Fig. 1.4
The sea and land breezes. (Drawing by Chase Langford)

Almost daily, and persistently throughout the year, the sun heats the coastline of the delta, and the land, in turn, warms the air above it. During the day, as the warmer air rises, cool and heavier air blows in from the sea—especially in the afternoon and early evening—and across the overland low-pressure area thus created (sea breeze). In the lower delta, which topographically offers few obstacles, this onshore sea breeze penetrates as far as 50 kilometers inland, reaching practically all traditional Warao settlements. A reverse process evolves during the night, when the heat-retaining sea warms the air above it. As the warmer air rises, a cool and heavier stream of air blows off the land in the morning to take its place (land breeze).

Local Winds

Known in Venezuela as *barineses* (after the western Venezuelan state of Barinas), these strong local winds are called *ahakabari*, "turn-about winds," by the Warao. Unlike the predominantly easterly (trade) winds of the delta, they blow periodically westerly and southwesterly from sunset.

The *barineses* are caused by pressure differences, from May to August, and between the excessively hot Orinoco plains, or llanos, and the cold regions of the Andes in western Venezuela. Converted into a large low-pressure area, the llanos experience an influx of cold air from the Andean high-pressure area. Over the inundated llanos the *barineses* absorb humidity and drop it in thunderstorms on the lower Orinoco and its delta (Marrero 1964, 175).

Trade Winds

Rather than moving back and forth across a relatively narrow band of shoreline, as the breezes do, the trade winds are on a planetary scale and blow across both the subtropics and the tropics. The northern trades are a dominating factor in the dry seasons, just as the southern trade winds reach the delta in the rainy seasons.

Owing to its being near the equator, the Orinoco Delta is an area where warm, moist, and unstable air rises skyward, often in the condensed form of cumulonimbus clouds (fig. 1.5). The high degree of heat in these convective columns increases the buoyancy of the air and, upon release, the warming of the upper tropical atmosphere. As the air reaches the tropopause it is cooled and deflected in a northerly direction. Through a continuing process of cooling by radiation, the air moves along a steep pressure gradient between the equatorial low- and the subtropical high-pressure zones until eventually, at about thirty degrees north latitude, it sinks to lower elevations. From there the air, as the northern trade winds, flows back, in part, toward the equator, closing the vertical overturning loop referred to as a Hadley cell. Heated and raised once again near the equator, the air is then sent back on its cellular journey within this system of equatorial convection.

A Hadley cell, like the one just described for the Northern Hemisphere, exists also between zero and thirty degrees south latitude in the Southern Hemisphere, functioning in an identical way (southern trade winds). Owing to the rotational effect of the earth, the trade winds acquire a steady easterly component, blowing from the northeast in the Northern Hemisphere and from the southeast in the Southern Hemisphere (Ahrens 1985, 294–95; Atkinson and Gadd 1987, 42–43; Snow 1976, 296–97).

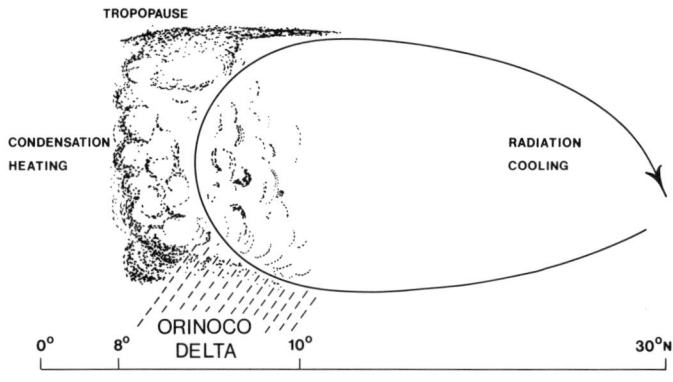

Fig. 1.5
Northern Hadley cell.
(Drawing by Amalie Orme)

Land and Weather

Whirlwinds

Although not situated in the immediate path of Atlantic hurricanes, the Orinoco Delta lies on the southern periphery of the hurricane maturation grounds. Atlantic hurricanes originate close to the equator and mostly in the eastern half of the ocean. They travel then on the tropical easterlies to the West Indies (Atkinson and Gadd 1987, 24). Thus, at least from the sidelines, the Warao experience the windstorm's roaring force, torrential rain, and ocean surges when, between July and October, hurricanes may pass by or may originate in the Lesser Antilles and proceed across the Caribbean, the Gulf of Mexico, and eastern North America.

Sometimes tornadoes materialize on the fringe of a hurricane, but more often whirlwinds appear in the delta as waterspouts rather than as tornadoes, less violent but equally awe-inspiring. In view of the similarities between these two convective vortexes—which differ from each other quantitatively more than qualitatively—the Warao are not mistaken in regarding them as two manifestations of the same spirit (Golden 1973, iii). Although the meteorological conditions that spawn tornadoes and waterspouts are rarely the same, the latter may also be associated with hurricanes. The Warao must have been convinced of the essential sameness of the two storms, however, because in the tidewater of the Orinoco Delta tornadoes may transform into waterspouts and then change back again.

The height of a waterspout ranges from a few hundred to several thousand meters; its width varies from a few meters to several hundred. Waterspouts invariably look like serpents, descending vertically or obliquely in a twisted fashion from the clouds to the surface of the water. Sometimes waterspouts have the shape of an hourglass, with the indentation roughly at the midsection. Some waterspouts are double-walled or even triple-walled, with dark or semitransparent interiors. They travel across the water at an average hourly speed of twenty or thirty kilometers, but they may move as slowly as two or three kilometers or as rapidly as eighty or more kilometers an hour. While moving along, waterspouts sigh and hiss, make sucking sounds, or roar and crash. Most disconcerting to the Warao boatman is the fear that waterspouts may form and overcome him at almost any time or in any place, day or night, at sea or on a wide river, with or against the surface winds. Worse still, whether in the guise of a tornado or a waterspout, whirlwinds may appear singly or in groups of several. Even in the weaker form of a waterspout, a twister can lift up a person or a boat and cause enormous damage (Lane 1986, 63–69).

Floods and Tides

The hydraulic regimen of the Orinoco is strongly governed by the rhythm of precipitation throughout the vast river basin (fig. 1.6). A period of "low river," beginning in September, culminates in March, toward the end of the primary dry season in the delta. There is also a period of "high river," beginning in April, and peaking in August, toward the end of the primary wet season in the delta. In addition to this annual flooding the Orinoco is noted for its long-range (7-,

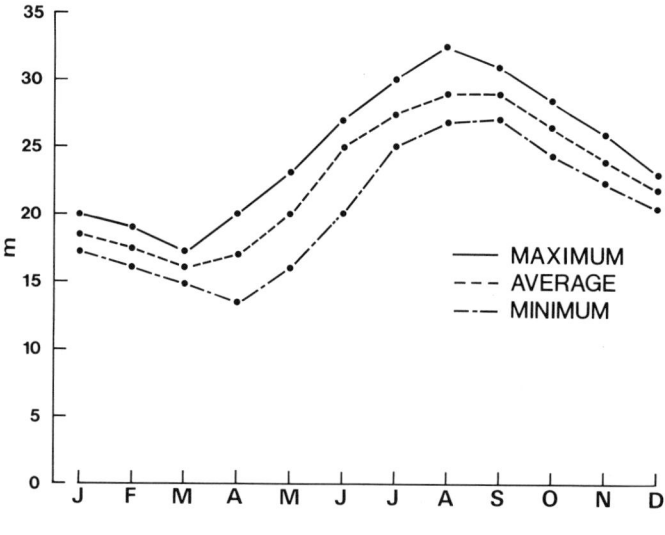

Fig. 1.6
Orinoco regimen at Ciudad Bolívar: monthly mean levels, maxima, and minima at monthly intervals. (After Marrero 1964, 122; drawing by Amalie Orme)

20-, and 50-year) cycles of high floods (Barral 1964, 438–40), and the occurrence of a 100-year return frequency of catastrophic floods has recently been discovered (Pfefferkorn, Fuchs, and Hecht et al. 1988).

Complementing the fluctuations of low and high river levels across the delta are those of low and high ocean tides. During the long dry season the reduced river volume is overpowered by the tides, which can be felt throughout the delta and even upriver beyond its apex. Saltwater penetrates the littoral and intermediate zones, causing the water in the Warao habitat to turn brackish as far inland as 60 kilometers. In contrast, during the long wet season and following the northern solstice, the increased volume of the Orinoco River keeps the tides at bay. Saltwater does not enter the delta; rather, water in the Gulf of Paria and the Atlantic Ocean near the river's estuary turns fresh (Marrero 1964, 120–23).

Chapter Two

Narrow Passages

Within the labyrinthine mesh of deltaic waterways, the Warao, protected by mangrove swamps, the wet savannas, and the rain forests, have found refuge from a host of existential perils. Unlikely as it may seem because of their geopolitical location, they have managed to overcome the dangers and to survive the battles against extremely heavy odds. Some of the ordeals that have impacted the course of Warao history are pre-Columbian invasions, incursions by warrior cannibals and slave raiders, interference by missionaries and colonial authorities, and such ills as imported pestilence, forced labor, bondage, expatriation, and rejection. Because evangelization is particularly relevant to this study, the role of mission life in reshaping Warao weather religion and related practices is emphasized in the account that follows.

Pre-Columbian Invaders

Indians ancestral to the Warao may have occupied the northeastern littoral of South America for a very long time. Indeed, I place them among the foraging populations that, some seven thousand years ago during a widespread intensification of a shoreline life-style, occupied the region between eastern Venezuela and Surinam. Early on they began to build canoes, an innovation that gave them maneuverability in the tidal zone, the coastal waters, and eventually in the interinsular passages of the Lesser Antilles (Rouse 1986, 132). The maritime emphasis thus given the northeastern seaboard generated a nautical tradition of migration, travel, and trade (Rouse and Cruxent 1963, 46; Royo y Gómez 1960; Wilbert 1977a, 1977b).

Some three thousand years ago Arawakan migrants, traveling down the lower Orinoco, occupied the area around the apex of the delta. As tropical rain forest farmers, they cultivated their crops on the area's floodplains and possibly on the fingerlike levees in the riverine drainage system in the upper delta. Eventually they were uprooted by a second wave of Arawakan migrants who, following them downstream, pushed their precursors along the Rio Grande onto the coastal plain of Guiana. The displacement strengthened the Arawaks' contact with the nonagricultural people of the coast, including the delta, and in the ensuing acculturation the river-traveling farmers became as adept at offshore navigation as the littoral pre-Arawakan foragers had ever been. Beginning about the time of Christ, successive waves of Arawakan invaders pushed off from Guiana, Trinidad, and possibly from the east coast of Venezuela, to conquer the West Indies. They occupied the Lesser and the Greater Antilles, overrunning the inhabitants who had peopled the islands thousands of years earlier. Like the nonagricultural populations on the Guiana coast, the foraging islanders were unable to repel the intruders. Except for a few isolated groups like the Guanahatabey of western Cuba, most of the islanders perished in the struggle.

Internecine warfare in the West Indies, however, had not yet come to an end. During the first half of the second millennium after Christ, invaders with Cariban linguistic affiliation began to encroach on the Arawakan settlers in the Lesser Antilles. Like the ancestors of the Arawak, Cariban war parties launched their attacks mainly from the Guiana coast and from Trinidad, killing the arms-bearing menfolk and settling down among the women and children of the vanquished men (Boomert in Rouse 1986, 151). Their descendants subsequently harassed their Arawakan neighbors in the Greater Antilles to the north and, somewhat less aggressively, the coastal people of the mainland to the south. Only after the Europeans had arrived in the West Indies did the long-standing turmoil subside. Like the nonagricultural settlers of earlier times, the farming islanders gradually became extinct throughout the West Indies. Of the nonagricultural littoral navigators, only the Warao in their deltaic refuge weathered the protracted storm of conquest and subsequent demise (Rouse 1986, 106–56).

Warrior Cannibals

Their location at the bridgehead of perpetual population movements makes it unlikely that the ancestral and historical Warao of the Orinoco Delta entirely escaped the danger of invasion. Early on they may have had to abandon the upper delta and parts of the lower delta, which had natural levees, to Arawakan intruders (Voorhies, Wagner, and Arvelo 1981). They may also have had to accommodate within their sanctuary refugees uprooted by the agriculturalists along the Guiana coast. Such events could well have introduced to the delta Indians the kind of warring observed there by late-sixteenth-century explorers (Raleigh 1970 [1596], 108).

In historic times, according to tribal tradition, the Warao were intermittently subjected to attacks by war parties approaching the delta from the islands of the Caribbean and from Guiana, possibly in continuation of pre-Columbian invasions. The Warao distinguish two such foreign invaders: the Musimotuma (Red Faces), also called Dariatuma (Warriors), and the Siawani. In their oral lore both groups are identified as Carib. The singer of one song asks:

> Where are they coming from this time?
> The Red Faces, the Red Faces are coming from the sea this time.
> From the islands they have come. They come in search of our flesh, to eat it as their food. . . . This very moment they have arrived from the crab beach [mouth of the Orinoco]. Full of contented anticipation, this time, the Red Faces have come (Barral 1964, 538–39; my translation).

A number of Warao songs and narratives deal with the subject of such invasions. Besides identifying the attackers and their places of origin, the tales also point out that a major objective of the raids was cannibalism (Roth 1915, 273; García 1947, 45–46; 1971, 192–202; Barral 1960, 134, 250, 259; Wilbert 1970, 135, 141; Lavandero 1991, 29).

Reports of cannibalistic practices in the Caribbean entered the literature early in the logbooks of the Columbian voyages (Andree 1887; Koch 1899; Volhard 1939, 334–38; Métraux 1949b, 403–4; Whitehead 1984; 1988, 172–80). And recent expressions of skepticism notwithstanding (Arens 1979), indications are that cannibalism was indeed practiced in the immediate vicinity of the Orinoco Delta.

In Warao country in northwestern Guyana, kitchen middens of the so-called Alaka culture have been documented by early investigators (Brett 1852; Im Thurn 1967 [1883]) and by modern researchers (Osgood 1946; Evans and Meggers 1960) as revealing evidence of successive occupations, ranging from a preceramic lithic period more than two thousand years ago through a pre-European ceramic period to a historic Tropical Forest/Caribbean cultural tradition. Besides debris suggestive of seafood, such as clam, oyster, and mussel shells, crab carapaces, and fish and animal bones in the lower strata, other findings indicated that cultivated food plants had been introduced at differing periods and that contact was eventually established with Arawakan traders from the region around the distributary point of the Orinoco Delta.

At the lower and middle levels of several mounds, human skeletal remains were scattered haphazardly throughout the midden refuse. Although Evans and Meggers (1960, 63) were unable to determine whether cannibalism was practiced by people of the Alaka culture, earlier writers had confirmed its occurrence from human bones found strewn about, many of them cracked open. For example, Brett (1868, 423) described the condition of the Waramuri shell midden:

> These bones were not found stretched out, either in horizontal or perpendicular positions, but huddled and jumbled together in a manner impossible to describe. The skulls, some of which were of great thickness, were in fragments;—the long bones had all been cracked open and contained sand and dust.

Brett (1868, 427, 451) was convinced that the condition of the skeletal remains indicated cannibalism. He hypothesized that the mounds were probably constructed by a "preceding race" of cannibals whom Guianan Arawak used to call Méyanow. Im Thurn (1967 [1883], 410–21), whose description of the shell mounds is similar to Brett's, believed that the "human bones occur in a condition which clearly indicates cannibalism."

Besides the oral histories of the Arawak and the Warao, which speak of cannibals on the Pomeroon coast, a specific historical record of 1597 says that the Kalinago of Dominica and Grenada in the Lesser Antilles went periodically to the mainland region of the Barima, "where they are on terms of peace and friendship with other

Carib, and where they go to divide their spoil and offer sacrifices, and eat those Indians that they have captured" (British Library, Department of Manuscripts and Venezuelan Papers, MSS IV-15, London [Whitehead 1988]).

Although documentation of cannibalism in the vicinity of the Orinoco Delta and in the West Indies is sparse, early historical accounts of its occurrence cannot be ignored. Mention of the designation "Carib" in the presence of contemporary Warao causes concern among both young and old. Moreover, the lumps of red pigment found in the Barima refuse mounds vividly evoke the image of the Red Faces which, according to Warao oral lore, originated in the region near the mouth of the Orinoco (Im Thurn 1967 [1883], 414).

Furthermore, the Cariña Carib of the Venezuelan llanos to the west of the Orinoco Delta were long feared by the Warao as cannibals (Barral 1964, 161–63). In their colonial mission contacts the Warao have had firsthand experience with the devastating combativeness of the Cariña, and it is from their enemy's stronghold on the Guarapiche River that the Jesuit missionary Pierre Pelleprat documents the occurrence of ceremonial cannibalism. "People worthy of consideration" were offered morsels of cured human flesh taken from an enemy. The French priest himself was witness to such a practice when a Cariña chief invited him to eat of a hand and a foot taken from a slain Arawak (Pelleprat 1965 [1655], 71).

Slave Raiders

The seizure of slaves by Arawakan and Cariban groups in the delta and in the West Indies probably goes back to precontact times. With the coming of the Europeans, however, slavery on both mainland and islands intensified sharply in response to the growing demand of conquistadors and colonists for slave labor. In the first half of the sixteenth century the conquistadors enslaved Indians of mainland Venezuela and the Caribbean in large numbers. They either hunted slaves themselves or traded for them with Indians who had obtained them through intertribal warfare or barter. The Arawak to the west of the delta and the Guianan Carib to the east, both functioning as intermediary traders, posed a serious threat to Warao survival.

Operating from their home base at Barrancas, near the apex of the delta, the Arawak supplied the Spanish settlers of Margarita and Cubagua with provisions and slaves in exchange for iron tools, weapons, and other European goods. Perpetuating the age-old trading tradition established by early Arawakan settlers, their descendants continued to control that trade throughout the sixteenth century (Boomert n.d.; Rouse and Cruxent 1963, 81–90; Rouse 1982). Consistent with the pre-Columbian trading pattern connecting the Paria and Cumaná coasts, Trinidad, the Windward Islands, and northwestern Guiana in a far-flung network, the Arawak joined the Spanish slave hunters on Trinidad. Arawak Indians also guided the Spaniards of Margarita on slave-trading expeditions through the Orinoco Delta to Venezuelan Guayana and beyond to dealers on the Barima, Pomeroon, and Essequibo rivers (Salas, 1964 [1520–70], 55; Raleigh 1970 [1596], 39; Ojer 1966, 1, 332–35).

To the east of the delta, the Warao were increasingly threatened by resident Carib and Arawak slave traders of Guiana. Between 1613 and 1678 the Dutch constructed a network of fortified trading posts on the "Wild Coast" from the Orinoco to the Amazon. Operators of the posts established friendly relations with these indigenous traders, and Indian slaves were a valued commodity. Especially the Carib of Guiana supplied the European settlers with large numbers of Indian slaves (Goslinga 1971, 409, 578 n. 3). Extending the range of their raids from the lower Orinoco and the Guianas to the llanos and deep into the interior of the Dutch and Spanish colonies, Carib slave traders became a menace to independent tribes and to the encomienda and mission Indians of the entire region. Whatever social and political objectives might have motivated the prehistoric slavery of Arawakan and Cariban peoples, in colonial times its principal purpose was simply mercantile (Gumilla 1963, 324). With the Dutch colonists providing an insatiable market for slaves, the Carib relentlessly plied their trade, thus contributing significantly to the disorganization and the demographic decline of the Indian population of northern South America (Morey 1979). In 1735 an estimated six to seven hundred slaves were taken from the llanos of western Venezuela and eastern Colombia alone (Rey Fajardo 1971, 1:55 n; Morey and Morey n.d.: Morey 1979). And Garriga (1898 [1758], 147) reports "that the Caribs sell yearly more than three hundred children, leaving murdered in their homes more than four hundred adults; for the Dutch do not like to buy the latter because they well know that, being grown up, they will escape." According to Garriga (ibid, 148), "this slave trade has so completely changed the Caribs, that their only occupation is constantly going to and returning from war, selling and killing Indians."

Eventually, in 1746 and 1748, the Warao responded to the harassment by Carib slavers by taking up arms and attacking their oppressors in their own homes along the Guaní and Cuyuni rivers. Then in 1752, about a year after the Carib had raided "three Spanish missions and murdered four or five priests," the Warao joined with the Spanish to deal the Carib of the lower Orinoco so decisive a blow that they were forced to seek the protection of their European allies on the Essequibo (British Guiana Boundary Case 1898, 2:45, 57, 70; Butt Colson 1971, 68). By that time, however, the human resource of indigenous populations had been exhausted. According to Governor Manuel Centurión (1979, 132), "within a distance of one hundred leagues [from the Guayana capital at Angostura] there remain no Indian tribes other than the Warao of the Orinoco Delta." Protected by their swampy habitat, the Warao, despite their closeness to the centers of slave trade, had escaped the scourge of slavery which had ravaged the lands around them. Members of other tribes had perished in the armies of the conquistadors or in the pearl fisheries of Margarita and Cubagua, or they had been deported to plantations in Hispaniola, Puerto Rico, the Guianas, and still other locales in the West Indies. A number of them had even been taken to distant Peru (Villamarín and Villamarín 1975, 115). Not until the eighteenth century, when slaves of African origin began to replace Indian slaves and to work on plantations and in livestock industries, did the demand for Indian labor decline.

Colonial Missionaries

Early in the Discovery period, Dominican, Franciscan, and Capuchin monks arrived in Venezuela to attend to the spiritual needs of their compatriots in the towns and villages along the country's northeastern seaboard. The presence of the Europeans and their descendants, the Criollos, aroused the aboriginal populations of the hinterlands to repeated aggression against the newcomers who, in turn, retaliated with all the force they could muster. In order to break the drawn-out cycle of measures and countermeasures which followed, Franciscan (1656) and Capuchin (1657) missionaries from Spain began to evangelize the Indians, hoping to achieve by means of the cross what had failed through the agency of the sword.

Between 1713 and 1817, the padres settled the Indians of the general region in pueblos and secular villages along the southern coast of the Paria Peninsula and on the savannas west and south of the Orinoco Delta. To bring the Warao as well into the Western ambit, missionaries and colonial authorities mounted a series of invasions of the Orinoco Delta, intent on uprooting the Indians from their homes. Over a period of more than a century and as residents of thirty-three separate and mixed communities outside the Orinoco Delta, thousands of Warao came into either prolonged or short-lived contact with other aboriginal groups (Acawaio, Cariña, Coaca, Chaima, Cumanagoto, Locono, Paria, Saliva, and various Carib groups of Venezuelan Guayana) and with Spanish missionaries and colonists in the missions of Cumaná, Guayana, and Píritu. Apparently Warao contact with missions was most intensive between 1768 and 1817, almost fifty years (Armellada 1957; Carrocera 1968; 1979; Gómez Cañedo 1967; Lodares 1930, 2:241; see also appendix). The colonial mission connection was thus one of the most critical episodes in Warao postconquest history. Its impact on Warao culture, and the adaptive significance it has had for Warao rain shamanism and weather-related ritual, requires a more detailed explanation.

Evangelization and Colonization

Throughout the years of their mission work in northeastern Venezuela, the Capuchins have often characterized the Warao as more strongly disinclined to mission life than most other Indian groups with whom the fathers dealt. They were always eager to escape into the Orinoco Delta. The priests attributed this disposition to the Indians' love for their homeland, prompting them to prefer a roaming, foraging existence in the delta to a sedentary farmer's life on the mission's savannas.

This preference, however, was not the only reason for the reluctance of the Warao to join the padres. Of the various incentives offered by the mission—iron tools, defense against traditional enemies, protection from abuse by European colonists—none was guaranteed or sufficiently enticing to woo the Indians permanently from their homes. For instead of merely abandoning their land, they were in fact expected to surrender their entire existence to European-Christian rule, thus relinquishing both their ethnic and their cultural identities. Furthermore, far from being safe havens, missions were places fraught with corporeal dangers such as pillorying, incarceration, and death by oppressive capataces, as well as hunger, epidemic disease, soldiering, and predation by enemies of the mission. All these dreadful consequences would potentially be visited upon the Indians in exchange for the advantage of drawing closer to the Europeans and their manufactures and for yielding to the padres' zeal to align them with the Christian God and sovereign. Finally, as will be explained, mission life would impose an onerous psychological toll.

Perusal of the contemporary ecclesiastic and colonial sources reveals a blatantly prejudicial bearing of the European actors which no frontier Indian could ignore. To paraphrase and quote from archival documents, the Indians, especially those outside the mission pueblos, were viewed as people without reason whose animal-like existence in the forest offended God in all its evil ways. To be reconstituted as Christians they would first have to be turned into humans, because in their barbaric, ferocious, and unmannered heathenism they represented a "new human species apart from humanity." They were "rational fauna" in need of domestication to rid them of their superstitions, vices, and idolatry. Only in this way could they acquire the prerequisites of human existence, and only then would they attain a level of development at which it would no longer be appropriate to call them "Indians" (Carrocera 1964, 150; 1968, 1:198, 509; 1968, 2:52; 1979, 2:289; Gómez Cañedo 1967, 1:187–90).

Given such radical debasement, Warao historical consciousness is bound to have retained the memory of the colonial frontier as a critical bottleneck in the tribal past. In constructing a postmission ideology of contact, they have committed their harrowing experiences to myth, song, shamanic cosmology, and ritual, expressing them in various facets of their culture, including weather lore. A few telling examples will illustrate the degrading effects colonial missions had on the Warao and will set the stage for the subsequent analysis of the role they played in recasting Warao weather religion.

The myth of misbegotten origin:—Nowadays, in their interaction with strangers, the Warao are likely to display a demeanor of submission, dejection, and melancholy. And, despite some light-hearted intervals, Warao life evolves in a predominantly minor key. Part of the trauma of the mission experience has been preserved in mythological etiologies regarding the origin of Warao and Europeans. From the Arawak whom they met in several mission villages, the Warao seem to have adopted the view that their tribal origin resulted from a union between an ancestral man and a dog-woman (Brett 1880, 176; Koch-Grünberg 1916–28, 2:290; Coll 1907-08, 484; de Goeje 1943, 129; Drummond 1977, 847).

South American mythology is replete with stories of unions between humans and animals. In fact, essential sameness in the face of formal heterogeneity of all living creatures constitutes a virtual ontological orthodoxy of indigenous mythology throughout the continent, one that is largely unconditioned by developmental arrows, as from lower to higher forms of life or vice versa, and unencumbered by differential values attached to one form or another. Specifically, the motif of descent from a human-dog union is widespread and of considerable antiquity in South America and elsewhere (Latocha 1982, 323–47; Wilbert and Simoneau 1992, 866).[1] Abasement of the Warao by treating them as "rational fauna" in and around the missions, therefore, is not associated with the autochthonous mythologem of essential ontological equality of living forms. Rather, it is grounded in the interpretation of the tale according to the European concept of hierarchical genesis and the moral stigma of bestiality.

---

[1] Elsewhere the dog-ancestor mythologem occurs in Mesoamerica (Horcasitas 1953, Furst 1993), North America (Jackson 1929), and northern Asia (Koppers 1930, Kretschmar 1938). In avian guise, it is akin to the Eurasian "Swan Maiden" motif (D361.1) (Thompson 1955, 58) and "The Swan Maid" tale-type (400) of Aarne-Thompson (1964), which as motif K1335 occurs also in South America (Wilbert and Simoneau 1992, 1232).

The Warao know at least three different myths of human origin. One follows the common tale type of ancestral descent from heaven on a rope—an age-old myth of pre-European vintage (Osborn 1958, 158; Wilbert 1969, 30–35). The second etiological story focuses on the canine *Ur*-mother (Barral 1960, 214, 323; Vaquero de Langayo 1965, 253–55; García 1971, 79), and the third explains the origin of both Indians and Whites (Turrado Moreno 1945, 303; Barral 1960, 339; 1969, 32–34; Wilbert 1970, 243). The latter two versions are of particular validity in the present context, for they epitomize the psychological pummeling the Warao sustained.

The narrative of the human-dog couple tells of a bachelor who, somewhere outside of the delta, encountered a dog in an abandoned house where strangers had lived. As he is alone with the dog, the man is perplexed when finding that someone has prepared food for him. He discovers that it is the dog who, removing its hide and changing into a young woman, has done the work. The dog-woman owns manioc gardens and knows how to process the tubers into cassava cakes. After the man throws the woman's hide into the fire, it is impossible for her to revert to her animal form. He then takes possession of the dog-woman and lives with her. Their union gives origin to the Warao people.

This human-dog couple resembles many other versions of the myth from South America. The reason for my suggesting that it originated in Guiana with the Arawak rather than with the Warao is that the dog-woman obviously has a farming background and thus differs from the nonagricultural Warao. Although most Warao did not adopt agriculture in the Orinoco Delta until a century or so ago, however, they had earlier become intensely familiar with cultivation in mission pueblos and colonial settlements, where they often associated not only with cultivating Europeans but also with indigenous farmers like Arawak and Carib. And Carib (Cariña) mythology appears to agree with the assignment of the canine origin story to the Arawak (Magaña 1992:65). It is in the closing explanatory motifs attached to several versions of the human-dog myth that the moralistic European overtones ring out: "From that time on the Warao say that it is an abominable vice for an Indian to marry an animal" (Barral 1960, 215); "Since that time most Warao are very ashamed because they are the descendants of this canine Indian; they live full of fear"; and "For this reason. . .we Warao are distrustful and flee from people as dogs flee, because we are of the same race (Barral 1960, 324; García 1971, 80). Latocha (1982, 341) is probably correct in suggesting that moralizing missionaries latched onto the story of the human-dog couple to admonish the Indians of the vice of sodomy, which they presumably counted among the Indians' God-offending ways. In the eyes of the missionaries, Indian nudity was a scandalous provocation, an abuse of the innocent, and an affront to Christian modesty. Though it had been regarded as intolerable from the beginning of mission activity in northeastern Venezuela and elsewhere, combating it as an expression of the Indians' barbaric nature became an issue in the 1700 ordinance of mission government (Carrocera 1968, 2:278–79; 1979, 3:148). Under European influence the shamelessness of nudity was symbolically transferred to the domestic dog (Lavandero 1991, 151). That the events behind the human-dog story took place in mythological times—when animals and humans related to each other as varieties of a single race—was conveniently forgotten. Mythical history gave way to contemporaneity, wherein dogs are dogs but where Indians condemn bestiality for their own moral reasons.

The myth of inferior judgment:—Another demeaning historical narrative contrasts the inferiority of the Warao in intelligence, linguistic skills, and culture with the superiority of Whites in these areas. This myth shows how the mental and physical otherness of the European became rooted in the *illo tempore* of Warao mythology, how it was interpreted by their ancestors in colonial times, and how it is internalized and justified by the Indians of today. Its salient points, gathered from a number of Warao variants, are presented below in a synoptic version (Barral 1960, 323–24, 338; 1969, 147; Garcia 1971, 233–34; Turrado Moreno 1945, 303).

> God our Maker created first the Warao and then the Criollo. Addressing the firstborn in various bird idioms, God finds him monolingual, whereas the second-born is capable of understanding several languages. Of two types of dwelling which the Creator offers the brothers, the Warao chooses a rickety structure lacking walls and furniture, whereas the Criollo opts for a well-furnished, solid house with floors and walls of boards. God asks the Indian whether he wants to live on dry land where he can build cities and engage in large-scale trafficking and lucrative business. The Indian favors

the marshes away from cities and their confusing bustle; the Criollo chooses the life of wider dimension. Next God offers the Warao decent (i.e., Western) clothing which the Indian rejects outright, preferring to go naked. His younger brother agrees to being dressed. In a succession of tests God sends different kinds of domesticated animals to the Indian, encouraging him to catch the cow, the goat, the horse, the donkey, and the camel, which he will own forever. But the Warao is afraid to capture anything larger than the dog and the chicken. He also elects to stick to the small dugout canoe, which lacks an outboard motor, to serve as an appropriate means of transportation in his quest for food. His younger brother more courageously goes for the large animals as mounts, the motorboats, and the schooners.

After reprimanding the elder brother for his lack of intelligence and his cowardice, God explains to the Warao that despite his sympathy for the Indian and his willingness to help him live an easy life, he must allot the better things to the cleverer and more courageous Criollo. Prophesying that the Indian would have to work hard to earn his livelihood, God admonishes him to be like a man, outspoken, clear-minded, and alert, and not to be like a woman, unable to think and discourse upon a subject. To aid the unfortunate Indian, God hands him a package of useful things that may assist him in his arduous life. But the Indian, succumbing to his natural inquisitiveness, opens the package against God's will, and he is overwhelmed by a houseful of useful merchandise. However, the following morning, the Indian finds that all the goods that God had given him are no longer there.

Thereupon the Creator rules that henceforward the Warao must work under the sway of his smarter brother, the Criollo. As the Indian bows in resignation, he receives three hard bumps on the head which God had ordered the Criollo to give him for not having known how to choose. As God had ruled, the Indian will unremittingly receive such blows from the progeny of his brother, and he accepts his deprivation and cultural retardation as the consequences of his own imperfections. Since this day of judgment, the Warao lives in his hut in the forest, but the Criollo, who had mounted his horse and ridden away, built his house elsewhere, giving origin to the great nations of the world.

Demystification of the Creator-God of the myth (Turrado Moreno 1945, 299) by replacing him with the missionary, his representative on earth, reveals the ambivalent historical relationship (1) between the protector-priest and those who accepted his God-given rulership, and (2) between the avenger-priest and those who rejected the life he proffered. Rather than merely the amenities of daily life, God's gifts to the brothers exemplify the typical accoutrements of a foreign cultural system, including linguistic, logistic, technological, socioeconomic, and mental elements. The Warao spurns the offer but the Criollo welcomes it. By making this choice, the elder brother abdicates his birthright, yielding it to his younger brother whose cunning has reversed the original God-willed order of seniority. As Hugh-Jones's (1988) analysis of a similar Tucano myth confirms, such inversion of rank and status between two brothers is not restricted to Warao mythology, and its motifs of "two brothers" and the "fateful choice" appear to be grounded in postcontact history. They show that the clever younger brother outsmarts his dim-witted elder sibling, accepting foreign goods and a corresponding European life-style. Furthermore, rather than having the status difference, as in reality, caused by the intruding missionaries and their powerful allies, in myth the reversal of divine order is attributed to the native man himself. It was his own mental deficiency that determined his mediocre position vis-à-vis the missionaries and other Western agents.

How deeply internalized in Warao culture this belief has become is exemplified by the custom of contemporary shamans to revert in times of crises, guilt-stricken, to "true Warao" behavior. When the gods show their anger by sending epidemic disease, the healers seek to mollify them by shedding all Criollo clothes and by eliminating from their diet cultivated and salted foods. Wearing clothing and eating the meat of larger animals, foreign or domestic, is inconsistent with the humble life-style their primordial forefather had chosen for himself and his descendants. Similarly (as will be shown later), the Warao have been known to feel uneasy about acquiring Western technology. When outboard motors, for example, now owned by Warao without any qualms of impropriety, first became available to the Indians, many felt that their purchase was irreconcilable with the original design of their life-style. Instead, objectors were deemed to have been mindful of their mythical ancestor's rejection of Western artifacts.

Mission soldiering:—Particularly calamitous barbs along the Warao's historic gauntlet were mission soldiering and the danger of becoming the target of the Cariña, the dreaded enemy whom they had mythologized into man-eating were-jaguars likely to attack and kill or enslave them at will. Warao oral literature explains that the Cariña were the unnatural prodigy of an incestuous union.

The sister of the first group of siblings who had descended from the sky inadvertently became pregnant by her younger brother after bathing—against his wishes—in the men's bathing place. Upon entering the water she had embraced a pole her brother had planted there for support. She carried a half-human, half-snake child that remained in her body after term, emerging only temporarily to help its mother gather fruit in the forest. On one such occasion the mother's brothers killed their monstrous child with arrows and then cut its serpentine body into four pieces. The grieving mother made the maggots that emerged from the decomposing parts of her quartered child crawl up to the top of poles she placed around herself and then, transformed into Carib people, jump down. In a battle between them and the Warao, the Carib were slain, but they were resurrected as were-jaguars by their invincible mother. The poles were transformed into the posts of their communal house, and the Carib multiplied to become a monstrous people (Vaquero de Langayo n.d.; Wilbert n.d).

As intimated earlier, Warao myth, song, and lore proclaim that for centuries the Orinoco Delta has lain like a boulder in the traffic flow of Carib trading and that the Carib trade network encompassed the Lesser Antilles and the coastal regions of northeastern Venezuela and the Guianas. The Carib trading area also included the offshore islands of Granada, Tobagua, Trinidad, and Margarita and led through the *caño* Manamo, the Orinoco River, and the river systems of the Guiana highlands deeply into the interior of Greater Guiana (Civrieux 1976, 212 bis; Whitehead 1988:10; see also map 2.1). "Where are they coming from this time?" is the anxious query expressed in a Warao song (quoted earlier). And, as map 2.1 reveals, the feared enemy might have skirted the delta or entered it from any direction. Historic encounters with Carib (Cariña) in the missions of Cumaná, Guayana, and Píritu sharpened the traditional

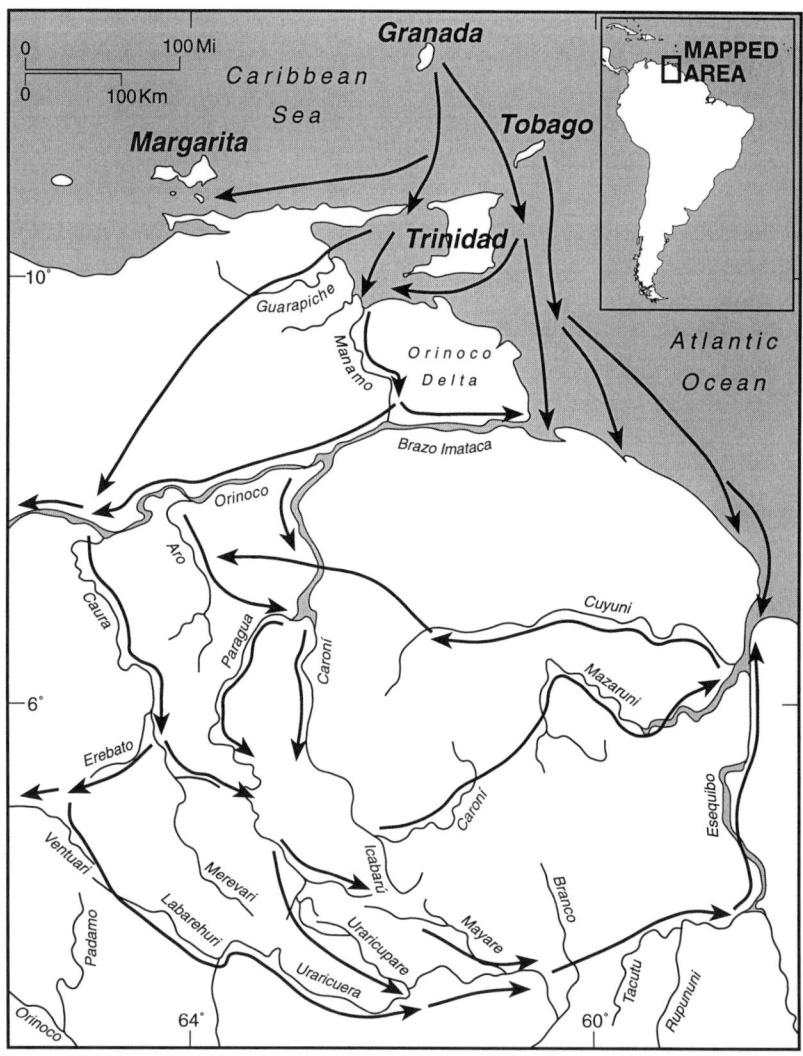

MAP 2.1
Principal traffic routes of Caribs in northern South America.
(After Civrieux 1976:8bis; drawing by Chase Langford)

fear until it became deeply embedded in the historical consciousness of the Warao. Warao were occasionally placed with rebellious Cariña in the same mission, and Cariña repeatedly assaulted mission settlements established with Warao and/or other non-Cariña Indians and annihilated them. Whether stemming from their ongoing resistance to the missionary presence or expressing outright rebellion against Spaniards and Criollos, Cariña attacks were serious enough to cause grave concern to mission Indians. It is worth noting in this connection that in northeastern Venezuela, as elsewhere along the fringes of Western frontiers, indigenous populations were usually drawn into European conflicts, particularly those between expansionist European states (Ferguson and Whitehead 1992). I suspect that such embroilment was yet another reason persuading many indigenous groups to stay away from Spanish missionaries and colonists in northeastern Venezuela who became increasingly involved in wars of resistance with Cariña Indians and their French, Dutch, and English allies. Two mission raids that concerned Warao settlers (San Miguel de Unata and Payaraima) are listed in the appendix. The Mamo massacre, another militaristic incident, is particularly well documented.

The massacre took its name from the Mamo lagoon, located west of the Orinoco Delta apex, near Ciudad Bolívar and inland from the north bank of the Orinoco. Prior to the battle the Spanish missionaries and colonial authorities had attempted to create an auxiliary force to fight the Cariña. As part of the effort, they rounded up twenty Warao families living near the lagoon and settled them, in 1732, at the Chaima Mission of Santa Rosa de Ocópi. Here they were trained to become part of a local militia. The Warao remaining at the lagoon, who were then taken to another mission, were reinforced, on 24 March 1735, with a contingent of Warao who had recently been expatriated from the delta. They were also trained for ethnic soldiering in an anti-Cariña militia (Caulin 1966, 2:215; Whitehead 1988, 113). Mustering these contingents into mission militias, however, put the Warao into a particularly dangerous situation. As research on warfare in so-called tribal zones (areas affected by the continuous presence of a state power without being administered by it) amply demonstrates, the alignment of an ethnic group with imperial power has utterly destroyed aboriginal peoples along the early North American frontier and elsewhere (Fitzhugh

1985; Perdue 1979; Utley and Washburn 1985; Ferguson and Whitehead 1992). The Mamo incident is a further example of this kind of state expansion (Whitehead 1988, 1992). It also helps to explain quite specifically the preference of the Warao, so lamented by the missionaries, for life in the uncharted hinterland of the Orinoco Delta.

The Mamo massacre took place on 18 September 1735, in the newly founded Mission of Nuestra Señora de los Remedios, situated on the shores of the Mamo lagoon (Caulin 1966, 2:218–20; Whitehead 1988, 114). Early in the morning the mission was attacked by a force of more than four hundred Carib warriors who came, in some thirty large dugouts, from the Caura and Barima rivers. They seized the resident padre, cut off his arms, and hung his mutilated body from a tree. Thirty-seven Warao (mostly men) were killed during the raid and, in accordance with Carib practice, the women and the children were carried off by the attackers. The fact that the Warao of the Mamo and other missions had become known as ethnic soldiers may possibly have provoked the attack or aggravated it after it had begun. In any event, violent assaults like the one at Mamo and those at other mission sites occupied by Warao have helped to form the Warao's image of the Cariña as a rapacious and martial tribe. Their war paint of red annatto gave them the name *musimotuma*, "Red Faces," in Warao historical narrative and song, where they are also called *mamo araotuma*, "People of Mamo." As noted earlier, the memory of these slave-taking adversaries as perverse human beings, were-jaguars, and cannibalistic evil spirits has remained alive among contemporary Warao, hundreds of years after the Mamo incident and other mission-mediated Cariña encounters (Barral 1964, 161–64).

Old World Pestilence

Another serious threat to Warao survival were the exotic diseases brought to the New World by Europeans and their imported slaves and indentured laborers from Africa, India, China, and Indonesia. Soon after the discovery, the Caribbean islands and northern South America were ravaged by pandemics of such diseases (Morey 1979). Witnessing the destructive effects on the islands, in the delta, and along the lower Orinoco, the Warao had yet another valid reason to withdraw into the isolation of the swampland. Their Cariña enemies also retreated into the least accessible areas of their territories, but cholera and other plagues eventually caught up with them because of the relatively large number of foreigners in the colonies (Saint Clair 1834, 1:299; Brett 1868, 225; Crévaux 1883, 505; Roth 1924, 703). The Warao, in contrast, by retreating from their outlying regions into the delta did not move from one contami-nated area to another. The lower delta, where they tended to concentrate, remained virtually free of Europeans, Africans, and Asians and thus free of Old World contagion. While many Caribbean and mainland Indians were succumbing to disease, the traditional life-style of the Warao helped to check the spread of communicable pestilence and to keep suffering and death within tolerable bounds (McNeill 1976; Wilbert 1983). Significant factors were their low population density, partly owing to a 50 percent prepuberty mortality rate; the practice of infanticide (Barral 1964, 464–65); and the organization of nomadic local groups averaging about fifty people each. Bands of this kind were kept apart by the fear of contagion and the dread of sorcery. Only occasionally did the Warao congre-gate for ritual purposes, and then only about 250 of them convened for short periods of time (Wilbert 1980a). Band boundaries were also maintained because of, and were reinforced by, dialectical variations in language, kenning, and allegiance to subtribal patron deities (Wilbert 1975a). Relative isolation, low population density, and division into small bands thus were crucial demographic factors in Warao survival, enabling them to achieve relative immunity by the elimination of susceptibles from successive generations and selection of less virulent pathogens over lethal strains which died with their hosts (Murdock 1980).

Epidemic disease did, of course, afflict the Warao, as demographic isolation was less than complete. Periodically, Warao navigators crossed the epidemiological frontier on trading expeditions to Trinidad and to European centers near the delta. Many of the expatriated Warao who escaped from European missions and Criollo towns rejoined their communities in the delta. Still others traveled back and forth between their own communities and those of European colonists to work as shipwrights, lumberjacks, and plantation laborers. Referring to Warao boat makers, for instance, who lived outside the delta between Moruka Creek and the Orinoco, Hilhouse (1978 [1824], 33, 125) reports that "of late years, the Warows have suffered dreadfully from measles and smallpox, which last has been owing entirely to the neglect of their protectors, in not spreading the *vaccine virus*, at a time when the other tribes were saved by the inoculation." Hilhouse describes the health situation among these extradeltaic Warao as "a scene of mortality." Arboviruses and other pathogens entering the delta on their own also devastated local bands. Alarming as such flare-ups must have been, however, the various disease agents seldom encountered populations large enough to sustain infectious chains. Contemporary Warao remember times when entire local groups were extinguished by virulent disease. And they tell a historical myth about a young man who, after years of working for the Criollos outside the delta, returned home to find that his kinfolk had all succumbed to an epidemic (Vaquero de Langayo n.d.).

Thus, although the Warao may have been aware of the virulent force of Old World pestilence in early postcontact times, probably not until the eighteenth century did they fully realize its enigmatic power. By that time the European colonies had taken root and the mission complex had been established in northeastern Venezuela with populations large enough to perpetuate viral contagion. In the words of an eyewitness, virgin soil epidemics began to race through the aboriginal populations of the coastal hinterland and the Orinoco basin "like fire through a dry cane field" (Vega 1974 [1744], 104–6; Whitehead 1988, 28; Ferguson and Whitehead 1992, 8–9).

As is well known, serious population decline in the Western Hemisphere in general and in various subcontinental regions of the New World in particular has been attributed to exotic epidemic diseases.[2] Morey (1979) specifically documented the destruction such pestilence wreaked upon the aboriginal populations living on the Orinoco plains, where smallpox, measles, malaria, and possibly influenza apparently had the most lethal effects. The population decline during the eighteenth century alone is conservatively

---

[2] Dobyns 1966, 414; 1983; Sweet 1969; 1974; Cook and Borah 1971, 411–29; Crosby 1972, 38; Denevan 1970a, 70; 1970b, 251; 1976a, b; Ramenofsky 1987; Purdy 1988; Butzer 1992; Lovell 1992; Stannard 1992; Verano and Ubelaker 1992.

estimated at 50 to 60 percent, and many autochthonous cultures became disorganized or extinct. Throughout their history, the missions of Cumaná and Guayana also reported frequent outbreaks of smallpox, measles, malaria, dysentery, and possibly dengue (Carrocera 1968, 1:297, 299, 375; 3:378, 492; 1979, 2:25, 27, 157; 3:320, 339; Turrado Moreno 1945, 275). Accordingly, the mission effort suffered repeated setbacks owing to epidemic outbreaks of one sort or another, leading to the abandonment of many stations by horrified Indian residents.

What must have struck the Indians as particularly uncanny was the seeming immunity of Europeans and Criollos to pestilence. In 1658 more than two thousand slaves and Indians died in Caracas during an epidemic of *puntada*, yet only twenty Spaniards and Criollos died (Carrocera 1968, 2:55–57). The missionaries succored the afflicted and walked among the dying, but, as most of them were spared, it was common for Indians of the Orinoco plains to blame the priests and their God for all the evil that had befallen them. In general, however, the padres also believed in God-sent illnesses, imputing them to his ire over the Indians' moral corruption (Carrocera 1968, 1:299; 2:55–57; Morey 1979, 85, 89, 90, 95). As missionaries ritually assuaging the wrath of God and entreating him in public prayer were common sights in mission villages, Indian residents came to understand pestilence as a coercive rod in the hand of an indignant divine power. This experience may have resonated with, but not necessarily originated, the Warao's theory of illness through mystical retribution incurred by the individual for having violated moral injunctions. The idea is widespread in South America as it is elsewhere (Murdock 1980, 22–26); sickness is held to be caused by human neglect of the supernaturals who vent their wrath by punitive pathogenic action. Warao weather shamanism also operates (as noted later) on the basis of mystical retribution, especially when the code of altruistic conduct has been violated. The theory of spirit aggression is involved in this area because the rain lords' ire is deliberately aroused by a shaman's conjuring.

To integrate new diseases into the shamanic and cosmological order, the Warao mythologized their etiologies and—as in the missionary tradition—placed them in divine hands. The pertaining myths are structurally stereotypic and resemble, notwithstanding stylistic and formal mythic idiosyncracies, historical accounts of first appearances in their midst of individuals contaminated by febrile, respiratory, gastrointestinal, cutaneous, or other contagious diseases.

At some time in the past the Warao became aware of an individual in their midst who had symptoms of a particular contagious disease. Whether a local or a stranger, the infected person insisted that he was a Warao, even though he seemed to be a stranger and familiar with European-style adobe houses, featuring windows and doors. As the contagion began to spread, the villagers brought the infected person to the attention of the shaman, who, after visiting him, decided that he resembled a spirit rather than a human being. After consulting his tutelary spirits, the shaman teleported the diseased stranger to a distant place in the Warao universe. Before departing, however, the spirit of the disease involved promised to return periodically to contaminate the villagers (Wilbert, W., 1986, 116–84).

Thus, whereas the attribution of affliction to wrathful supernaturals is unique neither to Christians nor to Warao, the amalgamation of indigenous and foreign contagions into a single complex pathology and the construction, after the impact of European pestilence, of an idiosyncratic disease ideology are distinct accomplishments of Warao postcontact shamanism (see also chapter 3). Their disease ideology reveals an intermingling of exotic and endemic pathogens, indicating a blending and a restructuring of health traditions, probably in colonial times.

During the last several decades of the colonial era, the Capuchins waged an all-out campaign to induce the entire Warao population to leave their deltaic homes. The effort was curtailed by the failure of the Crown to give financial support and by the outbreak of the Venezuelan War of Independence, temporarily terminating mission activity in the region. In 1769 expatriated Warao, in their quest for freedom, began to escape to the delta and to Dutch Guiana. Their effort continued for several decades, even though the Spaniards did recapture some of the escapees (Garriga 1979 [1769], 99). In 1817 the Dutch authorities in Guiana became concerned about the growing number of refugee Indians who kept in touch with their homeland on the Orinoco, "to which they look forward at some future period to return" (Hilhouse 1898a, 23). In 1834, however, refugee Warao were still in exile, and some of the present-day Warao of Guyana and of the southeastern delta are probably descendants of their displaced ancestors of colonial times (Hilhouse 1889b, 52; Turrado Moreno 1945, 17).

When patriotic forces liberated eastern Venezuela from the Spanish in 1817, the Warao resembled a battered population relic. After visiting them in the mid-nineteenth century, Level (1898, 164) drew a sorrowful picture of the Warao and their overall situation:

> Ever labouring, and ever naked; frequently ill paid, and always in objects reckoned at three times as much as their value; as a rule, more than half their pay in spirits, and the spirits always preliminary to the rest of their pay; their wives and daughters always persecuted, their sons torn from their breasts and handed over to strangers, their men dispersed, their tribes and families weakened, their wretched belongings snatched away, and they themselves never considered worthy of the smallest care, for he that fell sick died, and the family of a man that died was given the least care of all; all this could lead to no other results than those which we deplore to-day. This inconsiderate and inhuman people who prepared and precipitated these results were proceeding down a dangerous declivity to their own ruin in that of the Indians, relying upon an indefinite continuation of the humility and silence with which the latter submitted to everything. To everything, the unhappy wretches! They did not belie that reliance, it is true; but they fled to the woods seeking the refuge which nature held out to them. Providence has armed that against every kind of oppression; there were their woods, their innumerable islands, their intricate creeks inviting them to come. In saying they fled, I use the word most commonly employed. They turned their backs upon treachery, as all things do, when having relied upon a given promise they find themselves wickedly cheated. They returned, I will say, to their homes, heartbroken at seeing themselves dismembered, separated from all they held most dear, and dispersed.

Forced Labor and Servitude

Retreating to their homes in the lower tidal zone was of little benefit to the Warao when, at the turn of the twentieth century, the rubber boom reached the Orinoco Delta. No matter how far inland the

Indian settlements were, armed mercenaries found them and carried the villagers off to their rubber stations and plantations in the western delta and in regions south of the Rio Grande. While the men were forced to collect rising daily quotas of latex, or to work in sugar, cacao, or coffee production, the women and children were detained in camps, a ploy to keep their husbands and fathers from escaping. Severe corporal punishment, starvation diets, and wanton abuse afflicted many subtribal groups. Even a widespread bloody revolt staged by the Indians (Barral 1972, 290–95) might not have stemmed the avalanche of human greed had not the collapse of raw rubber prices on the world market come to their assistance. Plant pests, floods, and other adversities hastened the abandonment of the plantations (Barral 1951b, 109–11; 1964, 550–52). Conditions of servitude were also imposed on the Warao by self-appointed Criollo caciques and their version of encomiendas, as well as by the notoriously exploitative practices of company stores at lumber mills and other industrial enterprises (Escalante González and Moraleda 1992, 181–205).

Postcolonial Missions

In 1922, approximately a hundred years after the closure of colonial missions in northeastern Venezuela, Capuchin missionaries left Castile to return to their former colonial missions of Cumaná and Guayana. With the permission of the Venezuelan government, they founded the Vicariate Apostolic of Caroní, encompassing much of the territory of the former Guayana Mission and of the then federal territory of delta Amacuro, homeland of the Warao. Later, in 1954, the territory, after separating from the Caroní vicariate, was recognized as the Vicariate Apostolic of Tucupita, named for the capital of the federal territory (now a state) where its seat is located.

At that time the Warao of the Orinoco Delta were the only major group of Indians remaining in the coastal hinterland of northeastern Venezuela. The missionaries therefore decided to move into the delta, even though their colonial predecessors had found it impossible to work there. The first delta mission, established in 1925, was named Divina Pastora de Araguaimujo. Two more missions, San Antonio and San José, were founded in 1925 and 1927, respectively, in the southeastern outskirts of the delta. These two, like several others the fathers tried to establish, were short-lived. In 1942 the second mission in the delta, named San Francisco de Guayo, was inaugurated. It still survives, as does the founder station at Araguaimujo. At the northwesternmost and southeasternmost corners of the delta, respectively, the Capuchins founded the Criollo parishes of Pedernales (1952) and Curiapo (1957). By 1928 the mission personnel also included Third Order Capuchin nuns (Bustamante 1946, 131).

Before Vatican II

Before the Second Vatican Council was enunciated in 1962, evangelization by missionaries in postcolonial times differed little from its practice in colonial times (García 1940, 517; Turrado Moreno 1945, 137, 290–92).

 Agriculture continued to be regarded as the essential economic basis of mission life, even though hydraulic circumstances and soil conditions in the delta should have dissuaded the missionaries from putting so much emphasis on this activity, especially in the places they had chosen for their foundations. The first selected fields for their agricultural efforts were wiped out by high seasonal floods in 1927. Soon thereafter, however, the missionaries made a heroic effort and planted even larger fields of maize, banana, cacao, taro, and sugarcane (Bustamante 1946, 132). Besides seeking economic self-sufficiency for the mission, the padres also intended to use intensive cultivation as a way of teaching the Indians how to work. Increasing agricultural production in the late 1930s and early 1940s was achieved by using the colonial method of communal labor, except that this time the missionaries paid an honest daily wage to the twenty or thirty laborers working for a month or so in the fields. In another difference, the proceeds of the fields helped to feed children in the mission boarding schools. In 1942 the padres introduced large-scale rice cropping, again depending on collective labor, including nearly everybody living in the four areas where rice was grown. The project failed when the Indians, instigated by outsiders, refused to harvest the crop. In the following year the missionaries abandoned collective farming and, more appropriately, fostered large-scale production of *morocoto, bagre*, and *laulau* fisheries (Las Muñecas 1949, 398).

As in the colonial missions on the savannas, the lay brothers were often the inconspicuous heroes of the modern Capuchin establishments in the delta. When reopening their present missions, they were again among the pioneers (Carrocera 1941, 233; Bustamante 1946, 103). And in the 1950s and 1960s, I watched them leave the mission in the morning and again in the afternoon, with their work teams of teenage boys, heading for the fields. Most of the children in the missions were in boarding school, and the recruits requisitioned for work teams were resident boys rather than, as in colonial times, able-bodied males between the ages of fourteen and seventy.

Another continuation of colonial mission activity was the creation, in 1942, of a political organization for all Warao living in the delta, featuring three *gobernaciones*, seven *capitanías*, and twenty-three *fiscalías*. In the same year the padres appointed the governors, captains, and fiscals and introduced the new post of *arukari*, "the one with the cudgel," also referred to as *borisia*, "police." Each of these officeholders was issued a commission paper and instructed that his duties were to keep order in his village, to punish delinquents whose infractions were relatively minor, and to provide an adequate number of children for the mission boarding schools; boys for the wing run by padres and lay brothers, girls for the wing operated by nuns (Las Muñecas 1942; 1949, 395–96). The missionaries were fully aware that their political organization continued, and even broadened, the policies of their colonial forerunners. The boarding schools were probably even more traumatic for the students than the colonial schools had been for the youngsters of their time. For most of the delta children, attending a boarding school meant living separated from their families for several years. Hard as it was for the students, the padres felt that a lengthy separation from parents was necessary to eradicate the Indians' traditional ways and replace them with the customs and the values of Europeans or of Criollos. The trauma occasioned by this separation can be seen in the children's rebelliousness and in their occasional attempts at mass suicide (Marino 1939, 395–96; Barral 1947; Carrocera 1949; Ceñogal 1949).

After Vatican II

Since the enunciations of the Second Vatican Council (1962–65), the delta missions have been run more like modern parishes except that Capuchin missionaries rather than secular priests are in charge of operations, now that no Indians remain to be pacified. The missionaries have given up large-scale, communal labor projects in agriculture, fishing, and lumbering. Classes in nationalized schools (not boarding schools) attached to the missions are taught by missionaries, Indians, and Criollos employed by the state. Present-day missionaries have long since rejected the ethnocentric, self-righteous, and paternalistic attitudes of their predecessors, no longer considering it their obligation to "reduce and civilize" the Indians, as decreed by the old Law of Missions (Heinen 1988, 675–79). After two thousand years they find that the Church in Venezuela is no longer the Church of Spain and the West (i.e., Europe). Rather, since the decolonization of America in the nineteenth century and of Africa and Asia in the twentieth, the Mission of the Church has shifted to the Southern Hemisphere, where independent states will have the majority of Catholics (70 percent) and other Christians (60 percent) by the end of the twentieth century. As conceptualized by Vatican II, Catholic missions are being replaced by local churches that function increasingly under native prelates and clerics rather than under White mission bishops. These local churches accept their role as missionizing agencies but welcome any help that foreign missionaries can give them. In Latin America religio-sociological institutes such as CERIS (Centro de Estatística Religiosa e Investigações Sociaes) and DESAL (Centro para el Desarrollo Económico y Social de America Latina) and organizations like CELAM (Consejo Episcopal Latinoamericano) and CLAR (Confederación Latinoamericano de Religiosos) have exposed the static conditions of the clerical church and have promoted initiatives designed to end the centuries-old spiritual dependency of the people. Missionaries who today question their role in a changing world know that a new mission epoch will dawn only if the Church, rather than isolating itself and becoming irrelevant, accepts the challenge of the Universal Church and its missionizing local churches that actualize her. Missions that presently continue to operate in the colonial spirit of reducing and civilizing primitives and idolaters are believed to be coming to an end. In this era of readjustment within the Universal Church, missionaries are adopting a more ecumenical attitude and, in addition to their spiritual duties, are finding new roles as teachers and promoters of health care, development, and liberation. No longer considered inferior beings, the Indians are treated as coequals whose participation in a local church is not assured by a Catholic monopoly, but who are increasingly recruited in Latin America by missionaries of other denominations and faiths (Bühlmann 1976, 141–64; Costello 1979; Gorski 1985).

Contemporary Survivors

The Warao entered the twentieth century with a population of probably less than six thousand. Between 1936 and 1962 population estimates went as high as 11,712,[3] although this figure was almost certainly inflated (Barral 1949, 337; 1964, 1; Carrocera 1939, 202; Turrado Moreno 1945, 14). Thus the recovery of the Warao population is of recent standing and reflects, in part, the availability of modern health service through mission dispensaries and rural clinics. Western medicine, besides saving lives among the reproductively active generation (mothers in childbirth, for instance) and prolonging the lives of the elderly, has also reduced the rate of juvenile mortality through immunization. A more humane attitude by outsiders toward the Indians and the permanent protective presence, since 1925, of Capuchin missionaries in the delta have given the Warao a measure of security from wanton violence and persecution. From the diminished state in which Level (1898, 164) found them in the mid-nineteenth century, they have become the thriving population of today.

[3] It is only since the National Census of 1960 that numbers higher than 11,500 have become credible, and only since then has the Venezuelan Warao population begun to increase at an accelerated pace (Wilbert 1980a, 4). The impact of untoward circumstances during the colonial era can be gauged to some extent by examining the demographic data available for the Warao east of the delta, in Guyana and Surinam. Estimates for the former region have ranged from more than 3,000 in the mid-nineteenth century (Schomburgk 1840, 50–51) to just a few hundred in modern times (Butt 1965, 75). The Warao of Surinam, never known to have been numerous in the past, are today, as noted earlier, extinct.

Strange as the tardiness of researchers may seem for a relatively large tribal society at the gates to South America, professional anthropologists did not begin studying the Warao Indians until the 1950s. The older generation of the Winikina subtribe I researched for the first time, in 1954, had all been born in the secluded wet savannas of the deltaic islands, where they had existed as non-agricultural swamp foragers from time immemorial (Wilbert 1980a, 13–47). In the late 1920s, after taking up residence along the shores of nearby rivers, they had turned to swidden agriculture in the gallery forests around the islands. Eventually, in the 1940s, missionaries and Criollos running a timber mill entered Winikina territory, each group wanting for its own reasons to bring the Indians out of the morichals into a more accessible river environment. Many men and women of the reproductively active generation thus had originated in the refuge of deltaic islands, though others had already been born in exposed river settlements. Together they became first-generation village farmers in the central and western delta, thereby following the Warao of the southeastern delta. The latter, because of the location of moriche groves in their territory, had always favored a riparian environment; they probably adopted agriculture in the latter half of the nineteenth century. Thus, for the delta Warao, who are more traditionally diversified swamp foragers and fishermen, farming is a relatively recent occupation which they acquired from their Arawakan neighbors and their Guianese relatives.

Sago of the moriche palm, the preagricultural staple of the Warao, is supplemented by a variety of wild foods (palm cabbage, herbs, pineapple, fruit, honey), aquatic fare (manatees, alligators, fish, crabs, snails), terrestrial game (rodents, iguanas, turtles), and birds. Large species of mammals are traditionally hunted only reluctantly as they are considered to have "blood like our own." Leaving the interior swamp savannas of the lower delta for riparian habitats, where many of these edibles are unavailable or occur farther away, dictated a sharp change in subsistence procedures. The Warao, replacing sago with a newly introduced root, taro (*Colocasia antiquorum*) (plate 2.4), relied increasingly on this crop and on other agricultural products like sweet manioc (*Manihot dulcis*) and bitter manioc (*Manihot esculenta*), maize, bananas, and sugarcane. The old fishing techniques—bare-hand catching, spear and weir fishing, basket dragging and scooping, and gorge angling in shallow backland waters (plate 2.1)—had to be adjusted to function in deeper riverine water and for larger species of fish. Harpoons (plate 2.2), harpoon arrows, multipronged arrows, hooks, and nets became the preferred implements. Bows and arrows and lances are the most useful hunting weapons, and women go after small rodents with the help of hunting dogs. Although formerly unaware of the advantage of domesticated animals, the Warao now, besides using dogs, raise chickens and occasionally a pig, mainly for sale to non-Indians. With the introduction of agriculture, the methods of preparing food changed substantially. Once restricted to roasting fish and meat directly on an open fire or on rectangular barbecues, the Warao now boil food in imported iron casserole-type pots (plate 2.3). Round lumps of dried clay serve as fireplaces in the kitchens and under hammocks, where fires are kept burning through the night.

Modifications were also needed in house construction and settlement patterns. On the interior savannas nomadic bands lived in temporary camps of lean-tos, beehive huts, or simple rectangular thatched-roof pole structures without walls. Along the river, the more sedentary local groups took to constructing small rectangular single-family or large extended-family stilt houses with palm-thatched gable roofs (plate 2.3). The houses are arranged in one or more rows subparallel to the riverbank, with, possibly, a shrine on the eastern end and a hut reserved for menstruating women on the western end of the village.

As nomadic foragers, local groups or bands comprised probably less than 50 people. Of the sedentary agricultural bands in the gallery forests, roughly two-thirds (68 percent) still average no more than 54 inhabitants although some are much larger, numbering between 50 and 250 (31 percent) or more (1 percent) residents (Censo Indígena de Venezuela 1985). Now as before, however, Warao populations are composed of young people, with about 50 percent below eighteen years of age. Band members belong to interrelated nuclear and extended uxorilocal families. They follow the advice of the oldest man in the group, though his political power is sharply limited. Polygyny, which is often sororal, is not uncommon, and men may be married to two or more women at the same time. Several local bands belong to a subtribe which, under mission influence, began to recognize chiefs who were responsible to governors in charge of larger aggregates. Traditionally, bands and

Narrow Passages

PLATE 2.1

Demonstrating ancient method of fish gorge angling. Live bait is tied to end of fishing line on rod. Small backwater fish bite and are flipped into basket before they can let go of bait. Gorge works less well in rivers with larger species of fish and was replaced by iron fishhook. (Photograph Johannes Wilbert)

PLATE 2.2
River fishing required adoption of iron-tipped composite harpoon. Bait is held dangling from stick, close to water's surface, while harpoon is held on the ready. (Courtesy Lucy Millowitsch)

PLATE 2.3
Sago flat cakes being baked, using bottom of traded casserole-type iron pot, in camp of provisional rectangular huts built to celebrate sago festival (1954). (Photograph Johannes Wilbert)

PLATE 2.4

Woman removing taro roots, brought home from garden, from folded-leaf basket. Taro and horticulture are relatively recent acquisitions of the Warao, introducing global culture change. Weather shamanism becomes obsolete because of this change in food economy. (Courtesy Peter T. Furst) subtribes were loosely held together by a group of elders specializing in different types of shamanism. Contemporary villages, therefore, still possess a strong religious leadership officiating side by side with political leaders. Often enough, however, the offices of chief and shaman are held by the same person. Men predominate among officeholders, but women also practice as shamanesses and herbal healers.

By Hawaiian type-kinship reckoning, bands are mostly exogamous, since cousins are considered as brothers and sisters and thus are subject to the incest taboo. Young men must therefore seek marriageable partners in neighboring bands or wait for occasional reunions when the bands of a subtribe congregate, two or three hundred strong, to hold a sago festival or participate in other religious or secular ceremonies. On these occasions young people meet potential spouses, always anxious to avoid subtribal exogamy, which occurs only infrequently among the Warao.

In their modern houses, hammocks netted from moriche-palm fiber have replaced the old leaf-stalk hammocks formerly used in the morichals. A variety of baskets are made by both men and women, but landmark crafts like weaving, pottery, and metallurgy are nonexistent. In colonial times Warao women wore sleeveless ankle-length cotton dresses whenever their men brought home fabric, thread, and needles from trading expeditions across the sea to Trinidad or after overland journeys to Criollo settlements. Although today all women wear these or similar dresses and men sport European-style pants, shirts, and hats, before the 1930s most women and men lacked such outfits; instead, they wore pubic covers of homemade bark cloth or palm stipules. Except for these covers they went naked, adorning their bodies with necklaces of seeds, bones, shells, or animal teeth. They also wore bands of moriche bast on their arms and legs and occasionally painted parts of their bodies with red roller-stamped vegetable dye.

The single most important item of Warao material culture is the paddled dugout canoe (plate 2.8). It is essential to the Indians' livelihood, especially now that they live on the banks of big rivers with most life-sustaining activities requiring transportation by water.

The Warao have developed a complex system of shamanism. Shamans cure endemic as well as exotic diseases. This medical activity has allowed them to remain just as successful as they had

PLATE 2.5, River frontage village of pile dwellings housing semi-sedentary endogamous band. Three or four such villages constitute an endogamous subtribe of 200 to 300 people. Political leadership of villages and subtribes is more accentuated than in nonagricultural times. (Courtesy Peter T. Furst)

Narrow Passages 59

PLATE 2.6. Interior view of large pile dwelling sheltering three nuclear families of uxorilocal extended family. Houses like this belong to wife of founder couple. Observance of avoidance taboo vis-à-vis in-laws of either sex requires interpersonal communication to flow from the male founder through his wife and his daughters to their husbands. (Courtesy Peter T. Furst)

PLATE 2.7
Mealtime for women and children in kitchen house. Men eat in separate group. (Photograph Johannes Wilbert)

PLATE 2.8. Nuclear polygynous family returning from the garden. Dugout canoes of all sizes below 12 meters are used for daily chores. Canoes 12 meters and over, once used for overseas trading, are built by shamanic craftsmen in complex ritual procedure. (Courtesy Lucy Millowitsch)

been before the arrival of Old World pathogens and to escape the enduring loss in reputation their colleagues suffered throughout the Americas. With their prestige intact, it also afforded them the time necessary to construct a cosmological theory of illness which made intellectual sense of the formidable threat the new diseases posed to their survival.

Both endemic and exotic diseases are attributed by the Warao to divine beings at the cardinal points, the zenith, and the nadir. To some degree, this compartmentalization has promoted shamanic specialization in diseases specific to these directional powers (fig. 2.1). More specifically, the priest-shaman (*wishiratu*) relates to the gods of the south, the north, and the east. The god of the south is responsible for febrile diseases like "the fever of many granules" (smallpox and measles), "the shivering spirit" (malaria), and "the hot skin" disease (yellow fever). The god of the north specializes in endemic and exotic respiratory ailments like "the bad cough" (bronchitis), "the hurting lungs" (pneumonia), and, above all, the "cough of the howler monkey" (whooping cough). The god of the

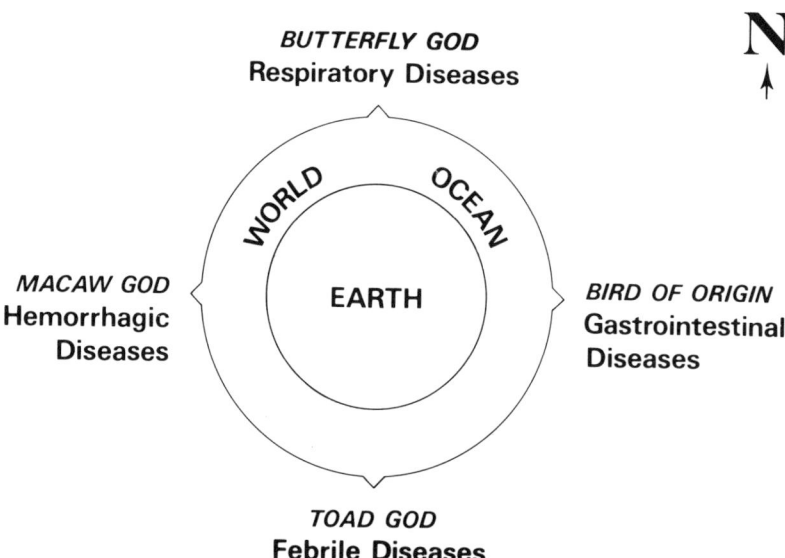

Fig. 2.1
Warao ethnopathology and epidemic disease. (Drawing by Noel Diaz)

east controls gastrointestinal disorders like hookworm, enteritis, and other diarrheal diseases. His most devastating weapon, however, is cholera.

The dark shaman (*hoarotu*) serves the god of the west who magically "kills" by means of hemorrhagic diseases like bloody dysentery, both amoebic and bacillary. He is a strangler who asphyxiates his victims with the "incurable cough" (pulmonary tuberculosis).

The light shaman (*bahanarotu*) relates to Mawari of the zenith whose image, in the form of a wooden mannequin, he activates to cause sporadic epidemic outbreaks that purportedly wipe out entire villages (Wilbert 1983).

The rain shaman is not a healer but a sorcerer. He engages the rain lords to produce weather conditions that enfeeble the people of his own or any other target community. Exposure to inclement atmospheric and concomitant hunger conditions predisposes the victims to be smitten by the directional gods with *hebu, bahana*, or *hoa* sicknesses. These may or may not be curable by the corresponding healers (*wishiratu, bahanarotu, hoarotu*), depending on the endemic or exotic nature of the disease pathologies concerned (see chapter 3).

Accordingly, each shamanic specialist addresses or relates to both native and foreign diseases and learns in the course of his practice not only how to distinguish among them but how to gauge his prospects of healing them. For the patient and his or her kin, however, the stark reality between curable and incurable diseases remains largely hidden, so that ministrations by the herbalists and the hope of recovery will relieve the patient's suffering and move him or her beyond the crisis toward recovery or death.

Shamans in the missions were probably aware that the padres, observing the pathologies of disease and its distributions throughout the land, began to suspect natural causes of epidemic illnesses as well. There were sickly and healthy locations for mission foundings and stale and airy climes. Some early writers even mention a possible correlation between febrile diseases and the presence of swamps, seasonal precipitation, flooding, and mosquitoes. They also implicate "gaseous emanations" from swampland as causal factors of recurrent epidemics as well as "pestilent exhalations" rising from the rocks (Morey 1979, 86, 94, 97). Similarly, in their present

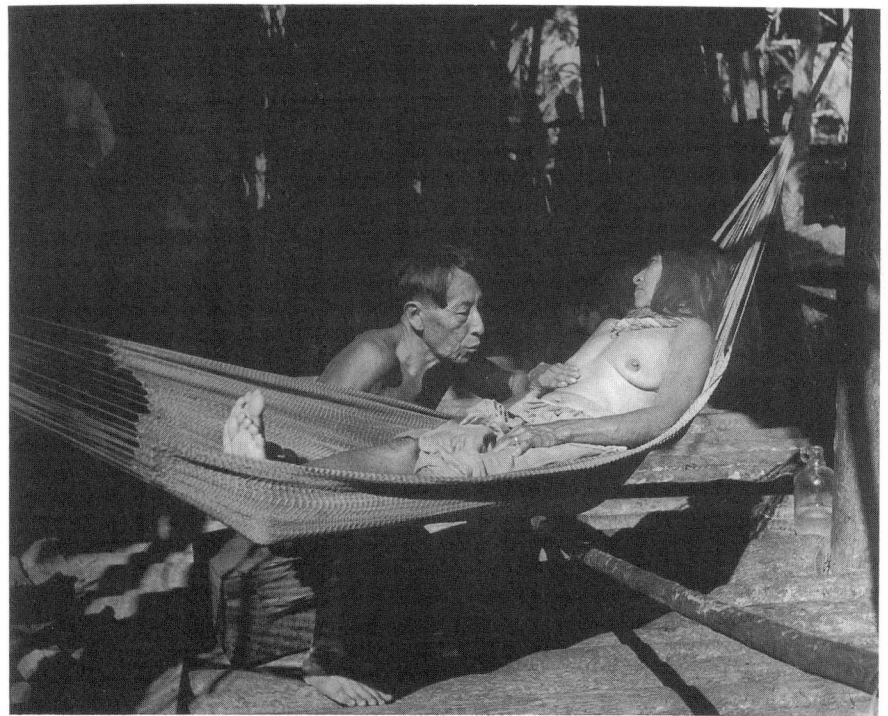

PLATE 2.9

Shaman curing woman through massaging and magical blowing of ailing body part. Pathogens are sucked out and blown away to remote part of forest. Despite access to Western health facilities, Warao shamanism continues to be fully functional; with increased mobility due to outboard motors, however, Warao now frequently consult Western health personnel. (Courtesy P. J. Ziegenaus)

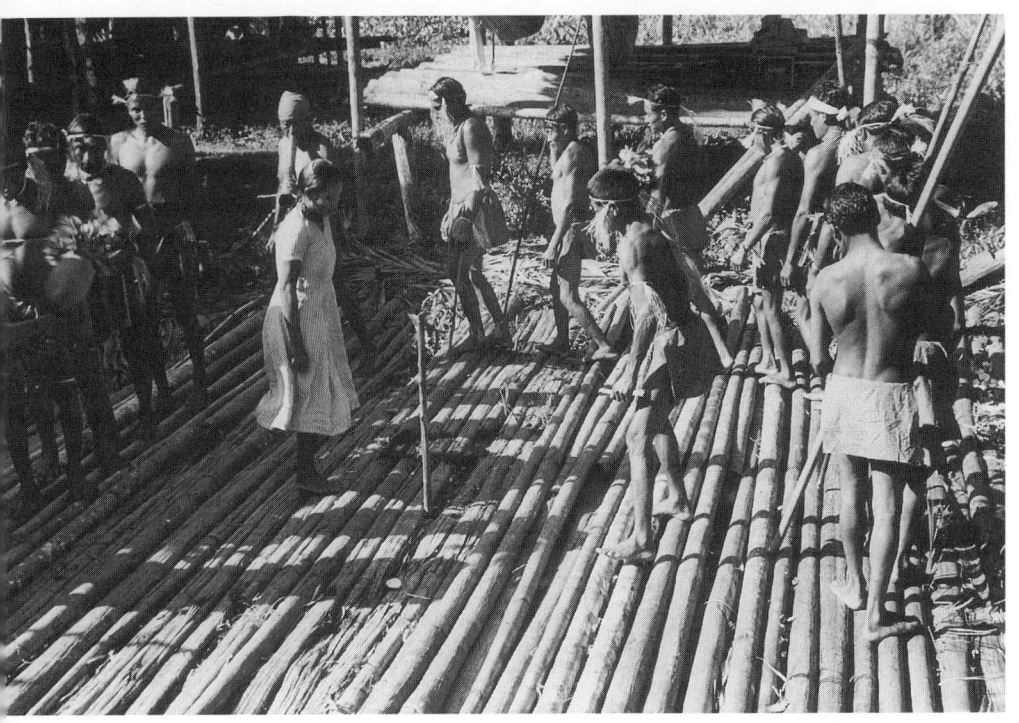

PLATE 2.10
Preparatory to sago festival, player of sacred trumpet leads men in a counter-clockwise circle dance. Woman has entered circle where she jumps up and down with locked feet, fixing gaze on sacred central pole. On other side of pole, partner steps sideways, swinging sacred rattle. Sago rite connects living with dead and propitiates "Grandfather" deities to protect the children from dying during rainy season. (Courtesy Sociedad de Ciencias Naturales La Salle, Caracas)

PLATE 2.11

Early morning during sago festival (1954). Three baskets containing sago offering stand in middle of dancing platform constructed of moriche bark strips. Sets of large and small sacred trumpets and rattles rest near the central pole. Large "rattle of ruffled feathers" is sacrosanct instrument used on festive occasions. (Photograph Johannes Wilbert)

PLATE 2.12. Primary and secondary burials of priest-shamans are miniature houses with walls of palm fronds lacking doors or windows. (Photograph Johannes Wilbert)

understanding of epidemic diseases, the Warao connect some of them with blustery winds in the rainy season and ground their entire system of herbal medicine in a theory of pathological and salutary airs (Wilbert, W., 1986). According to this "pneumatic theory" of illness, pathological agents of putrefaction, filth, and macula are transported by turbulent winds, the trade winds, polluted water, crusted mud, spoiled food, and other vehicles into the patient's body, where they transform into fetid gas. Here the foul air is attacked by fragrant air emanating from ingested or applied herbal remedies. The two airs engage in battle and the good air, if successful, expels the bad air before it departs on its own, leaving the patient healed. It is likely that the missionaries and their fellow patriots were no strangers to the Mediterranean folk theory of fetid air or evil wind (*mal aire*) as a cause of disease in humans (Foster 1953a; 1972). And it is conceivable that this concept was incorporated into Warao disease etiology. But similar theories of bad wind illness are also prevalent among other South American Indians (Kogi, Reichel-Dolmatoff 1985, 237; Puruhá-Quichua, Aguiló 1985, 19; Cashinaua, Abreu 1938b, 310; Campa, Weiss 1969, 146; Shipibo, Roe 1982, 121), and, as pointed out by W. Wilbert (1986, 378; 1987, 1144–45), the pneumatic theory of the Warao is much more intricate than the simple Mediterranean notion of disease-causing winds. A number of idiosyncratic structural and systemic differences can be marshaled to demonstrate that relatively simple Old World concepts of wind pathology, as they were pondered by colonial missionaries, were possibly absorbed by the Warao but then reworked into a more complex paradigm of phytotherapy.

For the Warao, an important side-benefit of leaving the secluded wet savannas for the riverbanks was access to Western medicine in the mission clinics. This entrée has had a significant impact on priest-shamans and their elaborate sago rituals petitioning the directional gods to spare the children from dying in the rainy seasons. "Now we have the nuns [in the mission dispensary]," I was told by the headman of a southern delta village; "we don't have to placate the gods anymore, because it is the medicine of the missionaries which protects our children, not the annual sago festival." Shamanic curing is gradually losing ground among groups that live in permanent contact with missionaries and Criollos, not only because of the efficacy of Western medicine but also because of the differing theories of illness held by the two systems. For the Indians, animistic causation (spirit aggression) and magical causation (object intrusion) are deeply rooted in the cosmogony and shamanic ideology of foragers. At the time of this writing, agriculture and commercialization are eroding the traditional socioeconomic system of Warao society, and there is a noticeable decline in the Indian's quality of life (Heinen 1988, 672, 682). Population growth, cultural disorientation, and outmigration challenge the cohesion of several subtribal groups. Partially uprooted Warao are entering the wage labor market of Criollo towns, and groups of men and women are occasionally bussed to the country's capital, Caracas, there to panhandle for their personal benefit and, one suspects, for the enrichment of some entrepreneurs.[4]

---

[4] Newspaper article by Miguel Layrisse in *El Nacional*, October 11, 1994, p. 4.

Chapter Three

Warao Weather Lore

Polluting Rain

Rain Maidens and Rainbow

The Warao distinguish among various kinds of celestial water and consider all of them to be potentially harmful. Rather than being related, as such waters usually are, to purification and fertility concepts, rain for the Warao has the antithetical connotation of pollution, infirmity, and death. It is also mythically associated with the acute suffering caused by rape, uprootedness, murder, bereavement, and subordination.

Dew, drizzle, and soft rain, for instance, are more often than not manifestations of the cloud people. They materialize as drifting mist, as veils of spray in the forest canopy, and as swishing droplets on river, swamp, and soil. Though apparently gentle and benevolent, cloud people in these guises enfold the world in a deadly embrace. According to Warao tradition, from behind this curtain of moisture, cloud girls sometimes appear. They laugh engagingly and are so fair that young men, enthralled by their charm, are tempted to possess them. After the fleeting moments of intimacy, however, a human lover will find that he has acquired the watery nature of the cloud girl's body. Having turned into a water person himself, he perspires incessantly and finally dies of exposure to the cold of the night (cf. Lavandero 1982).

Another kind of moisture are soft showers that fall when the sun is hot and often accompany the appearance of a rainbow. Rainbow is believed to be a male personage with a columnar body not unlike that of a serpent. In fact, his name, *hubanasiko*, is indicative of the likeness, inasmuch as it includes *huba*, the word for snake, combined with *nasi*, necklace. *Hubanasiko*, then, meaning "serpent with necklace," designates a vain and flirtatious young man (Barral 1964, 456).

No longer a bachelor, Rainbow is married to a daughter of the Forest Mother. Uprooted from the place where he grew up, he lives uxorilocally along the sun's path at the southern solstice. Here, stretched out between sunrise (southeast) and sunset (southwest), reclines the body of the Mistress of the Forest in the form of a felled red *cachicamo* tree (*Colophyllum lucidum* Benth.), the wood that shamanic boat makers prefer to use for dugout canoes. To these craftsmen the Mother of the Forest appears in a trance as a colossal horned serpent. Her head, containing her immortal soul, is located at sunrise. Her abdomen, in the form of a tree stump—from which the trunk has been severed—is located at sunset of the winter sun and contains her reproductive powers. Although all trees, generically speaking, are daughters of the Forest Mother, only red *cachicamo* trees are the female offspring specific to her kind. And it is to one of these young women that Rainbow is wedded.

Whereas Rainbow, as a married man, lives in the southern realm of his in-laws, his place of origin is actually in the north, along the path of the summer sun. At times he may be observed raising his chromatic body skyward and bending over across the firmament to reach the opposite northern region of his childhood. Distressed by the separation from his consanguineal kinfolk, he longs to slake his excessive thirst with the water of his homeland. After he has done so and is fully saturated, he can be seen relieving himself over the earth in showers of urinary rain. The Warao sing facetious songs about this abuse, imploring Rainbow to tighten his loincloth and stop the drizzle (Barral 1948; 1964, 455). In a more serious vein, however, rain shamans blow against the incontinent Rainbow, shouting:

Hubanasikoo,	Rainbow,
Hubanasikoo.	Rainbow.
Diana tai.	That is enough.
Maribu noko.	Listen to my words.
Diana tai.	That is enough.
Maribu noko:	Mark my words:
Nakanaka takunarai.	Let it [the "rain"] fall no more.

Sometimes Rainbow, accompanied by his beautiful wife, travels to his home country. They can be seen spanning the firmament as a double arch, with the male bow above the female one (Barral 1960, 94–95). On these occasions it rains, because somewhere on earth a red *cachicamo* tree has been felled to be turned into a dugout canoe. Showers of this kind are the tears of the female rainbow and of her mother, the Forest Mother, and other close uterine kin. Overcome by grief and bemoaning the death of their kinswoman, the tree women accuse humans of having made necessary, once again, the sacrifice of a *cachicamo*-maiden (Wilbert 1977b, 31–38). Precipitation accompanied by a rainbow, or only by sunshine, is feared for its pathological qualities. The sunshowers are taken especially as a sign that the spirit that causes them is about to send such illnesses as diarrhea, typhus, and vomiting, among others, into the homes of the people. Moreover, sunshowers also herald danger from an approaching jaguar (whose roar produces thunderstorms) or from a large group of foreigners (whose presence brings dreaded pestilence).

Gentle rain showers of a similar nature also fall when a shaman dies or, for that matter, when any member of his family passes away. Even upon the death of an ordinary person or of a child, the women's lament can be so mournful that the tears and the grief of the bereaved may bring on a weeping sky. Gentle rains therefore are usually intermittent. They may come at any time of the year, be it during the rainy seasons or during the dry seasons.

The Lords of Rain

In contrast, storms are typical of the rainy seasons. They originate with supernaturals referred to as *kabo arotutuma*, "Masters of the Night Sky." The Warao recognize eight such gods, or Lords of Rain, who reside on the same number of mountains at the cardinal and intercardinal points along the horizonal edge of the universe (fig. 3.1). Bracing the sky, the mountains are seen as enormous petrified tree stumps modeled, it would seem, after the flat-topped table mountains (*tepuis*) of Guayana, south of the Orinoco Delta. The tops of these truncated mountains, shrouded in clouds almost every day, give the impression that the sky rests on them. Some Warao shamans, as well as some ordinary men, are familiar with the *tepuis* and associate their cloud-gathering nature with the wind people and the rain.

The rain gods live on the mountains in mansions with doors and windows facing the center of the earth. During the dry seasons the doors remain permanently closed, but during the rainy seasons they are wide open, with the resident lords sitting on stools in the doorways looking toward earth. A peculiarity of the rain gods is that their life-style is distinctly non-Warao. To begin with, it is obvious that the traditional pile dwelling, featuring raised floor, roof, and wall-less sides, cannot have served as a blueprint for the mansions of the rain gods. Rather, the shamans compare their architectural

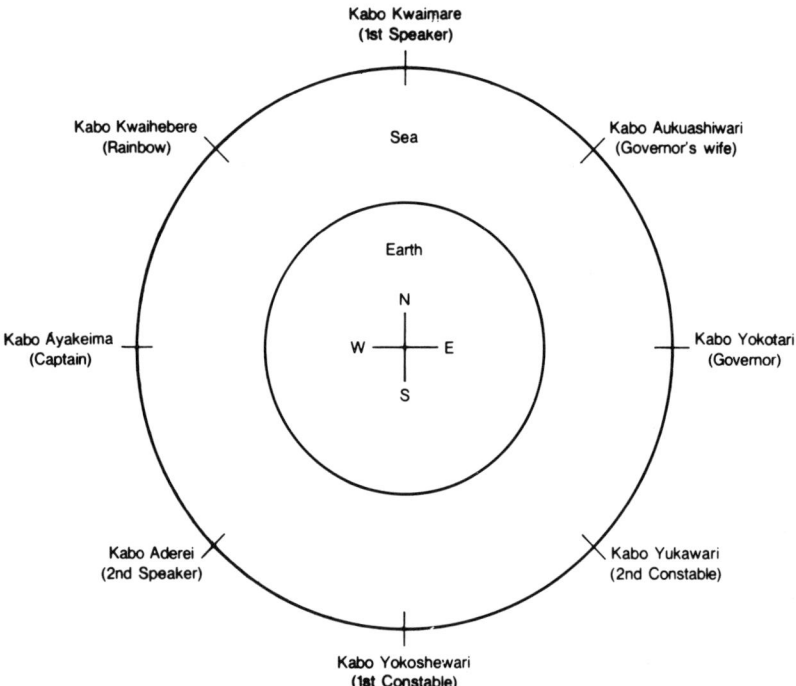

FIG. 3.1
The eight Lords of Rain and their stations. (Drawing by Noel Diaz)

style with that of the houses of wealthy Criollos. Like the Criollos—whose ancestors interbred for several generations and in differing degrees with whites, Indians, and blacks—the rain gods have a complexion that is lighter than the dark skin of the Warao; it is said to be almost white. Still, all the rain gods have a common human physiognomy, except for their enormous flaring heads.

The apparel of rain gods is also distinctly different from that of the traditional Warao. In the dry seasons the gods wear long white tunics, which they exchange for black ones during the rainy seasons. Their eyes are framed by spectacles, their mouths hold elbow pipes, and their feet are protected by sandals. To complete their wardrobe, the gods wear black, wide-brimmed hats, and in their right hands they clutch sturdy walking staffs with which to steady their gait.

At the onset of the long rainy season, sometime in April, the Lords of Rain begin to stir inside their houses. As they walk about, they are heard to moan, making rolling thunderous noises. After their seclusion during the preceding dry season, they need to urinate, and eventually they push open the doors of their mansions to relieve themselves. The southerly lords become especially restless, and their actions cause the rivers of the Orinoco basin to overflow and flood the land.

When indoors, the rain gods pass the time sitting on their stools and smoking their pipes. From time to time they hear the weather shaman's voice, provoking them into action. Then they rise singly, in groups of two or more, or all at once and stride toward the top of the sky vault, which is the center of their village. As they engage in dancing and chanting on the plaza, they perspire rain and provoke storms of thunder and lightning.

The rain gods constitute a hierarchical assembly of one female and seven male supernatural beings. The titles of rank in Table 3.1 are English translations of their Waraoan equivalents, most of which come from Spanish. In the Warao language the governor is referred to as *kobenahoro*; the governor's wife as *kobenahoro atida*; the captain as *kabitana*; the first constable as *bisikari* or *fisicali* (Sp., *fiscal*); the second constable (*bisikari's* assistant) as *borisia* (Sp., *policía*); the first speaker as *dibatu aida*; the second speaker, as *dibatu sanuka*; and the rainbow as *hubanasiko*.

In colonial times, missionaries first used titles of Spanish origin, as noted, to designate members of indigenous local councils or

TABLE 3.1
Warao Lords of Rain, Their Ranks, and Locations

Name	Rank	Location
Kabo Yokotari	Governor	East
Kabo Aukuashiwari	Governor's wife	Northeast
Kabo Ayakeima	Captain	West
Kabo Yokoshewari	First constable	South
Kabo Yukawari	Second constable	Southeast
Kabo Kwaimare	First speaker	North
Kabo Aderei	Second Speaker	Southwest
Kabo Kwaihebere	Rainbow	Northwest

cabildos, and later, in the time of the republic, to designate leaders of Indian communities under their jurisdiction. Today the Warao recognize the governor as the supreme leader of a region or a subtribe; the captain, serving as the governor's deputy, is in charge of one village or of several villages. He usually succeeds the governor in office. The first constable functions as a foreman in carrying out communal projects. The second constable metes out punishments ordered by the governor or the captain. The speakers are traditional rhetoricians who present, at public sessions of dispute resolution, summaries of the cases before the assembly. They mediate with considerable oratorical skill, admonishing the disputants to uphold the values of their people (Briggs 1988). Usually only one speaker in a local group plays this most important role of peacemaker, yet two of them belong to the assembly of the rain lords. The second speaker's title, *dibatu sanuka*, meaning "lesser speaker," designates an occasionally significant position as an alternate or a substitute. Finally, Rainbow is the nickname of the rain lord of the northwest who marks the homeland of the meteoric spirit visible from earth. The rainbow is thus an image of the northwestern lord, but they are not identical in nature.

Following a hunch that the order in which the rain gods are ranked and placed along the horizon might be deliberate rather than random, I compared the mythical layout with climatological wind roses from various locations in and around the Orinoco Delta. It was with some surprise when my suspicion was confirmed by the wind rose of Güiria situated on the southern shore of the Paria Peninsula in the Gulf of Paria, opposite the delta (fig. 3.2).

Warao Weather Lore

TABLE 3.2
Relationship of Rain Lord Ranking and Wind Conditions

| | | Wind | | |
Rank	Location	Frequency (percent)	Direction	Average Velocity (kph)
Governor	E	20	Easterly	5
Governor's Wife	NE	10	Northeasterly	5
Captain	W	7	Westerly	3
Constable 2nd	SE	5	Souteasterly	3
Constable 1st	S	3	Southerly	3
Speaker 1st	N	3	Northerly	2.5
Rainbow	NW	3	Northwesterly	2.5
Speaker 2nd	SW	1	Southwesterly	1.5

Source: *Atlas de Venezuela*, 1979, 195. Meteorological data corresponding to Güiria, Sucre.

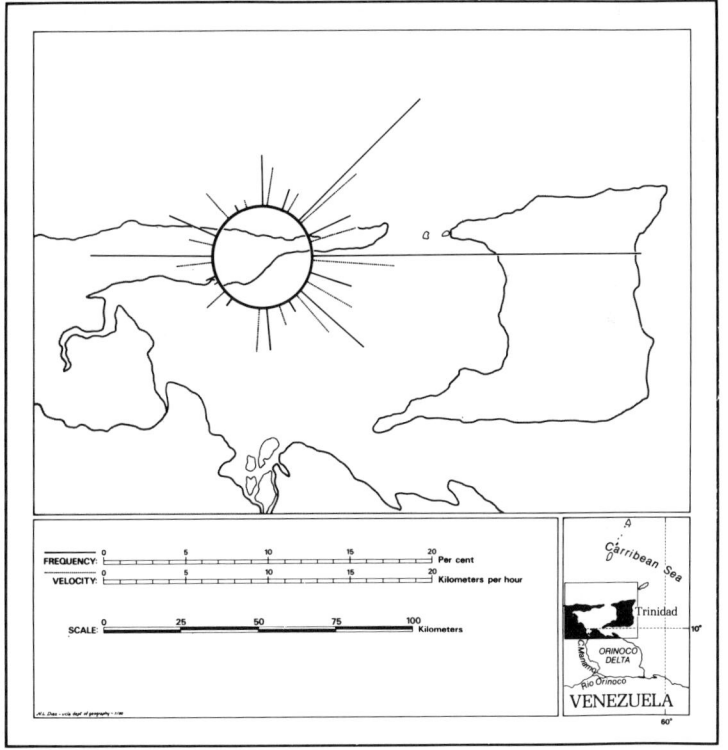

FIG. 3.2
Wind rose, Güiria, Gulf of Paria. Wind data for period 1951–70.
(Drawing by Noel Diaz)

The Güiria wind rose was published in the *Atlas de Venezuela* (1979, 195) and is based on data recorded during the time period of 1951–1970. With minor deviations, the rank and power of each lord corresponds to the relative frequency and velocity of winds along the delta littoral and the Gulf of Paria (table 3.2). In the middle of the eighteenth century, small groups of Warao lived in the missions of Santa Isabel and La Divina Pastora de Catacuao near Güiria (map A.1), and delta navigators frequented Güiria and its environs on trading expeditions. On these and similar occasions they may have become familiar with the European compass and inspired to enthrone eight rain lords on as many mountains located at the cardinal and intercardinal points of their universe. As will be shown later in the study, mountain rain spirits in South American mythology did not necessarily have to await the arrival of the Europeans to be brought into existence; they occur in several places throughout the continent. But compliments of eight directional spirits of this kind (at cardinal and intercardinal points) in a single tribal cosmology appear reminiscent of the Old World compass tradition, especially if the roles of several of them are only vaguely defined. In Warao mythology the rain lords are not identical with the directional wind spirits (see below). But, they convey the precipitation they cause on the winds that frequent their world quarters; the more frequent and forceful the wind the more powerful the rain lord who makes use of its service.

The Long Rainy Season

When, in mid-April, the northern trade winds lose their vernal equinoctial vigor, the Warao take the change as the first sign that the long rainy season of travail and sorrow has begun. In the headwater region of the Orinoco—overall the rainiest part of Venezuela—the rain is especially heavy. Probably caused by a rapid transit of the centerline of the equatorial trough between the Amazon and the llanos region, these monsoonlike conditions soon reach the llanos, west of Warao territory, where muffled thundering is heard in the distance. The center of the equatorial trough is moving northward toward the Orinoco-Apure line (Snow 1976, 337–38). By the end of May precipitation in the delta has risen to above 200 millimeters, and Kabo Ayakeima, the rain lords' captain in the west, has begun to demonstrate his overpowering rage. Between that time and August, he intermittently inflicts tempests of uncommon violence on Waraoland.

To the Warao, these local western storms (*barineses*) are driven by the anger of this powerful third-ranking rain lord. Kabo Ayakeima's mansion is located near the underworld of the Warao universe, where *miana* magic is at home and where the anger of weather stress, both physical and mental, has its taproot. For it is not only physical suffering, such as hunger, sickness, and death, to which the Warao expect to be subjected during the wet seasons. Equally dreaded is the emotional torment that creeps like fog into their villages, triggering outbursts of disruptive behavior.

Another unmistakable sign of the rainy season's arrival is the whining, buzzing, and biting of blood-sucking insects which take to the air with the onset of the rains, when their bites are more painful than at any other time. The Warao associate this tormenting plague with the occupants of the underworld because, like them, the insects feed on human blood. Mosquitoes, horseflies, and *golofa* (Bombyliidae) flies are simply metamorphic forms of a mythical young man who murdered his wives by sucking out their blood through a hollow cane. He performed this act at night when his victims were asleep, using a technique akin to that of underworld denizens.[1] When discovered by one of his intended victims, the murderer of women was burned to death by the people. But from his ashes arose a score of different bloodsucking insects which continue to torture humankind with spiteful vengeance (Wilbert 1970, 50–51, 199–201; n.d.). Arriving with the Orinoco floods and the first thunderstorms from the west, they all inflict painful bites; the mosquitoes may even introduce debilitating and sometimes fatal illnesses to the upper delta and the regions south of the Rio Grande.

---

[1] The spirits of the underworld employed for the same purpose an umbilicus-like artery that automatically attached itself to the crowns of sleeping humans to drain out their blood (Wilbert 1975b, 173). *Hoarotu* shamans are believed to suck blood from their victims by mouth before transporting the cadavers on their backs to the underworld for consumption.

The Indians are also consternated by the disappearance of the Pleiades (April 30 to June 9) and of Orion (May 27 to July 5).[2] From the beginning of May to the first week in July, these two asterisms are either invisible or "separated" over the Orinoco Delta, their absence or separation coinciding with a sharp upswing in the rate of infant mortality. Food shortages caused by the lack of sago in moriche stems and the flooding of the forest bring severe gastro-intestinal disorders which "draw" the children up to the sky when the constellations are not watching. Orion is the son of the sun and the husband of the Pleiades; Orion's belt represents the phallus that fertilizes the womb as recognized in the cluster of the Pleiades (Heinen and Lavandero 1973, 12).[3]

According to the Warao, in primordial times Pleiades rescued her husband from being eaten by her mother, a monstrous swallower

---

[2] Calculated for nine degrees north over the Orinoco Delta, the course of the Pleiades is as follows: last visible setting in west after sunset, April 30; first visible rising in east before sunrise (heliacal), June 9; last visible rising in east after sunset, November 10; first visible setting in west before sunrise (heliacal), November 26. The equivalent positions for Eta Orionis (central star in Orion's belt) are: last visible setting in west after sunset, May 27; first visible rising in east before sunrise (heliacal), July 5; last visible rising in east after sunset, December 12; first visible setting in west before sunrise (heliacal), December 7.

These dates are approximations within at least plus or minus eight days. The margin of uncertainty is owing to variations in water vapor and dust in the atmosphere. I am indebted to Dr. Edward C. Krupp (director, Griffith Observatory, Los Angeles) for these calculations, which are based on the appropriate tables in Aveni (1972).

[3] The constellation of Orion is called *nohihabasi*, "one of two thighs," in Waraoan. It also means phallus. The constellation of the Pleiades is called *kuramokomoko*, "little stars." It also means vulva. The double entendres are apparently not current among all the regional subgroups of the Warao. In areas where the double meaning for Pleiades is understood, however, it is risqué to use the term in the presence of women, especially the mother-in-law, who would be gravely offended by having her matriarchal respect shamed and compromised in this way (Barral 1979, 281). Instead of *kuramokomoko*, sons-in-law say *hahesebe*, "many paddles," *wirimusebe*, "many paddlers," or *domu*, "bird" (Heinen and Lavandero 1973, 12).

A narrative similar in kind to this stellar episode of the Warao "Origin of the sun" was recorded by Magaña (1978a, 185) among the Trio Indians of Surinam and Brazil. See also Koelewijn with Rivière 1987, 26–30; Magaña 1978b, 220–22.

who had already devoured her husband's twin brother. Orion was a successful fisherman who tried to satisfy the insatiable appetite of his mother-in-law with huge catches of fish (cf. Magaña 1988, 191–92). Eventually realizing that he could not provide adequate sustenance for the gluttonous woman, he murdered her and escaped to the sidereal sky. Before he reached the firmament, however, his wife caught up with him and cut off one of his legs with a machete. She too went to the sky, where she may be seen walking ahead of her disabled husband.[4]

In one particular version of Warao genesis, Pleiades, the wife of Sun's son, was destined to become the generative locus of humanity, the birth canal through which the ancestral Warao descended from heaven to earth (Heinen and Lavandero 1973, 14). As the passageway was obstructed by his pregnant wife, the priest-shaman, along with other ancestral Warao, was unable to descend. Envy of the trapped shaman is what causes people to fall ill and draws many of them up to the sky-world (cf. Lavandero 1975, 63). Thus, whereas the presence of the Pleiades and Orion symbolizes fertility and life to the Warao, the absence or separation of these asterisms during the culmination of the long wet season indicates physical decline and the precipitous loss of human offspring.

Among the various heralds of the primary wet season are also the constellations of Cancer, when it appears at dusk in the western sky (Heinen et al. 1995, 323), and of the Southern Cross. The latter asterism, which dominates the night sky over the delta from April to June, has a special meaning for the survival of Warao children (as noted below). Finally, when the *waiwari* butterflies arrive at the beginning of the period, the floodwater of the Orinoco basin begins to invade the upper delta. The rivers become turbid, and the swamp streams adopt the dark brown color of so-called blackwater rivers. Now the big rainy season (*nahanaka,* "fall of rain," or *hoida,* "high water") begins in earnest.

---

[4] This summary of an episode in a lengthy myth about the origin of the sun was collected, in 1970, from the Siawani-Warao (Wilbert n.d., 177–95).

The Thunderbird

As a consequence of the northward translation of the intertropical convergence zone across the Orinoco Delta in June, the Warao habitat comes to be situated in the southern meteorological hemisphere. Concurrent with this meridional translation, the skies over Waraoland are stirred up as the southern trades gain access to the region and clash with their northern counterparts. The powerful rain lords of the northeast, the southeast, and occasionally of the west (*barinés*) battle it out and send heavy precipitation on their winds in nimbostratus clouds with continuous rain or, more often, in towering cumulonimbus clouds with periodic downpours.

The Warao believe that the trade winds hail from the ends of the world, where the rain gods have their mansions. The ruler of the monsoonlike southern trade winds is Tuyuna, the sun bittern (*Eurypyga helias*), known in Venezuela as *tigana* (Yépez 1979, 66: 22–23). Hia, the striated heron (*Butorides striatus*), known as *chicuaco cuello gris,* is master of the northern trades. Although the southern trade winds, meteorologically speaking, may be of lesser frequency in the delta than the northern trades, it does not follow that Tuyuna, mythological master of the former, is considered inferior to Hia, ruler of the latter. As a matter of fact, because of his relationship to the wet seasons, and especially because of his association with hurricanes and other tropical storms, Tuyuna, like the western rain lord, provokes turnabout winds (*ahakabari*) and is a rather formidable ally of the rainmaker (Heinen et al. 1995, 322).

In Western taxonomy the two avian rulers of the trade winds are grouped in different families (*Eurypygidae* and *Ardeidae,* respectively). The Warao, however, consider them as two birds of a kind. And, as suggested by biologists themselves, the two species do actually resemble each other in appearance and behavior (Meyer de Schauensee and Phelps 1978, 65; Slud 1964, 37; Grzimek 1969, 107). The sun bittern, except for its long tail, looks very much like a small short-legged heron, and both are solitary wading birds which inhabit swamps and forest rivers and streams, where they feed on fish, frogs, and insects.

Ethnographic literature usually describes the sun bittern as a semidomesticated bird that walks about the yard like any other fowl.

Schomburgk reported the bird among the Guyanese Warao (1847–48, 2:185), and a century later Turrado Moreno (1945, 104) mentioned it as one of several kinds of birds kept by the Warao of the Orinoco Delta. The sun bittern is invariably described as having exceptionally colorful plumage and a meek and "melancholic" bearing (Codazzi [1841], in Alvarado 1953–58, 1:334), with a plaintive piping voice.

The Warao, however, focus their attention on the distinctly different characteristics of the sun bittern in the wild. They see its deep red eyes flashing in a perpetually turning head. They see a serpentine neck and a daggerlike beak lunging out to snatch its prey with lightning speed and deadly accuracy. In addition to its mournful cry, they also recognize the sun bittern's aggressive and penetrating double whistle that rings out when the bird is startled or attacked. Finally, the Warao have seen the sun bittern step out of the darkness of the forest into a clearing where, in full daylight, it spreads its richly colored wings, displaying their "sunburst" effect (plate 3.1). The forward-tilted wings and the raised tail that fills the space between them form a canopy of plumage which, in frontal view, prefigures the mental model of the bell-shaped universe of the Warao. While the bird holds this impressive position, its rear part weaves uncannily, providing a background for the sinuously curved neck on which its head and beak, thrust skyward, stand rigidly in the midst of an imposing tableau (Skutch 1985, 568).

The first time I heard the *tigana* (sun bittern) mentioned was in a chant of Yokoshewari (see below, pp. 105–9), the powerful rain lord of the south. By pronouncing the bird's name the rainmaker intended to gain the lord's angry attention, just as an unsuspecting boat traveler hugging the river bank is startled when the *tigana's* voice suddenly rings out, shattering the quiet of the gallery forest. The knowledge that the *tigana* is Tuyuna, ruler of the southern trades, gives the occurrence of the bird's name in the shaman's chant a much deeper meaning than it would have had as merely a cause of fright.

The cosmological connotation of Tuyuna is derived from the fact that the southern trades convey billowing rain clouds with thunder and lightning. No wonder, then, that in Warao weather lore Tuyuna is a thunderbird, albeit not in this world but in the netherworld. During the long rainy season the peculiar trills of the sun bittern

PLATE 3.1
Sun Bittern. Warao Thunderbird of the Netherworld. Father of Southern Trade Winds and Master of Solstitial Rains, Sun Bittern is the ally of the rain shaman. (Painting by Walter Arp. Arp 1980, 133. Courtesy Fundación La Salle de Ciencias Naturales, Caracas)

sound like thunderclaps and crackling discharges of lightning to the inhabitants, *kanishawarao,* of the lower world, who propitiate their ancestral gods with brown *temiche* (*Manicaria saccifera*) sago rather than with white moriche starch (Wilbert 1976a, 326).

Kaunasa

Some six weeks after Ayakeima, rain lord of the west, has assaulted the Orinoco Delta with the first annual thunderstorm of *barinés* fame, Kabo Yokotari, supreme rain lord of the east, rises from his bench and "speaks" with thunderous voice. The winds turn sharply easterly, auguring storms of heavy rain, thunder, and lightning. In addition to breezes, the trades, and local winds, the Warao are no strangers to coiling winds of hurricanes, tornadoes, and waterspouts. Referring to them as *ahakaida*, "big winds," the Indians recognize in them a powerful spirit called Kaunasa. Warao oral literature recalls two occasions when, in remote times, Kaunasa destroyed the world with awesome power (Barral 1960, 9; Wilbert 1970, 180–81).

> In the beginning the earth was populated. Then very strong winds blew and carried away the houses and the trees. . . . [Subsequently there came again]. . .in those remote times a terrible storm of wind and water that demolished all the huts and tore up all the trees and plants by their roots. In this cataclysm all Indians were lost, no one survived except one lone pair, a man and a woman. All the others died.

Sometimes Kaunasa appears in the form of a tornado striking south of the hurricane path. On these occasions, as at other times, his enormous head (covered by a black wide-brimmed hat) and his dark, columnar body span the sky and the earth. At other times Kaunasa shows up as a waterspout traveling across the coastal waters and along the waterways of the delta. In the words of Lane (1986, 63):

To the onlooker, the formation of a waterspout is an awesome spectacle. From the sky, which is generally cloudy, a funnel-shaped mass descends toward the sea. The sea itself is disturbed, and immediately beneath the dipping funnel the water may foam and turn white. As the funnel comes lower, spray rises to meet it. At last the rising cone of water and the low-swinging, writhing tube of air meet, and the waterspout is fully formed. Around the base is the "cascade," or circular whirl of spray, which is considerably wider than the spout.

The following eyewitness account[5] of a water-spout/tornado sighting was given by one of my Warao friends.

> This happened a long time ago when I lived in Nabasanuka. While I was there, I had several children. Their mother was Felicia.
> One day I said to Felicia, "Felicia, it is the season of the crabs. We should go to the beach to collect many crabs. We have no meat to eat. We have sago but no meat."
> "Very well," she said.
> So I prepared many baskets to hold the crabs we were going to eat at the beach. This was the season of the crabs. We would get many.
> At dawn we left for the beach. I put the baskets in the middle of the canoe. We had ten. Felicia brought sago because crabmeat always tastes better with sago. So we went paddling down the Araguao River and to the beach. Paddling, paddling. Felicia was the captain and I sat in the bow.
> By the time the sun was directly overhead we arrived at the beach. We pulled the canoe high up out of the water. If you leave your canoe at the waterline when the tide is low, you will have to walk through a lot of water if you want to leave at high tide. So we tied the canoe to a tree stump. Felicia said, "Tie it well."
> "Yes, yes, Felicia, I will tie it very carefully."
> We began collecting crabs in their holes. It is dangerous work, because if a crab grabs your finger, you could lose your fingernail. We filled one, two, three, five baskets. Then we could not find any more crabs. Usually there are many. There should have been many. But they had disappeared.
> "Where are all the crabs?" asked Felicia.[6]
> "I don't know. There is something wrong here."
> Suddenly, from the place where the sun rises we heard a loud noise. We looked but did not see anything.

---

[5] The account and the chant that follows are courtesy of Werner Wilbert.
[6] Fiddler crabs take refuge in inland burrows hours before a whirlwind hits the coast.

Then Felicia said, "Look, Antonio, there is something huge coming on land from the water. What is it?"

"It is the spirit Kaunasa," I told her.

"Is he after us?"

"I don't know."

It came closer. Right along the beach, closer, closer, and closer.

"Do you know the proper chant to pray?"

"Yes, yes, I do. Let me think."

I sat down, covered my eyes, and chanted the prayer for Kaunasa, over and over and over. You cannot look a spirit in the eyes. If you do, you will be taken for sure.

The spirit was breaking the trees standing in its way. Huge mangrove trees were falling in its path. Some of the smaller trees were taken right up into the wind of Kaunasa and thrown far, far away. I could not think "spirit," because then he would have come straight for us. He comes from the roots of the world mountain to the east, the roots of the sky vault. Sometimes he comes to hunt us Warao. Sometimes he only wanders about. But one never knows, so it is best to say the right prayer. I prayed it over and over again, and finally, when he was very close, he shifted and went up the Araguao River. If I had not chanted the prayer, we would not be here today.

That is all.

At the time of this encounter with Kaunasa, the Indian reporting the event had not yet distinguished himself as the famous local chief and light shaman (*bahanarotu*) he would become in later years. As a commoner, then, and not as a religious practitioner or a rain shaman, he relied on a magic chant to rebuke the menacing spirit. I mention this because I was told that there used to be priest-shamans who specialized in producing strong winds. And Heinen (1988, 668) learned of a female priest-shaman of our acquaintance who was known among the Arawabisi-Warao as a practicing *kaunasa arani*, "Mother of Whirlwinds." Whenever I have raised the topic with rain shamans, however, they equated their own ability to attract rain with their power to call strong winds. And they do, of course, have a point, as we shall see. In any event, however, here is how, years later, the above eyewitness repeated for the anthropologist the protective chant he uttered:

| Hebu Kaunasa | Spirit Kaunasa |
| Ihi hebu Kaunasa | You are spirit Kaunasa |

Hebu Kaunasa	Spirit Kaunasa
Hebu Kaunasa hebu	Spirit Kaunasa spirit
Hebu Kaunasa hebu Kaunasa	Spirit Kaunasa spirit Kaunasa
Hebu hi wai hi tamaha	Spirit your name is this
Hi wai hi tamaha	Your name is this
Hebu Kaunasa hebu Kaunasa	Spirit Kaunasa spirit Kaunasa
Hebu hi wai tamaha	Spirit your name is this
Hi wai karamuna	Your name, hear it clearly
Yanokonu yanokonu	Listen, listen
Hi wai hi tamaha	Your name is this
Hi wai hi tamaha	Your name is this
Hi wai yanokonu	Your name listen
Hi wai yanokonu	Your name listen
Hi wai tamaha	Your name is this
Hi wai tamaha hi karamuna	Your name is this, your sound
Ine wari hekore	Distance yourself from me
Memosaba naritabenu naritabenu	Leave me, turn your back, turn your back, look away
Memosaba maiabanu naritabenu	Leave me, turn your back, look away, turn your back, look away
Naru nonau naru nonanu	Go far away, go far away
Memosaba meyobaremu meyobaremu	Leave me, turn around, turn around
Hebu Kaunasa	Spirit Kaunasa
Hebu Kaunasa.	Spirit Kaunasa.

In Warao mythology, whenever one hears about the master serpent of an animal species, a plant form, or, for that matter, about any natural phenomenon, one encounters a guardian spirit of the highest ontological order. The supreme master of these species of serpents is *hahuba*, the Snake of Being, who encircles, in *uroboros* fashion, the earth disk in the world ocean and whose voice, incidentally, can unleash stormy weather (Wilbert 1977b, 40). The designation *huba*, "snake," for the rainbow is actually part of the meteor's name. Although the same is not true of the proper names of the eight rain lords, it is probably fair to suggest that the image of their cylindrical bodies, including that of Kanamuno, swallower of initiates, and his consort Tarita, the Thunderer (see below, p. 114–

15), is modeled after the serpentine configuration of tornadoes and waterspouts. This theory would also explain the anatomical peculiarity of the flaring salient heads ascribed to these personages, which admittedly baffled me the first time I heard it mentioned. I had not expected to hear the word *bere* ("salient, projecting, jutting out") applied to human physiognomy. But the rain lords are believed to possess the cornicelike heads of the clay figurines in the Valencia style (A.D. 1000 to 1500), whose heads are saliently curved or rectangularly jutting out (flat-topped like the anvil of a cumulus cloud), whose bodies are sometimes elongated and cylindrical, and whose arms are rudimentary (cf. Pérez Soto de Atencio 1971, 109, 110). In fact, the northwestern rain lord, Kwaihebere, carries the designation in his personal name.

Kaunasa, as manifested in hurricanes, tornadoes, and waterspouts, belongs to a class of weather denizens whose formal and behavioral features seem to be modeled after the serpentine twister storms. Mature waterspouts are huge in size and columnar in shape. With funnel-shaped collar-clouds and enormous cumulus heads, they appear in black or in white and move across both water and land. They produce rain, displaying their violent nature by means of thunder, lightning, hissing, and roaring. The spirits, like the whirlwinds, possess overwhelming strength. They can lift humans, such as shamanic initiates, and swallow them. In a semitransparent waterspout one can see the hollow core, like a huge digestive tract, through which the novice must travel on his initiatory journey. In a spout of hourglass shape, the midpoint depression marks the waist of the giant's body.

The suddenness with which waterspouts and tornadoes appear lends them a particularly ghostly character. At an early stage in their development they may, in fact, be invisible, at least at their lower levels. All that can be seen in nascent waterspouts, for example, is a churning ring of spray, and as such it may appear, without warning, right beside a boat on the ocean or on a river. Warao oral literature tells about a hair-raising experience of such phantom storms when two winds meet in human form, each boasting to the other that he can appear suddenly and invisibly. In the ensuing contest the invisible challenger, a waterspout, is discernible only in ripples on the water's surface. The other wind, a tornado, gives a less convincing performance.

Protecting the Children

While the Warao suffer through the worst of the long rainy season, the Pleiades-woman of tribal origin reappears in the sidereal sky over the delta. Unlikely as it may seem to the Indians at a time of hardship and dying, her heliacal rising marks a turn for the better, and they salute her arrival as the beginning of a new year (*kura hido*). From then on they look forward to the arrival of Orion, husband of the Pleiades, who will rise heliacally in early July to rejoin his wife. Despite the deaths of children prevalent during this season, the couple's appearance promises that the group will survive all trials and tribulations. Hunger will again be rebuked as soon as Hearani, the Mother of Crabs, rises heliacally in July in the guise of the crab nebula, marking the onset of the crab season.

Toward the middle of the long wet season, through the short dry season, and into the second wet season, children continue to die from diseases conveyed by the polluted floodwater of the Orinoco, from other weather-related diseases, and from epidemics like whooping cough and measles. In 1954, when I began to report demographic statistics of the Winikina, I found that, of the 172 prepuberty offspring of the active generation of 195 individuals, eighty-seven were living and eighty-five were dead, a mortality rate of 49 percent (Wilbert 1980a, 25). But to gauge the level of individual suffering caused in large part by climatic conditions, one must look at family mortality statistics, which reveal prepuberty mortality rates of more that 80 percent and an almost unending procession of parents carrying dead children to the graveyard. Furthermore, a substantial number of adults and elderly people succumb to the stresses of the rainy seasons. It is not only the loss of life that causes suffering, however, it is also the realization that most of the deaths were caused by the assaults of rain shamans whose debilitating action makes people susceptible to illness sent by the directional gods (not the rain gods) and who use adults but especially children as pawns to exact compliance with the contract between the gods and humans. This contract stipulates that gods depend on humans for food (tobacco) and ritual moriche sago (for rejuvenation) and that humans receive health and longevity from the gods. No love is lost in this interrelationship, which clearly recognizes the harsh conditions of survival facing both partners.

Victimization of children in this tug-of-war between humankind and the supernaturals lies at the root of the mental anguish of parents, who can place their hope only in the art of herbal curing, magic practices, and compliant behavior in serving the needs of the gods.

Among the magic practices designed to protect children is a brief ritual that takes place almost every night in June and during the short rainy season, when Orinoco floods cover wide stretches of the delta with contaminated water and when intestinal disease and/or epidemic pestilence may kill as many as two-thirds of the child population of a local group (Barral 1964, 69). Parents place their trust in the constellation of the Southern Cross after it has stopped appearing in the night sky at the peak of the long wet season in June. More specifically, it is the mystical bird the Indians see behind the asterism, which, like humans, is perpetually pursued by the gods (α and β Centauri). In a ritual context the bird is referred to as *shiborori*, "the beautiful one," and is pictured as resembling the oscillated turkey (*Agriocharis ocellata*) endemic to Belize and Guatemala. Discussion of the ethnohistorical question posed by the appearance of this exotic bird in the oral lore of South American peoples (Wilbert 1975b, 182–84) would be out of place here. More pertinent is the fact that Shiborori is believed to fly from his garden at the foot of the eastern world mountain to the center of the sky every night to chant for the protection of the girls. During the day he returns to sing for the protection of boys. The avian hero performs this ritual despite the disapproval of the cardinal gods, who see their power over humans diminished by the bird's action. As they want to stop Shiborori's protective activity, they expect their hunters to catch the bird, pluck it, and thus ground it forever. Worn out by the relentless chase, Shiborori, as evidenced by his periodic absence in the night sky, is believed to be inclined to cease his flights. For that reason he needs encouragement from someone who has suffered similar persecution by the gods. And who would be better qualified for the role than a postmenopausal woman. Throughout her reproductive life she has feared the supernatural pursuers who were constantly on her heels. She has experienced the oppressiveness of the gods' actions and knows that she has managed, against all odds, to save several of her children from the celestial hunters. Thus Shiborori and the mothers are fellow travelers who give each other mutual encouragement.

In the dark nights of the rainy seasons, when the *pauji* turkey calls in the forest, one can see an elderly woman rise from her hammock and go from the platform of her stilt dwelling to the village plaza. Silhouetted against the dark background of the forest, she faces in the direction whence the bird's call came, awakening her from her light sleep, and shouts:

Shiborori,	Shiborori,
Shiborori, naru!	Shiborori, go!
Detanaka,	Don't tarry,
Shiborori, naru!	Shiborori, go!

Apparently nobody in the quiet houses pays much attention to the duet of the bird and the woman. And yet the adults would be concerned in the morning if they had missed the old woman's call, for Shiborori is believed to find enough solace in this response of an understanding mother to take heart and eventually resume his protective flight and his song.

A second ritual for the magic protection of children takes place during the annual sago harvest festival, called *nahanamu*, when large reserves of ritual sago are distributed to the hungry people. Viewed as a religious rite, this festival features propitiation of the directional gods (not the rain lords), who receive their annual gift of food and "bathing water" and listen to the supplications of the shamans on behalf of the children. Toward the end of the long rainy season, the people's attention is directed to the store of palm sago in the sanctuary and its redistribution. This revitalizing medium for the ancestral gods was prepared at the end of the long dry season preceding the big wet season of food shortage and physical enfeeblement. Requiring communal labor, the process of recovering the ritual palm starch is directed by the windmaker or *isimoi arotu*, "owner of the sacred trumpet," one of the two religious practitioners to be treated in this study. The *nahanamu* cycle evolves in two phases: preparation in the long dry season and redistribution at the beginning of the short dry season. This child-saving ritual (described later on pp. 151–57) shows that the people have high hopes that the sago offering will propitiate the gods. From a purely economic point of view, the redistribution of the temple sago could not come at a better time. It takes place in the crab season, when sago and crab tide the community over the most critical food shortage of the year.

The Rainmaker

Like all shamans, Warao rainmakers feel perennially challenged to demonstrate their talents in order to maintain shamanic status. The efficacy of their specialty as a famine preventive depends in good measure on their success in meeting this challenge. It is, therefore, somewhat disconcerting to meet a rain shaman for the first time, as the image he projects is certainly far from that of an apotheosized personage who holds the lives of his fellow villagers in his hands. On the contrary, resembling an elderly mendicant, he walks about seeking empathy and solicits food, goods, and favors. He asks for parts of a catch of fish, of game, or of other staples. He wants trading expeditions to bring something back for him, and he expects to be offered ready-made shelter in provisional camps. In short, a man who threatens people with a dousing whenever he feels hurt or neglected projects an air of pettiness. Yet rain shamanism, like all powerful sorcery, is born of weakness, suffering, and neglect. The Warao seem to think of it as a form of ritualized revenge practiced not so much for personal benefit as for the common good. Surprisingly, in a society whose elderly people once faced abject neglect (Wilbert 1972, 107–8), everybody caters to the wishes of the old man to keep him from turning his power against them. In any event, the delta's erratic local storms, which influence the reproductive cycle of the moriche palm, are seen by the Warao as a validating token of the rainmaker's magic power over their staple food supply. He causes rain to fall upon the leaching stands of the women, preventing the sago from settling at the bottom of the trough. He also is believed either to provoke a sago shortage by causing it to rain on their local morichal or to fail (voluntarily or involuntarily) in warding off the storms that hostile neighboring colleagues have invoked. The rain shaman makes his people aware of the interrelationship among climatology, botany, and human behavior, pointing out that regional and local famines are the result of his anger and the rain lords' wrath provoked by human stinginess and egotism. Constantly calling on his people to be considerate of others by sharing food and helping the disadvantaged, he conjures up the frightful images of hunger and starvation to enforce selfless normative behavior.

The humble outward appearance of the rain shaman and the

meekness he projects were among the reasons it took me so long to realize the full extent of Warao rain shamanism and appreciate its full impact on Warao culture. That the ranking rain shaman of the Winikina, whom I had known for decades, held simultaneously the prestigious office of sacred trumpet player made awareness of his significance even more difficult. Much of what he did, I wrongly assumed, was related to the office of trumpeter. Like other shamanic specialties, both offices can be held by the same person; although they complement each other, however, they are separately rooted in Warao religion and are not identical.

Earlier ethnographers have reported isolated instances of rain magic from both the delta and the Guianese Warao. Most of these incidental observations were unconnected, referring as they did only to a rainmaker's function of rebuking stormy weather. Brett (1868, 169), for instance, came across an old man who was fishing from a canoe:

> The clouds threatened rain, and when he perceived it, he began to use extraordinary gesticulations, flourishing his arms, and shouting his incantations to drive it away. It soon cleared up, and the old sorcerer rejoiced at his success, as he deemed it.

Passages like this one reveal the people's faith in the magical power of the shaman. But they are mute as to the content of the spells, and reveal little of the underlying belief system that prompts a weather shaman to act in the manner described.

The first actual text of a Warao rain spell was recorded by Turrado Moreno (1945, 147) in his ethnography of the delta Warao. He writes that the priest-shaman (*wishiratu*), or, in his absence, an old man, would blow forcefully against the clouds, gesturing with open hands and making wry faces at them, saying:

Uf, uf!	Uf, uf!
Naha naru.	Rain go away.
Naha naru.	Rain go away.
Naha ekoranu.	Rain be done with.
Naha ekoranu.	Rain be done with.

On numerous occasions I had, of course, witnessed Winikina shamans acting in the same way and had heard about certain practices of rain shamanism. But in accordance with the (mostly casual) suggestions in the literature that similar procedures prevailed throughout South America and the Caribbean (Roth 1915, 267–68; Weiss 1969, 490–91 n. 143), I had assumed that such behavior was the extent of Warao weather shamanism. In any village an old man can often be seen sitting on the edge of the house platform, his body silhouetted against the gray pall of an approaching storm (plate 3.2). Holding his joined palms to his mouth, he rubs them together and

PLATE 3.2

Rebuking a rainstorm. Warao rain shaman sitting on edge of pile dwelling, blowing against coming storm. (Courtesy Sociedad de Ciencias Naturales La Salle, Caracas)

blows, with or without tobacco smoke, between them. With a sudden thrust he then stretches out his arms, raising them skyward against the clouds, the lightning flashes, and the thunderclaps and shouts:

He! Wara hisikoo.	Eh! Talking to you.
Wara hisikoo.	Talking to you.
Ine hi dima.	I am your father.
Diana tai.	That is enough now.
Hi obohana iabanu.	Calm yourself.
Hi natoromo sanera.	Your grandchildren are weak.
Ine sanera.	I am miserable.

The action and the invocation are repeated at intervals until the worst of the storm has passed.

Empowerment of the Rainmaker

When focusing on the weather shaman's ascribed ability to influence precipitation, the Warao refer to him as *naharima*, "Father of Rain." Rainmakers are usually elderly men and, rarely, elderly women. A female practitioner is called *naharani*, "Mother of Rain."[7]

Young men are denied induction into the shamanic profession for fear that they might frivolously misuse their power. Thus gender and maturity are two important considerations for those who want to be rain shamans. A third requirement is that the candidate be able to raise the means required to compensate a teacher for his instruction. It may seem impossible, at first glance, for a member of a foraging society to be both old enough and affluent enough to have disposable surplus goods, yet this caveat is removed by probing the specific definition of "old," "elderly" in the present context.

In the 1950s, when I began researching the Warao, only 5 percent of the Winikina subtribe of 195 individuals had survived the age of fifty (three men and seven women). This survival rate seems to be in keeping with reports for earlier time periods (Turrado Moreno 1945, 14). Even by the decade 1966–1976, in a larger sample of several subtribal groups, including the Winikina, the ratio had

---

[7] Female rainmakers are said to begin practicing spontaneously without undergoing initiation. I return to the subject of women's careers later on, focusing here only on the empowerment of male rain shamans.

increased only slightly, to 6 percent (Layrisse, Salas, and Heinen 1980, 61; Wilbert 1980a, 26). Yet a number of both men and women lived to the age of sixty or more. The increase is best explained by attributing it to the improved health services to which the Warao have gained access in modern times; the earlier reality with respect to longevity is more realistically reflected in the data of the mid-1950s, when adult Winikina had only sporadic contact with mission dispensaries or government-established clinics. In those days the number of men over fifty in any local group or band was none to extremely few and of women of comparable age, one or two. When advanced age as a criterion of eligibility to the office of weather shamanism is considered, therefore, the terms "old" and "elderly" must be understood in the context of Warao demography.

This conclusion does not mean, of course, that it is easy for an individual to raise the required induction fee. Anyone who is able to do so, however, is likely to be in his forties. To convince a master shaman that he is mature enough, a candidate must be about forty years of age and must also be the father of both small and grown children and the grandfather of several. Although his strength is declining, he is still active and eager to enhance his standing in society by acquiring shamanic status.

The decision to become a rain shaman does not depend upon a special call to office by supernatural powers. Rather, it is the individual's free will and his initiative that lead to his choosing the vocation and seeking instruction. He begins the process with some trepidation, as the quest most frequently entails a journey to the settlement of another band or subtribe. As fear of sorcery makes a Warao extremely reluctant to cross subtribal boundaries, disregard of this precaution presupposes a special purpose and a strong motivation.

To become empowered as a rain shaman, a man must study with a competent master and must undergo mystical transformation. Some modern practitioners, however, are said to possess only superficial knowledge of their trade or even to have dispensed with the initiatory transformation. Having corrupted tradition, such untrained and uninitiated shamans find their prestige substantially diminished in the eyes of their fellowmen.

In recent decades the number of fully trained and initiated rain shamans has steadily declined. My principal informant complained of the difficulties he had to overcome, even in the 1930s and 1940s, in finding a competent master. Instead of apprenticing himself to one teacher, he had to seek out several men, each of them possessing some knowledge of weather lore. In fact, my informant told me he had successively studied with as many as six masters, paying five of them ten bolivares each and one as much as thirty bolivares (about twenty dollars at that time). For years he saved the small change he had earned selling fish and game. He had also worked in lumbering and rice production for the Criollos. Because a substantial portion of his wages had to be spent in the "company store" on notoriously overpriced provisions for days when he was unable to fish or gather food for himself and his family, the strenuous effort to save up for his tuition fee dragged on for months. One of his six teachers I knew personally, the others, by name and reputation only. One was his uncle, shaman and ranking elder of the Winikina; the second was a priest-shaman (*kanobo arima*) of the highest rank; the third was a famous shaman of a kind unknown to me. They were all members of my informant's own band and subtribe, but they were not recognized as experts in weather magic. To complete his studies, my informant ventured across subtribal boundaries to employ three additional shamans of the Mariusa, a subtribe reputed to have special knowledge of magic and sorcery. Of these three, one was a dark shaman (sorcerer) of my acquaintance whom I had observed, during a brief visit, blowing against a storm. The second Mariusa was nondescript, as far as I could tell. It was the third teacher whom my informant acknowledged as a true Father of Rain and who finally pulled the entire assemblage of disconnected details together into a coherent system of weather shamanism.

If, during this prolonged quest, shamans other than those who would seem to be specialists offered to train my informant, it was not entirely because of the declining number of properly initiated weather shamans. Rather, any curing shaman, drawing on his supernatural powers, may blow against a storm and may also decide to become a rainmaker. Thus the priest-shaman, aided by his tutelary spirits, blows and waves away all kinds of evil, including foul weather. After sucking pathogens out of his patients, the light shaman, by exhaling, blows the disease-causing organisms into the most remote forest. He blows in the same way to repel an evil storm. It is therefore incumbent upon a novice rainmaker to familiarize himself with the techniques and ultimate purposes of these exorcistic practices lest he confuse them with a rain shaman's art. This requirement is especially valid for a sorcerer's cloud-blowing which, upon closer inspection, reveals a rather complex connection with rainy weather.

Both the dark shaman and the rainmaker indulge in public sorcery, albeit with social rather than personal motivation. The outward sign of their relationship to necromancy is encoded in the terror-inspiring word *miana,* with which their magic chants ordinarily begin and/or end. *Miana*, "darkened vision," refers to the twilight of the underworld at sunset, where only a dim white or yellow light casts a faint glimmer on the macabre doings of its man-eating inhabitants. These frightful denizens live entirely on human flesh and blood, catered for them by the dark shaman. The prospect of becoming the food of the underworld is said to be the lot of many human beings, who would then suffer the annihilation of body and soul. To hear the sorcerer or the rain shaman intone a *miana* chant augurs equally ill; sickness caused by different agents may result in a similar fate for the victims.

The pharmacological connection between the magic of "darkened vision" and nicotine-induced amblyopia may not entirely be recognized by either the master shaman or the student, although it is common knowledge that tobacco is indispensable for shamanic practice (Wilbert 1987, 167–71). Equally disassociated, at least for the neophyte, are bits of information accumulated in the process of growing up, like certain notions he acquired through listening to transformation stories (*namonina a re*) about apparent and hidden forms of the objective world around him. Some of these doubles and metamorphic forms are particularly germane to his shamanic specialty, and it is incumbent upon the master to teach his student the shape-shifting nature and transformational histories of these natural models. Only a coherent comprehension of these alternate shapes enables the practitioner to make full use of their inherent power. More important than just knowing the identity of a natural model's hidden form through storytelling and perhaps through dreams, however, is learning from a trance-initiated shaman how to interpret the significance of its interaction with the visible world. Several such metamorphic shifts pertaining to weather lore are revealed and explained in the course of this study. But one lesson of specific relevance to rain shamanism entails the hidden alligator imagery that conceals the essential necromantic alliance as it exists between rain shamanism and dark shamanism.

It begins with the awareness that the alter ego of the crocodile (generally referred to as alligator) is a human being, that is, a dark shaman.[8] One may dream, for instance, of an alligator that, when about to be killed, turns into the sorcerer of the dreamer's own group. It "is something like the soul of the sorcerer," say the Warao, and between the two there exists a nagual kind of relationship: whatever happens to one—whether in a dream or in reality—inevitably happens to the other.

To gauge the depth of this relationship between alligator and sorcerer and to explicate the connection that exists between these two forms and the rain shaman, one must realize that although the alligator is a fiercely aggressive opportunist which, like the sorcerer, strikes its victims indiscriminately whenever and wherever it can, its eye is nevertheless best adapted to a crepuscular and nocturnal life. Thus it is a most fitting double for the dark shaman, whose life evolves equally in the twilight of the underworld. The alligator is feared by the inhabitants along the riverine channels of the prelittoral delta and the estuaries, especially when the annual flooding of the Orinoco rises above the riverbanks and carries the reptile overland. It is during the rainy season, then, that both the alligator and the sorcerer arouse terror among the people as man-snatching creatures which drag their victims into the underworld to die. And it is precisely this common characteristic that determines the essential nature of the covert correlation between the alligator and the sorcerer as life-devouring. The essence of this baneful affliction inheres particularly to the reptile's teeth. Women wear them as amulets around their necks; hunters exchange the teeth of alligators they have overcome as a sign of spiteful alliance against the odds of fate.

---

[8] Although three crocodilian prototypes are involved, they are treated here as one: the Orinoco Crocodile (*Crocodylus intermedius*) of the Venezuelan and Colombian llanos, which may reach downriver to the Orinoco Delta; the American Crocodile (*C. acutus*) in the coastal habitats of the mouth of the Orinoco River; and the Common Caiman (*Caiman crocodilus*).

The relationship between the alligator-sorcerer and the rain shaman is revealed—more clearly than by the term *miana*—by the fact that both are considered mighty thunderers, the shaman because of his magic power, the alligator (especially the Common Caiman) because of its social display of bellowing in the form of deep roaring vocalizations; hence, the alligator's onomatopoeic name *duruduru*, "Thunder." Pulsating noise like distant thunder stimulates alligators to respond with resounding bellows, and it is not uncommon for several of these reptiles to break out in a loud bellowing chorus simultaneously, in dialogue with thunderers in the sky. Furthermore, male alligators, through subaudible vibrations produce "rain" in the form of spray that rises more than twenty centimeters from their backs, recalling the spraying of a nascent water spout (Vliet 1989, pers. comm; John Thorbjarnavson, pers. comm.; F. Kent Reilly pers. comm.). The bellowing alligator double of the sorcerer is, then, endowed with powers not unlike those of the chanting rain shaman. The reptile's maliferous magic, uniting it with the sorcerer, manifests itself when an alligator tooth is thrown into the water: it provokes incessant rain for long periods of time. Thus, continuous precipitation caused by a sorcerer's use of his alligator power, although not conjured up by the rainmaker, is considered harmful and bad.

In sum, all kinds of shamans can be observed blowing into a storm and uttering their versions of spells. The indiscriminate observer may therefore be easily misled into believing in the existence of different classes of rainmakers, such as defensive *wishiratu* and offensive *hoarotu* rainmakers (Barral 1979, 327). This idea, however, is only conditionally correct. Although all shamans blow defensively against the rain, the institution of Warao rain shamanism is much more complex than any outward similarity might suggest. Beneath the usual posture of shamans vis-à-vis bad weather lie deeper differences which distinguish the practices of all shamans, including those of the rain shaman, from one another.

To learn to understand these overlapping relationships is, of course, part of the instruction a shaman receives. When an aspirant is eventually accepted by a master, the two men agree on the time and place of meeting and on the fee for initiation. During his apprenticeship the student lives in his teacher's settlement, although the preferable location is a provisional hut near the master's home. The isolation is intended both to provide an environment conducive to learning and to protect the community from the dangerous practice of powerful magic. The study period, including initiation, may last from six to twelve weeks, depending on, among other factors, the physical resistance, the learning ability, and the mental fortitude of the apprentice. The indoctrination includes the cosmography of weather shamanism; the theology of weather deities, including their interaction with the world and humankind; and invocational skills.

Once the period of indoctrination has begun, the teacher admonishes the apprentice to eat little but to smoke many cigars. In earlier days, when Western cigarettes and the smoking habit had not yet been widely adopted for hedonistic purposes, tobacco was consumed exclusively for magico-religious ends. As a means of communication between people and supernaturals, it was used primarily by shamanic practitioners—healers and expert craftsmen—to fulfill their respective mediating roles. Rain shamans were no exception to this rule, and a substantial part of the initiation fee was used to obtain enough tobacco to cover the needs of both master and pupil during the training period and, especially, the final act of trance initiation.

Of course, much of what is expressed here in the past tense is current today. The difference is that up to the mid-twentieth century tobacco was an exceedingly precious commodity in the Orinoco Delta. The principal species of tobacco available in the delta and in the Caribbean area were the two cultigens *Nicotiana rustica* and *N. tabacum*. In areas around the delta, several feral species were also to be found, although wild nicotianas were missing altogether. As a nonagricultural people, the Warao lacked the expertise to cultivate tobacco. Even had they known how to raise the plant (as through mission experience), it is difficult to grow in the swampy littoral and intermediate delta zones. Thus tobacco, so indispensable to Warao religion, had to be imported into Waraoland via an overland route of several hundred miles from, among other centers of Criollo occupation, Angostura (Ciudad Bolívar) and Tucupita, or by sea from the island of Trinidad.[9] In the past the scarcity of tobacco and the difficulty of importing it must have been a serious

---

[9] Voyages to Trinidad for trading purposes, first reported by Raleigh, are of long-standing tradition among the Warao (1970 [1596], 52).

stumbling block for an aspirant eager to undergo shamanic induction. Compensation in cash or in kind would have been acceptable only when the master had his own reserves of tobacco or had access to a supply in exchange for goods.

Tobacco is indispensable to the Warao in their practice of religion because the smoke it produces is the food of the supernaturals, who are completely dependent on humans for their sustenance. This is why tobacco offerings are an effective way of coercing the spirits. Yet, although this interrelationship makes the supernaturals pliable to the wishes of humanity, it also creates a liability for mortals. The spirits expect to be provisioned by humans, and any negligence is believed to arouse the wrath of the spirits, who vent their anger by inflicting sickness, death, and destruction on the people.

Fully initiated healing shamans are said to have occasionally been inducted into the office of rain shamanism. (Holders of both offices could certainly have confused the casual observer.) But if the *naharima* neophyte has never trafficked with the otherworld, he is hardly likely to have experienced, personally, the effects of nicotine on the human body. For days, or even weeks, his physical resistance is severely challenged by the pharmacological effects of ever larger doses of the drug. Nauseated and retching, he is incapable of eating, has no appetite whatsoever, and certainly needs no persuasion to curtail his food intake. After this harrowing initial test, the candidate, as he becomes more habituated, experiences the nicotine-induced inhibition of hunger pangs which together with other like effects makes it easier for him to substitute the spiritual food of tobacco for his normal diet. The more plentiful and the stronger the drug consumed, the longer the lack of hunger lasts. A change in chemistry thus takes place in the student's progressively emaciating body, a process that prepares him for his initiatory transformation as the culmination of the induction procedure (Wilbert 1987, 171–72).

Suffering from nicotine-induced physical distress, the student not only rejects food for his body; he is also disinclined to absorb spiritual fare through learning processes. Instead, the teacher and the student lie beside each other in their hammocks while the teacher reminisces about his experiences in his own apprenticeship. Thus, much of the indoctrination consists of the master recounting lessons he has learned during his own career, lessons that have helped him interpret the messages contained in the weather elements. He may also practice weather magic in the presence of the apprentice, reminding him that drifting mist, gentle rain, and continuous precipitation can occur without intervention by a weather shaman. On such occasions shamans have only defensive powers, restricted to stopping the rain or diverting its course by using their incantatory formulas. In contrast, over stormy rain—the second major class of precipitation in Warao weather lore—the rain shaman possesses apotropaic power, enabling him to avert precipitation or to attract it, either to protect or to harm his people. Both kinds of precipitation, however, the student is told, provide the rain shaman with opportunities to apply his arsenal of painful torments that include, besides hunger and famine, weather afflictions like gastrointestinal "sun shower" diseases (vomiting, diarrhea, typhus), as noted; rainy season diseases like coughs of all kinds, fever, colds, muscle ache, arthritis, rheumatoid arthritis; and dry season diseases like bronchitis, asthma, conjunctivitis; as well as chronic anuria that afflicts many Warao throughout their lives, owing to exposure to inclement weather conditions of wind and rain.

Invoking the Rain Lords

The power to invoke the rain gods (*nahanatakitani*) to unleash stormy rains, thunder, and lightning sets the weather shaman apart from those who only practice blowing against a storm. Special skills and supernatural alignment are required to achieve this power. After internalizing the names, nature, and locations of the Lords of Rain, the student must learn how to communicate with them by uttering magical chants, which differ from exorcistic spells in being necromantic in essence and instrumental in achieving an evil purpose. As noted earlier, the initiation master prefers to teach the chants in a house some distance away from the people, lest they become alarmed by the singing and by the repetition of the word *miana* and of the rain lords' names. Even whispering the names draws their attention, and the consequences for children and adults may be disastrous.

Several days after the induction period begins, the master shaman starts to teach his student the words and the music of the chants to the eight rain lords. As the eight chants are similar, one example suffices to convey their basic nature.[10]

Chant to Kabo Yokoshewari

I

Ihi kabo arotu ihi	You are the lord of heaven
ihi weyo a buaranoko arotu	You rule where the sun comes aflame
ihi tata arotu	you are the lord of yonder
otuida arotu	lord of remoteness
hi [wai] karamuna	I shall pronounce and
nanoarate ine.	repeat your name.
Hi karamuna	I shall raise it
hi wai ka- karamuna	your name I shall raise
hi wai ka- karamuna	your name I shall raise
nanoarate	and repeat
hi wai karamuna	your name I shall raise
nanoarate ine.	and repeat again.
Otuida arotu	Lord of remoteness
ma nobo diawara	my grandfather god
ma nobo diawara	my grandfather god
hi karamuna	I call upon you
manobo diawara ihi	my grandfather god
kabo arotu ihi	you are the lord of heaven
kabo arotu	lord of heaven
otuida arotu:	lord of remoteness:
YOKOSHEWARI.	YOKOSHEWARI.

---

[10] I transcribed the text of the "Chant to Kabo Yokoshewari" from a cassette recording. Translation was aided by field notes and by the commentaries of two Indian assistants, Antonio Lorenzano and Cesáreo Soto. Dr. Dale Olsen kindly provided the musical transcription from a copy of the field recording. Transcription entailed slowing the music down from 7.5 ips to 3.75 ips. Several text corrections made by Dr. Olsen in the process of musical transcription are gratefully acknowledged. Close examination of the original recording at reduced speed by Dr. Olson (pers. comm.) revealed the personal name of the rain lord addressed in the chant as Yokoshewari rather than as Yokotari as previously reported (Wilbert 1981, 136; 1993, 225).

II

Karamunai	You trembled
hi karamunai	you trembled
hi karamunai	you trembled
hi karamunai	you trembled
nanoarate ine	I shall repeat your name
hi kanamane	so you will rise
hi kanamane	you will rise
hi kanamane.	you will rise.
Hi natorobo aida	Your mighty staff
orebekane	preceding
orebekware	ahead of you
kabo sisi awitu	right on the road of heaven
orebekane	ahead of you
hi urunaka tane	will not weigh you down
hi urunaka tane	will not weigh you down
neriwakate	so you be content
neriwakate ine	and I be content
hi urunaka tane	it will not weigh you down
neriwakane.	being comfortable.
Neriwakane	Being agreeable
hi anatoro aida	your mighty staff
memo sabane	pass me by
memo sabane	pass me by
hiyakakune	to the *cuajo* tree
doko mara	with its windblown leaves
nisinatahine	there you plant it
hi abate ine.	I shall leave you.

III

Hi nasaribu tane	With your voice like
domu turu tuyuna	the *tigana* bird's
tuyuna ware	the snake-necked *tigana*
taisi a yekoita	with its cry
ahi hatekore	its piercing cry
mu yaritanu	become enraged

mu yaritanu	become enraged
hi tehori	your body
mu yaritanu	become infuriated
mu yaritanu.	become infuriated.
Ori kanamanu	Arise
hi kanamane	to your full height
hi kobukane	stand up
hi kobukane	stand up
kabo sisia	on the road of heaven
hi kobukanewitu ine	stand straight [I say]
hi kobukane	stand up
hi kobukane	stand up
hi kobukane	stand up
kabo sisia.	on the road of heaven.

IV

Kabasimo hi tehori	Your body like a fiery wasp
hi te abane	brace your body
mu yaritanu	become enraged
ma nobo diawara	my grandfather god
ma nobo	my grandfather
ma nobo diawara	my grandfather god
ma nobo kabo arotu	my grandfather lord of heaven
kabo arotu diawara.	lord of heaven.
Kabo meho kasaba yana	Now then at the bosom of heaven
kasaba yana toate ine	there then shall I place
ma weraribuyawitu	my tongue's own words
ma nasaribuyawitu	my very words
kabo arotu	lord of heaven
isa ine nanoarane.	wherewith I repeat your name.
Ne mu yaritanu	Eh! Become infuriated!
mu yaritanu	Become infuriated!
Miana	Dim-visioned
diana.	that is all.

Inciting the Anger of the Rain Lords

Chants sung by Warao rain shamans to conjure up a storm are generally evocations that proclaim the placement and stations of the lords, climaxing with the pronouncement of their names (Olsen 1975a, 75; 1975b). These calls reveal the lords' existence and, by knowing and uttering their secret names, the rainmaker, like religious practitioners everywhere, proclaims himself their master (Budge 1973, 1:173). Upon hearing their names the lords rise, become increasingly more infuriated as the chant spurs them on, and stride with pounding heels toward the celestial plaza below the top of the cosmic vault. During the walk and while dancing on the plaza, the gods perspire copiously, causing heavy rainfall. Their stomping thunders through the universe, and their staffs discharge sky-rending thunderbolts.

To incite the ire of the rain gods further, the rainmaker attempts to provoke them with threats and violent imagery. This motive is certainly behind the suggestion that the lords cast their staffs like lightning into the *cuajo* tree (*Virola surinamensis*, Ro. Warburg; Waraoan: *diaru*).[11] For the shaman, besides reminding the average listener that *Virola* trees are frequently struck by lightning and incinerated, intends to leverage the power of the rain gods by the vengeful reaction triggered in the forest people through the loss of one of their own. The student learning about this association is reminded of the hyperactivity that overcomes a patient upon application of the latex of this species of *Virola* as a remedy for buccal sores or toothache (W. Wilbert 1986, 649). But he also remembers that those who eat honey from the nectar of the tree lose muscular coordination, experience a general numbness in their limbs, and have a heavy, nauseated feeling as if they were inebriated.[12]

---

[11] The species *Virola surinamensis* in the Orinoco Delta was identified by botanist Dr. Steven Tillet of the Universidad Central de Venezuela, Caracas, on the basis of a fresh specimen. His determination was confirmed by Dr. Richard Evans Schultes of Harvard University after the inspection of a mounted herbarium specimen at the Botanical Institute of the University of California, Los Angeles. Both samples were collected by Werner Wilbert.

[12] Inspection of the bees' nest from which insects, honey, and pollen were collected (*Trigona hyalinata branneri*, Cockerell) revealed various kinds of pollen. Besides *Virola* pollen there was pollen of *sangrito* (*Pterocarpus officinalis*) and of *mamure* (*Anthurium flexuosum*); neither one of the two plants is known to be hallucinogenic.

The insect that produces the honey is a small, black, stingless bee known in Venezuela as *pegón (Trigona hyalinata branneri,* Cockerell) and in Waraoan as *hoi*.[13] It builds its bulbous nest preferably in the tops of tall trees such as riparian mangrove or *cuajo* in the deciduous forest on the levees behind the mangrove belt. Although stingless, it is a fiercely aggressive insect whose attacks cause panic in human intruders when their scalps are bitten, their hair is twisted, and their facial orifices are painfully invaded. In addition, an unidentified ant that frequents the tree near the bees' nest also attacks human interlopers. Small and harmless-looking as the *pegón* may be, there is an air of what the Warao call *ayari,* "noxious ill-temperedness," about it and its buzzing nest, a poisonous aura that enrages the rain lords and instills in humans an uncanny feeling of dread.

The initiate has, of course, been familiar with this phenomenon since early childhood. From listening to the storytellers, he knows that Warao oral literature explains the charged atmosphere surrounding the *pegón*'s nest as the essence of base humiliation and sexual frustration. The nest is the shriveled, painfully contorted body of a blind man who, distraught with sexual urge, was led by his sighted fellowmen into a rushing river rather than to a rendezvous with young women. The student also remembers the many occasions when women and children accompanied the men on honey hunts and when, to protect themselves from the infuriated bees, they covered their heads and faces with hoods made of plant materials (Wilbert 1980b, 109). The novel aspect of the student's situation, however, is that, once initiated, he will be permitted to eat honey in its natural state, not diluted with water as, at least traditionally, commoners must ingest it.

As for the *pegón*, rain shamans know that behind the angry bee there stands an assertive youth named Joioana. Defying the ridicule of his fellowmen, he decided to have a young moriche palm grow vertically from his head. He extracted from the central leaf the bast fibers, letting them hang down from the top of the leafstalk to the crown of his head. The tree looked like a furled umbrella. Walking

---

[13] Identification of insects mentioned in this study is courtesy of Dr. Roy R. Snelling of the Natural History Museum, Los Angeles (hymenoptera) and of Dr. Kumar Krishna of the Museum of Natural History, New York (termite).

around thus adorned, both in sunshine and in rainy weather, the young man dared the thunderstorms overhead to strike him down with lightning. (As noted above, rainmakers use Joioana's lightning rod as a model for person-directed sorcery.) Eventually, however, the youth became so maddened by the scorn of his people that he decided to change into a different form, opting for the body of the *pegón*. He could find no more suitable place to surround himself with rejection than the gnarled body of the blind old man. For this reason the *pegón*'s nest is often built around a branch of a tall tree, as far away from humans as possible. From below it looks like a person's head, and the branch penetrating the nest shows that Joioana still has a tree growing from his crown. This "tree," supposedly, is what attracts lightning into the *cuajo* and other tall trees, and people struck by lightning are said to have experiences reminiscent of *Virola* honey and nicotine intoxication, which strikes a person down as muscle coordination is lost. The victim lies unconscious on the ground as if dead. Recovery is often spontaneous, and the sufferer remembers the charge of lightning he experienced. Of course, death or burns and other injuries are said to occur at times, but more often bodily strength is completely restored. With luck, the sightless old man of the *pegón*'s nest does not permanently leave his mark of blindness on the victim.

The connection of the *pegón* with tobacco intoxication results from its position as the most powerful of the four tutelary spirits of light shamanism (*bahana*). Together with three other social insects (a wasp, a different stingless bee, and a termite),[14] it resides in the ovoid house of the supreme *bahana* spirit on the platform near the zenith, functioning as chief of the house's occupants. *Pegón* was selected to occupy this exalted position precisely because of its fierceness and its noxious powers (Wilbert 1985). These qualities likened it to the supreme *bahana* spirit—who is the Master of Tobacco—and to all the fellow inhabitants of the *bahana*'s lofty house, which is comparable in form and elevated location to the *pegón*'s own nest. The master shaman reminds his pupil that the tobacco spirit's house is located on the celestial platform where the

---

[14] Wasp (*Stenopolybia fulvofasciata* DeGeer; Waraoan: *tomonoho simo*); second stingless bee (*Trigona capitata* F. Smith; Waraoan: *asebe*); termite (*Nasutitermes corniger* Motschulsky; Waraoan: *ahi simo*).

rain gods congregate to dance and where their feelings of frustration, bitterness, and malignancy culminate in a fit of anger that produces lashing thunderstorms.[15]

Yet another image conjured up by the chanting weather shaman to incite the Lords of Rain is that of a fiery wasp (*Stenopolybia fulvofasciata*, DeGeer; Waraoan: *tomonoho simo*). This insect is the second-ranking tutelary spirit of the Master of Tobacco, who resides in the ovoid house at the zenith. Wasp, the younger brother of *pegón*, is charged with the role of constable. The specific *ayari* or ill temper of this wasp is a strong noxious venom which produces fever and nausea in humans. Carnivorous in its feeding habits, the wasp often attacks its prey at considerable distances from its nest. Some human intruders who have a particular attraction for the insect find themselves besieged by it without intentional provocation. Its spiritedness and aggressive attitude, as well as its potential man-eating and noxious nature, turn the wasp into exactly the vexing symbol expected by the weather shaman to provoke the Lords of Rain. Furthermore, the figure of the wasp's previous existence, hidden behind the insect form of this poisonous spirit, is recognized by the initiated. Before turning himself into an insect, the spirit was an exceptionally hateful youth who lived in a perpetual state of rage. Incapable of controlling his aggressiveness, he injured everyone he

---

[15] To become aware of such bitterness of heart at the root of Warao weather magic and of its retaliatory nature was a revelation to me. Yet the first faint hint of the sentiment underlying this lore was given more than a century ago by Bernau (1847, 267) for the Warao of Guiana:

> On the Kamwatta Creek, in the Moruca River district, there is a half submerged tree stump, known as Ibúma (lit. "young woman," in the Warrau language), believed to be the site where either an Indian murdered his wife or where she killed herself. In dry weather the tree is exposed, and as the Indians pass it in their corials, they call out, "Ibúma!" and slash their cutlasses into it, with the avowed purpose of making the woman vexed, and so causing the rain to fall.

Although the reasons suggested for calling the tree stump "Ibúma" seem contrived, the aggression displayed by the travelers and the imaginary suffering inflicted to provoke the rain are quite in keeping with Warao weather magic. *Iboma*, meaning "puberal girl," is the term a shamanic shipwright uses to address a *cachicamo* tree destined to be made into a dugout canoe. Such trees are believed to be the daughters of the Mother of the Forest, and it is possible that the travelers meant to incur the wrath of the bush spirit and the goddess.

met and devastated everything he encountered. To increase his potential for tormenting others, he eventually took the shape of the wasp he is today, but shamans still recognize his origin and consider him a spirit of wanton violence.

Initiation

Once the lore of weather shamanism has been internalized to the satisfaction of both teacher and student and the novice has demonstrated his mastery over the evocational chants, the apprenticeship culminates in the student's initiation. This process is always used when the candidate wants to acquire the art of rain shamanism not only by "listening," as the Warao would say, but also by "dreaming." Although it is difficult to prove that in the past all properly installed weather shamans were dream- or trance-initiated, the uninitiated practitioners of today are symptomatic of culture loss.

To induce a trance in the emaciated novice, the master prepares three or four ritual cigars by peeling off leaves from a length of rope tobacco and rolling them into a wrapper of manaca stipule (*Euterpe* sp.). The finished product is 60 to 90 centimeters long and 2 centimeters in diameter. Smoking the cigars by hyperventilation, the novice points them toward the rain lords around the world, offering the smoke as a gift of nourishment and satisfaction. The increase in the amount of nicotine thus inhaled puts him into a comatose state, and, because the trance usually occurs at night, noises from the nearby village are muffled and the danger of awakening the novice prematurely—and "killing" him as a consequence—is minimal.

While in his trance the initiate, facing east, waits for the arrival of Kanamuno, a black giant of colossal proportions. As the ghostly figure approaches the fearful novice, his serpentine body and widely flaring head come into view. The spirit, drenched in rain, is accompanied by thunder and lightning. He reaches down for the initiate, lifts him up, and drops him into his gaping mouth. Once inside the giant's body the novice embarks on a long journey, during which the essential nature of the devourer is revealed to him: Kanamuno is the manifestation of Kabo Yokotari, who has come to induct him into the ranks of the Lords of Rain. Thunder and bright lightning reverberate in the traveler's body as he realizes that through them he is encountering Tarita (Thunderer), the consort of Kanamuno and the manifestation of Kabo Aukuashiwari, the supreme rain lord's female companion. Upon leaving the giant's body (via the rectum) the new shaman meets Kabo Kwaihebere, who enters his body and henceforth resides in his breast as his personal patron and his familiar. This god will be the "father" of the shaman and call him by his own name, just as the "son" is now entitled to use the god's personal name.[16] The new shaman returns from his initiatory journey a changed man, as a human endowed with *kabo* power. Having aged at an accelerated pace during his otherworldly travels, he rejoins his people as a wise old man, the equal of the rain gods.

Dying in the Rain

To offer a close-up view of the suffering and the dying that afflict the Warao in the wet seasons, I propose to reminisce, with the aid of my diaries and in correspondingly intimate style, about my first experience, in 1954, of heavy rains and their aftermath among the Winikina-Warao and the emergency ward atmosphere that prevailed during these months. In villages along the river, shamans busied themselves with blowing and raising their hands against the clouds. Nevertheless, during the short dry season rain fell with unexpected frequency. In October even the short rainy season seemed to have started unusually early; it rained often, and heavy downpours rattled through the forest like freight trains.

Away from their traditional home in the morichal, people who had fairly recently taken up residence along the now black Winikina River were unable to catch the small fish in the interior water holes and the drainage channels which usually relieved their hunger in such periods. Food was scarce, and teenagers collected the hardened

---

[16] The protagonists do not address each other as "Rainbow"; when applied to a person, their nickname alludes to flirtatiousness and coquetry. For this reason, my principal informant, though known among his people by the same appellation, was too embarrassed to utter the spirit's name. In other words, as the lord of the northwest is held to be the "rainbow" among his peers, so was my friend considered a "rainbow" by his people. I was unable to verify how widespread this naming practice and taboo was.

temiche palm fruit that came drifting by the village. When thunderstorms were approaching, the women covered or turned over their cooking pots, and the rain shaman warned the villagers to extinguish their fires or to keep the flames low, lest the rain lords, begrudging them their food, would strike their houses with lightning (cf. Lévi-Strauss 1988, 48–58).

Widespread coughing and aching afflicted the hungry people, especially during the long nights when rain pelted the rooftops. These rains were not the warm ones that fall of their own accord. Instead, they were the "real" rains brought on by the magic of rain shamans and the fury of rain lords—cold rains that are accompanied by bone-chilling winds. (These rains are one example of the weather shaman's bringing rain and wind.) The smoldering fires gave little comfort, and even the dogs were suffering. The priest-shaman treated his wife's hunting dog by swinging his rattle and chanting over the animal, just as he did over many human patients. The shamans of the village were called upon repeatedly to conduct healing seances during which, incidentally, adults are expected to stay awake lest the shaman's curing power prove ineffective. As the wet season advanced, the entire community began to suffer from lack of sleep, becoming progressively more irritable. Overtired, the curers dragged themselves from house to house and village to village. "All the gods are evil," the *wishiratu*-shaman of my village told me when he returned from yet another all-night battle without apparent success. With the alertness of a combat soldier, he tuned his senses to all the voices—conversation, complaints, laments—in the village. He had packed the shirt and the half-sweater I had given him weeks earlier in a basket and wore only his loincloth. He had gone back to living in true Warao style (*waraowitu*, as it is called in their language): no European clothes, no salt in food, and no cigarettes (only homemade cigars of rope tobacco rolled in wrappers of palm stipule).

Women who had become full-time herbalists were preparing remedies made of barks, leaves, and roots. They discussed and exchanged recipes, and administered medications even as the shamans were chanting for the recuperation of their patients. An epidemic of whooping cough, which struck in September of that year, had the worried mothers digging with their fingers into the little mouths to pull out the strings of phlegm that were choking their children. A man and a boy were bitten by poisonous mapanare snakes. A woman had given birth without passing the placenta; she lay in her hammock, as stiff as in rigor mortis, and then had to be taken through pouring rain in an open canoe to a neighboring settlement of Mariusa-Warao, where shamans were reputed to be able to take care of such life-threatening complications. (And they did do just that.) A young girl was suffering from two boils, one in her right armpit and the other on her left buttock. Her father lanced them with a palm-wood dart. A shaman in a downriver village bashed his sacred rattle against a house post in frustration over his failure to cure a girl's dysentery and fever, which he had been treating for days. The news of this sacrilege echoed through the settlements like the pall of death itself. Similar cases in the past, when large numbers of children had supposedly been killed by the offended spirits, were recalled. The women, frantic with fear, lamented the outrageous act, which they thought would only make matters worse.

Rumors began to circulate about a neighboring rain shaman who had cursed a stingy man by causing a tree to sprout from his head, thereby eventually killing the culprit who had brought on many rainstorms (see above, p. 111). One morning toward the end of September, a man from a distant village arrived, reporting that he had learned of a heinous crime: a woman had been buried alive, he said. She had come back to life during the funeral, but as she was trying to scramble out of her coffin, the terrified men supposedly pushed her back, struck her with a machete on the head, and closed the grave over the still living woman. Hearing this gruesome story, the people began to protest in loud and angry voices. All agreed that the messenger should carry out his plan of traveling from village to village to spread the news and to make sure that Venezuelan authorities were brought in on the case.

Family quarrels erupted, as when a fiscal had decided to take a second wife. At the end of November, after smoldering for weeks, a fight broke out when the first wife exploded in anger, packed her belongings, and left the village.[17] On another occasion a sudden

---

[17] The uxorilocal residence rule of the Warao would normally make it unusual for a woman under these circumstances to leave her village where she could count on the support of her matrikin. In this case, however, the woman had married her husband in the mission and lived virilocally with his family.

burst of anger on behalf of my immediate neighbor rocked the house. The man grabbed a piece of smoldering firewood and threw it after his scurrying son who had dropped the little sister he had been carrying. The girl would be afraid of her brother for the rest of her life. Public disputations were frequently called into session. The speaker and the headman (who was also the priest shaman of the local group) had to resolve conflicts of various kinds. A husband had beaten his wife. There were cases of adultery and of theft. Three women were convicted and punished for tale-bearing.

Without doubt, events like these may take place in a village at any time during the year, but rarely does quarreling reach the intensity of the highly charged debates which occurred during the wet season and the short dry season immediately following it. Invariably, after incidents of this nature had been heard and settled by the speaker for the village, the heavily smoking assembly turned to a discussion of the weather, the rain makers, and their fellow sorcerers, the *hoarotu*, whose actions caused suffering and death and had to be stopped. The sessions often ended with someone expressing the hope that the fifteen huge baskets of moriche sago the Winikina had offered the directional gods on September 15 would soon diminish the wave of ill health. Nevertheless, the suffering brought about by diverse weather diseases continued. For some reason the nights seemed to be more hectic than the days. Only during the early morning hours did the whimpering, crying, and screaming of children briefly die down. But then, toward sunrise, coughing was again heard in many houses. The shaman resumed his chanting to interpret his dream for the sick and the dying; at times he chanted softly to soothe a delirious child.

Besides the children who died during this difficult season, several adults among the Winikina and their kin in nearby settlements succumbed to the stresses of the period. An intimate look at one such case reveals the tension and the mental anguish that prevail when someone is believed to be dying from the effects of the rain.

Juan was the son of the ranking priest-shaman of the Winikina, keeper of the sacred rock of Uraro, god of the south.[18] Juan's mother, Ana, was an elderly woman who had given birth to eight live children, four of whom had died of measles, bronchitis,

---

[18] Personal names have been changed.

diarrhea, or vomiting. The family lived in a village upriver from the place where I was staying in 1954. Juan, whom his parents had brought safely through the vicissitudes of childhood, was about nineteen years old when he became gravely ill. He had joined his uncle and several other men of his local group to work in the rice fields of the Criollos. They were doing this hard work in order to earn enough money to buy a twelve-horsepower outboard motor they would own in severalty. Such a motor had been acquired the year before by men of my village, who had formed a temporary cooperative for the purpose (with their earnings supplemented by credit from the Criollos). But now, disassembled and lacking in spare parts, the motor was idle while its owners were still toiling to pay off their debt. Juan and his uncle wanted an outboard motor badly enough to emulate their neighbors, despite the latter's predicament.

The men had planted the rice fields for the Criollos in March when, in addition to hard labor in preparing ritual sago for the annual sago festival and in providing for their families, they traveled between the morichal, the village, and the rice fields in their paddled canoes. Work in the rice fields included cutting out underbrush and felling trees on two parcels of land, burning dried wood, and sowing rice. During the *nahanamu* festival, in September, while at a camp near the coast, Juan told me about their work, but I realized at the time that the young man was seriously ill. Unable to participate in the energetic dancing, he was just sitting in a small provisional house. He had lost weight from the heavy labor; he felt feverish and not at all well. He coughed a lot every morning, and the shamans identified his ailment as the "bad cough" (bronchitis) caused by rain, rather than the "hurting lungs cough" (pneumonia), another frequent weather disease. Halfway through the festival the young man's father asked me to take Juan home in my motorboat (a canoe with outboard motor) and put him in the care of his grandmother. The boy and I left in the late afternoon, and as the skimpily clad patient was suffering from exposure to the cold wind of the falling night, I gave him my blanket to keep him warm. Traveling through the early night hours to Juan's village, I began to fear that the young man might actually be suffering from pulmonary tuberculosis (the "terrible cough"), which had reached the Winikina area during the late 1940s or the early 1950s by way of Criollo immigrants who had settled among the Indians.

It was cold in the open canoe and I was suffering from an acute streptococcal pharyngeal infection with bouts of fever and throbbing headaches. For several days after getting back to the camp, I repeatedly boiled a glass syringe to inject myself with penicillin. While the people were petitioning the gods for the lives of their children, my thoughts went back at times to Juan and his village. His parents agreed with the shamans that he was dying from the rain. A month earlier, the men had returned to the rice fields to bring in the harvest. For several days they had been exposed to repeated heavy downpours, and they worked and slept in wet clothes until they had completed the task.

Not all the participants in the *nahanamu* festival had returned from the coast when, one evening in September, a messenger from Juan's village arrived to summon the resident priest-shaman. The shaman asked me to give him a ride in my motor-driven canoe. Towing the messenger's boat, the three of us arrived at the patient's house toward ten o'clock. We were rushed by a pack of dogs as we made our way across the swampy plaza and up onto the platform of the sick boy's stilt house. A fire was burning on the hearth near the hammock in which he lay. The parents were sitting in their hammocks, swinging gently back and forth. The patient's younger brother and his brother-in-law stood at the edge of the platform facing outward, each with one foot set on top of the other while holding onto the crossbeam above their heads. I joined them while the shaman from my village walked over to the patient's father to talk about the case. They both began to smoke long cigars as their conversation became more animated.

As yet nobody had even looked at the patient. He lay, naked but for a loincloth, with both arms thrown overhead and one leg pulled up to his stomach. He had my woolen blanket crumpled up under his head. His eyes were closed; he was coughing; his body was wasted to the bone.

The visiting shaman was crouching on the floor, his basket containing the sacred rattle placed in front of him. Speaking without raising his eyes, he repeated the term *obo monida*, "terrible cough," over and over again, and he refused to undertake the cure. The same was true of the sick boy's father, who said he could cure only injuries, not this kind of disease. The boy's mother was less resigned. She kept insisting that coughing caused by rain was curable and that she knew for certain that rain had brought on the cough while her son had been working in the rice fields of the Venezuelans. Nobody paid much attention to her except for her sister and co-wife, María, who was sitting near the fireplace in a neighbor's house.

Neither of the two *wishimo* who were present felt competent to cure what they said was *obo monida*. While the women's gesticulations and speech became more agitated, the shamans became increasingly less talkative. Finally, they remained only sitting silently in the twilight between the fire and the patient's hammock, drawing on their faintly glowing cigars.

After some time had passed, the dogs again rushed to the riverbank, where a boat full of men was arriving. Among them was Mario, the most respected dark shaman of Mariusa descent. Also climbing up to the platform was a famous young dark shaman of the Winikina and his brother, the most accomplished *bahanarotu* on the river. They all sat along one side of the patient's hammock, and after having been informed about the case by the two priest-shamans and encouraged by Ana, all four shamans—the *wishiratu* from my village, the two *hoarotu*, and the *bahanarotu*—agreed to join forces and to chant in the hope of getting information about the case from supernaturals around the world. Only the patient's father (a priest-shaman) refused to join the others. He now sat on the floor with his legs stretched out and his chin on his breast. The officiating shamans had come from four different villages.

Mario's sonorous voice rose out of the dark on a high note and then, falling in a plaintive cry, was joined by the voices of the other shamans. Reminiscent of a Gregorian chant, it was the most impressive chorus I had ever heard Warao sing. It went on for four hours, as the shamans visited the distant corners of the world in quest of the disease-causing agent. Only once did they pause to roll new cigars and stoke the fire. Toward early morning the chant began to weaken until it finally stopped, with Mario's voice being the last to fall silent in the quiet night.

The shamans then began to consult with one another. The *wishimos* had learned of the spirits' displeasure with the young man's efforts to acquire an outboard motor. But there continued to be confusion about the kind of cough they were dealing with. Eventually, however, they all agreed that in the case of Juan's affliction they were confronted with the "terrible cough" of tuberculosis, precipitated by a hostile sorcerer. Taking advantage of the young man's weather-debilitated state, he had "shot" him with a magic arrow of the western cannibal god. It was decided, therefore, that the *hoarotu* shamans among them should undertake the cure.[19] While they were still deliberating, Juan had stopped coughing and had fallen asleep.

After an hour had passed and the brilliance of the stars had begun to fade, the sick youth opened his eyes and spoke for the first time, saying he needed to urinate. To everybody's amazement he scrambled out of his hammock and stood for awhile like a statue of death. Then he began to walk toward the front of the house and, silhouetted against a pale sky, we saw him balance himself as he walked across a seven-meter-long bridge of poles to a kitchen house, above the river's edge. After returning, he crouched next to the fire, looked around to see his mother, and said, "I am hungry."

Immediately the women rushed to the baskets hanging from the ridgepoles to search for leftovers of taro. They placed cold lumps of the boiled root in front of the boy, who slowly ate two or three pieces. "He is well!" they said. "He is eating." The shamans also seemed relieved. They now knew the identity of their adversary; sometimes even terrible coughs were curable. Then suddenly the boy collapsed. He lay like a pile of bones, right next to the hearth. They picked him up and lowered his limp body into the hammock, where he slept quietly without coughing. The shamans departed at dawn, feeling a degree of hope, for the young man had already walked a little and eaten some food.

Five days later I received an unexpected visit. Two Italian physicians, having heard about me in the boy's village, had come to spend the night in my hut. They had examined the young man

---

[19] The initial confusion of the ministering shamans was due to the various possible disease etiologies of cough. Were they dealing with one kind of common weather disease (bronchitis, pneumonia) that befalls a patient through the action of a priest-shaman (*wishiratu*) and the agency of the cardinal god of the north? Or were they confronting the bloody cough (pulmonary tuberculosis) with which sorcerers (*hoarotu*) smite a weather-weakened, susceptible individual for the benefit of the cannibal god of the west? Both kinds of cough can be the result of a rain shaman's initial action. But other shamans take advantage of the victims' weakened disposition to strike on behalf of the respective gods they serve. As previously noted, "alligator-sorcerers" or *hoarotu* are akin to rain shamans.

and had diagnosed his ailment as pulmonary tuberculosis, as I had suspected. At this stage in the consumption, they said, there was nothing anyone could do for Juan. The next day, after my guests had departed, I conveyed their pessimism to the priest-shaman of my village. He looked past me across the river.

The two dark shamans, however, were less resigned and continued chanting for days to extract *hoa* pathogens from the patient's body. On October 4, for instance, the healers sang six times and sucked out an equal number of evil *hoa* spirits. These were trying weeks, not only for the struggling patient but also for the parents, whose lives were filled with tension throughout the shamans' fight against evil.

On October 19, at nine o'clock in the evening, a messenger arrived in my village to report that the *hoarotu* shamans, who had given up hope for the young man's life, had ceased curing him. The patient kept on spitting blood. Everybody, young and old, took to their boats and, crying and wailing, made their way on a starlit night to the village of misfortune. One heard such lamentations as "My friend!" and "My grandson!" The women cried as we disembarked, crowding into the house of the moribund boy. He lay in the mellow light of a lantern that swayed from the crossbeam above his hammock. He had been completely consumed by tuberculosis, his abdomen caved in, his extremities without flesh. His black hair seemed too heavy for the bony face and his black eyes too large. He jerked his head from side to side and, every so often, opened his mouth in immense yawns. His legs were stretched out and his hands clawed the hammock above his head.

The men sat or stood on one side of the youth, the women on the other. Just at the edge of the hammock sat his mother, his co-mother (his father's second wife), and his aunt. Behind the wailing mother stood a woman who was clutching her long hair; two other women held her by the shoulders to steady her. Also behind the "other mother" I saw a woman who was holding her hair firmly with two hands. Juan's father sat on the opposite side of the hammock, behind the younger brother of the dying young man. The brother, resting his head on the edge of the hammock, wept quietly.

Around this central group of relatives stood forty-five or more persons, smoking, talking, and staring into the light. Suddenly loud laments were heard. "Wait, my friend," screamed the women. "I am your mother," shouted the mother. "I am your father," the father called out. These outbursts pierced the high-pitched, inarticulate wailing of the crowd, which lasted for several minutes, reached a crescendo, and then ebbed. The lamenting rose in waves as the men smoked their pungent cigars and the women took turns on a cigar being circulated among them. The adults spoke in an argumentative way, pointing fingers, addressing one another in staccato utterances, and stressing final syllables in a characteristic way. People milled around, shoving one another; men urinated from the house platform; small children tried to sleep through the commotion in hammocks that had been slung along the outer edges of the house.

Then a new wave of lamentation erupted. As it reached its high point, the men grabbed their heads with both hands and shouted the kinship terms that expressed their respective relationship to the dying boy: "My son!" "My elder brother!" or simply "My friend!" And the men and women standing behind the parents came to the assistance of the bereaved, holding back the mothers by their hair and shoulders and attempting to calm them.

Suddenly a deep silence fell throughout the house as Juan began to speak. "My uncle," he said, "come here." Paulo emerged from the crowd and asked, "What is it?" Juan, looking at him, answered: "We owe debts at the rice station. If we cannot have an outboard motor, all right. We'll just go by paddle. For us is the paddle [not the motor]."[20] "You are right," said the uncle. "The motor is bad for us. For us is the paddle."

Then Juan asked his brother to take good care of his (Juan's) field of bananas. Turning to his father, the boy just looked at him. "It's me, your father," he said in a strong voice, turning his face away from Juan. In his hands he held a large white rag, which he used occasionally to mop his face. "Who killed you?" asked the father. There was utter silence in the house and then came the answer: "Mario!"

This accusation by the dying youth provoked fury among the people. Everybody had heard the name clearly and everybody knew that the boy was right. Mario's name had come up in the course of

---

[20] Through the ministering shamans' consultations with the ancestral spirits, the patient had learned about the gods' censure of his and his companions' efforts to acquire an outboard motor (see chapters 2 and 6).

many disputation sessions, and public opinion was openly hostile to the elderly dark shaman. The protest of angry men and women was so violent that I was relieved to see that Mario was not there.

Eventually the people quieted down. Near midnight the dying youth's voice was heard once more. "Father, I am going." Turning to his mother, he said, "Mother, don't cry. I am going." "Wait! Wait, my son!" cried the desolate woman, and the general wailing started anew. Meanwhile, groups of other people had arrived at the scene, and with each group the wailing rose to new heights.

Juan's body was now flailing about in his hammock. He kept yawning, his mouth gaping. From time to time his voice was heard to say, "For us is the paddle, my brother. For us is the paddle." He was in his last moments of life. His uncle lowered the lantern over the hammock while the lamenting swelled again with force. One of the men grabbed the boy's legs and held them down in a stretched-out position. Another man grasped the blanket that had propped up the patient's head, pulled it out from under the youth, and wound the boy's arms firmly into the overhanging ends on either side.

As Juan's head rolled to the side, his uncle placed his hand on the boy's heart and, saying the inevitable "*wabai*," pronounced him dead. The women instantly broke into wild screaming. They threw their arms up in the air and clapped their hands, but the men were comparatively calm and restrained. One of them stepped away from the group and blew four long hoots on a shell trumpet to carry the message of death to distant villages.

In the ensuing melee the mother of the dead boy attacked her co-wife. She kept hitting her on the head with both fists and screaming at the top of her voice, "It is your fault! You never fed him when he was hungry!" Several men intervened to separate the women. In her grief the mother threw herself over the corpse, sobbing and crying, "My son, my son!" A small girl was hurt in the tumultuous confusion. The mother brought her to me, asking fearfully whether the damage was serious. "It's nothing," I reassured her. "Just a bleeding lip."

Then I saw Juan's father step outside onto the elevated causeway between house and kitchen; holding his head between his hands, he yelled across the dark river, "My son! My child!" Behind him the two co-wives could no longer be restrained; again they lunged at each other and pulled each other's hair. One of the men stepped forward and struck the mother in her face; the blow was so hard that blood ran out of her mouth. Other men pressed close to the aggressor and shoved him back into the crowd.

Eventually the frenzy died down and the crowd became silent. One of the men turned down the light and hoisted the lantern to a higher position under the roof. The dead boy's uncle closed the deceased's eyes; his aunt held his jaw up and straightened his hair. Two other men dressed the naked, emaciated body in a pair of trousers and a shirt. Juan's arms were so placed that his hands rested on his lap.

When the mother finally approached the hammock, she was surprisingly collected. She painted her dead son's forehead with red vegetable dye and wound a ribbon of white cloth around his head. She marked the middle of the forehead with a red Saint Andrew's cross. The hammock was then lowered until the body touched the floor of the house. The father wrapped a similar white ribbon around his own head, weeping loudly. Toward morning Juan's brother came to place two flashlights and a metal dinner plate on the corpse's lap. Someone else brought the young man's fishing line to be put with the body. By that time the women had grouped themselves around the hammock, weeping and wailing until dawn.

At six o'clock in the morning rain began to fall. It started, people told me, because Juan had died. More and more mourners, some three hundred and fifty in all, arrived at the scene, having been attracted by the sounds of the shell trumpet from villages on the Winikina, the Arawabisi, and the Araguao Rivers. At about nine o'clock, the fiscal of the Winikina called the mourners to order. All *hoarotu, bahanarotu*, and *wishiratu* shamans present were told to line up in the back part of the house, and they complied. One of them, who was wearing a shirt, took it off. The shamans began to rub their hands over their chests while assuring the crowd, "I am all right. I am all right."

The early morning visitors included Mario, for whom everybody had been anxiously waiting. As soon as he opened his mouth to say "I am all right," the people began to accuse him of murdering Juan. Had the deceased not been spitting blood for weeks? Had he not been consumed by the western spirits before their very eyes? Had he not named Mario as the sorcerer who had taken advantage of

Juan's weather-beaten state and suffocated him with a *hoa* snare (cf. Wilbert 1993, 129–31)?

In a demonstration of unexpected authority, the fiscal kept the mob from attacking the shaman. Thus, nobody could vent his anger except by shouting at the accused. The other shamans were allowed to leave the lineup and mingle with the crowd. Mario was told he would be held in custody for eight days and would be watched until he was either acquitted or convicted of killing the boy. "Your breast is pale like that of the dead man," the people shouted. The other shamans in the crowd also joined in the general accusation, while Mario, staring at them with swollen eyes, kept repeating, "I am all right. I did not kill him."

Some two hundred meters downriver from the village a group of eighteen men were busy cutting a clearing in the gallery forest. They fashioned a rectangular platform from palm stems in juxtaposition and in an east-west direction placed a canoe-coffin in the middle of the platform. Next to the platform the men piled up palm leaves and several lengths of liana.

The preparatory work completed, the men returned to the village and went directly to the house of mourning, pushing the screaming women out of their way. They had brought a thin stem of manaca palm which they slid through the end ropes of the dead boy's hammock. Two men lifted the pole onto their right shoulders and carried the corpse in his hammock to a large canoe at the village dock. While the men had been preparing the corpse for transportation, some thirty women had embarked in a large boat and were waiting there to receive the body. All these activities followed the normal routine. Within minutes the funeral boat, carrying the sorrowing women and the corpse, was drifting to the nearby grave site. Most of the mourners followed in a cluster of boats of all sizes.

After the corpse had been placed in the coffin, the hammock and the blanket were pulled out from under him and were buried next to the grave. Rain fell on the corpse while the spaces at the head and the foot of the coffin were filled with mud and the top was covered with slats. Mud was put on top of the cover and the entire coffin was wrapped in palm leaves tied with bush rope. Resting on the platform of palm stems, the coffin looked like a giant cigar (plate 3.3). Soon the grieving women, men, and children walked the short way back to the river, embarked, and returned to their villages. The

PLATE 3.3
Juan's primary burial made from hollowed-out tree. Coffin is wrapped in temiche palm fronds and covered with layer of clay. Clay cover serves as trap for sorcerer, who is believed to visit grave of victim to suck blood from corpse. (Photograph Johannes Wilbert)

sun had broken through the clouds. It was almost noon, about twelve hours after Juan had died. We arrived at our village half an hour later. Although we had been away for only a short time, all the fires had gone out in the village. "*Akai*," yelled the woman who noticed it first. "Help!" It was a bad omen.

The next day the Winikina, assembling in the chief's dwelling, insisted that Mario had to spend eight days in that house. Like all other houses it had no walls, so the accused sorcerer could be observed on the elevated floor of the pile dwelling. His wife and daughter were the only ones allowed to go near him.

Mario arrived at about noon on October 21. He slung his hammock in the chief's vacated house and slept for long periods of time. The people expected him to vomit blood, an act that would be the ultimate proof of his guilt.

While Mario was being detained, the village shamans decided to return to the grave site in order to inspect the layer of clay on top of the coffin. I went along to witness the inspection and to take photographs of the grave, which I had felt unable to do the day before with the mourners present. In the cracks of the dried clay the shamans clearly discerned Mario's footprints. This discovery was not surprising, because he had also been named by a man and a woman who had died the same week on another river. At the woman's grave, Marios's tracks, together with those of two other shamans, had also been found on the coffin. (A dark shaman is believed to go to the graves of his victims to suck their blood before transporting the bodies to the world of the macaw god of the west.)

When we returned from the grave and the shamans announced their findings, the people were satisfied: they had known all along that Mario was a powerful dark shaman. Now they had only to watch him carefully until he vomited blood or until blood ran out of any open wound on his body. They fed him well to prevent him from turning against them. In the low tones of his baritone voice, Mario chanted during the night, but his songs were only protective, not malevolent.

The old shaman (of Mariusa, not Winikina, origin) was kept in custody until October 31. He never vomited blood—or at least nobody caught him doing so—but his chest was still pale, the color of a corpse. Everybody in the village breathed a sigh of relief the day Mario departed with his wife and daughter for the isolation of the palm forest. They told the shaman to stay there and never come back, and the old man left without protest. I heard of him in later years without ever seeing him again.

Juan's death, of course, did not mark the end of the 1954 season of suffering among the Winikina and their closely related neighbors, the Arawabisi. Toward the end of the short rainy season, men and women walked about as in a daze. Apparently, even some attempts at suicide were made by surviving kinsmen who could no longer cope with the strain. I heard of a father, for instance, who was said to have grabbed a loaded shotgun the moment his grown-up daughter expired, held it against his breast, and tried to shoot himself. When the short wet season had finally come to an end, it was an emotionally drained and weary people the gods had left behind on the Winikina River.

Pollinating Wind

The Warao recognize a group of spirits (*ahakatuma*) that govern the winds of the major world directions. Aligned with both the directional gods of the cardinal and solstitial points and the rain lords of the cardinal and intercardinal corners of the universe, wind spirits are of cosmic significance. The northern trade winds blow in the delta in the dry seasons; local winds, southern trades, tempests, and whirlwinds prevail in the rainy seasons. In contradistinction to the predominantly destructive and pathological winds associated with the denizens of the rainy season, however, the trade winds of the dry season are related to beneficial protagonists identified with fecundity and regeneration. The breezes, in turn, present over the delta in both the dry and the wet seasons, are associated with the terrifying masters of earthquake and water spirits.

Armadillo and Earthquake

The Warao are, of course, keenly aware of the different kinds of wind that govern their homeland. And, although wind (*ahaka*) is now an expected everyday occurrence, it nevertheless had a beginning, according to the Warao scheme of things, and soft winds like the sea and land breezes were the first to come into existence. Wind began with the gentle flow of those breezes, called *ahaka boto*.

Before that time there had been no wind at all; the trees stood motionless in sweltering heat. No movement could be sensed, no rustling of leaves could be heard. Profound silence lay over the land.

Then, one day, a noise was discerned approaching overland. Laughing, shouting, and singing filled the air as a multitude of animals drew near. As they jumped and danced along the way, the sound of joyful anticipation echoed across the world. The animals, having lived until then in the west, were on their way to the east, intent on giving origin to the wind. On their journey they had met Oka (Armadillo), who, because of his superior strength, had become the leader of the animal trek.

When, upon reaching the east, the travelers inquired about the master of the region, they were taken to meet Huru (Earthquake). Both leaders, Oka and Huru, were powerfully built and of gigantic stature. Now that one of them had come to invade the land of the other, the two giants intended to determine which one should be master of the realm. In preparation for the contest, each leader fabricated a convexly curved rectangular combat shield of juxtaposed moriche leaf-stalks[21] (fig. 3.3).

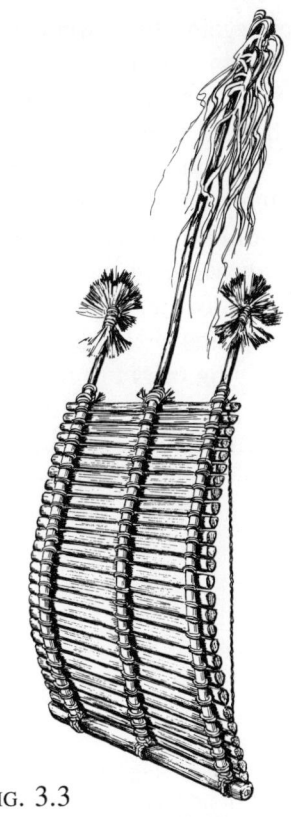

FIG. 3.3
Dueling combat shield.
(Drawing by Helga Adibi)

---

[21] The word *oka* designates the nine-banded armadillo (*Dasypus novemcinctus*). It lives in burrows it excavates in the levees along the rivers in the upper delta, preferably close to a tree. In the unstable levee soil, the roots of trees are often undermined by the river, causing the trees to topple into the water. In narrow waterways they obstruct navigation.

The typical burrowing behavior of the nine-banded armadillo is precisely what

Resting their shields on the ground before them, each bracing one foot against the lower edge and, with arms outstretched, clasping their hands around the two handles on the upper edge of their weapons, the champions began the contest. They pushed and shoved from behind their shields, attempting to throw their respective opponent to the ground[22] (plate 3.4). Back and forth went the duel, each champion alternately advancing and retreating. As the thumping of colliding shields resounded in the air, it became evident that the rivals were of equal strength; neither was able to push his opponent off the field. Their alternating movements in opposite directions and their heavy breathing, however, stirred the atmosphere, giving origin to the breezes.

In the pell-mell of battle, Oka eventually was pushed back to the river. He lost his footing and slid into the water, thus ending the contest in an inconclusive draw. As the objective of each man in the duel had been to overpower his opponent, not to gain advantage over him accidentally, Huru hastened to help his rival out of the water. He bent down several trees along the riverbank for Oka to hold onto, but none of them was strong enough to support the giant spirit's weight. One by one the tree trunks snapped, and the clambering Oka dropped back into the river. Finally, throwing his

---

relates it as a natural model to Oka, the leader of the water spirits. To differentiate the animal from the mythological hero, the Warao refer to it as *oka sanuka*, "the lesser Oka," and to the hero as *oka nabarao*, "Oka, the water denizen."

Other characteristics of the nine-banded armadillo make it especially suitable as a natural model for Oka. Even a strong man must strain to pull the animal out of its hole, as it braces itself with its legs and its shield against the walls of the burrow. The small animal demonstrates uncommon strength for its size. Underwater, the nine-banded armadillo can hold its breath for up to six minutes and is capable of walking short distances on the floor of the riverbed. Finally, the armadillo as an insect eater is related to the moriche-palm complex of the Warao, inasmuch as it opens the bark of a fallen palm to extract palm borer's larvae, a food preferred by the Warao. In fact, it may very well be that the shield fight between Oka, the invader, and Huru, the local chief, hints at competitive territorial fighting over the right to exploit a morichal which took place in the past between two groups.

[22] The rounded carapace of the armadillo, with its nine bony bands, may have served as a model for the unique shield fight (*nahakara*) the legendary heroes employed in their man-on-man shoving contest. Furthermore, while holding their curved shields in front of them, the combatants charged each other with spasmodic thrusts reminiscent of the sudden reflex jumps of armadillos when they are excited.

Warao Weather Lore

Plate 3.4. Ritual shield fight. (Courtesy Sociedad de Ciencias Naturales La Salle, Caracas)

shield onto the bank, he decided to stay in the water permanently, there to become the supreme spirit of the water people (*nabarao*) who are associated with the sea breeze. Evidence of his and his people's presence near land can be seen in the trees uprooted by his hands digging into the riverbank in his effort to get out of the water. The trees may remain there, obstructing navigation, for months or even years, slowly becoming recognized as landmarks. Their denuded branches bob ceaselessly in the current, making the crews of passing boats apprehensive. Menstruating women avoid such places for fear that water spirits may attack and rape them. The relationship of Warao women to water spirits is explained in the lore of many narratives and songs (Barral 1964, 467–69; Wilbert 1970, 600). In mythical times human societies and water people exchanged women with each other (Roth 1915, 250–51), and to this day mythological heroines are believed to govern the tides and the water levels of rivers. Huru, for his part, went underground and lay down to rest at the center of the earth. People perceive his presence when, with the slightest movement of his body, he causes the earth to tremble.

Oka and Huru have remained rivals ever since that first encounter, and their back-and-forth contest continues in perpetuity as the daily alternating pattern of sea and land breezes across the edge of the earth. As in their first duel, Huru sometimes overpowers Oka, thus momentarily checking the sea breeze. On such occasions the people know that they will soon feel Huru's muscle flexing to form an earthquake, shaking their houses and rumbling through the bogland.[23]

The Father of Wind

During the long dry season the soft rain, carried inland by the sea breeze, quickly evaporates under the rushing trades in the heat of the day. The breeze itself is also muffled by the northern trade winds

---

[23] The northeastern coast of Venezuela, including the northern two-thirds of the Orinoco Delta, is earthquake country. The Paria Peninsula is one of the most active seismic zones in Venezuela. Quakes felt in the delta are most likely the effects of seismic activity in this general area of high exposure (Fiedler and Rivero 1979, 172–73, map).

(*ahaka taira*). Pure wind with almost no rain, the northern trades are subject to the original *Ahakarima*, "Father of Wind," who manifests himself in the form of the striated heron (*Butorides striatus*).[24] At the beginning of the year and especially at the time of the vernal equinox, this highly vocal heron engages in lively mating behavior, the aggressive male chasing the female in vigorous pursuit as both birds engage in duets of sharp calls that fill the air. The vigor of the birds' courtship and display marks their nesting places in coastal and insular mangrove belts. More important, their wing flapping movements and noisy calls unleash the northern trade winds.

Before Hia, the Wind Father, adopted his avian form, he was a priest-shaman who specialized in producing strong winds through loud vociferations; he was a shamanic *ahakarima* (windmaker). He is said to have been living in a large settlement when, in the sultry weather of August, his fellowmen asked him to produce a cooling wind to refresh their bodies and dispel their melancholy (*arawanera*). Instead of a softly fanning wind, however, Hia unfortunately produced a storm too strong, too cold, and too destructive to bring the desired relief. The people implored the shaman to still the tempest and lull the wind so that they could enjoy it. The shaman then invited the people to come to a designated place the next day to witness the beginning of the kind of wind they wanted. Before the assembled crowd, Hia flapped his arms like wings and transformed himself into the bird he is today.

The heron is certainly no stranger to Caribbean weather lore. Island Carib knew the green heron (*Butorides virescens*) as a storm-related bird. Both herons, *B. striatus* and *B. virescens*—considered conspecific by some scientists—are prone to interbreed in areas where their ranges overlap (Hartert 1920; Harris 1973; Hancock and Kushlan 1984, 179). The Caribbean name for the green heron is listed in Breton's (1892 [1655]) dictionary as *ioboura* (*yábura*), a form that may even, at least in part, be cognate with the Waraoan term *hia* for the striated heron of the Orinoco Delta. Both birds are crabiers. The Island Carib associated the green heron with the rising of Orion in August and September and thus with stormy weather

---

[24] The vernacular name for the green-backed (striated) heron is *chicuaco cuello gris*.

and the crab season (Taylor 1946, 217–18; Robiou-Lamarche 1986, 484).

Hia, the Warao mythical Father of Wind, is the ruler of the northern trades. As such, his influence upon the Indians' life is strongest in the months of the vernal and (much less so) the autumnal equinoxes, when the weather of the Orinoco Delta goes through, respectively, its primary and secondary annual dry seasons. Especially during the first quarter of the year (January through March), the northern trade winds blow with force across the coastal plain. That is when the Indians turn their faces into the wind to listen for its buzzing sound, a muffled humming noise, which tells them that the Sago Mother, in her home at sunrise at the northern solstice, dehisces to discharge her bounty of moriche starch. A season of well-being and abundance is brought by Hia, the mythical heron, as he produces the wind to carry the sago across the sea to earth.

In Warao weather lore the heron is a culture hero of singular importance. He is the creator of the moriche palm (*Mauritia flexuosa*), the same plant that was celebrated as the tree of life by early observers, who marveled at the central role it played in Warao economy (Gumilla 1944, 1:143–49; cf. Schomburgk in Raleigh 1970 [1596], 49). In primordial time Hia, while still in human form, was a close friend and neighbor of Kasisi, the rufous crab hawk (*Buteogallus aequinoctialis*), who in turn was a *bahana* shaman.[25] At one of their frequent meetings, the hawk wondered whether the heron might be capable of creating the moriche palm. Planting a seed, Hia made it germinate and then grow with miraculous speed. As trees and plants in general derive their nourishment from the wind,[26] heron, as the Father of Wind, found it easy to accelerate the growth of the palm. Because the first fully grown palm was a female plant, the heron called it *ohiarao*, "bearer of moriche fruit."

---

[25] The vernacular name for the rufous crab hawk is *gavilan de manglares*. As a coastal species, it frequents the littoral mangrove forests, where its habitat coincides with that of the striated heron.

[26] Underlying this belief in the miraculous growth potential of the wind may be the empirical effects of wind pollination on plant reproduction (see Lavandero 1980a). The influence of the wind on plant fertility is extended to humans when an unmarried girl is found to be pregnant and her sexual partner remains unidentified. People refer to her as *ahaka arani* "wind mother." Her son and her daughter are called, respectively, *ahaka auka* and *ahaka aukatida*.

The male palm, created next, the heron named *haukwaharu*, "producer of moriche pollen." Finally, Hia ordered old Spider Woman (*Ayara*) to deposit starch in the stems of both palms.

Kasisi, the hawk, delighted with his friend's handiwork, suggested that a sago ritual be arranged. Hia agreed, and the two crab-eating heroes came to appreciate moriche sago as the ideal complement to their favorite diet. Through these events the Warao learned of the relationship between moriche sago and the northern trade winds. It is the wind that makes the palms grow and conveys the starch from the northeasterly mountain of the Sago Mother into the palm stems. Ever since the original agape of the bird heroes took place at the beginning of time, the Warao have continued to celebrate the sago ritual. And, because sago and crab were served at the first banquet of the culture heroes, they have become foods of sacramental nature.

The Long Dry Season

There is hardly a time in the year when the Warao can be more relaxed and more confident about the future than during the long dry season from January to April. Plenty of food is available, and the people enjoy good health and benign weather. The strong northern trade winds join the daily breezes to mitigate the heat of the season, known as the time of "dry land" (*inawaha*). The sunken interiors of the deltaic islands do indeed dry out, notwithstanding occasional shower activity.

The moriche palm that Hia, the Father of Wind, is reputed to have created is one of several Old and New World palm genera that are exploited for sago, the starch in their stems.[27] The extraction of starch from palms, reported earlier from tribes in southern Brazil, the Gran Chaco (*Roystonea oleracea, Arecastrum romanozoffianum*), and the Orinoco Delta (*Mauritia flexuosa, Manicaria saccifera*), is now practiced to any significant degree only by the

---

[27] On the mainland and the islands of southeast Asia, in parts of Melanesia, and in Micronesia, native peoples exploit species of the genera *Corypha, Arenga, Eugeissona, Caryota,* and *Metroxylon*. In lowland South America and the Caribbean, Indians learned to extract sago from palms of the genera *Roystonea, Arecastrum, Mauritia,* and *Manicaria* (Wilbert 1976a; Ruddle et al. 1978, 5–10).

PLATE 3.5
Moriche palm (*Mauritia flexuosa*). "Tree of Life" of Warao and centerpiece of weather shamanism. (Photograph Johannes Wilbert)

Warao of the Orinoco Delta. In preagricultural times, sago from *Mauritia* (moriche) served as a staple in the delta, whereas starch from *Manicaria* (*temiche*) played only a secondary role as an emergency food (Wilbert 1976a, 275–78).

The moriche of the Orinoco Delta is a regal palm with a smooth and unarmed columnar trunk twenty-five to thirty meters tall and sixty centimeters thick (plate 3.5). Its crown consists of some twelve palmate leaves, which unfold from sturdy three- to four-meter-long leafstalks. These leaves measure about three meters in diameter and consist of numerous stiff segments that droop at the tip. The moriche is a dioecious palm; male reproductive organs grow on one kind of tree and female (sometimes hermaphrodite) organs on another. The more than one-meter-long persistent and pendulous flower stalks grow among the leaves; they have numerous short tubular bracts and are heavily branched. The one-seeded fruit of the moriche is spherical, the size of a small apple, and is covered with reddish-brown scales that form a geometric pattern (McCurrach 1960, 136–37; Heinen and Ruddle 1974, 121).

In the Orinoco Delta the moriche palm grows in freshwater swamps, where the trees cluster in groves (morichals) whose size—large or small—depends on their relative distance from the major rivers and on varying microenvironmental conditions. The abundance of sago in any given morichal is not always predictable, although in general starch is most plentiful in the long dry season (see fig. 1.3).

The Warao, emerging decimated and browbeaten in early January from beneath the oppressive cloud canopy of the preceding season of bad weather, enjoy renewed vigor in the sunny, dry, wind-freshened months of the vernal equinox. As the overland equatorial trough has moved far to the south of the equator, the northern trade winds, unopposed by their southern counterparts, blow across the delta with maximum strength. To the Warao these winds signify that the Sago Mother is beginning to send her gift of palm starch into the moriche groves. In search of sago, scouts leave the settlement for the morichals. They drive their axes deep into the trunks of palms so that the blades penetrate the soft pith beneath the bark. Sago sticking to the withdrawn ax head indicates its presence in the stem. Should several probes prove positive, the scouts hurry home to alert their people. The good tidings spread like wildfire to neighboring

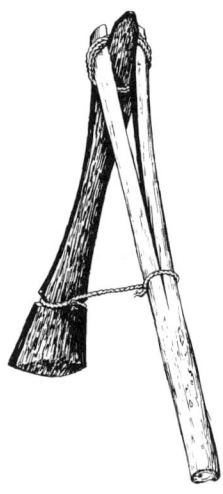

Fig. 3.4
Moriche sago hoe.
(Drawing by Helga Adibi)

Plate 3.6
Man using moriche hoe to chop pith of moriche palm, while woman kneads pith to leach out sago. (Courtesy P. J. Ziegenaus)

bands, where young and old ready themselves for the big trek into their respective subtribal morichals.

Soon after they arrive, the men begin to fell the palms. They are surrounded by the women and children, who urge them to cut the first terminal shoot of the season. The nutritious and crunchy palm heart, or cabbage, of moriche, weighing several pounds, offers an instant meal. But, facing a larger task, the man of the family takes his ax and removes the bark from the upper side of the fallen tree. He steps onto the trunk and, using a special hoe (fig. 3.4), begins to chop the exposed white pith (plate 3.6).

The women's responsibility is to scoop the crushed pith into tuba-shaped, fine-meshed carrying baskets (plate 3.7). Each woman takes her load to a nearby washstand, a dishlike basketry sieve that rests with its reinforced rim on four vertically implanted sections of green moriche leafstalk. The washstand is placed astride a hollowed-out moriche stem which serves as a trough. Packing several handfuls of pith into the sieve, the woman pours calabashes of water over the white pile of ligneous material and starts kneading it with both hands (plate 3.6). This activity frees the starch particles contained in the pith and washes them through the sieve into the trough below, where they settle to the bottom. From there the starch may be collected and eaten in its fresh, moist form, but more commonly it is spread on the bottom of a hot casserole and baked into flat cakes.

Thus, with relatively little effort, a large supply of sago can be extracted day after day. The air around the settlement is filled with the appetizing kitchen smells of toasting sago and roasting fish. Several species of small but plentiful backwater fishes are gathered from pools and creeks. Depending on the region, the Indians fan out in search of iguana and land turtles, often bringing home large catches of these edible reptiles. Enormous amounts of palm-borer (*Rhynchophorus palmetum*) larvae, as thick and long as a thumb and rich in fat and protein, are also harvested from fallen moriche palms. Children frolic about with handfuls of these grubs, which can be eaten raw or cooked. To wash down food and to quench their thirst, the Warao tap the old felled moriche palms for gallons of sweet sap. The availability of this refreshing drink comes at a most opportune time, especially in areas of the delta where, because of the decreasing volume of river water and rain, brackish seawater penetrates deeply inland. Morichals of the lower delta, however, usually retain

142 *Mindful of Famine*

PLATE 3.7. Women collecting chopped pith of moriche palm. (Courtesy Peter T. Furst)

fresh water; because of this circumstance and because of a generous supply of moriche palm sap and other plant juices, such as the liquid contained in a thick liana (*waikuba*) or the "milk" of *temiche* palm fruit, any major crisis of thirst is averted during the primary dry season (Wilbert 1976a, 300). On the contrary, far from signifying life-threatening privation and death, the low water level of the river and the simultaneous invasion of the littoral and intermediate zones by the sea connote fertility and life. As the origin myths of the tides and of low- and high-river seasons assert, in primordial times the world on this side of the ocean was populated only by men. Living near the outer fringes of the world sea (Caribbean), however, a woman and her two high-spirited daughters wanted to find husbands. Setting out to cross the ocean on a raft of moriche leafstalks, they managed to get closer and closer to the earth. When they were near land, however, a hurricane destroyed the raft and killed the mother. The two daughters swam ashore, where they joined the men. All present-day Warao are the descendants of these two mothers and the grandchildren of the old woman who drowned at sea. She is Hoarani, the Mother of Tides. When she approaches land she pushes the water in front of her, thus causing high tides (*hoidabaka*). When she returns to the sea she takes water with her, causing low tides (*homanuka*). The two temperamental daughters of the Mother of Tides became, respectively, the Mother of Low River and the Mother of High River. The Warao hold them in high esteem because of their power over the waters of the delta (cf. Lavandero 1991, 157–61).

The presence of brackish water in Waraoland during the long dry season is, thus, really a visit of the ocean grandmother with her grandchildren. It reminds the Indians of the momentous arrival of the ancestral mothers in this world. When the river is low the river women come to mate and to conceive. During the rainy season, when water levels are high, they are pregnant and give birth (Barral 1960, 118–21; Wilbert 1970, 233–35).

A frequently heard reference to the long dry season alludes to the blossoming of the *sangrito* tree (*Pterocarpus officinalis*). The fondest memories are commonly associated with this phenomenon when, in December and in January, along the riparian levees on the deltaic islands, the world of the Warao is ablaze with the exuberant yellow flowering of this tree. Besides being a feast for the eyes, the golden blooms attract swarms of bees which signal the approach of the honey season. With the possible exception of moriche sago and crabs, the Warao enjoy no other food as much as honey. Certain men, called *shimomu*, are known to be especially knowledgeable about bees and their ways. The men's uncanny ability to locate beehives in the interior hollows of hardwood trees suggests to the Indians that the specialists are supernaturally endowed. Whenever they reach for their axes or indicate in any way that they are preparing for a honey hunt, a flurry of excitement stirs the women and children, who are always ready to follow the men into the forest.

Warao lore of honey-producing hymenoptera is rich (see Lévi-Strauss 1969). It classifies many species of bees and wasps as interrelated kin in extended families (Wilbert 1985, 165–66). The complexity of this apian lore is commensurate with the importance of bees and bee products in the Warao economy. From February through April honey is regionally available in large quantities. In preagricultural times the abundance of honey initiated prolonged expeditions of entire local groups in search of the delectable food. A tree containing a hive or several hives was felled and opened, the combs or honey pots were removed, and the harvest was stored in containers made of folded manaca palm stipules. Honey, larvae, and smoked backwater fish provided a fare so rich in proteins and so high in carbohydrates that the Warao "would breakfast. . .and go all day without getting hungry again," according to an elderly informant. "Sometimes we even turned in at night without feeling hungry enough to eat. Honey was the blood of the Warao."

Taking full advantage of the cornucopia of the dry season, the Warao indulge themselves to build up their strength. In the midst of plenty and of copious consumption, however, the rain shamans and other elders of the tribe read the signs of seasonal change with experienced eyes. As the days go by, the force of the northern trades weakens, rain showers become more frequent, and the sago content of palm trees gradually diminishes. Aware of the inevitability of the rainy season, the priest-shaman calls upon his people to remember that the time of plenty will come to an end. He reminds them that their best chance of surviving the hardships of approaching bad weather is to placate the gods with the gifts they crave. Foremost among such offerings are moriche sago and, traditionally, honey. As neither of these commodities is available in large enough

FIG. 3.5
Temple with enclosed upper compartment, where sacred paraphernalia are kept, and lower compartment (shown half-open), where the sago container is stored. (Drawing by José Luis Ulibarrena)

amounts during wet seasons, the priest-shamans in the central delta advise their respective communities to conduct a harvest ritual in March. In this central region (as possibly elsewhere in preagricultural times) the ranking priest-shaman of a subtribe is known as *kanobo arima*, "Father of the Ancestral Spirit." He is the keeper of the sacred rock crystal, a manifestation of the directional god and patron deity of the subtribe. The guardian-shaman keeps the rock in a basketry tabernacle on the upper floor of a two-story temple (fig. 3.5), where he also stores his sacred rattles, wooden effigies (fig. 3.10), the resonance chambers of the sacred trumpet, and other paraphernalia. It is likely that in this sanctuary the priest-shaman will have a dream vision of the patron deity represented by the sacred rock, reminding him that the sago-gathering ritual of the *nahanamu* should commence.

The Windmaker

Other then to its rainmaker, Warao society entrusts the management of the climatological conditions in the Orinoco Delta to a second religious specialist: the windmaker. As the rainmaker relates to Tuyuna, the thunderbird of the southern trade winds, so does the windmaker relate to Hia, the Wind Father of the northern trades. The former practitioner, using the imagery of his shrill-voiced avian double (sun bittern), unleashes thunderstorms destructive of life. The latter, by means of the piercing trills of his bird model (heron), provokes winds propitious to survival.

The windmaker practices as the sacred trumpeter (*isimoi arotu*) who, thanks to his instrument (*isimoi*), enjoys the boon of creative breath. Replicating the mating calls of his natural double, his musical exhalations, as channelled through the trumpet, produce the cosmic wind that fertilizes the sago deity and enables her to bestow upon humankind her life-sustaining gift. Even the ancestral gods of the world directions depend for their existence on the windmaker's breath, contributing thereby to the psychosocial taming of the elements and their powerful protagonists.

Sacred trumpet players among the Warao of the Orinoco Delta have been known since the 1920s, when missionaries repeatedly referred to the hallowed status of the instrument and the prestigious position its owner holds (Barral 1964, 60). But, like the character and the purpose of rainmakers, the importance of ritual windmakers and their functions has often been misrepresented, belittled, or entirely misunderstood. Authors who report that the *isimoi* was played for general entertainment and popular dances in Guyana must have seen it used on secular occasions, thus profaning the sacred purpose it enjoys among Warao of the central delta (Roth 1924, 460; see also Aretz 1967, 267).

Though intimately associated with the supernatural world, the player of the sacred trumpet does not need to undergo shamanic initiation in order to assume his duties. Instead, like other experts, both male (boat makers, basket weavers) or female (herbalists), he is considered a professional (*uási*) of the highest order whose practices accord with the religious precepts of his specialty (Wilbert 1975c; 1977a). His supernatural patroness is Isimoi Arani Ariawara, or simply Isimoi Arani, Mother of the Sacred Trumpet, who originated *sui generis* at sunrise of the northern solstice. Her body is imagined in the form of a gigantic trumpet, with a brazen (blow) tube or "leg," said to be forty meters long and twenty meters thick. Her nickname is *hebunaka arani*, "Mother without Illness."

The knowledge of Isimoi Arani's existence goes back to primordial times, when a priest-shaman is said to have traveled to Mount Karoshimo, at the southern rim of the earth. His mission was to request from the residing god (of the same name) and from Uraro, his senior fellow god on the world mountain at the southern border of the world, a son to live with the shaman's people at the center of the earth. (Other shamans purportedly journeyed north to Nabarima and Warowaro to request the same favor of these directional gods.) The gods consented by "giving" him a rock crystal to take back to his community. Agreeing to care for his supernatural foster son (the rock), the shaman became the first *kanobo arima*, "father" or "guardian of our ancestral spirit."

Uraro's son, however, proved to be an unruly spirit, killing one guardian after another as well as numerous men, women, and children. These killings and other equally vicious deeds were so catastrophic that the people felt obliged to return the rock and forfeit the advantage of the god's presence among them. They had tried everything conceivable to pacify the rock spirit; they had built a beautiful shrine, had given him a spacious tabernacle basket, and

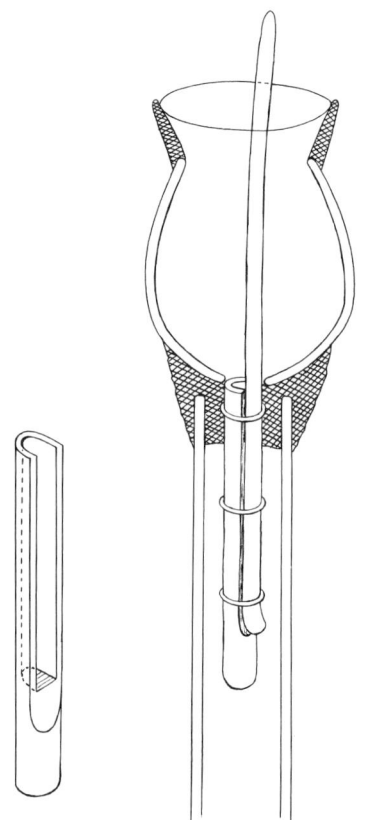

FIG. 3.6
Cross section of the sacred trumpet.
(Drawing by Helga Adibi)

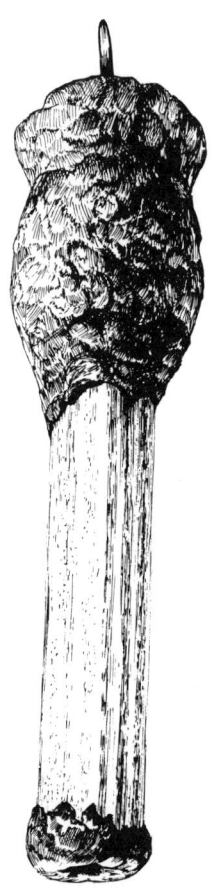

FIG. 3.7
The sacred trumpet.
(Drawing by Helga Adibi)

had fed him a large amount of tobacco. Whatever it was that had provoked the spirit's anger, it could hardly have been physical discomfort or neglect.

Distraught and having reached the limits of his wisdom, the ranking shaman went to the temple to consult the ancestral spirits in a dream. There the son of the Sacred Trumpet Mother suddenly appeared to him. He told the shaman that the rock spirit would calm down and remain with them if he were addressed with musical notes rather than with spoken words. More precisely, he said the spirit was longing to hear the signals of the sacred trumpet announcing the imminence of a sago offering that would serve as a rejuvenating bath for him and for other ancestral spirits. The body of Isimoi Arani's son, of a size more appropriate for mortals, is the prototype of sacred trumpets now in use by the Warao.

Technically a clarinet, the *isimoi* is 50 or 60 centimeters long (figs. 3.6, 3.7). The 30- or 40-centimeter-long blowtube (*aká*, leg) is made of moriche leafstalk, whose diameter measures 4 to 5 centimeters. The calabash serving as a resonance chamber (*ateho*, body) is 10 to 13 centimeters long; its maximum diameter is 8 to 10 centimeters. The funnel-shaped end (*arokoho*, opening of the neck), or bell, of the clarinet is made of carbonized beeswax; it is 4 to 5 centimeters in height, and its maximum width is 10 centimeters. After a valve device (*dausitore*) made of *himaheru* wood and a lamella (*ahono*, tongue) of *itiriti* (*Ischnosiphon* sp.) or bamboo have been inserted into its interior distal end, the resonance chamber is glued to the blowtube with wax. The mouth end of the blowtube is sealed with a thin layer of blackened wax applied at the blowhole. On ritual occasions the bell of the trumpet is decorated with a beard (*arokohi*) consisting of 40-centimeter-long temiche spikes or moriche leaf ribs which are stuck into and around the funnel of the endpiece. Each spike is decorated with small cylindrical pieces of pith of moriche leafstalks (fig. 3.8). Decorations of bird feathers, flowers, and seeds have also been seen on ritual trumpets of this kind (Barral 1964, 60). The basic pitch of the instrument is determined by the length of the free vibrating end of the lamella tied to the voice bridge. Although the *isimoi* has only one basic tone, higher tones and trills can be produced on the same instrument by overblowing, usually at the end of a sequence. As a ritual wind instrument the *isimoi* of the Warao is similar to sago-related instruments (*yuruparí*) known from South America (Kapfhammer 1992; Orjuela 1983; Reichel-Dolmatoff 1986, 1989) and from the tropical Old World (Ruddle et al. 1978, 91).

When toward the close of the long dry season the local priest-shaman anticipates the end of the sago period, he expects to receive a dream vision in which the manifested spirit of the sacred rock reminds him to begin the cycle of the sago festival. In areas outside the central delta between the caños Macareo and Araguao, the sago festival is referred to as *noara*. It is essentially the same ancestral cult festival as the *nahanamu* ritual of the central region (Mariusa, Winikina, and Arawabisi), except that sago redistribution and consumption follow promptly upon its harvest. By adopting horticulture first, the Warao of the peripheral delta regions undermined the economic importance of sago, making it unnecessary to stock stem starch for delayed consumption in the rainy season by relying on taro or, possibly, on manioc flour stashes. If not based on a historically staggered adoption pattern of agriculture within the delta, the difference between the *noara* and the *nahanamu* sago

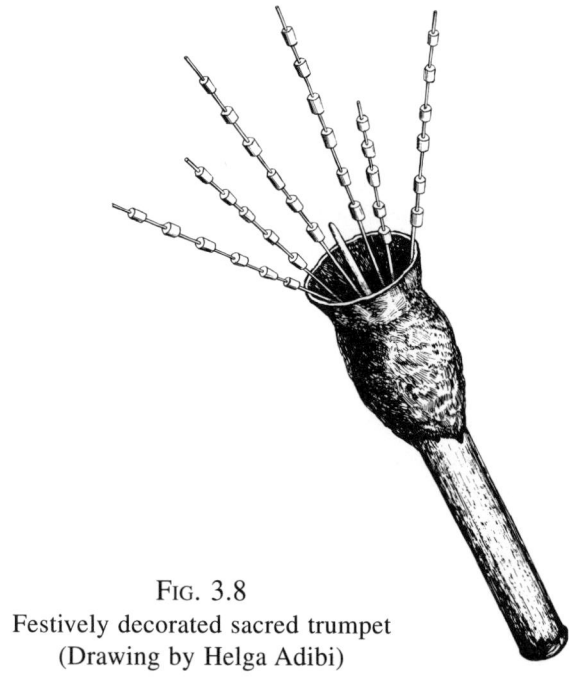

FIG. 3.8
Festively decorated sacred trumpet
(Drawing by Helga Adibi)

rituals may reflect varying regional influences of the colonial frontier (see below, pp. 253–57; Lavandero and Heinen 1986). Described here is the two-phasic cycle of the *nahanamu* dance ritual as it is celebrated in the central delta: its sago gathering or preparatory ritual, *nahanamu anamunaya* (toward the end of the long dry season), when the sago is offered to the ancestral spirits; and its propitiation ritual, *nahanamu* proper (at the beginning of the short dry season), when the sacrifice is consummated. The player of the sacred trumpet is the director of and the lead actor in the ritual. He is conversant with the intricate details of its protocol and knows how to build and tune a trumpet. Tuning may take days, especially when two trumpets are intended to be played simultaneously. Determining the pitches of the duet is an exacting task that can go on for days but which has remained beyond the capability of the fieldworker's understanding. "The *isimoi* is sacred," explained my informants. "No woman must touch it and children cannot play with it. It has to hang freely suspended in the wind, away from kitchen fumes and fish odor." It should never be kept in a basket or a similar container, where it would be hidden from the view of the spirits.

The Sago Ritual

The sago harvest ritual:—Upon receiving the dream vision, the ranking priest-shaman informs the player of the sacred trumpet who, late the same day, selects four axmen (*akabamu*) and four male hoers (*naharutu*) for the season. The next morning, when the axmen, accompanied by the trumpeter, leave the settlement, walking single file under the drawn-out notes of the trumpet, the harvest phase of the sago ritual has begun. Before returning home that day the axmen cover the felled and opened moriche stems with the large palmate fronds of the palms.

On the second day, before dawn, the team of hoers goes to triturate the exposed ligneous pith in the stems. This time the *isimoi* player does not go along, because at sunrise he must take to the work site his wife and five other *namomo,* women chosen to leech out the sago from the shredded pith. On the way the trumpet is played continuously, stopping only when the women begin their work. The workers, men and women alike, are ranked according to their social status as household heads. Ranked above everybody else, however, are the *isimoi* player and his wife, who process only one moriche palm and whose labor is essentially symbolic.

Later in the morning the trumpet sounds again, this time to summon the axmen to come to the morichal in order to fell more palms for the next day's processing. They leave their houses and walk toward the instrument; the playing continues while the second lot of palms is being cut. Then the men, after taking baths, follow the playing *isimoi arotu* back to the women, who are still working on the palms felled the preceding day. The men rest. The trumpet, carefully placed on the stump of one of the felled moriches, is silent.

Shortly after noon, when the women have finished their work, the trumpet sends them and the men back to the camp. In single file, the women go first and the men follow; last in the procession is the *isimoi arotu*. This time his playing is accompanied by the singing of the men and the falsetto voices of the women. At home, the trumpet is returned to its usual place above its owner's hammock.

Again as the trumpet sounds, the women go out on the third day to wash the sago from the second lot of felled moriches. On the fourth day the men bring in the heavy basket of harvested sago, which weighs about 150 pounds. In the first working period, now completed, one large basket of sago has been produced. A flute made of the tibia of a deer (fig. 3.9) is played to mark the joyous occasion. On the fifth day the workers rest and prepare "secular" sago for themselves and their families. They then begin a second round of sago recovery, following the same procedure as before. Altogether ritual sago production takes place in

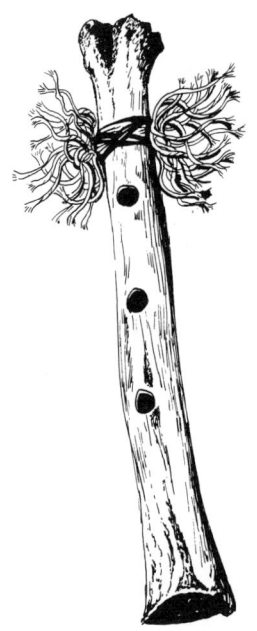

FIG. 3.9. Deer-bone flute (Drawing by Helga Adibi)

four periods of four workdays and one day of rest. Four large baskets of sago, with a combined weight of approximately 600 pounds, are recovered.

The harvest baskets, with their moist contents, are placed next to the sanctuary in the open, where a *himabaka*, or guardian spirit, takes charge of them. *Himabaka* spirits, in the form of large praying mantises, are reminiscent of those in Arabic, African, European, and native American mythologies, where they are invested with supernatural powers (Budge 1973, 1:159; Campbell 1968, 90; Reichel-Dolmatoff 1971, 169).

In Warao religion, the mantis acts as an omniscient guard of either the northern or the southern directional gods. He travels with lightning speed between the world mountain and the human vassal communities of his master to enforce the latter's will. Modeled after the insect's body, and with its combative fierceness in attacking even its own kind, the swivel-headed ogre carries a halberdlike weapon combining an ax and a pike (armed forelegs) mounted on a long handle (sticklike body). Some also say the ogre wields a saber. He applies his formidable weapon whenever humans need to be prodded in their efforts to cater to the wishes of his master. The victim feels the painful prick or blow and, depending on the shortcomings of which he or she is found guilty, expects to fall ill or to die.

During the harvest ritual the enforcer stations himself next to the sago baskets and repels anybody who seeks to steal from them. The long period of *isimoi*'s playing has reassured him and his master that a sustained effort has been made to procure an ample amount of sago. *Himabaka* is said to be extremely fond of *isimoi* music, and some Warao go so far as to say that he actually owns the instrument. He is believed to be everywhere at the same time, as are the strident sounds of the trumpet during the gathering of ritual sago. An unusual silence of anticipation pervades the settlement when, at the end of harvesting, the trumpet stops playing.

The silence is short-lived, however, for it ends the moment the men finish repairing the dance floor, a platform (8 x 10 m) of juxtaposed planks of moriche bark centrally located between the temple and the houses. Their strength restored by resting, the impatient workers approach the trumpet player and ask him to entrust the instrument to their care. Then for two days they dance as a preliminary to the actual feast. As any man may play the *isimoi* during this period, commoners take advantage of the occasion to learn how to perform on the instrument. In the nineteenth century, Schomburgk (1847–48, 1:152) reported one such instance when the "music master" taught "the young boys and the men of the place to blow on a kind of oboe." In fact, the master may single out a particularly promising youth to whom he will pass on his skills in playing and his knowledge of an *isimoi arotu*. Good musicianship and a measure of discipline are the essential prerequisites for succeeding in the profession.

Once the two days and nights of merrymaking have ended, the master repossesses the trumpet for more serious work. The barrel-shaped container that holds the sacrificial offering of sago must be manufactured and placed on the ground floor of the sanctuary (fig. 3.5). The men selected for the task work quickly and quietly while the trumpet again fills the air with its sounds. This time, however, the music attests to the presence of the god in the upper compartment of the temple. From now on, the people will avoid raising their eyes higher than the *isimoi* at the lips of the musician. Only the player himself is free to look up, and he does so deliberately, for his presence is pleasing to the god, especially at this time when two of the four large sago baskets are emptied into the new container under the raised temple platform. The sago in the other two baskets is subsequently distributed to the various households in the community. To this end the people approach the sanctuary in solemn silence and the *isimoi arotu* plays ardently to announce their presence and to ingratiate them with the god. While the people are accepting their shares of sago and during the dance that follows, the fronds at the entrance to the upper room of the shrine are pushed aside so that the resident god can overlook the platform and watch the dancing. Men and women who take part in the ritual before the eyes of their supernatural patron enter into a vassalage relationship with him by pledging allegiance and by promising to produce a specific number of large baskets of sago according to their families' abilities. The promissory affirmations are made in public by the male heads of households, who thenceforth are known in the community as having pledged certain amounts. The more generous the pledge, the higher the prestige of the household head and his family for the rest of the year. In this pledge system entire bands may come to enjoy a high status within the subtribe, as a group whose members are capable of hard work and are eager to strengthen the bonds among subtribal bands, their patron deity, and the directional gods at large. After the final night of dancing to the trumpet's sounds, the people rest for a few days and then set out to fulfill their sago pledges before the end of the long dry season. The sago collected is packed on top of the two-basket foundation already in the temple container. The prestige ranking of households, based on differential giving for the common good, spurs optimum production and helps to minimize the drudgery of the intensified production process. At times, an estimated 3,000 pounds of firmly compacted sago have accumulated in the temple, to remain there throughout the approaching long rainy season and until the short dry season begins in early August or September (Heinen and Ruddle 1974, 127). The sacred trumpet remains silent during the three- and four-month interval while the sago store is being protected by *himabaka* and the shaman's two invisible temple guards in the form of jaguars.

In times past, as noted earlier, priest-shamans also sent people out in their communities to gather honey with similar intent. Around the vernal equinox, when production is at its peak, hundreds of liters of honey were collected for a sacrificial offering. It was stored in a small (1.5 m long) trough placed next to the sago container in the temple's lower compartment. Surplus honey, like surplus sago, was ritually collected to be presented to the supernaturals as a gift of propitiation and to be consumed later during the fertility festival. Shamans ate the honey in its natural (nonalcoholic) state, whereas commoners ingested it diluted as honey water or fermented mead. Thus, in addition to serving as highly nutritious daily fare, honey, like sago, was a sacramental food.

The sago distribution ritual:—The store of sago in the temple is kept dry and compact throughout the long rainy season, when food becomes extremely scarce. The moriche palms contain no sago, and only small emergency rations of starch can be extracted from temiche palm stems to help the hungry people survive the most acute period in their annual food cycle. Throughout the months of heavy rain, until late August or early September, the temple sago holds out the best hope for temporary relief, although since late July large numbers of crabs have been running on the beaches. The members of the subtribe openly query the reason for the delay in beginning the second phase of the harvest festival, when the sago offering is consecrated by the gods and the starch is finally redistributed.

As in the initial harvest phase, the sequence of events in the phase of sago distribution is triggered by the priest-shaman's dream in which the rock spirit appears to him in the temple. The spirit explains that he has immersed himself in the sago and now wants to eat tobacco smoke. Near that month's full moon, the guests from neighboring subtribes arrive to participate in the ritual dancing. Two wooden images, each on top of a stick (1.5 m high), are placed in the center of the dancing platform (fig. 3.10). Called *daunona* (made of wood), the images represent two high-ranking ancestral personages residing at sunrise of the northern solstice. Usually referred to in the singular as Daunona Arani Ariawari, or simply Daunona Arani, "Mother of the Wooden Image," they are believed to manifest themselves, in the sky-world as well as on the dancing platform, as a couple (a woman and a man). Without these two images the ancestral spirits cannot see or hear the dancers.

During the distribution ritual of the *nahanamu* festival, two sacred trumpets are played: one is small with a high voice and the

FIG. 3.10. Daunona images. (Drawing by Helga Adibi)

other is a larger one with a low voice. Instead of being male and female, however, the two trumpets are sons of Isimoi Arani, "Mother of the Sacred Trumpet." As always when she hears the music, the great spirit rejoices and begins to dance. The wind produced by the instrument being played and by the swaying body of the giant spirit pollinates Aru Arani, the "Mother of Sago," engendering copious reserves of fresh sago in her. Thus, at a time when hunger, pain, and death hover over the Indians like apocalyptic vultures, the sago ritual points to mating crabs and pollinating palms as the guarantors of survival by a sufficiency of food and by procreation. Robust eroticism stirring in the dancers manifests itself in suggestive signs and explicit actions, allusive cross-sexual comportment, as well as in the symbolism of ritual paraphernalia, including sacred rattles and trumpets as conjunctive models (Suárez 1968, 79, fig. 52).

After the singing and smoking by the priest-shaman and his assistants in the sanctuary, and after nightlong dancing to the sounds of rattles and trumpets, part of the sago store is distributed to the participants according to their social status. More dances follow until the feast eventually comes to an end and the sacred trumpets are blown (by the headman) for the last time. They are said to be weeping out of sadness over their impending death (Barral 1964, 60). After almost continuous playing throughout both phases of the *nahanamu* cycle, someone (i.e., any man) takes the two instruments and breaks them apart. The blowtubes are stuck like bones of game animals into the roof thatch, but the resonators belong to Isimoi Arani who watches over them so as to protect them from desecration. The player of the sacred trumpet handles them with care and speaks of them fondly. "They are companions, brothers," he says. "The eyes of Isimoi Arani are upon them." After the feast any remaining temple sago will be gradually doled out over several days until the store is finally exhausted. The dispensing shaman is careful to see that every family receives its fair share. The eyes of many hungry persons are watching his every measure, and quarreling ensues if he shows any partiality. The Warao hope that soon after the *nahanamu* festival ends, sago in small amounts will once again become available in the morichals, thus preventing acute hunger for at least another year.

Provisioning the Ancestors

To keep hunger and famine away from his people is only one of the trumpet player's main objectives; provisioning the ancestral spirits is the other. He accomplishes these goals, as noted, by means of musical wind that issues from his instrument, causing the Trumpet Mother to dance and sway. This pollinating performance impregnates the Mother of Sago with the staple food of the living and coincidentally generates the spring of life for the ancestors.[28]

Metaphorically, palm sago represents an osseous medium of inherent seminal power (Briggs 1992, 344). And when the directional gods, "Our Grandfathers," come to bathe in the temple's sago container, they yearn to immerse themselves in the moist and pure (odorless and white) substance to assimilate its regenerative energy.[29] As semen is believed to nourish the fetus, so is sago-semen considered to function as a source of vital sustenance for the dead. Thus the player of the sacred trumpet participates in a bonding ritual that manifests the essential properties of an ancestor cult, including offerings, communication, placation, and supplication (cf. Heinen 1993, 176). The trumpet itself functions as the agent that actualizes the symbiosis between the community and its ancestors.

Warao lore draws attention to the metaphoric significance of sago as bone on two different levels of mythic history. On the oldest plane, as previously noted, it presents Hia, "Wind Father," who created earth's first moriche palm in the image of Aru Arani Ariawara, the giant "*Ur*-mother of Sago," fashioning the stem's starchy core from the silk of Old Spider Woman (*tihidamo ayara*). Spider Woman's origin, in turn, was owing to a creative act by Kanobo Yaukware (god of the noon sun), who formed her from the bleached bones of ancestral Warao. Thus the first sago contained

---

[28] Sound waves emitted by wind instruments have been implicated as precipitating dehiscence (Huxley 1978, 136–38). Awareness by Tucanoan groups of the causal relationship between trumpet- or flute-blowing, chanting, or addressing trees in loud voice on the one hand and palm pollination on the other has been suggested by Reichel-Dolmatoff (1989, 109–10).

[29] Only the cardinal gods of the east, north, and south are invited to bathe in the sago of the *nahanamu* festival. As the lord of the underworld, the god of the west is excluded from the ritual. The sorcerer (*hoarotu*), however, is said to prepare two large baskets of sago to be used as bathwater by the denizens of the west.

in the primordial palm was the essential "osseous" exudate of her body symbolically connoting, like moriche sago, seminal ancestral power.

On a more recent mythical level, moriche sago originated in the transformation of an ancestral woman, Natue (Grandmother), and an ancestral man by Hahuba, "Mother of Being." About the time of the couple's transmutation and after their children had already populated the land, a man who died in an ancestral village was buried in the hollowed-out stem of a moriche palm. His bones became the sago-containing fibrous pith (sometimes referred to as *ohidu a muhu*, "bones of the moriche palm") that entered the bodies of the moriche couple, completing Hahuba's creation. The transformed Natue, also in the form of a gigantic palm, is Aru Arani, "Mother of Sago," whose trunk is white because of the sago starch it exudes.

FIG. 3.11
Tuba-shaped carrying basket formerly used to transport human bones.
(Drawing by Helga Adibi)

Ancestral bones are precious to the Warao. They are given a second burial after most of the corpse's flesh has decomposed in the tree coffin, *(wa)bahoro*, "skin of the dead" (plate 3.3). The graveyard (*bahahoro*) is the place where the dead exchange their human skin (*horu*) for the bark (*horu*) of a tree. Until recently Warao groups of the central delta packed the life-containing bones of their forebears in closely meshed baskets (*uhumutu*) in a quasi-fetal position. Carrying them along on their seasonal wanderings, they hung the baskets from the crossbeams of their houses or from the rafters in special charnels (Gumilla 1944, 1:201; Barral 1964, 8; 1972, 258) (fig. 3.11).

Thus, there exists a functional and metaphorical analogy between the recovery of ancestral bones and the gathering of moriche pith. Women bend over the opened coffin to collect the osseous remains of the desiccated, white fungi-covered corpse and put them into a large basket, just as they bend over the opened stem of a felled moriche to extract the white, "osseous," sago-containing pith and put it into a large basket. Transformed in their cocoonlike tree coffins from humans into spirits, the dead emerge from this chrysalis as bones invested with supernatural life. After the ancestral gods and spirits have gained renewed vigor through immersion in the sago, the transubstantiated stem starch is released as life-giving sustenance for their descendants. This communion, then, unites the world of the living with the world of the dead and, conforming to religious orthodoxy, it does so by means of a mystical sacramental meal with divine participation. Seen from this perspective, the *isimoi arotu*'s role as author of pollinating wind assumes a position of profound eschatological import.

Chapter Four

South American Weather Lore

This chapter on comparative South American weather lore records beliefs of 128 aboriginal societies about practitioners, techniques of climatic control, and weather denizens (map 4.1).

Weather Practitioners

Weather is usually considered either beneficial or harmful on the basis of its critical role in a society's daily struggle for survival. Throughout native South America men and women have been observed as exercising apotropaic powers over weather, manipulating it for the better or for the worse of their communities. Some practitioners adopt attitudes of submissiveness and supplication to evoke the benevolence of the weather lords. Others mark the outward expression of the relationship between humans and the elements with antagonism, making those confronting the weather defiant in their efforts to compel the clouds. In either situation, however, underlying the interrelationship between human beings and weather spirits is an animistic worldview. Weather phenomena are perceived as sentient beings with needs and emotions like those of human beings, rather than as mere atmospheric conditions. Weather denizens fear for their safety, require sustenance, and become enraged, hateful, fearful, sorrowful, joyful, amorous, or compassionate according to their nature, to mood swings, or to changing relationships. Humans, counting on these characteristics, evoke the respective emotions, exhibiting suppliant or belligerent behavior. The techniques adopted in either attitude vary from one society to another. To Western onlookers who have derided this seemingly

MAP 4.1
Comparative South American weather lore. Approximate locations of tribes treated in Chapter Four. (Drawing by Chase Langford)

Comparative South American Weather Lore:
Legend to Map 4.1

(Numbers in parentheses correspond to numbers on the map)

1. Akawaio (9)
2. Amuesha (59)
3. Andoque (44)
4. Anserma (33)
5. Apinaye (70)
6. Apytré-Mbyá (128)
7. Araona (86)
8. Araucanian (Mapuche) (67)
9. Arekuna (11)
10. Awaikoma-Kaingang (120)
11. Awa-Kwaiker (34)
12. Aymara (64)
13. Ayoreo (97)
14. Bacaïri (80)
15. Bará (Northern Barasana) (25)
16. Barasana (Southern Barasana) (26)
17. Bororo (82)
18. Botocudo (126)
19. Caduveo (109)
20. Callinago (1)
21. Camayura (77)
22. Campa (56)
23. Camurú-Cariri (125)
24. Canelo (Penday) (42)
25. Canelos-Quichua (43)
26. Carajá (75)
27. Carihona (27)
28. Cariña (5)
29. Cashinaua (53)
30. Cayapa (37)
31. Cayapó (72)
32. Chacobo (88)
33. Chaima (4)
34. Chamacoco (106)
35. Chané (99)
36. Chapacura (89)

37. Chiquito-Manasi (Chiquitano) (96)
38. Chiriguano (98)
39. Chorote (100)
43. Craho (71)
44. Crengez (122)
45. Cumanagoto (3)
46. Cuna (31)
47. Desana (23)
48. Embera (32)
49. Guajiro (28)
50. Guaraní (116)
51. Guarayo (95)
52. Guató (83)
53. Guayakí (117)
54. Guiacurú (111)
55. Huarayo (63)
56. Ica (30)
57. Inca (62)
58. Ipurina (84)
59. Jivaro (47)
60. Kogi (29)
61. Kumana (91)
62. Lengua (113)
63. Lokono (8)
64. Machiguenga (60)
65. Macuna (24)
66. Maka (115)
67. Maku (21)
68. Manao (20)
69. Maroni River Carib (10)
70. Mashco (61)
71. Maskoy (108)
72. Mataco (102)
73. Mbayá (112)
74. Mbya (119)

75. Mehinaku (78)
76. Mocoví (105)
77. Mojo (94)
78. Munduruku (74)
79. Nambicuara (93)
80. Nivaklé (Chulupí) (110)
81. Otavalo (39)
82. Paéz (35)
83. Panare (12)
84. Parintintin (85)
85. Pasain (104)
86. Payaguá (118)
87. Pilagá (101)
88. Piritu (2)
89. Piro (57)
90. Puruhá-Quichua (40)
91. Quechua (55)
92. Quichua (41)
93. Sanemá-Yanomami (14)
94. Selknam (69)
95. Sensi (52)
96. Sharanahua (58)
97. Sharpa (48)
98. Shavante (79)
99. Shipaya (73)
100. Shipibo (54)
101. Shucurú (124)
102. Sikuani (13)
103. Siona-Secoya (36)
104. Surui (90)
105. Tacana (65)
106. Tamanaco (6)
107. Tapirapé (76)
108. Tariano (22)
109. Taurepan (16)
110. Tereno (107)
111. Toba (114)
112. Toromona (87)
113. Tukuna (51)
114. Tupari (92)
115. Tupinamba (121)
116. Umutina (81)
117. Urubu-Kaapor (123)
118. Vilela (Atalalá) (103)
119. Waiwai (18)
120. Wapishana (17)
121. Warao (7)
122. Witoto (45)
123. Yagua (50)
124. Yamana (68)
125. Yanomami (19)
126. Yekuana (15)
127. Yuracaré (66)
128. Zaparo (46)

preposterous posturing of frail humans vis-à-vis atmospheric powers, blowing, chanting, dancing, gesticulating, weapon brandishing, missile throwing, and still other techniques for influencing the elements seem pathetically inadequate. Yet native South Americans, like traditional societies around the world, have always tried to make the elements adaptable to human preferences instead of passively enduring them in fatalistic acquiescence.

In South America weather magic is practiced by the average man or woman, by regular shamans, or by specialized individuals. Generally functioning as healers and as intermediaries between the community and the spirit world, regular shamans are deemed capable of exerting their powers over weather denizens as well. To them, rain, thunder, lightning, windstorms and related atmospheric phenomena merely represent a class of potentially harmful agents that threaten human life and welfare. Common shamans manipulate the weather spirits, as they do any other supernatural cause of illness, by means of traditional techniques, and they care for the sick and the maimed the elements leave in their wake.

In keeping with the overall functions of shamanism, the essentially defensive role of weather shamanism is frequently exchanged for an offensive stance of weather sorcery. Through shamanic initiation, practitioners become the coequals, even the masters, of the weather lords; they are empowered to employ meteorological forces as offensive agents against all worldly enemies. Thus, to the Carihona, thundering is caused by the exchange of volleys between regional shamans who, interacting with one another, battle it out with counterparts in other world directions. In the process, regional shamans may dispatch thunderstorms to provoke havoc among their enemies or may direct lightning to cause an occasional death, to darken vision, to cramp a leg, and so on, in an adversarial community (Schindler pers. comm.). Bará shamans to the east of the Carihona used to protect themselves from similar attacks by taking cover behind a screen of tapir hide (Jackson 1983, 206–7). Witoto sorcerers send lightning to strike the houses of those who dare offend them (Maxwell 1961, 261), and to the attuned Jivaro shaman an approaching thunderstorm heralds a hostile colleague's imminent attack (Cotlow 1953, 43). Chacobo shamans and shamanesses use the wind to carry death over long distances to their victims (Hanke 1956, 22), and wind is one of several guardian spirits from whom Awaikoma-Kaingang shamans may obtain their supernatural powers. Even after death a shaman so empowered can send a frightening rainstorm to harass the people. In short, regular shamans engage in weather magic for defensive or offensive purposes, just as they practice in benevolent or malevolent ways in other professional contexts.

The same procedures are also used by specially ordained rain shamans whose office is considered as different from that of regular shamans. Ranking as their "father," the Warao rain shaman coerces the rain lords into unleashing their powers over their own people if he finds them lacking in altruistic or congenial behavior. He also commands them to send the clouds to hover above a rival's settlement if that rain shaman decides to redirect a storm away from home. Thus, like Warao healing shamans, rain shamans battle their counterparts in neighboring villages.

Special rain shamans have not been universally reported from South American societies. Other than among the Warao of the Orinoco Delta, they function in the Gran Chaco and Montaña regions. In some instances rain shamans are instated into office by undergoing initiation rites like those of the Warao. For example, Lengua candidates who aspire to receive the power must eat raw heron meat, that is, the flesh of Thunderbird. The Maskoy, their linguistic relatives, make their initiates ingest the uncooked heart, head, and wings of herons, storks, or other aquatic fowl, widely considered as stormbirds by Gran Chaco Indians (see below, pp. 206–8). Subjecting himself to a period of fasting, the neophyte drinks a foul brew of water mixed with plant leaves, bones, and rags. After undergoing this ordeal for several days, he begins to have alarming dreams. The emaciated apprentice then presents himself to a master. Only after the new rain shaman is certified by his teacher as an initiated colleague can he begin to practice (Stahl 1982, 45; Susnik 1984–85, 118). The Ayoreo call their rain shamans "shaman chanters," who as novices hear in dreams the special chants used to dominate the rain. They undergo a four-day-long initiation ritual during which each one practices his particular song until it is indelibly lodged in his mind. Once properly initiated, the shaman chanters are empowered to call the cloud birds from the high treetops, and they are warned by their masters not to do so in vain.

In the parts following this section, I discuss South American practices of weather shamanism in terms of the techniques employed in mastering the elements. As thunder, lightning, rain, and wind are often concurrent, however, this subdivision is somewhat arbitrary. Most of the techniques described address several or all four of the elements simultaneously, even though one practice is emphasized more specifically than the others.

Blowing against the Wind

For many South American Indians, blowing against an upcoming squall entails much more than pitting a puff of human breath against a blustering storm. Instead, the Indians have symbolically endowed the breath with supernatural power equal to that of the spirits. In magic, furthermore, blowing breath is believed to serve as a vehicle for protective missiles of various kinds which amplify its efficacy against all destructive forces, including bad weather.

In South America blowing against a storm and therapeutic blowing are both parts of a pneumatic ritual complex. In fact, they are essentially the same in practice and intent; both avail themselves of an inherent efficacious faculty of human breath and an arsenal of antidotes against attacks by pathogenic spirits.

Belief in the life-giving breath of humans, especially that of shamanic healers, is virtually universal in South America. Often administered with simultaneous exhalations of tobacco smoke, therapeutic blowing has the dual advantage of soothing the patient's pain and of reassuring the sufferer of the healing power of the curer's breath, made visible by the smoke. As Métraux (1949a, 593) explains: "The shaman's power was identified with his breath or with tobacco smoke. The purifying and strengthening power of breath and tobacco smoke played an important part in magic treatments and other rites." Besides manifesting the shaman's breath, however, tobacco smoke, through the pharmacological action of nicotine, provides the practitioner's breath with therapeutic properties (Wilbert 1987, 171–92). It alleviates a number of physical symptoms which are attributed to spirit intrusion rather than to natural causation. Thus, if nicotine administration by means of tobacco fumigation actually lowers a patient's fever, in an Indian's eyes it does so because the curer's breath is capable of evicting fever-causing spirits from the body. Similarly, if nicotine administered through tobacco smoke is really experienced as a soothing analgesic, its accomplishment is again owing to the pneumatic power of the shaman's breath to extricate pain-causing spirits. In addition to tobacco, curers and rainmakers also resort to hallucinogens, herbal medicaments, and food in their efforts to control aggressive spirits. All these counteragents have proven to be efficacious against spirits that cause human suffering, and they are believed also to be effective against weather spirits about to cause discomfort, illness, and possibly death. Thus, shamans, regardless of where they encounter these attacking spirits—in a patient's body or in the sky—force them to desist by subjecting them to human breath and remedial agents.

In blowing against a storm, practitioners face the squall, purse their lips, and puff as forcefully as their lungs permit. Some form a funnel with one hand and blow as if into a trumpet. As among the Tariano, "one holds the right hand like a funnel against the mouth and blows into the direction from where the rain threatens. While blowing, the hand is slowly opened and the rain cloud driven away with a movement of the outstretched arm" (Koch-Grünberg 1967, 24). Other practitioners place their hands in front of their lips and rub the palms together while blowing repeatedly between them. Then, thrusting their arms skyward, they shake the breath from their waving hands.

In describing the Warao rainmaker and his defensive routine earlier in this volume (see chapter 3), I gave a similar description of his method of blowing against an approaching storm. Warao rain shamans, elders, and some adults may engage in this preventive activity, as the following account of a Guyana case reiterates. The example also illustrates the cynicism, and even the ridicule, with which Western observers tended to witness such conjuring.

> All Clementi's [the headman's] spells to dominate the rain were fruitless. He stood in front of the hut gesticulating vigorously with his arms, his cheeks puffed up, as if to part the clouds with his gesturing and blow the fragments away with his breath. He continued doing this until his lungs gave out. Mumbling more spells, he gained new strength and resumed his blowing and waving. We had watched these silly goings-on for a long time, all the while holding back our laughter until it finally burst forth so forcefully that it could be heard even above the noise of the rain. Our hilarity, however, did not seem to perturb the sorcerer, whose movements became even more animated. It took him half an hour of exertion to convince himself of his powerlessness before he peevishly sneaked back into his hammock. Finally, toward eleven o'clock the

sky cleared a little and the rain lessened. Of course, this weather change was the result of the magic spells of Clementi, whose eyes lit up with pride and glee. [Schomburgk 1847–48, 1:186–87 (my translation)]

The extinct Callinago of the Lesser Antilles simply blew into the air and waved their hands when a storm cloud drew near. But when the weather turned stormy, they spat chewed manioc bread into the air and into the sea to placate the spirits causing the storm (Rouse 1948, 554). Among the Akawaio of Guyana, elderly women blow against the storm while uttering a spell. The women of the Maroni River Carib wave their arms against a squall and make a hushing sound (*shhh, shhh*), as if dispersing a flock of chickens (Kloos 1971, 220).

In the Vaupés-Caquetá region of the northwest Amazon, the various techniques of weather blowing are well documented. Thus, shamans of the Anserma blow and spit against the darkening sky while gesturing to drive the threatening storm away (Hernández de Alba 1948, 320). In this multilingual region of Amazonia, chiefs of the Tariano (Arawak) blow as hard as they can against approaching weather, ending each puff with "*te-te-te-te!*" Hoping to dispel the clouds with their hands, they shout alternately in Tarianan and in Tukanoan: "Rain, go away! Move on!" (Koch-Grünberg 1967, 24). The Yagua first blow large clouds of tobacco smoke against bad weather and then, in a low guttural voice, recite the formula: "Sun come out; clouds go away. Hrrrh . . . Hrrrh" (Fejos 1943, 92–93; Girard 1958, 46).

Weather blowing is practically universal in the Ecuadorian and Peruvian Montaña (Girard 1958, 211n; Izaguirre 1923–29, 9:174; 12). Indians on the Napo River attempt to banish rain and storms by magic blowing (Wallace 1853, 508). Groups like the Yagua, Zaparo, Jivaro, Canelo, and Sharpa and tribes on the Ucayali, the Mashco, and the Huarayu have abiding faith in an herb called piripiri (*Cyperus* sp.), widely used by Montaña Indians for medicinal purposes and as a repellent of bad weather (Baer 1984, 500). To apply rain magic, the root of the plant is chewed and blow-spat into the air. According to Stirling (1938, 121), Piribiri was a high-ranking supernatural figure of Jivaro cosmology, capable of both producing and stopping storms and floods. Jivaro shamans, blowing tobacco smoke toward the spirit's dwelling place, would chant appropriate songs to call upon this rain lord as if calling upon the spirits of disease. Although Harner (1962, 269), agreeing with Karsten (1954, 26), finds the existence of this personal rain god highly questionable, the Jivaro nevertheless make magical use of several species of piripiri; two of these, *yúmi* piripiri (rain piripiri) and *asáta* piripiri (dry-weather piripiri), serve in weather magic to produce both rain and drought.[1]

In the Montaña, of course, precipitation is plentiful and droughts are rare; therefore rain piripiri is employed in sorcery mostly to cause discomfort to other people or to swell the rivers to prevent hostile parties from crossing them (Harner 1962, 269). To make river parties labor as hard as he himself had under perpetually raining skies, a Jivaro member of the explorer Karsten's crew chewed the root of *yúmi* piripiri, jumped into the river, and took a mouthful of water. Then he blew the root fragments and the water forcefully toward the sky, confident that this act of magic would produce the desired downpours (Karsten 1935, 452–53). The Piro spit against the clouds (Sabate 1877, 254–55), and the Shipibo smoke a pipe to keep rain away (Karsten 1955, 171; 1964, 205). Spit-blowing and blowing the juice of masticated green tobacco are both practiced by the Campa for maximum effect (Weiss 1969, 490–91; 1975, 479). Warriors who are considered religious specialists among these Indians blow-spit in the direction of their enemy's village, expecting their action to bring fear-inspiring thunderclaps and lightning bolts (Weiss 1975, 255, 263, 275).

Psychotropic plants are also used by various tribes in eastern Bolivia to heighten the effect of their weather blowing. The Araona, for example, blow-spit a mixture of tobacco powder, coca, and unidentified herbs into the air to calm a thunderstorm or into the

---

[1] As a Cyperaceae, piripiri belongs to a large family of ninety genera and some 4,000 species of herbs. Harner (1973, 137) lists it among the various hallucinogens used by the Jivaro. Although the Sharanahua and possibly other Montaña groups add the powdered rhizome to a concoction of the ayahuasca hallucinogen (*Banisteriopsis caapi*), Cyperus is not known to have psychoactive properties (Schultes and Raffauf 1990, 257, 276).

water to keep the river from rising (Pauly 1928, 128; Métraux 1942, 44). The Paéz blow chewed febrifugal remedies, like black *yacuma* (*Myrcia* sp.), tobacco, and two unidentified plants (*chandur* and *ñushamuanda*), against the disease-causing rainbow. Curers blow tobacco smoke or other remedies toward a colorful meteor to cause it to fade quickly.

It was difficult to find information on weather blowing by Andean peoples. The Aymara of the central Andes, however, conduct a special blowing ritual known as *p'usarpayaña*, during which they sometimes blow tobacco smoke.

In central and eastern Amazonia, magic weather blowing is reported from the Parintintin (Gondim 1925, 16), the Bacaïri (Steinen 1894, 347; 1897, 302), the Tapirapé, and the Carajá (Métraux 1949a, 596). Among the latter group medicine men, doubling as rain shamans, chew a certain kind of wood and blow the pieces against the clouds (Ehrenreich 1891, 33). In the Gran Chaco the shamans of all tribes are rainmakers, sometimes shaking their rattles while blowing toward the clouds (Métraux 1944b, 307). Among the Lengua, weather blowing is done by shamans and laypersons alike: "one Indian will say to another, 'Iwatakáp,' blow! or puff! and the other will say 'Schwa,' and motion with the hand as if to push back the rain cloud" (Hawtrey 1901, 290).

As noted earlier, in some areas weather blowing forms part of a larger complex of ritual blowing, as it does, for instance, among several groups in Guiana. Thus, the Akawaio call their ritual complex *taling*. Though it serves different purposes, one of its objectives is to blow preventively against an upcoming storm, uttering intermittent spells between short, sharp exhalations (Butt, 1956, 49). Among the Waiwai, ritual blowing is also part of a larger complex of magical blowing. One of its aspects is the use of rain *eremu* (chants) by laypersons (not shamans) in order to dispel bad weather (Fock 1963, 112–13). Chants use one or more words or entire phrases repeatedly for lengthy periods of time. Each phrase is marked by the puffing of the word *pu-pu*. Blowing without chanting is considered entirely ineffective, but the exhaled puff of air gives the chant its thrust and its direction. When a rainstorm is approaching, the *eremu* singer turns toward the sky and shouts:

> Pu-pu rain go away,
> pu-pu to the mouth of the river,
> pu-pu go and make the beads wet,[2]
> pu-pu go and make the axes wet,
> pu-pu carry it [the rain] away in your ears, forest deer,
> pu-pu carry it away in your ears, savannah deer,
> pu-pu carry it away in your ears, tapir[3] [Fock 1963, 112].

Shamans of the Wapishana perform a small ritual that goes back to an encounter, in mythic times, between Kasum, the electric eel and Master Spirit of Rain, and an ancestral shaman. Contemporary shamans step into the open, face the storm, and exclaim:

> Tuminkar (the creator), in ancient times
> you gave Kasum power over the storm cloud to turn aside.
> You have more power than Kasum.
> Turn this storm away; it will do us great harm to have it come now [Farabee 1967, 120].

While reciting this formula the shaman breathes against the clouds and waves his right hand toward the south and his left hand toward the north to divide the storm into two parts.

The Bororo of Mato Grosso blow tobacco smoke therapeutically against spirits that have invaded a patient's body (Crocker 1985, 228) and protectively against the denizens of thunderstorms and meteors (Steinen 1894, 515). In other words, the blowing of a medicament of proven therapeutic value is analogically extended from the human body beyond local atmospheric conditions to sky-spanning planetary phenomena. The Bororo's meteor ceremony clearly demonstrates the common denominator of the South American pneumatic ritual complex; that is, differentially manifested spirit aggression is counteracted by similar procedures of ritual blowing.

As witnessed by Steinen (1894, 514–15), the ritual to neutralize the threat of a meteor began when a bright ball, a quarter the size of the moon, was sighted one evening in the southern sky. It was interpreted to be the "soul of a shaman" who demanded game and threatened to inflict dysentery on a member of the group (fig. 4.1).

---

[2] That is to say, go to the land of the Europeans, whence come the beads and the axes.

[3] All these animals have large ears.

South American Weather Lore

FIG. 4.1. Bororo meteor conjuring. (Von den Steinen 1894, plate 30)

The frightened people assembled around a number of newly started fires. Two shamans, their bodies painted red with urucú, spit-blew skyward in various directions in the same manner used to blow against the rain. Trembling and staggering, they held their cupped right hands before their mouths and screamed with threatening and terrifying voices in the direction of the meteor's appearance: *Vué! vué!* In his left hand with his arm raised, each shaman held a bundle of 25-centimeter-long cigars with maize wrappers, offering them to the ancestral shaman's soul and entreating him to leave the people alone. The trembling of the two shamans intensified, their bodies quivering and their backward-tilted heads shaking. They rubbed their bodies with abrupt movements as if to discard all evil from them. Several men lighted the bundles of cigars and smoked a few puffs before returning them to the officiating shamans, who sucked on the bundles, screamed even louder and more accusingly toward the sky, rubbed their bodies and scratched their heads more energetically, and sucked forcefully on their forearms as if to draw blood. Their legs were unsteady and their muscles quivered as they hollered *vué vuáu vuáu!* against the stars. Then the shamans, seeing a sick man (an old chief) in the crowd, treated him by spit-blowing into his face, yelling through their cupped hands, and smoking the bundled cigars down to the end. When the shamans retreated from the scene, the crowd broke the silence, shouting *huhá* in approval of their actions.

Chanting to the Rain

South American Indians have been said to control the elements by shouting at or simply talking to the respective weather spirits. In fact, speaking against an approaching curtain of rain is so common in South America that it would be difficult to detail all its occurrences. For example, the Campa (Weiss 1975, 479) and the Tereno (Oberg 1949, 42–43) tell a rain cloud to go away; Umutina Indians sit in the rain, invoking it to stop (Schultz 1961–62, 139); the Shucurú call out to Thunder, begging him to control the storm (Hohenthal 1954, 111); and the Awaikoma shout at the tempest, "Storm, go far away! I am afraid of you; go away!" or "Storm, go away from me; you are killing me and my children!" (Henry 1941,

4, 94). The Chorote, the Toba, and apparently all the Chaco groups shout loudly for the same purpose (Karsten 1964, 45). The Ayoreo bring rain by narrating the story of Cricket, the Mistress of Rain. Finally, the Yamana used to address their supreme being, Watauinewa, requesting him to get rid of the unfavorable weather.

Monotonic chanting is closely related to these various ways of calling for help. More often than the plain spoken word, however, chanting is used to communicate with the atmospheric spirits to convey messages and mental imagery. Thinking of rainmakers usually conjures up the image of dancing and chanting medicine men in arid places, beseeching the heavens to bestow new life on a parched land. Evidence of rain chanting from drought-stricken savannas and deserts in South America, however, is scarce, although in some instances shamans have been observed doing just that. In the semidesertic peninsula of La Guajira in northern Colombia and Venezuela, for example, where long life-threatening dry seasons are not uncommon, Guajiro shamans don a special garb, seat themselves on a bench, and, shaking their rattle, sing to the rain spirits (Pineda Giraldo 1950, 113; Bolinder 1957, 137). Similarly, in the arid scrub forests of the Gran Chaco, where soft rain is more desirable than flood-causing seasonal downpours, the Chamacoco sing a rain-producing song to the Son of Rain who, grateful for having been rescued and defended by their forefathers in mythical times (Cordeu in Wilbert and Simoneau 1987a, 99–106), grants their request. During their annual bird festival, the Ayoreo, western neighbors of the Chamacoco, commemorate Asoojna, a *dema*-deity, who brings them benign and rejuvenating rain (Susnik 1989, 55–56). And in the shrub-palm savannas of eastern Bolivia, local groups of the Guarayo petition Tamoi, their ancestral god, to end the droughts and grant them beneficial rain to make their harvest abundant. During a special rain-making ceremony men sit in a circle within their octagonal temple, staring at the ground while holding bamboo sticks in their hands. Ardently chanting, the participants mark the rhythm by beating the sticks on the ground. Seated behind the men are the women, who participate in the singing (D'Orbigny 1944, 395).

As noted earlier, Warao rain shamans also employ songs to invoke the Lords of Rain even if their purpose is neither to end a drought nor to call for fertilizing rain. Instead, their rain chants are general and standardized, and they are not the property of individual practitioners as are the chants of the Ayoreo. Unfortunately, the actual texts of rain chants and spells have rarely been reported in South American ethnographic literature. The Warao example given in chapter 3 is a rare exception.

Elsewhere in South America, rain chanting is seldom performed for the sole purpose of attracting beneficial rain; more frequently it is employed to repel rain. Rain-*eremu* chanting and blowing of the Waiwai is designed, like all *eremu* performed by laypersons, to rebuke evil rather than to honor good (Fock 1963, 113). The Yanomami fear both wind and rain, the former for lifting the thatch off roofs and the latter for bringing them illness. When a strong wind is approaching, the shamans congregate in the village center and shout incantations to Wadoriwä, pleading that he desist (Chagnon 1968, 28; Zerries 1964, 237). To stop the rain they chant an appeal to their culture hero Omaua, beseeching him to repel all fearful evils (Polykrates 1974, 11). Associated with evil and with attacks on enemies, Lightning reveals to the Surui the direction from which adversity is likely to approach them. Upon hearing a thunderbolt, all conversations and activities cease and Lightning is admonished in a chant: "Keep your evil influence away from me and my relatives! Sweep these evil winds far away!" (Mindlin 1985, 149). Toba shamans chant and converse in low tones with weather spirits, hoping to enlist their assistance against thunderstorms and other destructive forces, some of which ruin flowering trees on whose fruit all Chaco Indians depend (Karsten 1923, 76–77). The Cuna claim that their forebears knew how to chant the creation story of lightning and rain. Their chant was so powerful that it could be used only during the dry season unless the singer wanted to attract a thunderstorm. Formerly, Cuna shamans and diviners were renowned for their power to summon lightning and to provoke a flood (Nordenskiöld 1938, 86, 393–94).

Dancing away the Clouds

Weather dancing is usually performed to repel bad weather or to attract the rain that makes food plants and fruit trees grow, thus contributing to the welfare of the people. Corporeal images and scenarios of interaction are portrayed through metamorphic pantomimes that draw atmospheric denizens to earth and make them accessible to human manipulation. Rhythmic movement, chant, and music, as well as masks, disguise, and unusual garb, dramatize the metamorphic process that turns humans into gods and demons. Although sympathetic magic, analogous thought, and embarrassment of supernaturals are the coercive forces most often expressed in South American weather dancing, artifactual imagery, social custom, and anguish serve as its basic metaphoric props.

The Kogi dance to "turn the sun around" or "to bring a rain shower" in order to avert sickness. In songs the dancers refer to building fences to keep sickness away and to shut sickness out by closing doors. Dancers sometimes carry small brooms made of leaves, illustrating their intention to sweep away sickness and clean the village (Reichel-Dolmatoff 1951, 2, 142). Their neighbors, the Ica, seem to have adopted a similar dance from the Kogi. For nine days they restrict their food intake to maize porridge and water, hoping thereby to maintain their fields in good condition and to bring rain (Bolinder 1925, 261).

On the upper Xingú River, the Camayura engage in a rain dance that lasts for three days. On the first day, men attired in feather headdresses and moriche bast skirts, with leafy boughs attached to their arms and shoulders, dance around two musicians in the center of the village plaza. One of the musicians, seated on a stool, produces a booming sound by banging a large gourd on the ground; the other one, standing behind him, shakes a rattle. On the second day the women, wearing long-tailed pubic covers made of straw, perform circular dances. The ceremony concludes on the third day when a single woman, followed by men in bast skirts and headdresses, dances along the periphery of the village plaza, pausing in front of each house. The purpose of the Camayura rain dance is to further the growth of crops and of fruit trees like *piquí* (*Caryocar butyrosum*) and mangabeira (*Hancornia speciosa*). Oberg (1953, 56–57), to whom we owe the description of this dance, suggests that the thumping of the gourd may simulate thunder and that the men with their swaying boughs may represent growing plants. If unsuccessful in the first attempt, the dance may be repeated, but this time it is accompanied by a bull-roarer whose booming sound is believed to be particularly effective in causing rain to fall.

An equally elaborate rain dance used to be performed in the Gran Chaco by the Pasain and the Vilela (Atalalá) near the Río Bermejo.

After planting twelve stakes with colorful signs in the ground, the shamans identified a boy who was to personify Gos, a spirit, and a girl who was to represent the spirit's wife. A group of children served as assistants to the spirit couple. Two huts erected near the painted stakes were to house the two spirit personages and their retinue during the ceremony. On the appointed day the young people of the village, painted and covered with bird feathers, approached the spirit huts carrying pots of chicha beer. While dancing, they petitioned the spirits for rain and also for protection against epidemics. Thereupon, the spirit couple and their attendants appeared from a nearby stand of trees, where they had been hiding since the preceding day. Gos wore a large pyramidal head covering made of straw with two attached horns, and furs and grass bunches covered his entire body. Save for a loincloth, the girl impersonating Gos's wife was naked; the servants wore feather belts. All members of the group covered their faces with small, painted bands. Now the spirit couple and their escort danced around the painted stakes, yelling, grimacing, and hitting the stakes with the staffs they were carrying. After a while the dancers retired into their respective huts, only to emerge again at noon and in the afternoon of the following days to repeat their dance. Before sunset of the final day, the dancers broke the chicha jars (Métraux 1942, 308–9).

Rain dancing by the now extinct Selknam of Tierra del Fuego was performed, not to produce fertilizing rain for crops or fruit trees they may have had on the cold steppes of the Patagonian Plateau, but to melt the snow. "Rather rain than snow" was the motto of the Selknam, because protracted snowfall limited their foraging activities and imposed long hours of tedious idleness (Gusinde 1931, 685). The Selknam performed two different rain dances, one on a more or less regular basis during the winter months and the other occasionally during the boys' initiation and the men's ceremony, called *kloketen*, scheduled only at irregular intervals.

For the first kind of weather dance, known as *kóteten*, the members of a local band congregated in a hut appropriate for the purpose and selected a child, usually a boy, from among the children who were born on a day of bad weather. They painted the child's face red—leaving only the areas around the eyes and the mouth natural—and drew one thick vertical line from the throat to the genitals and two horizontal lines across the nipples and the navel.

Next, three bad-weather-born men painted themselves the same way, encouraging all other children and adults who, like them, had been born in bad weather to leave the hut and hide, lest the dance be doomed to failure.

Facing the fireplace, two of the painted men put the child between them, each holding him under an arm. The child's hands clasped a smoldering piece of firewood, with the live end tilted downward. While the line of dancers moved sideways, alternately stepping to the left and the right and executing little jumps in between, the third painted man stood behind them, continuously spraying water from his mouth and aiming it at their shoulders and at the firebrand in the child's hands. Meanwhile the assembly participated by repeating short sentences, such as "Now the snow must make way for the rain," or "If only rain would come," or "Soon the rain will drive away the snow." The ritual lasted for about thirty minutes during which the three dancers became soaking wet and the embers were extinguished. The three men and the child sat down to rest and to wash off their body paint. Only then were the bad-weather-born people invited to rejoin the group. Rain was expected to follow soon after the ceremony, if the firebrand had been doused quickly, but somewhat later if it had smoldered for some time.

A variant of the *kóteten* dance was performed to increase the likelihood of stopping the rain immediately. Men who were born when the weather was good made an adult-sized straw man. Two men, painted as described above, grabbed the figure and began to dance with it, moving back and forth. A crowd of people who had been born in good weather—the others had already left the scene—gathered around the dancers and began to spray or douse them with water while simultaneously deriding and mocking the rain. The taunting was intended to embarrass the rain and make it move away in shame. Eventually the jeering crowd began to disperse, with some participants remaining behind to tear the dripping effigy to shreds (Gusinde 1931, 684–86).

The second kind of weather dance of the Selknam, called čōwhtóxen, formed part of the *kloketen* mysteries during which men, among other ritual activities, impersonated various spirits that communicated with the women and children in the nearby settlement. The dance was performed when too much fog, rain, or snow interfered with the schedule of the boys' initiation and the men's rite. Selected by the master of ceremonies, eight young men took off their clothes and wound thick wreaths of grass around their heads. They formed a circle by placing their hands on the shoulders of their neighbors and began to wheel around the cold fireplace, first in one and then in the other direction (plate 4.1). After roughly five minutes the dancers formed a line, each man draping his arms around his neighbors' shoulder (plate 4.2). In this formation they left the ritual hut and moved toward the village watering place, where they regrouped once again into a circle, shouted a series of characteristic sounds, and began to wheel around with steadily increasing speed in one direction and then the other. Next a number of girls approached the men and took turns in pouring water mixed with ice and snow on the heads and naked backs of the dancers (fig. 4.2). Eventually the girls grew tired of their chore, and the men ended their performance with an extended hissing sound. Then, paying no attention to the girls, they formed a line as before and returned to their hut to dry and warm themselves near a big fire. The sequence was repeated at least three times at intervals of half an hour. If the desired change in weather failed to materialize, the entire dance was performed again the following day with increased ardor and dedication (Gusinde 1931, 1001–3).

Combative Responses

South American Indians express their anger at atmospheric spirits by making menacing gesticulations, brandishing weapons, and throwing missiles. Some even stage veritable battles with thunder-gods, dealing with them as with natural enemies, that is, by armed response. In these expressions of weather magic, therefore, the display of belligerence through ritual blowing, chanting, and dancing gives way to a display of physical martial resolve intended to intimidate the weather denizens.

Gesticulating against atmospheric spirits (mentioned earlier) sometimes coincided with other techniques of weather magic. As a dominant procedure it has been reported most frequently from groups in the Xingú-Tocantins region and in southerly areas of the continent. Typical of this kind of response is the behavior of a Shipaya man observed cavorting with two boys across the village plaza shouting, *Wap, wap*! and waving his right arm against the

South American Weather Lore 181

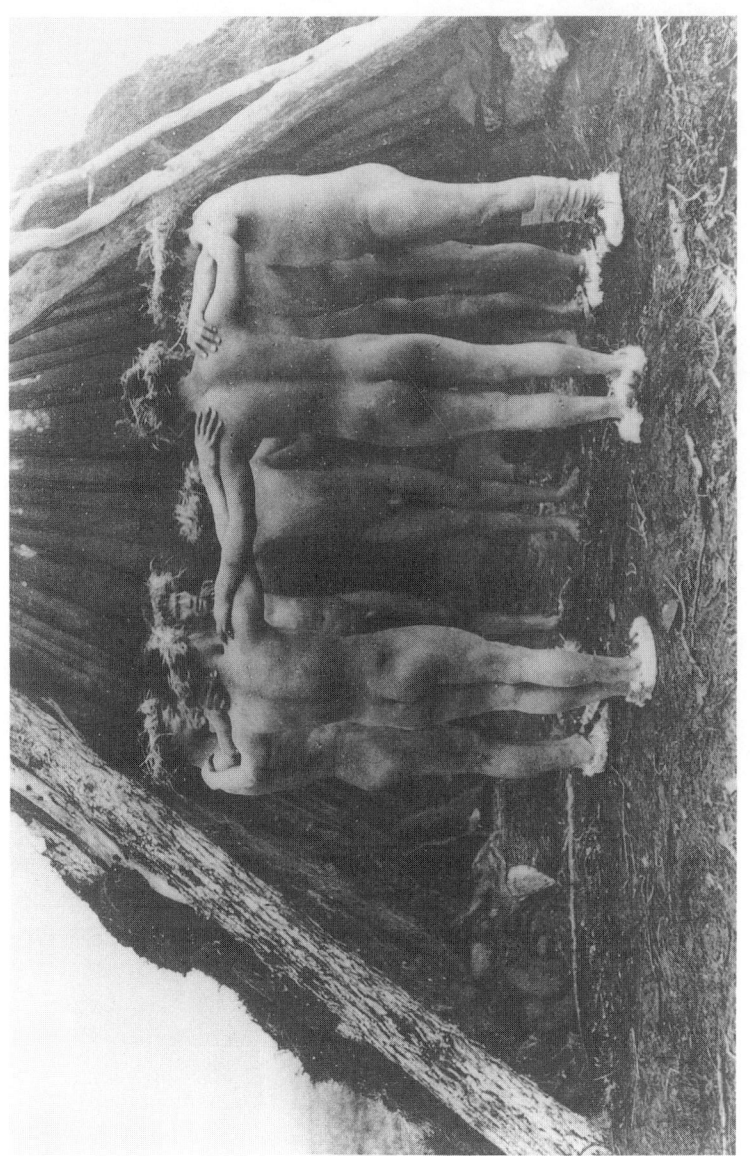

PLATE 4.1. Selknam weather ceremony. (Gusinde 1931, plate 37, photo 91; courtesy Anthropos Institut)

182 *Mindful of Famine*

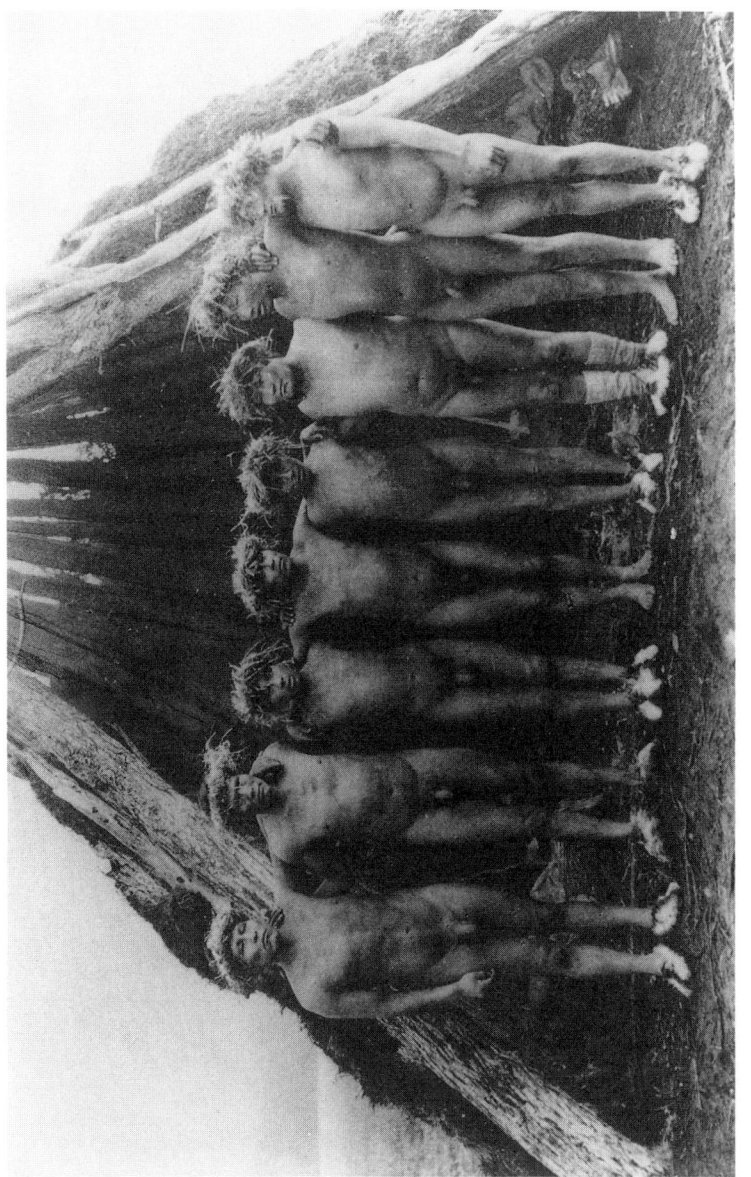

PLATE 4.2. Selknam weather ceremony. (Gusinde 1931, plate 37, photo 92; courtesy Anthropos Institut)

South American Weather Lore

FIG. 4.2. Selknam weather ceremony. (Gusinde 1931, fig. 88)

approaching squall as if to scare it away. "Go to the Jacaré! [who will be happy to see their swamps fill up with rain]," he shouted repeatedly until the storm subsided (Nimuendajú 1921–22, 16–17: 381). The Chiquitano extend their arms to the sky and shout in the direction of the approaching storm (Oefner 1940–41, 107). The Coroado dare express their anger at a thunderstorm only after it has passed. Venturing outside into the open, they raise their arms and fists at the weather spirits who destroy their fruit trees and kill their people (Booth Mabilde 1983, 135–36). Rather than waiting for an overhead storm to pass, the Selknam stepped to the front of their huts in the thick of a storm, beating the air with outstretched arms, leaping about, and shouting at the top of their voices. From time to time they paused to assume a characteristic defense posture by stretching both arms forward with clenched fists. Then, extending their fingers, they admonished the storm to move on (Gusinde 1931, 683).

The brandishing of arms against weather spirits takes several forms, perhaps the most common being the shooting of arrows or of modern firearms. Whereas on occasions this procedure is employed to attract the rain, most commonly it is an aggressive act intended to dispel severe thunderstorms or solar and lunar eclipses. The Guajiro, for example, shoot arrows or firearms hoping to pierce the clouds and cause them to release their precious contents over the parched land (Pineda Giraldo 1950, 113; Bolinder 1957, 137). The Sensi aim their arrows at the missiles of a storm spirit living in a distant lagoon (Coriat n.d., 80). By waving an arrow in the direction of the cloud, the Campa hope to waft the rain away with the lightness of the reed (Weiss 1975, 479). The Mashco brandish their arrows against Vaapuka, the wind, and his army of followers (Barriales and Toralba 1970, 59). Strong wind is also greatly feared by the Yuracaré as a cause of dangerous illnesses. After confining their women and children to the relative safety of their houses, the men shoot arrows at the fiery thunder spirit while reciting incantations to prevent it from destroying their shelters and gardens (D'Orbigny 1839, 1:365; 1944, 212; Métraux 1942, 12). The Cayapó dispatch arrows to the clouds, raise their fists, ram their war clubs into the ground, and, nowadays, fire shotguns to have revenge on thunder (Lukesch 1968, 193; Werner 1984, 169). Rather than war clubs, the Mundurukú display their bows to frighten the mothers of rain and stick them into the ground when an electrical storm threatens (Murphy 1958, 2). The ancient Botocudo dispatched their arrows at severe thunderstorms and against solar and lunar eclipses. Selknam shamans shot arrows into storm clouds and asked the missionaries to fire their handguns with the same objective. The brandishing of spears by the Cuna (Nordenskiöld 1938, 395) and the Jivaro (Karsten 1964, 46) serves the same combative intent of engaging the thunder spirits. Referring to thundering as "fighting enemies," the Jivaro leap into the air, challenging the spirits with words identical to those used in daunting their natural enemies. Describing how a Jivaro shaman engages in a half-hour ritual of weather magic, Cotlow (1953, 43) depicts him as attired in a monkey-fur headpiece, his face painted red with black streaks, and armed with a lance and a round wooden shield covered with hide.

> In a high, piercing voice he cried out at the black cloud and shook his lance at it threateningly. He started what seemed to be almost a dance, stepping forward with a hard thrust of the lance, a step back, another attack and blow with the lance. And all the time he chanted a loud series of imprecations at the cloud. Then he blew as hard as he could into the air, blew against the cloud.

Carajá medicine men double as rain shamans. Ehrenreich (1891, 33) saw one of these men step out of his hut, holding a tobacco pipe in one hand and a stick armed with a stingray spine in the other. Looking up to the sky, the medicine man uttered unarticulated sounds, repeatedly blew smoke against the clouds, and flaunted his weapon over his head. Finally, he shouted *bobutu*! and, his face grim, thrust his weapon in the cardinal directions.

Clubs are used by the Cayapó as well as by the Nambicuara (Oberg 1953, 100) and the Yamana (Gusinde 1937, 1305); paddles used by the Piro (Sabate 1877, 254) and the Ayoreo (Bórmida and Califano 1978, 154, 157) fall into the same category of offensive weather weaponry. Nambicuara warriors threaten storms by brandishing any weapon that comes to hand and by yelling loudly at the rain (Roquette-Pinto 1938, 258). But their sword-clubs seem to be particularly invested with the power to stop the rain. The same is true of Ayoreo clubs, which have been used to kill people or jaguars and to which adheres a deadly power to ward off storms. If a Yamana family was detained by a severe storm while on a foraging journey, they painted a club, a spear shaft, or a paddle with red earth.

Then they selected a child who was born in fair weather, walked him to the beach, and handed him the painted article, requesting him to flog the sea therewith and ask for favorable weather. Repeating after his father, the child spoke a formula somewhat like this one: "Bad weather, to make you move on instantly, a good-weather-born child has come to the beach to beat you up." The child reached out with his hands as if to grasp the clouds, part the fog, and push the rain aside, while simultaneously making a hissing sound. If the child was too young to carry out the request, the father sat him upright against his own legs and, moving the child's arms, recited the incantation on his behalf.

The winter ritual of the Yamana was a fierce attack on inclement weather spirits. When suffering from an usually harsh winter with high snowfall, the men used to make an image of winter in the form of a 1.20-meter-tall figure of snow. When it was finished everybody gathered about five meters away from it and began to pelt Winter with stones, logs, clubs, paddles, and spears. The frenzy lasted until the figure had been completely destroyed (Gusinde 1937, 1307).

Machetes are employed by the Campa (Weiss 1975, 287) to slash the air and cut off the wind, while the Piro use knives (Sabate 1877, 254) to do the same. The Payaguá of Uruguay use firebrands and shadowboxing to intimidate the storm spirits, whereas the Puruhá-Quichua of Chimborazo Province in Ecuador throw soil and ashes at an approaching hailstorm to divert it from their village.

A spectacular weather ritual, marked by aggressive gesticulation and a display of weapons, is the thunder ceremony of the Tapirapé. At the beginning of the rainy season, when heavy storms begin to threaten their gardens, the Tapirapé fight to protect their new maize crop and themselves from climatic violence (Wagley 1943, 84–91; 1977, 199–211).[4] They perform a pageant in which costumed participants gesticulate, prance, chant, and brandish their arms, engaging Thunder in a four-day-long ritual.

The beginning of the ritual is announced in song by a ranking village shaman and his wife who challenge Thunder (Kanawana), with his retinue of children (*topü*) and ancestral shamans' souls, to come and fight the village shamans and any neophyte or commoner

---

[4] Apparently the Tapirapé thunder ceremony is no longer observed. The late Charles Wagley (1977, 211) believed that he might have witnessed its last performance in January 1940.

courageous enough to join them. From noon of that day, nicotine-intoxicated shamans and novices continue to chant from their respective houses along the oval periphery of the village. Later in the day, continuing until nightfall, they and their wives—facing each other—assemble to chant on the dance ground in front of the ceremonial house at the village center.

On the second day the men open doors at the far ends of each longhouse to allow people to walk through them. A path is swept between the new doors of neighboring houses so as to form a closed circuit along the periphery of the oval village plaza. From noontime on, shamans, novices, laymen, and their respective wives walk the path around the village, the men heavily intoxicated from swallowing tobacco smoke from their pipes. At the center of every house, the man and the woman of each couple face each other and chant to the thunder spirits. Many of the men are unable to complete the circular rout because of their intoxication. After swallowing large doses of smoke, they vomit, shriek, suffer violent nicotine seizures, and stagger blindly through the houses. Some who experience cataleptic rigidity must be carried on the shoulders of young attendants to complete the tour of the houses. Encountering the thunder spirits in their trances, they are wounded by the spirits' arrows and lose the skirmish. As the day ends, the community gathers in a village house that has been cleared of inventory. A young man sings the songs of Thunder to the accompaniment of two rattles and a stamping tube. Becoming increasingly intoxicated by repeated draughts from the pipes of officiating shamans, the nauseated musicians, novices, and laymen walk back and forth in the house, vomiting and eventually collapsing. Wildly gesticulating and swinging their rattles toward the roof, some of them challenge Thunder and the *topü*-spirits to come and do battle with them. Gradually the shamans and the other men see the house being invaded by the spirits. Grunting *Hew! Hew!* and spurred on by the continuous rattling and the stamping-tube music in the background, the men tackle their adversaries, some with the aid of mirrors and red parrot feathers. The ranking shamans carry machetes and, walking to the ends of the house, threateningly wave them toward the roof, defying Thunder and the *topü*-spirits to come down and fight. Some of the men, in dodging the spirits' arrows, stumble, fall, and become entangled in a melee. The women pull their men out, prop them up against their legs, and induce other men to massage and fumigate them with tobacco smoke to make them regain consciousness. When the participants eventually walk along the circular path to their homes, they briefly halt in every house to sing once more. Finally, two boys brandishing the sacred rattles run around the entire circuit of the village to conclude the day's events.

The ritual of the next two days closely follows the pattern of the second day, except that the male dancers expose themselves to more serious danger by taking turns wearing a large headdress of red macaw tail feathers (plate 4.3). Because this is as "hot" as that worn

PLATE 4.3
Tapirapé thunder ceremony. Shaman in nicotine trance challenges Thunder. (Courtesy Charles Wagley)

by the sun, the men's headpiece infuriates Thunder. Even experienced shamans and all the men who dare to follow their example tremble with fear and succumb to Thunder's attack as they walk around the village and engage in battles during the afternoon. The two young men who, at the end of each daily ritual, carry the rattles through the houses expose themselves to the same danger by wearing feather headdresses. The carrying of the instruments in itself attracts the attention of the thunder spirits, but wearing the red feather headdress increases the likelihood of an attack by the spirits.

The ritual of the fourth day ends in the evening, when all the men of the village assemble on the dance ground. Facing north toward Thunder's house, the shaman touches their heads with the ceremonial rattle. The women and children also gather to be touched in the same manner, and everybody is assured of being safe from Thunder until the next year (Wagley 1977, 200–211).

Indians have occasionally been observed brandishing implements and contraptions made especially to use in opposing the weather spirits. For example, any Carajá man can practice weather magic by holding in his hands the ends of two one-meter-long sticks tied together at their distal ends in the form of a V (fig. 4.3a), with feathers attached by a layer of wax to the front end of the implement. Turning toward the approaching storm, the Carajá gestures with the device toward the clouds, uttering a certain formula. A second instrument consists of two fifty-centimeter-long switches tied together (fig. 4.3b). With this implement the Indian beats vertically toward the clouds (Krause 1911, 33, figs. 182a, b;

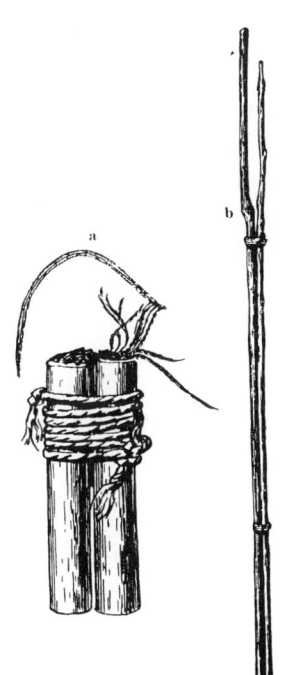

FIG. 4.3a, b. Carajá devices of rain magic (fig. 4.3a shows the cut off front end). (Krause 1911:33, figs. 182a, b)

Perrier 1948, 174). The Nambicuara apparently used a special wooden dagger in connection with rain magic (Disselhoff and Zerries 1974, 255–56). Toba medicine men employ a magic throwing-fork to bring a change in the weather. When twirled in the air, the instrument makes a noise like that of a bull roarer (Rydén 1933).

Homeopathic Magic

Homeopathic weather magic is widely distributed in South America. Its practice is based on the assumption that the mimicking of atmospheric phenomena will influence the spirits to conform to human wishes. Either thunder, lightning, rain, and wind are believed to have analogues in natural phenomena, or the elements are imitated as part of a variety of magical techniques of weather control.

Thunder is assimilated to such natural noisemakers as shrieking birds, bellowing crocodilians, hissing anacondas, croaking frogs, and erupting volcanoes. The human din caused by yelling, clapping, clanking, and rattling is intentionally produced for the homeopathic effect it is purported to have on weather beings. Both natural and human noises are resorted to whenever rain and stormy weather are considered to be either inexpedient or opportune.

Warao weather chants rely on the sun bittern's piercing call to infuriate the lords of rain. Bellowing alligators, according to the same Indians, practice weather sorcery by conversing with the thunderers. This interactive relationship between reptiles and thunder helps to explain the custom of Indians on the Pomeroon River of conjuring up the weather spirits by washing the scrapings of large alligator teeth (Rouse 1948, 554). According to the Warao, the awesome power vested in alligator teeth can cause protracted periods of rainy weather.

The croaking, honking, and pinging of frogs and toads are natural noises that also attract rain. Wassén (1934, 630–38) has demonstrated that the belief in this interrelationship between frogs or toads and rain is widespread among Utoaztecan, southwestern, Plateau, and Great Basin Indians of North America as well as among native populations of Central and South America. In part, this belief is almost certainly grounded in the natural dependency of these amphibians on temperature and humidity, but it is also related to the noisy ruckus they produce, which prompts the thunder spirits to respond in kind.

Because of their close relationship with precipitation, many Indians appreciate frogs and toads as convenient tools in their coercive dealings with weather spirits. As detailed below, some keep the amphibians under a bowl, where they can easily be admonished, reprimanded, or punished for failing to cater to the people's wishes. Others make small images of them to be put in propitious places. In the Montaña, the Sharpa credit the croaking of a toad or a frog with bringing rain (Girard 1958, 211). And the Aymara of Chucito, in order to end a drought, conduct a public ceremony to put frogs from Lake Titicaca into basins on the altar of a mountain shrine. As the water in the basins evaporates, the people, accompanied by panpipes, sing a special frog song. Because of the changing temperature and the increasing dryness in their environment, the frogs eventually begin to croak; these expressions of suffering are believed to arouse the pity of the rain spirits, persuading them to relent (Tschopic 1946, 567).

Like natural noises, human din is apt to attract the attention of the weather spirits. For this reason, the Guató refrain from making unnecessary sounds when crossing a large body of water in a boat, and they are apprehensive about noises made by others (Schmidt 1905, 150). Ayoreo shamans, undertaking spiritual journeys to the land of the clouds, sit down to meditate in silence and expect everybody else in their vicinity to do the same. Explaining the predicament their thirsty people face for want of rain, they admonish the spirits to come quickly (Sebag 1965, 28–29). Children of the Yamana who were born on bad weather days must eschew noisy conduct when romping at the water's edge, throwing stones into the sea, swatting the waves with sticks or paddles, or letting an object drop hard on the ground. Boisterous "bad weather children" were closely watched by the adults, who admonished them to behave quietly lest they cause a weather change (Gusinde 1937, 1306).

Some Indians like the Tupari, clap their hands to repel a storm. Fearing that the trees and bushes they felled in planning a new garden, if rained upon, might not burn before sowing time, they conduct a lengthy ceremony during which they ingest psychotropic snuff, chant in high-pitched voices, and rhythmically clap their hands (Caspar 1956, 129–30). To summon rain, the Camayura beat the ground with a large gourd and swing rattles and bull-roarers (Oberg 1953, 56–57). Banging on pots or pans has apparently been practiced by the Bará in imitation of the sky people and in an effort to counteract the dangers associated with thunderstorms and lunar eclipses (Jackson 1983, 205).

Noises like drumming and trumpeting are produced to imitate the roll and roar of thunder. The Guajiro, for example, play the drum in the evening and the early morning to attract thunder and rain (Pineda Giraldo 1950, 114; Bolinder 1957, 137). To repel rainstorms, Indians in northwest Brazil beat log drums, "first with heavy blows at regular intervals, then quicker and fainter until the blows fade into a series of light taps. This is repeated half a dozen times and everybody scatters" (Lange 1914, 219). Jivaro shamans imitate thunder by producing crashing booms, followed by a rapid series of lighter booms on a large drum (Cotlow 1953, 42). Gran Chaco groups like the Toba, the Mataco, and the Chorote also depend on drums to ward off tempests that have frequently destroyed the florescence of wild fruit-bearing trees (*algarroba*, *Prosopis nigra*) and shrubs (*chañar*, *Geoffraea decorticans*). Conversely, during a drought that threatens the fruit harvest, the Toba and possibly the Mataco use a drum to attract rain. "In some cases it seems as if the drumming Indian, by the very time in which he is beating his drum, were imitating the fall of the rain-drops" (Karsten 1932, 156). The Sharpa hope to attract rain with the blare of trumpets produced by blowing a horn or, formerly, a conch shell (Girard 1958, 211); the Aymara blow cow horns to frighten away crop-endangering frost and hail (Carter 1965, 38).

Lightning is likened to fire and hallucinogens. As among the Warao, fires must be extinguished during thunderstorms to avoid attracting a bolt of lightning. To change persistent foul weather the Selknam used to set a hollow, rotting tree trunk on fire and fan the flames until the whole trunk was aglow. They leaped around the flames and urged the bush spirits inhabiting the trunk to take the bad weather (Gusinde 1931, 683).

Rain is assimilated to such liquids as terrestrial water, tears, blood, urine, and alcoholic beverages and to smoke and magic stones. The Carib of the West Indies feared that splashing fresh water into the sea would provoke a storm and swell the amount of water (Rouse 1948, 554). When the Awaikoma-Kaingang or the Botocudo want to attract rain, they place their mouths on the water's surface and blow. Then they scoop up water with their hands and, throwing it upward toward the sky, cry out, "Look here! Do like this!" Hearing this appeal, the rain is expected to come down. Contrarily, to stop incessant rain from swelling the rivers and making them flood the land, the same Indians boil rainwater until it is completely evaporated (Henry 1941, 94). When Campa travel on a river, they splash water toward a rain cloud to induce it to discharge its load before it falls on them (Weiss 1975, 479). Aymara farmers go to mountain lagoons for water to sprinkle on their fields, hoping that this endeavor will bring rain (Monast 1972, 57).

The breaking of vessels or mysterious funnel-shaped packages containing rain brings tremendous downpours in Sikuani mythology (Ortiz, in Wilbert and Simoneau 1992, 219–25). The mythology of the Pau d'Arco Cayapó tells of a powerful sorcerer who causes a scorching draught. To counteract the magic a shaman throws a calabash full of water into the air; when it falls to the ground, it bursts and spills its contents, putting an end to the drought (Nimuendajú, in Wilbert and Simoneau 1984, 496). Ayoreo women cry out in order to stop the rain because, in mythical times, that is what the wives of the rain men did. While walking about in the sky, these men carried with them both small and large jars full of water, which spilled over to fall as drizzle from the small jars and as downpours from the large vessels (Califano, in Wilbert and Simoneau 1989a, 76–77). The Chané believe that putting a warmed jug into flowing water brings on a powerful storm (Nordenskiöld 1912, 296).

Imitative magic is also involved when ritually shed tears turn into rain. A Warao example of this process is the story mentioned earlier (p. 73) of the Mother of the Forest and her daughters who cry over the death of a tree woman whose body is being transformed into a dugout canoe. Another Warao example of the correlation between ritual tears and rain is the belief that the tears a woman sheds over the death of a loved one cause the sky to weep. Harassed by the pelting received in the rainy season, a Carajá shaman, assuming the form of an armadillo, once trapped the rain from behind the door of his house. On that occasion it was disclosed to the shaman and his people that rain is caused by the residents of the House of Rain. Of small stature, they stand around in the big house, sad and serious (probably expressing their pain and sorrow over the death of the rain-god's peccary friends at the hands of human hunters), producing the rain with their tears (Palha 1942, 48–49). Similarly, tears that fall during the Kwaríp ceremony of the Camayura in commemoration of their dead are believed to trigger the onset of the rainy season (Agostinho 1974, 165; Sullivan 1988, 547). Sometimes children are made to cry to arouse the pity of the weather beings. Aymara children, for example, are at times beaten for this purpose and to prevent the sun from dying. On other occasions they are taken to the fields, where they are stripped and hit to make the skies rain out of pity over their pain and tears (LaBarre 1948, 200). The Quechua also beat their children to make them cry and thus cause the rain to fall. As Disselhoff (1974, 49) has suggested, this practice may go back to earlier times when, during the water festival month of October, the Inca sacrificed hundreds of white sheep to principal huacas, entreating these powers to send rain. At the same time they tied up large numbers of black sheep in the public plaza and starved them so that their suffering might help the rain gods to weep. When dogs that were also tied up heard the people yelling and calling to the supernaturals, they began to howl and bark just as loudly. The dogs that did not join in noisemaking were beaten until they too gave voice. All men, women, and children, the healthy as well as the afflicted, asked the god Runa Camac for water from heaven:

> Ay, ay, let us weep,
> ay, ay, let us moan,
> from pain [anguish] are
> the children exhausted,
> only to thee can we weep!

After saying these prayers the people, weeping, cried out: "Oh, Creator of Humankind, what are you doing for those who eat, Huari Huiracocha God, where are you? Let loose your people, your waters, your rains, toward me!" (Poma de Ayala 1936, 255; Posnansky 1937; see also fig. 4.4). The Aymara custom of making frogs suffer from heat and desiccation until they uttered croaking sounds and the Carib practice of hitting their rain frogs are, of course, related to the Quechua and Inca conventions of punishing domestic animals to

South American Weather Lore 195

accentuate the widespread suffering and the intensity of the lament for rain. Appealing to the weather spirits for mercy is also behind the practice of a Yamana mother who, after painting one of her young daughters with red mineral dye, takes her to the beach to dunk her repeatedly into the sea until the child screams with pain. "You, bad weather," shouts the mother, "Take pity on that 'fair weather child,' leave at once and take this excessive snowfall with you" (Gusinde 1937, 1306).

Blood is analogously related to rain in the etiological mythology of the southern Yanõmami. The first four men were born from the leg of a female yellow-rumped cacique (*Cacicus cela*). As a manifestation of the female principal of the androgenous moon, she had intercourse with the four brothers and bore a son. He shot an arrow at the moon, producing a shower of blood in which all

FIG. 4.4
Inca rain ceremony.
(Pompa de Ayala 1936)

Yanõmami originated. The moon keeps shaking blood from trees in the sky; it falls to earth in droplets containing human souls, ready to be incarnated through sexual intercourse (Becher 1974, 14–15; 1976, 342). In real life the Sanemá-Yanomami seem to correlate menstruating girls, heavy with blood, and rain clouds, heavy with rain (Colchester 1982, 165). The menstrual blood and the urine of Romi Kuma, the female creator of the Barasana, are identified with rain (Hugh-Jones 1979, 179, 264). Blood, such as that of a certain duck is tossed upward by the Lengua in homeopathic weather magic to provoke the rain into falling (Nordenskiöld 1912, 296).

In likening urine to rain, the Barasana are certainly not exceptional among South American Indians. The Camayura believe that rain is caused by a small red bird (*dinínuwa*) that urinates into a shallow lake until it overflows (Oberg 1953, 99). (See also pp. 221–22 below.)

Mimicking clouds by billowing smoke from fires is practiced by the Lokono and the Warao of Guyana, who burn the carcass of a boa (possibly an anaconda, *Eunectus murinus*) to induce the rain to fall (Roth 1915, 267). In the northwest Amazon the Yagua burn lizards and termite nests, for the same reason, and the small *wicunda* palm because its spines, imitating thunder, explode in the fire. Black rain clouds are attracted by the Sharpa, who burn a piece of bark cloth on a tree trunk (Girard 1958, 211). The smoke of cedar wood is used by the Apinaye for protection against the danger of lightning (Nimuendajú 1939, 130). The Selknam attempted to attract rain clouds by setting the savanna on fire on windy days. "Now the rain must come to extinguish the fire," they would say. "He cannot see it burning here for long."

It is perhaps at this point that attention should be drawn to the fact that smoke from fires and burning animals and plants is not always primarily intended to simulate clouds. The principal purpose of producing fetid smoke pertains to the techniques of aggressive posturing or belligerent signaling, only that in this instance it is done by using a chemical weapon, that is, a deleterious odor. Odors are considered pathogenic by a number of South American tribal groups (Wilbert, W., 1986), and some Indians do not hesitate to employ stench as a means of magic weather control. According to the Barasana, the weather is governed by a celestial female shaman who manifests herself in the asterism of the Pleiades. Shamans who owe her their powers repel rain clouds by rubbing their hands in their armpits, blowing the smell skyward, and voicing a formula (Hugh-Jones 1979, 178–79). The same procedure is followed by shamans of the Apinaye who, after rubbing their hands in their armpits, hold them against an upcoming storm (Nimuendajú 1939, 149). A notion of offensive fecal odors is probably associated with the practice, by some Indians, of presenting their naked behinds toward the weather, as done by several groups of Guyanese Indians (Roth 1915, 268), the Piro (Sabate 1877, 254–55), and the Campa (Weiss 1975, 479). There are also indications that urine plays an important role in this chemical warfare. Fermented urine wards off various kinds of evil and weather spirits, such as harmful winds, for the Quechua of southern Peru (Lund Skar 1987, 281). Fear of offensive odors may also be the reason for the taboo among the Warao and the Fuegians, and possibly others, on discarding smelly refuse and food remains in the water so as to avoid upsetting the weather beings (Gusinde 1937, 1307–8).

Pertaining to the same category of odor-related techniques of weather control is the practice of the Nambicuara of tying the leaves of a certain plant (*yakúdenánsu*) into a cigar-shaped bundle. After lighting the bundle, the shaman waves the smoking leaves four times in the direction of the approaching storm, saying, "Go away, go away! Don't be angry with me." Should this conjuring remain unsuccessful, he lights three smudges by mixing *yakúdenánsu* with *pata toda* leaves. While the smoke is rising to the clouds, he takes a firebrand and shakes it against the storm, demanding that it move on. Unfortunately, Oberg (1953, 100), who observed this practice among the Nambicuara, did not further identify the leaves and the plants in question. Some plants used in weather magic are likely to be acrid and pungent, as probably are the branches of *aktaín* (*Capparis speciosa*) held up by the Lengua against twisters. Belonging to the Capparidaceae or the caper family of plants, *Capparis speciosa* and/or the unidentified wood and leaves burned by the Nambicuara may have an intrinsic smell in addition to the odoriferous smoke which is disagreeable to atmospheric spirits. In short, whereas in many instances smoke from fires is clearly intended to emulate rain clouds, at other times it is the odor of incinerated animals and plants which threatens the well-being of weather spirits, just as potential weather-related illnesses pose a threat to human health.

The Kogi believe there is an analogical relationship between precipitation and stones. Distinguishing among white, red, and green (or blue) rain, they crush white, glasslike stones and perform a rain dance with a green stone ax to call for rain. Dancing with a red stone ax is expected to produce periods of dry weather. By throwing white lime powder into the air, they seek to forestall rainy weather. Apparently, the precipitation/stone analogy of these magic practices rests primarily on color, although lime may have acquired additional power through the burning process which produced it (Preuss 1926, 103, 105).

Wind is analogous to breathing, vociferation, and aerophone and rattle music. The widely spread practices of forcefully blowing and bellowing against the clouds are related, to some extent, to the idea of fighting wind with wind. As noted for the Warao, the practice of fanning land and sea breezes came into existence precisely because of the heavy breathing of the dueling heroes, Earthquake and Armadillo. Characteristically, Armadillo and his animal followers arrived in Earthquake's domain as a loudly vociferating and singing group of invading challengers. Their clamor, together with the panting of the wrestling heroes, set the reproductive process of the entire forest into motion. Loud vociferation was also characteristic of the Fuegians, whose men relied on the homeopathic efficacy of their vocal and strutting display of valor to provoke the storm. Colored with charcoal and armed with clubs, they formed two groups that stepped out into the stormy weather, each band gathering behind a vigorous champion. The bodies of the champions confronting each other were painted with a white band from the chin downward. Around their heads they wore the skin of a kelp gander with white down sticking to it, and their hair was painted white. The two antagonists vociferated agitatedly and loudly against each other. Acting the part of the challenger, one of them carried a white stone in each hand. His antagonist, impersonating the wind, carried a club. Leaping toward his challenger, the "storm," as though thirsting for blood, kept demanding a human life. With his club at the ready, he engaged the opposing champion in a loud, impassioned dialogue. Then the challenger threw one of his white stones so that it fell about a meter behind the storm's heels, and presently he ran to pick it up again. While the duel was in progress, two other heavily painted men began to shout at and gesticulate toward each other. With one arm slung around his opponent's neck, each man kept bobbing his head while the spectators watched the confrontation (Bridges in Gusinde 1937, 1307–8).

Aerophones—horns, trumpets, panpipes, flutes, and clarinets—produce ritual wind as exemplified by weather rituals in the Montaña and the central Andes or from the Orinoco Delta, where the Warao connect the northern trade winds with the annual cycle of moriche starch production. The trades are believed to convey the sago as the Sago Mother's gift, extending from the northeastern world mountain. Every year the sago deity, in the form of a gigantic trumpet (clarinet), is made to sway in the wind of the sacred instrument.

The analogy between rattles and the wind is perhaps more difficult to detect, as the cacophonous noise of the shaken rattle, rather than the rushing windlike sound produced by the seeds or stones inside it, is the sound usually associated with the rattle. Rattles are even believed by the Cariña to house the four directional winds (Civrieux 1974, 21, 53). A special rattling device manufactured by the Araucanians (Mapuche) consists of a wooden container holding pebbles and leaves (*Boquilla trifoliata*) whose noise and associated movements bring a downpour.

Rulers of the Elements

Having discussed the role of weather practitioners, it is perhaps expedient now to scrutinize the mythical rulers whose outward expressions are the principal weather phenomena. That process reveals weather spirits to be modeled on the atmospheric elements themselves, on sundry other natural phenomena, or on zoological prototypes of characteristics that proved conducive to analogical imaging. Although not always apparent to outside observers, indigenous weather lore has been deeply informed by a sophisticated native capacity for analogical thought. It is all the more regrettable, therefore, that the world-making potential of the Indian's creative imagination has been sorely neglected by ethnographic inquiry, so that much of our current knowledge of South American weather religion is rudimentary and opaque.

Wind Demons

Generally invisible wind demons reveal themselves primarily to shamans and elders, appearing in drug-induced visions and in dreams. Whereas male spirits are often hairy, bearded, and grim-looking, Siona-Secoya mythology introduces a wind woman whose radiant smile is said to be typical of wind people (Cipoletti 1988, 117). Of less agreeable appearance, as envisioned by the Mehinaku, are the spirits of whirlwind and waterspout, featuring "giant heads, long teeth, eyes that glow in the dark, and hideous deep voices" (Gregor 1977, 321–22).

Like most atmospheric phenomena, light, heavy, and tempestuous winds are either ascribed to particular supernatural entities or conceptualized as different attributes of the same master spirit. To the Warao, Earthquake and Armadillo are responsible for the breezes, the heron and the sun bittern for the trade winds, and a chimeric demon with a serpentine body, human arms, and a huge flaring head for twisters of all kinds. The windless calm preceding an earthquake and the armadillo's ability to hold its breath under water for a long time made both actors ideal models for primordial heroes. They appeared at a time when wind had not yet come into existence and when, during their duel, both land and sea breezes were created by the panting of the contestants. The heron's and the sun bittern's distinctive calls, plumage, display behavior, daggerlike beaks, and other natural characteristics have caught the imagination of the Indians, who attribute them selectively to the rulers of the trades. The master of whirlwinds was obviously modeled on waterspouts and tornadoes.

The Yanomami spirits of strong winds include the variegated tinamou (*Crypturellus variegatus*), whose wailing whistle perhaps imitates the howling of the wind and the moaning of the people lambasted by a tempest; the spider monkey (*Ateles belzebuth*) that crashes like a storm through the foliage of trees and breaks their branches; the jaguar that claws the trees, leans against them, and bends them down; the jacamar (*Brachygalba* spp.) and the giant armadillo (*Priodontes*), which tunnel in the ground and uproot trees as a tornado does. Accordingly, the devastation caused by a whirlwind in both forests and settlements is attributed, not to a single wind, but to a swarm of raging spirits unleashed by the magic power of a hostile sorcerer (Colchester 1982, 164–65; Lizot 1976, 163–64; Polykrates 1974, 18). To the Cashinaua, other animal models for the wind include the speedy lizard (Abreu 1938b, 272).

Winds are often made to correspond to the world directions, underscoring their cosmic significance. Thus, the eight wind spirits, with different strengths in the Warao universe, were shown to be independent of but interactive with the rain lords of the cardinal and intercardinal points. Similarly, to the Apytré-Mbyá the master of the north wind is the Stiff-Bearded One who, while swinging in his hammock, drags his beard back and forth across the earth. Owner of the south wind is the Wafting-in-the-Air Bearded One. The east wind is personified as a pipe-smoking spirit whose puffing produces benevolent wind, and Tupan, the supreme spirit, is the master of the west wind. Tupan is related to his directional counterpart by the marriages his people have contracted with East Wind's daughters (Susnik 1984–85, 33–34). The Toba and the Pilagá also identify four wind spirits with the cardinal points (Métraux 1946c, 28).

The belief in personified north and south winds is widespread in South America. In Warao mythology, the stormbirds of the southern trade winds and those of the northern alternately invade each other's air spaces over the Orinoco Delta. To the Guarayo, North Wind is a powerful hero who in mythic times almost annihilated humanity with his club. The same Indians personify South Wind as two mythic kidnappers and abductors (Susnik 1984–85, 33). Archenemies of each other, the two directional winds are locked in perpetual hostility. The Ayoreo distinguish between directional wind spirits of the north and of the south. These, as well as directionally unsteady winds or soft breezes, are identified with primordial personages whose behavioral characteristics they express (Bórmida and Califano 1978, 169). To the Chamacoco the two contestants are women who come and go in pursuit of each other (Susnik 1984–85, 31). An epic battle was fought between Fuegian wind lords and their retinues of the south and of the north. Reminiscent of the fight between the (southern) land breeze and the (northern) sea breeze in Waraoland, the wind battle of the Selknam evolved as a contest over supremacy. In repeated attempts to invade the northerner's territory, and by means of one-on-one wrestling contests between champions of the two adversaries, South Wind eventually proved superior. Through perseverance, brawn, and clever strategy, he brought the battle to a successful end, carrying away North Wind's beautiful daughter as the victor's prize (Gusinde 1931, 606–12).

In some instances wind spirits have attained particular prominence as demonic beings. The Tacana and groups linguistically related like the Araona and the Toromona believe in Baba-buada, a wind god and the creator of heaven who lives in the sky to the south. He governs the march of the seasons, and the annual planting and harvesting festivals are dedicated to him (Armentia 1905, 136; Métraux 1942, 41; Schuller 1922, 164–65). A powerful wind personage is the Andean Huayra-tata, "Father of Wind," who manifests himself as different kinds of wind but especially as a whirlwind. He is a willful and autonomous figure of the Puruhá-Quichua whose personality fuses with Supay, the evil spirit in Quechua and Aymara mythology. According to the Aymara, the Father of Wind lives in a house high up on the mountains or in the deepest abysses. He is the consort of Pacha Mama, the Earth Mother, whom he fertilizes by gathering and transporting water from Lake Titicaca and releasing it over her in the form of rain. The lake is calm when he lies down to sleep in it, but it becomes dangerously rough when he stirs. Hurricanes are the expression of his anger over the suspected infidelity of his wife. Out of jealousy, the wind god rarely leaves the earth goddess; they are represented as a Janus-faced figurine, with Huayra-tata looking east and Pacha Mama looking west. Their effigy is covered with winding snakes that symbolize curling winds. Whenever he approaches a person or a village, the wind god spreads contagion whose evil effects can be averted only through propitiation, prayer, and ritual conjuring (Aguiló 1985, 19; Monast 1972, 59). Indeed, as noted earlier, the notion of pathological winds prevails not only in the Andes but throughout South America.[5]

---

[5] A widely scattered sample of tribes includes the Warao (Wilbert, W., 1987), the Kogi (Reichel-Dolmatoff 1985, 237), the Cashinaua (Abreu 1938b, 310), the Campa (Chevalier 1982, 393), the Shavante (Giaccaria and Heide 1972, 94), the Chorote (Karsten 1932, 113), and the Chamacoco (Susnik 1984–85, 31).

Demons of Thunder and Lightning

The demons of thunder and lightning adopt a variety of guises. Like spirits of the wind, they are normally visible only to shamans and old men. They appear in drug-induced trances and in dreams, through which they take form in myth. Often male and bearded, they can be either small, of normal size, or gigantic. Tapirapé thunder beings, called children or pets of Thunder, are small creatures, about the size of a hand. Their bodies are covered with white, hairy down and are adorned with headdresses of red parrot feathers, glass beads, and lip plugs. Thunder is described by the Apinaye as a male figure of normal size whose black painted body resembles storm clouds (Nimuendajú 1939, 139). A thunder-and-lightning personage of gigantic proportions is mentioned by the Ecuadorian lowland Quichua, who picture him as a male with disproportionately long legs, an enormous face, and bat ears (Santos Ortiz de Villalba 1976, 83; Oberem 1980, 293). Other Ecuadorian Indians, the Cayapa, visualize thunder spirits as giants dressed in blue. Some informants in the same group described thunder as being two uncommonly large, winged personages, a male and a female, with light-blue bodies covered with hair as coarse as hog bristles. In the mythologies of the Toba and the Pilagá, Lightning assumes different shapes. Appearing as a small, hairy old man or woman, the wind demon hates bush spirits and demolishes the trees in which they live. The Toba maintain that this being is actually an animal in human form, featuring a small head and a hairy body like those of an anteater. Regardless of the guise, however, whenever a storm breaks out one or more of the lightning spirits may fall to earth and ask humans to build a fire so that its smoke may waft them back into their sky (Karsten 1932, 215; Métraux 1944b, 295; 1946c, 27). The Chamacoco also regard Lightning as a woman, a shamaness of dark-purple color (Susnik 1984–85, 30), and the Sanemá-Yanomami tell of a sky woman who brings thunder to earth (Colchester 1982, 157). Like the Warao, who speak of a nadir goddess who manifests herself in the form of a four-headed serpent at the base of the world's axis, the Chapacura believe in a fish demon, visible only to some of their elders. The spirit appears to have four heads, alternatingly of fish and of serpent. Nobody dares hunt its natural prototype (*tupuiranca*) for fear of provoking a thunderstorm of rain, hail, and stones (Nimuendajú 1919–22, 1028; see also fig. 4.5).

Thunder-and-lightning spirits are usually conceptualized as living on mountaintops, as are the Warao, Yuracaré, and Makuna thunderers (Métraux 1942, 42; Trupp 1977, 55), or in the sky where, in a variety of ways, they produce the phenomena specific to them. Thunder resounds when these spirits speak, walk, bang on objects with their fists and staffs, throw stones, or hurl weapons. Lightning flares when they exhale, blink their eyes, lose their eyelashes, move their arms and ears, or beat their elbows against their bodies; it may also spring from their bursting heads or from reflecting labrets and mirrors. Streaks of lightning are also the resounding voices of spirits like the Warao rain lords, the thunderer of the Cayapó, the sky people of the Umutina, and others (Lukesch 1968, 191; Schultz 1961–62, 255). The anthropomorphic male and female lightnings of the Ayoreo express their anger by using their fists or throwing clubs or axes, contaminating the places they strike with illness (Bórmida and Califano 1978, 170). The long-legged lightning spirit of the Quichua engulfs his enemies in fire that billows from his mouth, and lightning bolts are produced by the movement of his batlike ears (Santos Ortiz de Villalba 1976, 83; Oberem 1980, 293). Featuring an axlike head, a wide chest, and an extremely small

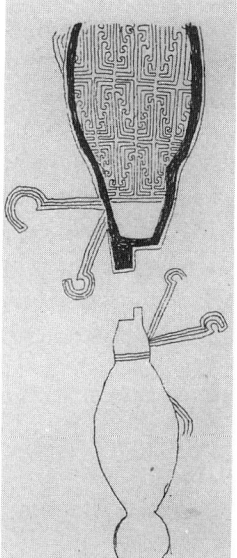

FIG. 4.5
Shipaya fish demon, Master of Lightning. (Nimuendajú 1919–20)

waist, the Tupari thunder-and-lightning demon splits trees with his jutting forehead and his nose. Lightning appears when he lifts food to his mouth, and thunder rolls when he throws stones (Caspar 1975, 193). The Siona-Secoya imagine Thunder as a white youth who walks about striking an iron rod against the wall of his house in the sky. When he blinks, lightning emanates from his eyelashes (Payaguaje 1990, 81–82). Similarly, the Caduveo speak of an ugly, big-bellied youth who sports eyelashes as long as his nose. A girl delighted in pulling out those lashes, as every time she did so her action brought loud thunderclaps and lightning. Unable to restrain herself, the girl plucked so many of the boy's eyelashes that lightning killed her and all the children who witnessed her frivolous act (Ribeiro, in Wilbert and Simoneau 1989b, 41–42). The Tupí-Guaraní think lightning is caused by the reflections of the rosin stalk that Tupan, a supreme being of small stature, carries in his lower lip (Grimal 1965, 483; Susnik 1984–85, 34). Instead of reflections of a lip plug, lightning to the Waiwai and the Andoque represents reflections from a mirror in Thunder's hands (Fock 1963, 85; Landaburu and Pineda 1984, 58). Tupinamba mythology explains that thunder originated in the treacherous and fiery death of their mythical grandfather. Disgruntled over their place in the scheme of creation, animal creatures from an earlier world subjected him to repeated fire tests. When he transformed himself into fire and flames, his head burst with so much force that the noise reverberated throughout the universe (Ibarra Grasso 1980, 146–47).

Zoomorphic master spirits of meteorological phenomena occur in the mythology and folklore of peoples throughout the world. Birds, however, are by far the creatures most frequently associated with thunder, lightning, and rain. North American Indians are well known for their complex beliefs in thunderbirds (Michelson 1930, 51–54), and the report, at the beginning of the twentieth century, of their absence from South America came as a surprise (Ehrenreich 1905, 15). To many, their absence seemed to reflect a lack of ethnographic information about them rather than the de facto absence of the concept as such. And, indeed, without perhaps achieving the same degree of importance as in North American mythology, avian thunderers from several parts of South America have since been documented. The findings are very similar to the thunderbird concepts of both North America and Asia (Métraux 1966, 132–35). Though not of universal distribution on the subcontinent, the thunderbird motif ranges from the Gran Chaco to the Caribbean and from Ecuador to the coast of Brazil. The concept's far-flung distribution indicates its antiquity in South America and suggests its wider diffusion in earlier times.

The thunderbirds of South American mythologies, though modeled after numerous ornithological species and pictured in different formal guises, all share the peculiarity of producing atmospheric phenomena from their bodies. The Island Carib of the West Indies identified the green heron (*Butorides virescens*), apparently linked with stars and constellations (e.g., Orion) visible in the rainy season, as the Master of Thunder and Hurricanes. The Warao seem to think he is related to the striated heron (*Butorides striatus*), the Father of Wind and ruler of the northern trade winds. His counterpart is the heronlike sun bittern (*Eurypyga helias helias*), which functions as a stormbird for the Warao on earth but as a thunderbird for the inhabitants of their netherworld. To the latter, the bird's peculiar calls sound like thunderclaps. Orion, the stormbird of the rainy season, is chased from the sky by the egret, a bird of the same family (Ardeidae) as the heron. This wind bird, which appears before the long dry season, is recognized by the Wapishana in a constellation composed of Gemini, Cancer, and Leo (Farabee 1967 [1918], 102). The noise of the rushing trade winds is made by the outspread wings of the egret.

The thunderer couple of the Cayapa in Ecuador are endowed with large blue wings whose flapping causes thunder (Barrett 1925, 2: 360–61). Across the continent in coastal Brazil, the Camurú-Cariri conducted rituals with the celebrants imbibing an infusion made from vision-inducing *yurema* root. Under the influence of the narcotic, they beheld the thunderbird generating peals of thunder with its footfall and shooting bolts of lightning from a huge tuft of feathers on its head (Nimuendajú, in Lowie 1946, 559).

Thunderbirds are much in evidence in Gran Chaco lore. According to the Nivaklé, they were hatched from the eggs of a hummingbird. As the original owners of fire, they were infuriated when Nivaklé and Lengua ancestors, with whom they had shared a dinner of roasted snails, stole the birds' fire. Deeply resentful of the thievery, thunderbirds became humanity's worst enemy, frightening people with thunderous voices, sparks of lightning from their wings, and thunderbolts they hurled at them. Thunderbirds also open receptacles filled with water and thus bring rain and floods to earth (for the Nivaklé, see Alarcón y Cañedo and Pittini 1924, 81; for the Lengua, see Grubb 1913, 98–99). Although invisible under normal circumstances, the human form and the life-style of the thunderbirds were revealed in mythic times to a man who, upon being taken to the uppermost sky by his twin lovers (Gemini), spent some time with the thunderbirds before returning to earth.

Several additional species of thunderbirds came into being through metamorphoses of humans. Offended by their wives and relatives who refused to bring them drink and food, Nivaklé forefathers asked a shaman to transform them into thunderbirds. After successfully joining the prototypical thunderbirds in the sky, the newly transformed ones settled in the four corners of the world, whence they bring rain and thunderstorms. When lightning flashes, the kingfisher can be seen in its light. Still another kind of thunderbird of the Nivaklé is identified as the stork or the heron. In an earlier and different form, the stork (heron) was a collector of honey who transformed himself into a bird because of the humiliation he had suffered from his brother-in-law, who had left him stranded on a high tree, suffering from thirst. Once in his avian form, he sent a roaring thunderstorm, killing his brother-in-law (or his sister) with a lightning bolt (Siffredi; Siffredi and Costa; Tomasini, in Wilbert and Simoneau 1987b, 219, 229, 258).

The thunderbird of the Toba is the so-called calandra lark (*Mimus modulator, M. orpheus*), a black-headed mockingbird. Jumping up and down when singing and always appearing when clouds approach, he is a powerful shaman closely associated with thunder (Terán, in Wilbert and Simoneau 1989c, 270). To the Chorote, thunder and lightning are caused by spirits called *ahuéna*, "the birds." Although not their proper name, the Indians refer to thunder and lightning simply as "the birds" (Karsten, in Métraux 1966, 132–33). The various bird peoples of the Chorote Master of Birds are locked in perpetual battle with one another and produce atmospheric phenomena by colliding in flight. Even small birds like the pigeon cause some rumbling. But loud thunderclaps and lightning are caused by the aquatic birds because of their greater strength (Siffredi, in Wilbert and Simoneau 1985, 22).

Gran Chaco Indians, the Warao, the Shipibo, and still others believe that, formerly, all human beings were birds (Girard 1958, 249), and the Nivaklé who became thunderbirds are pictured as winged persons. The Chané of the northern Chaco tell the story of a thunderbird in the form of a poor, rejected man who was given wings by the Great Spirit to help him become accepted by his people. Flapping his wings caused thunder, but raising them unleashed a devastating storm (Nordenskiöld 1912, 251–52). Dispensing with any ornitomorphic detail, but certainly appealing to the thunderbird concept, the Shipaya speak of mythical times when people killed a group of lightning spirits that lived in a hollow tree. When the sole survivor, a black boy, had grown up, he painted a red line along either side of his body, smeared the brain of a tortoise mixed with annatto dye on his hair, and beat his elbows against the line markings, producing powerful lightning, thunder, and rain (Nimuendajú 1919–22, 1012). Similarly, Thunder of the Ayoreo raises his arms to shoot lightning from his armpits and provoke catastrophic floods (Wilbert and Simoneau 1989a, 45–69).

In Maku cosmology, humanity was preceded by a society of fork-tailed flycatchers (*Muscivora tyrannus monachus*) whose members served as Thunder's assistants when he walked the earth. Invisible now, Thunder lives in the sky, where he can be heard playing the drum. Only shamans may travel to the sky to visit Thunder's birds and ask them for assistance in curing diseases (Silverwood-Cope 1980, 225). Similarly, Tupan, the Thunder-Rain demiurge of the Tupí-Guaraní, is believed to be inseparable from his fork-tailed flycatcher companions who are seen darting about before an approaching storm. Shamans wear tail feathers of the birds in their diadems to appeal for rain and perhaps to ask, like their Maku colleagues, for the bird's assistance in effecting a cure (Susnik 1984–85, 34). Finally, the Cashinaua Indians believe in the *xexeu* (cloud bird) that walks with the sun and has the power to produce thunderstorms and darkness (Abreu 1914, 429).

Traits peculiar to the denizens of thunder and lightning across the continent are their fear-inspiring anger, hate, and vindictiveness. Appropriately, the Bororo are said simply to call them "angry people" (Savage-Landor 1913, 252), and the Sanemá-Yanomami refer to rain as water that is being angry (Colchester 1982, 165). The masters of thunder and lightning brandish weapons (club, ax, rod, machete, whip, sling), stomp about on thunderous feet, and swing or throw their weapons in crackling lightning flashes. Frequently their power is said to be vested entirely in their weapons and that without them they remain powerless (for the Sikuani, see Maltoni, in Wilbert and Simoneau 1992, 191–201). Distressed by the deprivations imposed upon them by harsh, lean rainy seasons, the Warao project their anguish onto climatic spirits by way of their weather shaman's chanting. Infuriated, the rain gods respond with thunderstorms and tree-toppling lightning. Mainland Carib such as the Waiwai picture Thunder with a palm leaf whip, a large mirror, and a giant fan with which he produces thunder, lightning, and gusting winds, respectively (Fock 1963, 85). The Yekuana Master of Thunder and Lightning hunts with lightning bolts. To characterize his vindictive disposition, the Indians tell the story of how he murdered his sister's sons because their mother dared to disobey him. Their cooked hearts he saw transformed into a couple of terrorizing harpy eagles (Civrieux 1980b, 85–87, 186). The Kogi distinguish among different thunderers who express their rage with lightning. Only priests are able to deflect their ire, thanks to an agreement reached in primordial times between a priest and the thunder beings. But if provoked, as when, for example, no novices are undergoing training for the priesthood, the thunderers are still expected to enfold the world in chilling fog, destroy the forests, and scorch the fields (Preuss 1926, 81; Reichel-Dolmatoff 1985, 1, 237). On the Vaupés River thunder is considered to be an expression of the anger of Yurupary, the culture hero (Wallace 1889, 348, 500). The lightning demon of the Mashco lives on human blood, which his slaves are required to find for him. Whenever deprived of a fresh supply, he raves with anger and destroys trees in the forest (Barriales and Toralba 1970, 58). Also fear-inspiring is the ire of the Araucanian (Mapuche) god of thunder and volcanoes. If angered, he is wont to cause natural catastrophes, such as volcanic eruptions, rainstorms, and inundations (Susnik 1989, 67). The Selknam said that the distant rumbling of thunder signified the anger of their dead sorcerers, who send them plague and wars (Gallardo 1910, 343).

As noted earlier, a belligerent attitude marks humankind's relationship to the climatic supernaturals. From the weather spirits' point of view, this truculence seems to be conditioned by a general hatred of things, both human and telluric, and to be driven by a need for revenge for an identifiable or unspecified injury that the spirits suffered in the mythic past. Among themselves and vis-à-vis humankind, weather spirits are a militant lot; combativeness is their second nature. Lightning, say the Jivaro, is an ancestral warrior (Karsten 1964, 46), and thunder is produced by warring souls of the Guaicurú and the Mbayá who, in the form of stars, battle over their ultimate place in the heavens (Ehrenreich 1905, 15; Ribeiro 1980, 50). A perpetual battle is fought between the creator of the Urubu-Kaapor and his son, who lives in the sky with the souls of the dead. When he becomes intoxicated during periodic drinking sprees, he picks up his huge bow and shoots arrows of lightning and thunder in all directions (Ribeiro 1974, 20).

The motif of revenge comes to the fore in Cayapó mythology, which holds that a *dema*-ancestor, Bebgorotí, was cheated out of his legitimate share of a communal hunt by primeval humans. Insulted and humiliated, he ascended to the sky via a high mountain, killing his human pursuers with lightning bolts that he shoots from his sword-club. He became the master of thunderstorms who kills people wherever they may be (Lukesch 1968, 191). A similar event is described by the Crengez about a group of hunters who came across Thunderstorm in the form of a tapir. Finding their mark, their arrows produced powerful peals of thunder and killed some of the hunters. Deeply annoyed by the hunters' actions, the thunder tapir ascended to the sky, and since that time animals have stopped talking to humans (Nimuendajú 1914, 635–36). The Mashco believe that lightning is produced with the club of a slayer of jaguars, avenging the death of his mother who fell victim to their attacks (Califano 1982, 191). Abused and maltreated by Ayoreo children, a vindictive Thunder brings on a devastating flood and kills the perpetrators of the attack on him with lightning bolts, thus trans-forming them into frogs and other aquatic animals (Wilbert and Simoneau 1989b, 49–72). Examples portraying the vindictiveness of atmospheric beings could be cited from societies across the continent and from early postcontact times. One more typical example was recorded by Father Anchieta prior to 1560. To account for a storm that had devastated the area around São Paulo, a Tupinamba medicine man explained: "I knew God and his son. Having been bitten by a dog, I ordered the son of God to bring me medicine. He came immediately and, being angry at the dog, he sent a great wind which destroyed the forest and avenged me for the injury I sustained" (Anchieta 1812, 135).

As perpetual fighters, thunder-and-lightning spirits are closely associated with death and with the souls of the dead. The Cumanagoto, the Cariña, and the Yekuana fear Lightning as the master of life and death. Shamans invoke Lightning as a last resort to empower themselves with his charge to cure the sick (Civrieux 1980a, 186). Thunder, according to the Yanomami, functions as the judge of the dead, and in that role he is assisted by Lightning, his son. At the sound of loud thunder, the Sanemá-Yanomami say that someone has died and that the deceased, upon arriving in the land of the dead, will be greeted with welcoming celebration. The pounding of the revelers' dance steps is believed to cause the rumbling of thunder (Colchester 1982, 118, 157; Zerries and Schuster 1974, 155). Old Father, the Cashinaua's Ruler of Lightning, provides the souls of the otherworld with food (Susnik 1989, 71). The Shipibo also seem to believe that the demons causing thunder and lightning are the spirits of the dead (Karsten 1964, 445). The lightning beings of the Chiquito-Manasi are ancestral souls who stand in front of the temple that houses supreme spirits, including the Thunder God. Lightning bolts strike when the spirits come down from their dwelling place in the stars (Fernández 1895, 59; Métraux 1943, 21–22). Shamans descending from the sky to earth are also said to cause thunder (for the Mbya, see Sánchez Labrador 1910, 2, 84).

Among the Tupinamba and other coastal Tupí, the master of thunder and lightning, Tupan or Tupâ, figured as a very important demiurge. Early Catholic missionaries considered his place in native mythology to be so exalted that they used his name as a designation for God (Thevet 1944 [1557–58], 176; Métraux 1928, 52–56). As noted earlier, in modern Tupí-Guaraní mythologies Tupan is a small man, dressed in a resplendent labret, who is always accompanied by fork-tailed flycatcher spirits that announce—and then bring—rainstorms. Modern Guaraní petition him to withhold his anger and be more friendly toward them, but he is expected to be instrumental in the final cataclysmic destruction of the world of the living. This evil intent of Tupan relates to the vindictive nature (noted earlier) of atmospheric beings who hold a grudge against humans. Tupan's ill feelings began when he lived on earth in anthropomorphic form. At that time, he was married to a woman who was later killed when she frightened their three children to death. The father and his children climbed up an arrow-chain to the sky, where they became meteorological beings. Tupan's abode is located in the much feared western sky, where he keeps on grumbling, like distant thunder, over the misdeed of his terrestrial wife. His children cause thunderclaps by shooting arrows anointed with chonta palm oil at their father's behest (Susnik 1984–85, 33).

The Inca regarded Thunder as a deity of high rank. Roaming the sky, he produced thunder with his club and projectiles from his sling. His image appeared in the sky as the Big Dipper, with which he drew water from a long, wide river (the Milky Way) to pour out over the world (Grimal 1965, 483). The Indians of Cuzco venerated a representation of thunder and lightning together with those of Sun and Moon, considering them as their ancestors (Karsten 1926, 358).

Finally, the Aymara held the god of thunder and lightning in high esteem. Their modern descendants on the altiplano placate him with offerings and fetishes to protect their houses from being struck by lightning. Houses that have been hit are taboo, and their owners burn incense and sacrifice two black llamas every other year to propitiate the divinity. The Inca also abandoned houses struck by lightning, or they marked the spot where a bolt had hit the ground to keep unsuspecting people away from such places (Garcílaso de la Vega 1723, bk. 2, ch. 1). A person struck by lightning who survived was called "Child of the Sky" and was accorded deep respect. Some herbal doctors claimed to have acquired their art when knocked unconscious by a stroke of lightning (La Barre 1948, 170).

Rain Demons

Because of the primary association of rain symbolism with fertilization and life, it is perhaps not surprising to find rain and flooded rivers frequently associated with supernatural women and their reproductive cycle. Several of the meteorological denizens of the Warao are female, including the rain god of the northeastern world mountain; the water mothers of tides, high rivers, and low rivers; and the young women of soft rain. Hailing from an all-female land, the water mothers went to an all-male continent to mate with the men, giving origin to the Warao. Since then the reproductive cycle of these spirit women remains synchronized with the fluctuating hydraulic system of the Orinoco Delta. Reminiscent of the cloud girls of Warao mythology, who with their sweet voices entice young men into having sex with them, is the Goddess of the Waters of the Manao, who appears to young men in the form of a beautiful girl and, with her lovely voice, leads them to ruin (Cacella 1956, 240). Rain and floods, according to the Sanemá-Yanomami, are produced by female forces. Rain originates with elderly female spirits of the forest. In the rainy season or during the crepuscular hours of the day, these women send plumes of mist through the forest canopy into the sky, whence they fall as rain. In turn, the rainfall causes fluctuating water levels in the rivers of the Sanemá habitat, and the spirits of birds like the pigeon (*Columba subvinacea*) and the hawk (*Spizaetus ornatus*) lead the waters downstream. These spirits, collectively referred to as "wave women," appear in the dreams of Indians as small personages, dancing downriver on the water to announce future floods. The association of menstruating Sanemá women with rain clouds was noted earlier (Colchester 1982, 164; see p. 196 above). Rain, say the Kogi, is a woman who dances with Thunder; only when she sits down to take a rest does the rain stop (Reichel-Dolmatoff 1985, 1: 237). The Barasana correlate the entire rainy season with the menstrual period of Romi Kuma, their creator shamaness, linking her reproductive cycle, like those of the Warao water mothers, to meteorological periodicity (Hugh-Jones 1979, 179, 264). Among the cloud-dwelling gods of the Campa there are female spirits who, when inebriated, cause soft rain to fall by throwing water at one another (Chevalier 1982, 338). A savage sky woman is depicted in Lengua mythology as the angry bringer of cold and hail (Susnik 1984–85, 27). Apparently, the same woman appears to Ayoreo shamans adorned with a necklace of hailstones, which, upon falling to earth, forecast a propitious year. Another supernatural Ayoreo woman named Asohsná, was the first to send rain to fertilize the fields (Bórmida and Califano 1978, 170; Bórmida, in Wilbert and Simoneau 1989a, 222).

As exemplified by these cases of female rain denizens, rain demons, male or female, are conceptualized as living either terrestrially underground, in forests, in rivers, and on mountaintops, or celestially in the clouds and upper skies. Though often in human form, they also adopt the guises of insects, electric eels, amphibians, mammals, reptiles, and birds, or they are shapeshifters or chimeras.

Among anthropomorphic examples of supernatural rain demons are the famished dwarfs who lack intestinal tracts and who inhabit the subterranean world of the Sanemá-Yanomami. They cause devastating floods to punish women who conceal their menstrual periods (Wilbert 1963, 234). The rain spirit of the Carajá is a giant with a booming voice who lives in a subterranean lagoon below a large termite nest. In primordial times he launched a deluge to punish some overanxious hunters for killing a herd of peccary, his best friends, by covering the sky with the smoke from his pipe. As a form of perpetual punishment, the rain spirit does the same thing periodically, thereby determining the annual succession of the seasons (Sekelj 1950, 153–54). The Machiguenga Masters of Rain reside on mountaintops or in the cliffs of high mountains. Dressed in long, grey *cushmas* made of cloud yarn, they can leave their abodes in the form of mist and clouds, rise to the sky, and fall to earth as rain (Renard-Casevitz and Dollfus 1988, 17). Among the Campa of the same general region, cloud-dwelling spirits, including the God of Rain, wear white robes. When the rain god becomes inebriated from drinking too much sweet *masato*, rain falls from a large tank he keeps filled with terrestrial water (Chevalier 1982, 338). The culture heroes of the Yanõmami cause rain to fall by pouring water from a heavenly river onto the earth (Polykrates 1974, 11; Zerries 1964, 237). According to the Yuracaré and Chiquito-Manasi, torrential rains and ensuing floods are provoked by the irreverent behavior of a human soul toward Tatusiso, a celestial being. He inspects and directs the souls of young men who are en route to the Land of the Dead, but occasionally he asks them to interrupt their journey long enough to delouse his long, dishelved, scabby hair. If scorned and disobeyed, the demon seizes the soul by the leg and throws it into the celestial river, where its splashing causes excessive rainfall and floods on earth (Fernández 1895, 280; Métraux 1942, 131; 1943, 27). In Bororo cosmology a large group of bearded and long-haired spirits, masters of all kinds of precipitation, occupy a special sky world. Reminiscent of the stiff-bearded wind god of the Apytré-Mbyá, these Bororo spirits drag their streaming beards across the sky as rain. The Bororo say the primary home of these spirits is in the west, whence curtains of rain can often be observed approaching in the rainy season. Some rain spirits are believed to live inside jacaranda trees (*Machoerium* sp.), which continue to drip moisture through the beginning of the dry season (Crocker 1985, 130, 346–47). The Masters of Rain of the Ayoreo also occupy a separate sky, which is the middle level of a three-tiered sky vault. Water that streams from their bodies catches in the foliage of the trees on the lowest level, scatters, and falls in drops of rain to earth. Different kinds of rain are distinguished by sex and believed to have come about through the transformation of ancestral personages. Thunder is their chief (Bórmida and Califano 1978, 170). In Toba mythology, rain is personified as a male Cyclops who lives in an area toward the northwest. Clouds coming from the south stop at his place to request One-Eye's permission to let it rain. Thereupon, the Rain Master opens a door to his house and releases the water (Métraux 1946c, 26). Several Gran Chaco groups speak of a supernatural rain man who, for the Toba, brings heavy showers and short-lived downpours by moving about, adorned with a diadem of wet horsehair, on foot or on horseback (Susnik 1984–85, 28). The Chamacoco picture him as riding on a horse across the sky to make the rain fall (Métraux 1946c, 26). And the Mataco rain man rides a mule, his head and body wrapped in a red-fringed poncho to protect himself from the rain prefigured in the fringes. Never stopping on his way, his eyes flash lightning as he lifts his poncho to make certain of his path, while from his drum thunder rolls (Métraux 1946c, 26–27).

As to rain demons in animal forms, the electric eel (*Electrophorus electricus*), as previously noted, represents the Master of Rain of the Wapishana (Farabee 1967 [1918], 119–22). Representing insects, the cricket functions as the Ayoreo Mistress of Rain (Bórmida, in Wilbert and Simoneau 1989a, 79). Figuring very prominently in South American rain lore, however, are amphibians and reptiles. Northern Carib, such as the Chaima, Cumanagoto, Piritu, and Tamanaco, regarding toads as representatives of a divine guardian spirit, refrained from killing them (Civrieux 1980a, 187). They would keep a toad under a pot and scolded or scourged it with small sticks if it failed to send them rain (Caulin 1966, 1:152–53; Ruiz Blanco 1965, 45). Acting as an opponent of the rain among the Guajiro is a certain species of iguana. A special ritual is performed as the men close burrows of the reptiles to keep them from coming to the surface and preventing rain from falling. If rains fall abundantly, the Guajiro stage a combat between two men who personify *wanülü*, a supernatural being, and a rain cloud. The spectators cheer for the cloud because it promises an abundant harvest and the victory of rain over drought (Pineda Giraldo 1950, 113, 146; Perrin 1976, 120; 122). The anaconda (*Eunectus murinus gigas*) is regarded by the Sanemá-Yanomami as the master of rivers to whom all river creatures are related. Master snakes, such as anacondas and land boas, control the flow of rivers. If they are offended when chilies or food leftovers seasoned with pimento are thrown into the water, they agitate the waves and cause floods. In Warao weather lore, alligator spirits provoke prolonged rain and sudden river flooding just as they do when they are angered at the Sanemá-Yanomami for killing one of their kin in animal form (Colchester 1982, 164). In Sharpa mythology, the anaconda is the spirit responsible for bringing rain. Capable of moving in the air, in the water, and on earth, it has a function closely related to that of Lightning, who conveys the clouds. Lizards and boas, the rain masters of the Shipibo, cause rain to fall at a shaman's request (Girard 1958, 209, 249). The Tereno pantheon includes a number of evil monsters who are responsible for heavy rains and floods. One of them, Voropí, is in the form of a large serpent who has a human face. His home is on a large tree near a riverbank, and when he comes down to the ground he brings on a huge flood. This water spirit dislikes human scent, and when he smells it near his home, he becomes very angry. His anger makes the rain fall as lightning flashes from his sides. Tereno men and women remove their eyebrows, beards, and pubic hair because Voropí hates human hair just as much as he hates to see humans bathing in rivers and lakes. Another water spirit of the Tereno is Hihíaiuné, a female spirit in the form of a large serpent. During menstruation, women paint their bodies black to make their status known to others and to avoid any sexual contact. They themselves, as well as men who have copulated with them, are not allowed to bathe in lakes or rivers. That activity would make the serpent monster call upon the wind spirits to bring heavy rains and floods, which would destroy the houses of the offenders (Oberg 1949, 42–43).

Water spirits in the form of mammals include capybaras, weasels (for the Sanemá, see Colchester 1982, 164), and armadillos (for the Chorote, see Siffredi, in Wilbert and Simoneau 1985, 65–67).

Avian rulers of the rain are found mostly in the southern regions of the continent and more sporadically elsewhere. As already noted, there are dove and hawk spirits of heavy rain among the Sanemá-Yanomami, and the Cashinaua tell of a white heron spirit who controls the abundant water of a celestial river. Living in a deep lagoon, the heron uses his foot to close a hole at its bottom. It rains only when he removes the foot to walk away from his home (Abreu 1938, 309). Bororo mythology has a story about certain men who killed the clandestine snake lover of a woman. Playing ritual trumpets, they transformed themselves into hawks and flew up to the sky. The rain they send, even from a cloudless sky, is accompanied by the calls of the rain spirits (Albisetti and Venturelli 1962–76, 3:813–14).

Asohsná, the bird mother of the Ayoreo, lived on earth in human form before she adopted the guise of a nightjar (*Nyctibius grandis*). She commands both destructive and benign rains, and she can stop rain from falling altogether by simply opening her large mouth (Bórmida, in Wilbert and Simoneau 1989a, 222). The Ayoreo distinguish between several kinds of rainbirds which are responsible for different kinds of rain. White or gray (cloud) birds bring benign rain, whereas black (cloud) birds bring heavy rains.

Thunderbirds convey winds from the east, and tempest birds unleash powerful thunderstorms (Bernand-Muñoz 1977, 158). In Chamacoco lore, meteorological phenomena are the expressions of veritable ornithomorphic battles between white (cloud) birds of benign rain (whose bodies, according to one subgroup of Chamacoco, are filled with water and are shaped like cow tails) and black (cloud) birds that are thunderstorms. Nénto is the mistress of the white birds that flourished in a primordial world. The mistress of black birds is a dark-colored, violaceous shamaness. During the white bird–black bird battle, the stormbirds are blowing (thunder), staring (lightning flash), and licking (thunderbolt) at the earth. The male chief of the white rainbirds roams the earth in company with his son, searching for wells and pools which he keeps filling with water wrung from his long hair. The Toba also differentiate between birds that bring beneficial rain and those that bring destructive rain. The Nivaklé and the Maka envision bird spirits occupying a special layer in the sky whence they command rain, wind, and thunderstorms (Susnik 1984–85, 28–30). The mythical rainbird of the

Caduveo resembles a rhea that lives in the clouds. Known as Diguyálo, it causes rain by spreading its wings, but a drought ensues when its wings are damaged (Oberg 1949, 63). Finally, the Mocoví consider rain to be the spirits of wild geese who find water wherever they go (Tomasini, in Wilbert and Simoneau 1988, 265–66).

Rainbow Demons

Rainbow demons are conceptualized as male and female monsters of gigantic proportions, equal in size, that is, to their meteorological prototype. Other than as sky-spanning arches, they materialize in the cloud spray of waterfalls (Koch-Grünberg 1916–28, 3:15) and in halos around the sun and the moon (Aguiló 1985, 22). In whatever manifestation, however, as full arches or as partly or wholly circular bands, rainbows are envisioned theriomorphically in the form of large snakes such as land and water boas.[6]

Like their chromatic meteorological and many-hued serpentine models, rainbow demons wear colorful body decorations—poly-

---

[6] The concept of the rainbow as a land or water boa is widespread in South America. Examples other than those mentioned in the text include the Taurepan and Arekuna (Pemon), who regard the rainbow as a gigantic multicolored anaconda that lives in high waterfalls (Koch-Grünberg 1953, 30). To the Sanemá-Yanomami the rainbow is the expression of a cosmic anaconda (Colchester 1982, 145). The Tukano place the rainbow in a group of multicolored demons that, like other similar beings, inhabit the subaquatic world (Nimuendajú 1952, 120). Indians of the Montaña in Ecuador refer to the rainbow as the shadow of a giant anaconda (Karsten 1920, 70) or as a giant sea serpent that crosses the sky (for the Shipibo, see Girard 1958, 250). The Sharpa call the rainbow by the same name as that of the anaconda (Girard 1958, 250). Rainbows are the soul (manifested in breath) of the anaconda in Bororo cosmology (Crocker 1985, 64, 130), and the Panare identify the rainbow as the breath of a half-human and half-animal being that manifests itself in the form of a boa constrictor (Henley 1982, 140). Similarly, the Shavante explain the rainbow as the exhalation of a serpent that appears after a rainfall (Giaccaria and Heide 1972, 93). A huge land serpent is portrayed in Vilela cosmogony as crawling across the world swallowing humans and animals until the birds banded together and killed it. By donning pieces of his chromatic skin the birds acquired their variety of colors (Métraux 1946c, 38–40). Still other rainbow-serpent connections are made by the Arawak, Ipurina, Carajá, Cocama, Chiriguano, Guaraní, Lengua, Inca, and Mapuche (Métraux 1946c, 40).

chrome necklaces and feather crowns—and are associated with flowers, butterflies, and ferruginous water. Although this description applies to some extent to female beings like the rainbow mistresses of the Munduruku (Kruse 1951–52, 1104), it is especially true of male rainbows who, like those of the Warao, are flirtatious people who use their dazzling adornments to entice young women. The Amuesha, for example, tell the story of a girl of very early times who became attracted to Rainbow's beautiful flowers. Hiding them in her bosom, she became pregnant during a thunderstorm. The flowers disappeared until after the storm, when she saw them adorning the rainbow (Tello 1923, 128). In various South American mythologies, young women are admonished to beware of the rainbow's ulterior sexual motives. Instead of being a kind of harmless flirtation, his advances really amount to violent rapes of women or of solitary female travelers. Canelos-Quichua and other Ecuadorian lowland as well as highland women are admonished not to show themselves to the rainbow, lest he make them pregnant with a demoniac child (Karsten 1920, 70; 1935, 220). To elude his advances and the resultant defilement, Otavalo-Quichua girls are taught to beware of waterfalls, where Rainbow is frequently seen (Collier and Buitrón 1949, 95). Menstruating Toba-Pilagá girls are discouraged from stepping into a lagoon to avoid provoking Rainbow into drowning their village in a flood (Métraux 1946c, 29). As female manifestations, moon halos also pursue victims of the opposite sex, especially those who wander alone in the night (for the Puruhá-Quichua, see Aguiló 1985, 22).

When Rainbow joins his wife to copulate, or for some other purpose, they are seen spanning the firmament as a double rainbow. The phenomenon has already been alluded to in connection with the young rainbow husband of the Warao said to be traveling with his wife (see pp. 72–73). Similar interpretations of the atmospheric phenomenon are also reported among the Kogi (Reichel-Dolmatoff 1985, 237) and the Colorado (Calazacón et al. 1985, 173–74, 288–94). Bisexual connotations of the rainbow are seen in Desana graphic depictions of ayahuasco (*Banisteriopsis caapi*) visionary imagery. A semicircle of several parallel lines representing the rainbow intimates in some mythological contexts the Sun Father's penis and in others the notion of the celestial vagina (Reichel-Dolmatoff 1975, 171; 1978, 32).

Reminiscent of the Warao concept of the rainbow as the son-in-law of the Mother of the Forest—special protectress of large trees from which canoes are fashioned—is the Mojo's rain goddess, rainbow wife of the sun (Métraux 1943, 9), whose function it is to counteract the heat damage occasioned by her husband on earth. A monstrous swallower of rain and people, the arch of colors is her mouth behind which her immense body lies hidden in the clouds. The tall trees in the forest are under the rain goddess's special protection, and the Mojo fear offending the rainbow by felling them. Indians anticipated that dugouts made from trees would capsize, thus causing the death of their crews (Eder 1985[1791], 249–50; 1985, 117, 121).

Pervasively attached to the rainbow throughout South America is the meteor's alignment with sickness, death, and calamity. Regarded as the Rain Mother of the Mojo, the rainbow swallows people and causes illness by contaminating the places and houses she visits (Eder 1985 [1791], 117). The rainbow anacondas of the Sharpa cause fever and nightly vomiting in children (Girard 1958, 209), and rainbow boas produce noxious clouds which make the Shipibo sick (Roe 1982, 121). Rainbow seeks to abduct children in order to suck their blood (for the Embera, see Vasco 1985, 88), devour them (for the Sharpa, see Girard 1958, 209), or kill them, as well as people in general, by sticking out his tongue and turning it around his head (for the Mataco, see Métraux 1944b, 295; 1946c, 38). The Ipurina entrust their hopelessly ill patients to the water serpent that lives in the river but appears in the sky as a rainbow (Ehrenreich 1891, 68).

Drawing attention to the rainbow in any way is widely discouraged in South American weather lore. The Lengua believed they could hurt the rainbow by pointing at it with sharp objects (Susnik 1984–85, 27), and the Inca avoided pointing toward or even looking at the rainbow out of respect (Polo de Ondegardo 1816, 198). Dangers threatening those who dared to point at the arch include having one's hand covered with warts (for the Cuna, see Nordenskiöld 1938, 394) or having it wither and fall off (for the Shipibo, see Girard 1958, 250). The Machiguenga believe that rainbows are caused by the colorful ribbons some water demons use to adorn their *cushmas* before embarking on an ayahuasco-induced journey to the sky. Should a human so much as look at this colorful display, the demons make the prying individual's abdomen swell, thus causing the person's death (Ferrero 1967, 343; Renard-Casevitz and Dollfus 1988, 17). Similarly, the rainbow serpent of the Kumana angrily throws rocks at anybody who stares at him (Snethlage 1937, 82). But the worst calamities afflicted a nubile Cashinaua girl of mythical times, who pointed her finger at the rainbow. In doing so, she completely disregarded Rainbow's explicit command to the contrary, and in punishment she and all women began to have menstrual periods. Furthermore, since that time all women must endure the pains of childbirth, and all humans must suffer death (D'Ans 1978, 135). The rainbow serves as a bridge to convey a sorcerer's magical darts (for the Jivaro, see Harner 1973, 165) and sky travelers of different kinds, including souls on their way to the Master of the Dead (for the Tupari, see Caspar 1975, 195).

Appearing with sun showers before or after a downpour, rainbows are frequently associated with pollution and with the notion of drizzling urine. As noted earlier, the Warao liken sun showers to Rainbow's urine, which causes widespread sickness, and Paéz parents warn of Rainbow's "urine," which is believed to cause scabies in children (Bernal Villa 1954, 237, 238)—and possibly in adults—on whom it falls, if they fail to bathe immediately following the drizzle (Hernández de Alba 1946, 954, 955). Seasonally, when the fish swim upstream, Rainbow of the Macuna dons his feather crown. His daughters urinate into the rivers, and his son uses urine to color butterflies (Trupp 1977, 53). Like Rainbow of the Warao, he of the Craho appears when he wants to drink a lot of river water or seawater, which he later spills on the earth (Chiara 1961–62, 371). Rainbow's own urine is loaded with filth, "*polilla*." It penetrates and gradually decomposes the body until the victim dies (for the Shipibo, see Girard 1958, 250). The rainbow demons of the Machiguenga inhabit large subterranean boulders. Having slovenly habits, they urinate over the detritus they sweep from their houses into the rivers. The waste, which takes on a rusty color, can be seen in the sediments in ferruginous waters. The feet of a person who steps into the contaminated water will be afflicted with sores and tumors (Renard-Casevitz and Dollfus 1988, 17). Anyone who is polluted by Rainbow's urine suffers extreme pain, sending the victim to seek relief through herbal "rainbow" medicaments (for the Awa-Kwaiker, see Solarte 1986, 185). The Witoto believe that sun showers are caused, not by Rainbow's urine, but by the sun urinating on the clouds to repel the rain (Wavrin 1932, 138).

As an expression of the cosmic anaconda, the rainbow is described by the Sanemá-Yanomami as the light, the essence, or the feces of the snake (Colchester 1982, 145). The latter idea may be related to the description of rainbow excrement by the Toba and the Pilagá as small, variously colored balls that Indians find in the forest and wear in small bags around their necks (Métraux 1946c, 38).

The Guayakí think that Rainbow announces the imminent death by jaguar attack of a child or an adult (Susnik 1984–85, 31), and, according to the Taurepan and the Arekuna, he receives the souls after death (Koch-Grünberg 1953, 30). The Barasana also believe that sun halos herald the sickness which shamans of neighboring settlements cause by practicing sorcery or by teaching their pupils how to cast spells (Jackson 1983, 205). Some societies posit a close relationship between shamans and the rainbow; for example, the rainbow of the Macuna is said to be the teacher of shamans (Trupp 1977, 53). When under the influence of tobacco juice, Sharpa shamans chant to make the pathological rainbow serpent retire to deep waters, where her powers can no longer affect their children's health (Girard 1958, 209). Ingesting ayahuasco, Shipibo curers chant to dispel noxious, cold, evil rainbow clouds from the chest of a suffering child (Roe 1982, 121). And just as rainbow demons are required to curb their water intake to reduce "the drizzle," so must the weather shamans of the Warao and the Tupari refrain from drinking a lot of water so as to prevent cold, rainy days (Caspar 1975, 20).

South American Heritage

Throughout this chapter I have repeatedly drawn attention to parallels between atmospheric tenets of the Warao and those of other South American Indians. Ordained weather shamans, like the Warao's Father of Rain, were found to exist among Indians in highly pluvial areas like the Peruvian Montaña as well as in arid savannas like the Gran Chaco. Before anyone can assume the responsibilities of a weather shaman, he must undergo initiation, including seclusion, instruction in esoteric knowledge and in spells and chants, ordeals of fasting and/or ingestion of symbolic foods, psychotropic drugs, dreams, as well as symbolic death and rebirth. Although women practice defensive weather magic, only the Warao were found to have weather shamanesses. Like other shamans, ordained weather shamans practice with both benevolent and malevolent intent, and they are able to affect an individual person, the community as a whole, or a distant group.

The wind demons of the Warao share many properties with their counterparts in other South American weather lores, including differentiation into soft-wind and strong-wind beings. Although Warao rain shamans claim a full complement of eight cardinal and intercardinal spirits of wind, the forms and functions of several of them are only vaguely identified. Clearly profiled, in contrast, are the protagonists of light winds (land and sea breezes) and heavy winds (trades) who, like personified wind demons elsewhere in South America, are aligned with the north and the south. Following a common pattern, the members of each pair are antagonists who invade each other's territories to wage battles over territorial supremacy. The northern and southern stormbirds that are identified with the trades are very prominent in Warao mythology, the former as the creator of sago and the conveyor of abundance and life, the latter as the destroyer of sago and the bringer of want and death. The southern stormbird of the rainy seasons doubles as the thunderbird of inhabitants of the netherworld. As such it is related to the thunderbirds in various other regions of the subcontinent and beyond.

The Warao Lords of Rain are demons of thunder and lightning. As in various other places on the subcontinent, they live on mountaintops. They are clearly profiled in terms of physical features, attributes, and attire, and they are among the most prominent in South American weather religions. To communicate with atmospheric beings, Warao rain shamans follow a general South American pattern of chanting, blowing, and gesticulating in their attempts to persuade the powers to conform to their wishes. The widespread antagonism of South American weather shamans toward atmospheric powers finds verbal expression among the Warao in chants of anger-inciting images and pronouncements rather than physically in militant posturing and display of weaponry. Yet Warao rain chanting projects strong emotions of anger, hatred, and fear accompanied by notions of malevolence, spite, and pollution.

The primary intent of ritual dancing in connection with the Warao sago-harvest festival is to propitiate supreme beings other than the rain gods and it relates only secondarily to the rain god of the northeast. Its basic intent is, therefore, different from the examples of rain dancing given above.

Distinctly analogous to other belief complexes is the Warao concept of the male and female rainbow serpents, including their vanity, sexuality, association with colorful objects, need of abundant drinking water, and urinary sun showers. The parallel of the Mojo rainbow's connection with the protectress of the forest in general is particularly striking.

Additional parallels between Warao weather religion and South American atmospheric lore—differentiated soft- and hard-rain beings, cephalomorphic storm spirits, celestial and terrestrial water spirits, alluring fog or rain maidens, assimilation of wind and wind instruments with human breath, lightning with fire, tears and urine with rain, serpents/alligators with rain, floods with the female fertility cycle, among others—were shown to exist in considerable profusion. Thus, based on the large number of correspondences, it is warranted to conclude that the religious complex of Warao weather lore is essentially rooted in South American cosmology. Discounting those elements that are unique to the Warao owing to weather conditions in the Orinoco Delta and their relationship to the sago complex, still a number of ideational and technical innovations surrounding the rain lords, which do not exist in other South American traditions, seem to be syncretically intertwined with European cultural attributes.

Chapter Five

Recasting Weather Religion

Colonial Pattern

In his historical accounts of Capuchins in America, Fray Mateo de Anguiano (1649–1726), a prominent early chronicler in his order, writes about the shamans in the province of Cumaná and of their claim to be masters of the elements. According to the padre, these men affirmed that no rain would fall unless they willed it to (Carrocera 1964, 479–80). They claimed to be able to evoke rain and thunderstorms with beckoning gestures and facial expressions, giving onlookers to understand that they were the ones who attracted the weather. Conversely, when clouds appeared or when they heard a thunderstorm approaching, the shamans boldly confronted the upcoming weather, blowing vigorously and repeatedly into the air and thrusting their hands upward to dispel the storm.

In a different context, Anguiano writes about one of his confreres who, on successive occasions, admonished sizable congregations of Spaniards and Indians to abandon their sinful ways. When, after delivering his last sermon, he realized his preaching had fallen on deaf ears, the padre implored God to punish the impenitent people. Scarcely had he uttered his supplication when a violent tempest blew in, leaving the congregation clamoring for God's mercy. Moved by pity and compassion, the padre then entreated God not to unleash his ire against the people, and the storm was miraculously stilled.

In a third account, probably based on a field report by Fray Francisco de Tauste (Carrocera 1964, 189), Anguiano tells of a contest between the priest and a shaman. During the rainy season one year, the Indian planned to leave his village for a period of two weeks. To prevent rain from falling in his absence, he took a stone the size of an apple, colored it red, and buried it in his garden. With confident faith, the missionary, hoping to dissuade the shaman from his delusion, implored God to let it rain. Indeed, when the shaman left his house the rain began to pour down, and it continued until the Indian returned from his journey. Thus the priest attempted to convince the shaman of the futility of his superstition; but to no avail.

The Capuchin historian did not identify the tribal origin of the shamans of whom he wrote, but he did imply that they were probably not Carib (Cariña) (Carrocera 1964, 485, 488). In view of de Tauste's missionary experience, however, the shamans may well have been Chaima and were perhaps related through their weather magic to Juriquian (Yoriquian), the one-legged storm god Juracán of the Caribbean and Mesoamerica (de Tauste, in Carrocera 1964, 198; Ortiz 1947; Preuss 1986). But, as evidenced by Anguiano's descriptions of the shamans' conjuring, many South American rainmakers, including the Warao's *naharima,* would definitely have recognized their own routine in their colleagues' practice. And a contemporary rain shaman of the Warao, though naturally not appealing to the Christian God, would undoubtedly have understood the missionary's design of inciting the anger of a deity in order to punish an incorrigible congregation with heavy downpours. The point to be made here, however, is that the padre, conversely, had he been able to witness the present-day organization of Warao society, its weather shamanism, and its sago ritual, would certainly have discerned a common cultural note between them and a number of sociopolitical and economic institutions that prevailed in mission pueblos and secular villages along the Venezuelan colonial frontier. In view of the relative intensity of the Warao's colonial mission experience (see appendix), it is opportune to examine some of the political and ecclesiastic conditions of mission life and the influence they may have had on Warao culture.

The Cabildo

The cabildo, or village council, of the mission pueblos was composed of a hierarchy of officeholders. The Spanish titles of council members among the contemporary Warao were identified as having originated with the Capuchins of the twentieth century, indicating that the missionaries were following the conventions of the colonial government (see chapter 2). As an institution, however, the cabildo (or ayuntamiento) preceded the reign of Charles V, when it existed in Spain as a form of relatively democratic local government. Reviving the cabildo, the conquistadors brought it to the New World where, as in Spain, council members were put in charge of public works and empowered to exercise limited judicial authority. The council was a forum for the expression of public opinion on issues concerning the community's daily life. The cabildo members, originally appointed by the governor, commanded local respect and enjoyed considerable autonomy in running community affairs. Upon retiring from office, a cabildo member was replaced by a governor's appointee or the council itself chose a successor (Crow 1992, 168).

The appearance of local councils in mission villages in northeastern Venezuela was symptomatic of a process of incremental state hegemony charted by Spanish court authorities and favored in papal bulls of the 1520s for the New World. This change from religious to secular status of a village or a town began with the establishment of a mission settlement (*misión*) or the live conversion (*conversión viva*), the spiritual and temporal affairs of which fell exclusively under the jurisdiction of the resident missionary. According to law, ten or twenty years after its foundation, a mission was to advance to the status of a tribute-paying parish (*doctrina*). Ideally, the missionary was then replaced by a member of the secular (non-monastic) clergy, and his political authority was transferred to a magistrate or a corregidor who had to be a Spaniard (Gómez Cañedo 1967, 1:xxxiv; Carrocera 1968, 1:432). The missionaries, however, who were vehemently opposed to surrendering any mission to a political corregidor, would have preferred to continue working with a council—consisting of a governor, an alcalde, and a fiscal—typical of mission governments. To the missionaries, it seems, the reduction in size was less important than the fact that the power vested in council members flowed directly from them rather than from a secular body. Retaining the local power would also prevent the appointment of a corregidor, typical of cabildos in secularized parish communities, to an office that challenged the validity of mission work. Nevertheless, under pressure from governors, bishops, and the king of Spain, parishes from 1700 on were established, cabildos were chosen, and corregidors were appointed along the Indian frontier of eastern Venezuela.

In the early years after the king's authorization to establish parishes in 1700 (Píritu Mission) and 1702 (Cumaná Mission), a council of Indians was to be elected annually in every secularized mission village. The council's members would be a governor, two alcaldes (justices of the peace), an alguacil (chief constable), two alcaldes of the cofradia, two corregidors (magistrates), and a procurator (solicitor). True to the spirit of a Spanish cabildo, council members, once retired, refused to return to work with the commoners they had formerly governed, and the cabildo system soon proved too complex for Indian villages of a few hundred residents or less. In 1705 Fray Matías Ruíz Blanco wrote to the king that "in the few years that the ordinances [promulgated by Governor Ramírez de Arrelano of Cumaná and authorized by the king] have been implemented, in a village of one hundred Indians there exist already forty-five Indians who consider themselves retired" (Gómez Cañedo 1967, 1:180). Imitating their colleagues in cities and provinces, Indian village governors placed armed guards at entrances to their houses and insisted on being addressed as persons of rank (*señorías*). The worst aspect of cabildos operating in former missions, however, was the cruel treatment inflicted on the common Indian by a presumptuous corregidor.

Corregidor and Cabo

The corregidor was the enfant terrible of colonial frontier missions and villages. As an official charged with the administration of an Indian community, he was always appointed by the provincial governor and functioned as his local representative. As settlements were often too small to warrant a corregidor for each one, the court through its royal officers encouraged the consolidation of several villages into a "corregidorial" district (*corregimientos*) with a resident corregidor in the head village.

The corregidor received an annual tribute from the Indian residents of his village or villages. In return, it was incumbent upon him to promote the spiritual and material well-being of the community. He had to ensure that the Indians were prodded to attend religious services and catechetical instruction and that truants were publicly whipped by the fiscal. He could also have the Indians punished for failing to build a house or for not keeping one in good repair. The corregidor had to see to it that nobody entered the church naked, that the Indians lived chaste and sober lives, and that wrongdoers were sent to prison. He had to provide instruction for children in reading and writing Spanish. Adults were to be obliged to cultivate their gardens, form work squadrons to supply the communal food depot and chest, and provide services for Spanish colonists in the region. It was also the corregidor's responsibility to make sure that Indians were paid an honest daily wage for outside labor, that they were well fed by the colonists, and that they were not made to suffer from lifting heavy loads or walking long distances from home to workplace. Indians were not to be employed in sugarcane mills, and they were not to work for the personal gain of the corregidor other than annually cultivating a field for him. Traffickers, vagabonds, and nonmission Indians were discouraged by the corregidor from staying in the village for any length of time so that resident Indians could not be persuaded to escape and so that the harmony of the community was not disturbed.

Maintaining these regulations was, in theory, the major obligation of a corregidor. In real life, however, rarely did corregidors not mistreat and oppress their Indian subjects, most of whom were made to do hard work in colonists' fields and households or as porters or boat hands on the rivers. Often required to furnish their own tools, the Indians were perpetually indebted to the "company store," trying to repay their debts with labor and having no time to cultivate their own fields so as to provide for themselves and their families. The short rations of maize and cassava allotted to them by corregidors caused acute hunger among Indian peons, forcing them to beg for food from the colonists for whom they worked. In the words of the bishop of Puerto Rico (after visiting the missions of Cumaná in 1740–41), the hardships to which the Indians were subjected "reduced them to miserable slaves" (Carrocera 1968, 1:219–22, 432–35). Whenever possible, therefore, mission Indians managed to escape, thus undoing the work of missionaries who had made special efforts and had themselves undergone travails in gathering the Indians in settlements.

In 1770, in an effort to secularize the missions in his province, Manuel Centurión, the governor of Guayana, converted the civil position of a corregidor into the military commission of a corporal (*cabo de guerra*). *Cabos*, appointed by the commandant, reported to him in his capacity as head corregidor. The first villages affected by the reorganization (see appendix) were those the governor had founded near Angostura, the capital of Guayana, with Warao he had ordered taken for that purpose from the Orinoco Delta and its environs. But throughout Guayana, missionaries variously accused the *cabos* of depriving Indians of their liberty, of arrogating their property to themselves, and of forcing them to desert the missions.

The duties of a military *cabo*-corregidor remained essentially the same as those outlined for a civil corregidor, and the notion of a village *cabo* was not entirely alien to the missionaries. After being informed by the commandant general of the province of Guayana that the king had authorized a military guard of one officer and twenty to thirty men to protect the missions from Cariña attacks, the mission received a copy of a 1764 directive that had been drawn up to regulate the activities of the *cabo* and his men. The men were to be distributed in twos and threes to missions with resident priests. One soldier (preferably white) of each village detachment was to be appointed a local *cabo*, thus forming a network of peripheral *cabos* reporting to a head *cabo* in the central mission. The primary function of the *cabo* system, however, was to protect the community and to keep the peace; moreover, local *cabos* were substantially subordinate to the padre president of a mission. This arrangement was a far cry from the model Governor Centurión had planned for the commandant and the *cabos* of his Guayanan villages, whom he had invested with political, civil, and economic regulatory power. Although encouraged to heed the opinions of the resident padre, the habitual power of the missionary had thus been compromised, for the military appointees had been admonished to manage independently and to differentiate between "empire" and "priesthood." Apparently, the humane qualities of the local *cabos* left much to be desired. Hunger and deprivation befell Orinoco villages where Warao had been settled to farm infertile soil. They, as well as other Indians, were exploited, condemned to years of hard labor, and locked into stocks for attempting to escape, for being unable to pay their tithes, and for other offenses. As many of them did escape, a substantial number of Warao ended up in Guiana, where they became known as the Spanish Warao. Others were found in the savannas starved to death. Finally, in 1774, the king ordered Governor Centurión to withdraw his *cabo*-corregidors and so put an end to their oppression (Carrocera 1979, 2:40–53, 125–30, 149, 192, 206, 219, 238, 255, 262–67, 277, 279, 297).

Communal Food Repository

One important practice associated with the secularization process was the establishment in parochial missions of communal food depots of maize, manioc, and other storable victuals, in addition to cash crops like cacao, tobacco, and cotton. It was part of the *cabo*'s or the corregidor's duties to ensure that the work was performed and the food depot stocked. The depot, kept under lock and key, was carefully guarded by the local authorities. The stored food was destined to feed dependent villagers—the infirm, widows, and orphans—and to serve as a buffer against hunger and famine (Carrocera 1968, 3:474–510). The food reserves, however, were usually mismanaged by corregidors for their own benefit (ibid., p. 404). Later on (i.e., in 1783), with the installment of Indian protectors, the power of the corregidors was curtailed, so that communal food depots began to serve their intended purposes, as they did in missions like Purísima Concepción de Cocuisas, inhabited by Chaima and Warao (ibid., pp. 504–5).

Cofradias and Guilds

An inestimably important role in the mission effort was played by friars who dressed in habits similar to those worn by ordained monks but who were not priests. As members of the Capuchin order, these unordained lay brothers were mostly occupied with domestic and manual work and with assisting padres in all non-clerical obligations of the mission. They served as sextons, bellringers, and town criers, summoning the faithful to church and the children to school. They could catechize and, in the absence of a priest, baptize children and the dying. Sometimes they conducted entradas to found new missions, and in rare instances they served as heads of new establishments (Carrocera 1968, 3:372).

Lay brothers were often accomplished craftsmen—carpenters, weavers, masons, blacksmiths—who taught their skills to mission residents (Carrocera 1979, 1:xxiii–xxiv). In community service lay brothers educated Indians in farming, serving as foremen to field-workers cultivating traditional crops like corn, manioc, bananas, and cotton, as well as cash crops like rice, cacao, and tobacco. Lay brothers were particularly concerned with two aspects of communal life mandated by law: to grow cotton for clothing the Indians and to procure food reserves for the mission depot. They installed looms and taught the women how to use them in making clothes for themselves and their families. They introduced new agricultural methods and coordinated field-crop production with meteorological conditions, paying special attention to the precarious relationship between sowing and precipitation in maize cultivation. Because maize was the most important storable victual for the communal repository, the slightest inattentiveness to the rainy season (when sowing had to be done) reduced income for the communal chest and spelled hunger and deprivation for the community, especially the needy (Gómez Cañedo 1967, 1:183–84; Carrocera 1979, 1:xxiii, 79; 2:55). In missions that had no lay brothers and in secularized parishes, many of these functions were performed by the fiscal (Carrocera 1968, 2:271).

The missionaries taught the Indians how to read and write music and how to play violins, viols, flutes, drums, and trumpets so as to enhance liturgical services and add religious pomp (Carrocera 1979, 1:xxiv; 2:20). If the padres and lay brothers were unable to handle such skill training themselves, they employed non-Capuchin professionals whenever possible. To guarantee continuity of community work, including cultivation, the mission's Indians were organized into so-called cuadrillas, or work teams, who alternated between workdays and rest days. During their time off, the men were encouraged or pressed by the corregidors to work as wage laborers for Spanish colonists to earn money for the needs of mission life and to clothe their women (Carrocera 1968, 2:277).

As previously mentioned, lay brothers and non-Capuchin professionals of the mission taught the Indians their special skills and formed religious cofradias and gremios, also referred to as hermandades or religious brotherhoods. As a Spanish institution in the late Middle Ages, the cofradia served to integrate society and to meet communal crises (Foster 1953b, 2). It blended later into the gremio, or trade guild, thus emphasizing the economic aspects of local life while retaining many religious aspects of the cofradia. Both systems had earlier developments in northern European countries like Germany, France, Holland, and England, but it was the Spaniards who introduced them into New World colonies (Rumeu de Armas 1944).

Cofradias were voluntary organizations of laymen who pledged themselves to a particular saint and then cared for the religious images of their respective saints and other holy personages. They were also responsible for church ceremonies, including the Christian burial of their brothers, paid for from the communal food pantry or from membership fees. From early on, particular cofradias tended to attract craftsmen of the same trade or profession and began to integrate cult, mutual aid, and career. Members of a trade guild, besides practicing the same trade, venerated one patron saint. They received sickness and death benefits. Later on, economic trade guilds withdrew from cofradias, but they usually organized and maintained cofradias for religious purposes (Foster 1953b, 11–12). After suffering persecution from the thirteenth to the fifteenth century, the cofradias were legalized by Ferdinand and Isabella. In provinces like Andalusia and Navarre, cofradias or gremios became more commonly referred to as hermandad. They were exported as a regulatory device to the Spanish colonies, where they were frequently associated with such religious orders as the Capuchin. As in their missions in northeastern Venezuela and in Trinidad, both friars and lay brothers encouraged the formation of cofradia-guilds (Gómez Cañedo 1967, 1:180; 2:108; Carrocera 1968, 2:271–72; 3:468–69). Noel (1972, 20) says a sacramental brotherhood established on Trinidad in 1644 "for the purpose of maintaining some order among the converted Indians, served later as a basis for the effective control of the indigenous peoples." Toward the end of the seventeenth century, the political and religious governments were in place in a good number of missions in northeastern Venezuela. Fray Lorenzo de Zaragoza, a veteran missionary, gave a vivid account of the missions' festive display in his memorandum to the king (Carrocera 1964, 291–92).

> The divine offices are celebrated [in our missions] as if it were here in our Spain, attended by all the men, women, boys, and girls. Most of them are well dressed, in decent attire, the boys singing the mass in chorus. Throughout, they play viols and violins coordinated harmonically. Usually everybody participates in the celebration of the mass with sincere devotion.
>
> Not with less reverence do they join in the processions in honor of our Lord and his most Blessed Mother. The young people, dressed in gala clothing as their means allow, dance just as we are accustomed to in our Spain. During Holy Week they march in a parade, the captain with his lance, the lieutenant with his banner, and the rest of the other officers with their war badges. Beginning and closing the procession as they see fit, they march in lines of four or six men, everybody well attired and well armed, each soldier carrying his bow and twenty-five arrows. The sergeant-major walks at the head of the parade followed by the lance carrier. Many men consider it beneath their dignity to participate if they and their women are not dressed in their finest clothing and if they themselves cannot carry firearms. That's how they appear every day during the feast, the lieutenant striking the colors when indicated and the captain, similarly, wielding his lance. Looking at the participants one would not think, from their appearance, that they were Indians.
>
> Annually elected by royal decree, the missions' officers of the peace are two regular alcaldes, two field alcaldes, and their constables. The militia includes a sergeant major and his captains, lieutenants, sergeants, and adjutants, all having commission papers issued by the governors and their badges of office. That is why they are respected by fellow Indians as their chiefs and superiors. They have their privileged seats in church and, when the need arises, they know how to command resolutely and with the power they know is vested in them, seizing and castigating (upon consultation with the padre) the delinquents who deserve punishment. Also, the missionary treats them with respect because of your Royal Majesty's staffs they carry and the badges they wear. [My translation.]

The Warao Analogue

Cabildo of Rain Lords

Comparison of this arrangement of mission government with the organization and practice of the Warao rain lords shows them to be quite analogous. To begin with, it is of course suggestive that contemporary rain shamans of the Warao picture the Lords of Rain as opulent, light-skinned Criollos who dress in long robes and live in large Western-style houses with doors and windows. They smoke elbow pipes (*akashibo*), which in name and form are foreign to the Warao, wear eyeglasses, and carry staffs, just as officers do. The assembly of the eight Lords of Rain and their hierarchical structure, power, and function are reminiscent of the stratified body of cabildo members and their authority and roles. Like cabildos, the lords hold titles of governmental offices, although the titles differ in some respects from the more frequently heard titles of cabildos elsewhere in Latin America. Titular nomenclatures of cabildos vary from one region to another, but the differences are of little consequence to the present discussion. More importantly, the rain lords, like cabildo officers, exercise their various powers to promote solidaristic deportment amenable to community self-sufficiency and self-government. Thus, the assembly of rain lords relates to a Warao community as the cabildo relates to a colonial village or town.

Then there is the word *kabo* that is used as a title preceding the personal name of a rain lord. In the idiom of shamans, *kabo* (*kaborai*) refers also to the "sidereal sky" of which the rain lords are the proclaimed owners. The distribution of rain lords along the horizon of the Warao universe and their relationship to the rain shaman as their earthly master are suggestive of the distribution of local *cabos* throughout a mission district and their relationship to a superior in the head village.[1] In the process of mythologizing the

---

[1] The identification of eight rain lords according to the eight compass directions of a wind rose may have been influenced by mariners' compasses found on European ships frequenting ports in the Gulf of Paria and on the Island of Trinidad (see above, p. 76).

historical figure of the *cabo* and the terrifying impression he must have made on mission Warao, shamans seem to have sublimated his character and endowed it with otherworldly power.

Elevating the historical *cabo* to the stature of a mythical personage, however, may not have been the result of a direct associative transfer, for, as indicated by its ritual restrictiveness, in the Warao language *kabo* is a loanword. The Warao probably adopted it from the Chaima, the Cariña, the Pemon, and possibly from other Carib-speakers with whom they lived in several colonial missions for lengthy periods of time. In the languages of the various groups, *kapo*, or a form thereof, signifies "sky" (for the Chaima *capo*, see Tauste 1680, 16; for the Pemon and the Acawaio *kapo*, "in the sky," Butt-Colson, pers. comm.; for the Cariña *ka:pu*, see Hoff 1968, 405; for *kapu*, see Ahlbrinck 1931). According to Ahlbrinck (1931, 207), the meaning of Cariña *kapu* can be extended to designate "firmament," "horizon," "clouds," and "heaven." Cariban *kapo* (*capo*, *ka:pu*, *kapu*) is, therefore, cognate with Waraoan *kabo*,[2] and carries the semantic connotation the Spanish homonym *cabo* acquired in Warao rain shamanism. Furthermore, in its meaning "heaven," Cariña *kapu* designates "God's home" (Ahlbrinck 1931, 207), referring, as in Warao rain shamanism, to the cloudy sky as the dwelling place of supernaturals.

Corregidor-Cabo and Rain Shaman

In the context of colonial history, the rain shaman of the Warao is in many respects like the *cabo* (corregidor) of the mission. In his initiatory trance experience, the shaman is inducted by the governor of the rain lords and functions as their representative on earth. Through this enlistment he becomes the lord's peer, that is, a *kabo*. Similar to the official role of the colonial *cabo,* the shaman's function is to promote selfless congeniality and enforce rules for proper conduct among the members of his community. He demands respect, expects succorance, and punishes wrongdoers with hunger,

---

[2] In Waraoan the phoneme /p/ is limited to word-medial position and its pronounciation varies from [p] to [b] according to regional dialectical usage.

sickness, and death, which he calls down upon them from heaven. He may not be feared as much as his colonial counterpart was, but, like him, the rain shaman exercises great coercive power.

Communal Sago Repository

The Warao's experience with communal food reserves in colonial storehouses resembles that of their present-day descendants in the central delta, who store sago in their sanctuaries. Local groups with able-bodied members contribute large amounts of sago to a common reserve in the village silo, so that less able groups and incapacitated individuals receive a ration in the rainy seasons. Like the *cabo* or corregidor of colonial times, the rain shaman does not personally work to provide the food. But respect for his office and fear of his latent power bring forth the labor required for its procurement. The sago deposit in the temple is carefully protected by the shamans, and the resident directional god posts a sentinel in the form of *himabaka,* the mantis spirit, armed with such European weapons as halberds and sabers. As the personal enforcers of the northern and the southern gods, the *himabaka* function like the military *cabos* of the colonial governor.

Cofradia and Priest-Shamanism

Each subtribe of the central-delta Warao may be seen as a cofradia whose principal priest-shaman (*kanobo arima*) serves as its alcalde. The local priest-shamans (*wishiratu*) of constituent subtribal bands are members of the cofradia, dedicated to either the northern, the southern, or the eastern ancestral spirit (*kanobo*) as to a patron saint. The main purpose of this sodality is to pay tribute to its god with offerings of tobacco and sago and with the celebration of annual festivities. In return, the villagers, or cofradia members as it were, expect to be aided by their god in this life and in the hereafter.[3] In any event, however, as in Mexican *moyordomías*, present-day membership in the Warao cofradia is open to all men of the village.

---

[3] I plan to elaborate on this idea in a separate study that will deal with Warao shamanism as a whole and with its historical relationship to conversion.

In the central delta region they are expected to pledge themselves annually, with their families, at the foundation ceremony of the *nahanamu* (sago festival). Continuity of the brotherhood lies in the image (sacred rock) resembling the saint (divine patron) and in the group's priest-shamans who take care of it throughout the year, not in a set of statutes as in Spain (Foster 1953b, 19).

Guilds and Craftsmen

Similarly, craftsmen in modern Warao society may be seen representing guilds that are organized around an initiated master craftsman and his less competent, uninitiated artisans of the same craft (Wilbert 1993, 25–86). The guilds emphasize both the material and the economic aspects of daily life, and each guild member pledges to a particular deity, hoping that when he dies he will join his patron and his deceased predecessors (guild brothers) in the deity's heaven, wherever it may be located in the Warao universe. As in colonial mission pueblos, the number of specialists in modern Warao subtribes and bands is often small, and the presence of guilds, whose membership embraces both living and deceased brothers, is more covert than overt. But despite the inconspicuousness of guilds, attributes characteristic of them are clearly discernible in craftsmen like basket weavers and carpenters of canoes who relate to a deified power. For example, basket weavers are aligned with Mawari at the zenith, canoe carpenters with Dauarani at the southern solstice, and specialists like players of the sacred trumpet with Isimoi Arani of the northern solstice (Wilbert 1975c; 1977a; 1977b; 1993, 263–70). These artisans and specialists are oftentimes initiated commoners who seek to excel at their craft and strive for a life after death in the heavens of their supernatural sponsors, even though they are not practicing shamans. This system would also explain the bias in Warao culture against female specialists like hammock makers and herbalists, though a feeling of guild sodality attaches to female occupations as well. Yet, I have never met a woman practicing any of these specialties who had undergone the kind of religious initiation a male craftsman does. And I doubt that any of them would aspire to live near a supernatural patron after death. This bias was of course built into the whole concept of "brother"-hoods in Spain and other European countries, where skill training was typical for men rather than for women. There is no need to elaborate on the gender bias against women in colonial Europe and the colonies.

Like their European prototypes, the memberships of Warao cofradias and guilds overlap; only the emphasis of each sodality changes. Thus, subtribal Warao cofradias, like barrio cofradias in Cobán, Guatemala, for instance, are regionally segregated (Gouband et al. 1947, 119); they include professional guilds without apparently preempting them, as in Cherán, Mexico (Beals 1946, 132; Foster 1953b, 19). So it is, too, with the player of the sacred trumpet. As a musician he belongs to both the cofradia of his subtribe and the guild of professional musicians, serving Isimoi Arani, the *Ur*-mother of the instrument, as his patroness and expecting to join her and his deceased predecessors after death.

Lay Brother and Ritual Trumpeter

As will have become apparent, the lay brother of the mission and his functions coincide to a significant degree with the ritual trumpeter of Warao society and the role he plays at the annual sago festival. Both are expert practitioners who are connected through their art with the supernatural world. The lay brother is a religious but not an ordained priest, and the trumpeter is a religious but not an initiated shaman. His music summons the community to the *nahanamu* ceremonies in the rainy season, when the communal sago reserves, prepared during the harvest ritual in the dry season, are distributed. As the lay brother in the mission, the trumpet player pays serious attention to the meteorological conditions that govern the climate in the Orinoco Delta. During the long dry season he forms his cuadrillas of laborers who are to fill the sago reservoir in the community temple, just as the lay brother summoned his work teams during the sowing season to replenish the maize reserves in the community storehouse.

Brotherhoods and Ancestral Cult

In connection with the eschatological purpose of the communal food reserves in colonial times, it is worthwhile to reconsider the ancestor cult and the ritual sago reserves in temples in the central delta.

The most outward sign of this cult is the sacred trumpet or *isimoi*. Although it is technically a clarinet, I refer to it as a trumpet, because it is related to the so-called sacred-trumpet complex of lowland South America and because it seems to have been modeled (as noted earlier) on the European instrument. Its resemblance to the trumpet, as taught in colonial missions, lies mainly in the overall form and specifically in the waxen bell attached to the resonance chamber (fig. 3.8). Also reminiscent of mission practice is the instruction in playing the instrument which young men receive from the player of the sacred trumpet. Schomburgk (1847–48, 1:152) comments on the "Spanish Warao" of what is now Guyana:

> As a matter of fact every Warrau settlement has its own music master, *hoho-hit*, who teaches the young boys and men of the place to blow a kind of oboe. . . . Almost every evening the young men collect around their teacher, and under his guidance hold a concert in the middle of the settlement. According to the size of the bamboo stem and its reed, the height of or depth of the sound varies. A movement of the hand, a nod with the head, or a time beat with the instrument from the side of the *hoho-hit* to that of the musicians, either to commence or to chime in, regulates the whole concert. Although. . .each instrument only gives one note, the musical director knows the tone of the combined instruments exactly, and gives the directions so correctly, that a basis of harmony rules the sound. . . . [Translation by Roth 1924, 461; see also Appun 1868, 896.]

South American Indians play clarinets with resonance chambers as well as globular trumpets during fertility rituals and funeral ceremonies; the *isimoi* of the delta Warao fits into the same context as an instrument reserved exclusively for the ancestor cult of the sago festival. Emphasizing the *isimoi*-death relationship even more strongly is the idea that the denizens of the Warao underworld play clarinets with blowtubes made of human tibia and resonance chambers fashioned out of human skulls. Ethnographical pieces of this kind are known from the Huanyam on the São Miguel River in Rondônia, Brazil, who fashion an instrument out of a human long bone to which they affix a bell modeled in wax (Métraux 1948, 405; Izikowitz 1935, 233, fig. 113).

Both the sago store in the temple and the food depot in the mission have the ultramundane purpose of connecting the world of the living with the world of the dead. The mission store provided support for the widow and orphans and paid for the funeral of the dead man, properly blessed by the padre and protected by the patron saint of the mission. The sago store in a delta community guarantees the well-being of ancestors, and implicitly that of the living after they die, under the protection of their locally recognized patron god. Bridging the two worlds is the sacred trumpet, representing the Mother of Sago, patroness of the "cofradia" of ritual trumpeters in the subtribal community.

Colonial Pattern and Warao Analogue

To summarize this comparative account, I reiterate that, for a little more than a century, large numbers of Warao have had more or less intensive contact with colonial missionaries, colonists, and members of other ethnic groups in regions west and south of the Orinoco Delta (see appendix). The degree of participation in and exposure to colonization and evangelization seems to have been significant enough for the Warao to have retained, in their historical consciousness, the trauma of their experience and to have incorporated it into their religious life and overall culture. More specifically, a remarkable congruency exists between the pattern of the colonial mission and frontier life, on the one hand, and aspects of Warao weather shamanism and sago ritual on the other (table 5.1).

TABLE 5.1
Colonial Pattern and Warao Analogue

Colonial Pattern	*Warao Analogue*
Village cabildo of hierarchical officeholders	Subtribal cabildo of hierarchical officeholders
	Cabildo of Lords of Rain
Corregidor or *cabo*	Rain shaman
Communal food depot	Communal sago depot
Cofradia	Local subtribal group
Guilds	Careers of craftsmen
Capuchin lay brother	Player of sacred trumpet
Brotherhoods	Ancestor cult

The village cabildo or council as a form of local government was introduced by the Capuchins in colonial times to the Warao and to all other aboriginal societies in northeastern Venezuela and beyond. The Warao, in turn, seem to have applied the cabildo organization to the Lords of Rain, who constitute a council of eight ranked peers. They are described as light-skinned foreigners who hold Spanish titles and who live and function like Europeans and Criollos. When prodded by the rain shaman, they punish any untoward behavior of the members of their community or local group.

The corregidor and the *cabo* were local magistrates who wielded tremendous power. Like the rain shaman they coerced villagers into leading a life supportive of both the spiritual and the material well-being of their communities. Among other functions, the corregidor (*cabo*), like his contemporary counterpart the rain shaman, instigated the annual production of a food reserve.

Legalized by Ferdinand and Isabella, cofradias, or religious brotherhoods, and gremios, or craftsmen's guilds, were introduced by the Spaniards into the New World. Colonial monastic orders like the Franciscans and their branches (Capuchins, Observants), who were in charge of the missions of Cumaná, Píritu, and Guayana, actively promoted their creation. Cofradias were also operative in mission settlements occupied by Warao. Contemporary local groups of the Warao resemble cofradias, functioning under ranked priest-shamans as alcaldes and embracing all male members of a community. Distinct characteristics of guilds can be discerned in the modern Warao institution of professional careers, featuring specialties in canoe carpentry, basket weaving, and ritual trumpet playing. Women's careers as hammock makers and herbalists seem to be less well established. With his living coprofessionals, each craftsman or specialist relates to a group of ancestral career men of the same specialty and aspires, like a guild brother, to an afterlife in the company of a patron deity or saint. To achieve this goal, Warao career people adhere to a strict code of ethics which governs their actions as contributors to the prosperity of their communities and their performance as excellent craftsmen.

As a professional musician, the ritual trumpeter of the Warao seems to have much in common with the lay brother of the Capuchin order. Both men are religious practitioners, but the trumpeter, who receives instructions from the ranking priest-shaman, is not a shaman himself and the lay brother, who receives instructions from the local padre, is not a priest. As was customary for the brother, the trumpeter organizes the annual work teams, or cuadrillas, of communal laborers to provide a store of emergency food. Inasmuch as the missionary's supply provided for the widows and orphans of deceased men and paid for proper funeral arrangements of cofradia and guild members, the provision was of ultramundane significance. Similarly, the sago store prepared by the ritual trumpeter is of eschatological import, as it connects his community with the ancestral world.

Syncretistic Renewal

Comparison of the Warao's atmospheric lore with that of other South American societies has yielded two important observations: (1) Warao weather religion is essentially rooted in South American cosmology; (2) nevertheless, it includes important features surrounding the rain gods' complex and the *nahanamu* version of the sago ritual that are of foreign origin. Comparison of these anomalies with the colonial mission system has shown them to be exotic elements of European derivation, syncretistically adapted to the autochthonous atmospheric beliefs of the Warao.

Thus, the existence of directionally aligned weather beings in Warao cosmology is not extraordinary for South America. Nor is the fact that they live on mountaintops and in cloud-darkened skies, whence their voices sound like thunder, their sweat and urine fall like rain, and their staffs explode in lightning flashes. Even the monstrous size of the ranking male and female pair of beings is not unique, nor are the facts that the gods are anger-driven, are responsive to the shaman's threats, and regulate the people's food supply. Instead, what does stand out as nonindigenous is that the Lords of Rain—though superimposed on traditional weather denizens like Kanamuno and Tarita—are whites who live in Western-style houses, dress in long robes, wear eyeglasses and sandals, smoke elbow pipes, and employ guards who brandish European weaponry. Distinctly related to the ancestral Warao's acquaintance with the political organization of mission pueblos and frontier villages is the hierarchical structure of the rain gods, which emulates cabildos, including a power-differentiated nomenclature of statuses and roles. That the rain lords are referred to as *cabo* is probably only accidentally owing to Spanish influence; primarily it appears to have originated in contact with Carib-speaking mission Indians.

From a comparative South American perspective, neither is the existence of a specialized rain shaman in Warao society unique. His apotropaic weather regulatory function and his techniques in implementing it are common on the subcontinent. What is foreign about the Father of Rain, however, is that he uses his magic power like a divine rod to punish deviants and to exact obedience to his rules. This is not to say that the belief in a shaman's compelling power is uncommon in South America, but that its sociopolitical impact on a basically egalitarian forager society is remarkable. Fear of the rain shaman's lethal faculty to cause weather diseases, hunger, and death by starvation, exposure, or lightning is strong enough to enforce congenial behavior and to make men and women do strenuous communal labor to produce surplus food for later consumption and for the common good. True, it is not so much the rain shaman as the player of the sacred trumpet who ritually directs the harvest ceremony. And the trumpeter, backed by the priest-shaman, the directional gods (not the rain lords), and their halberd-wielding servants, would conceivably be able to muster the work force needed to replenish the sago repository. But to animate the men and women for so altruistic a task is certainly made easier, thanks to the coercive power vested in the rain shaman, and the two practitioners complement and reinforce each other like the benevolent and the malevolent faculties of a shaman. That is why the offices of the trumpeter and the rain shaman can be held so effectively by the same person simultaneously. Apparently, the concentration of extraordinary power in the hands of the rain shaman is itself a carry-over from the position of the colonial corregidor, whose modern counterpart the rain shaman seems to be. Without such empowerment, Warao weather shamanism would be less efficient in carrying out its socioeconomic mandate.

Forming part of a wide-ranging complex of sacred wind instruments (flutes, trumpets, clarinets), the sacred trumpet of the Warao is of pre-Columbian ancestry. Its function within an ancestral cult is not unusual for South America (Hugh-Jones 1987, 547; Reichel-

Dolmatoff 1989) and, notwithstanding postmission modifications, the instrument, as noted, is formally not unique. What appears to have been incorporated into the Warao *isimoi* complex, however, is the identification of the trumpet player as professional musician as well as possessor of a degree of formal political authority that allows him, like his lay brother counterpart of the missions, to enforce cooperation and to organize communal labor. Similar to that of the rainmaker, the office of the Warao windmaker has become a syncretistic institution, combining features of the South American sacred trumpet complex with aspects of Capuchin mission organization and practice.

To have musicians and artisans with well-defined careers and small-scale groups of foragers or village farmers who are governed by cabildos of appointed political officers is certainly uncharacteristic for South American lowland cultures. These political and professional offices were shown to have resulted from mission interference and influence, whether direct or indirect. Characteristically, however, Warao culture transformed the secular careers of mission craftsmen into religious vocations of shamanic artisans (Heinen 1993, 178).

Finally, there is the practice of large-scale food storage for lean times. Of course, it is entirely feasible that the Warao, like climatically stressed peoples throughout the Americas, developed the technique of their own accord. It is equally possible that sago storage among the Warao represents an adaptation of the aboriginal Amazonian farming practice of storing large supplies of sun-dried or toasted manioc flour and/or loaves for consumption in the rainy season. Packing them in leaf-lined baskets, native agriculturalists save these provisions on raised shelves in their family quarters or on the ground near the central posts inside their communal houses. The Warao store palm sago in similar leaf-lined baskets, and it is peculiar that they employ the Arawakan term for manioc, "*ure*," to designate sago, distinguishing between moriche-derived (*ohidu aru*) and true or manioc-derived (*aru witu*) flour.

Having said this, however, it is opportune to point to a number of differences that exist between sago storage of the Warao and manioc storage of Amazonian farmers. Sago storage is carried out by the member communities or bands of an entire subtribe of the Warao, while manioc storage among agricultural Indians takes place within the confines of the family. *Nahanamu* (*noara*) storage involves a sociopolitically structured harvesting procedure, while manioc storage entails a less organized economic routine. Significantly, sago storage among the Warao unfolds in a complex religious and ritualized context, while Amazonian village farmers go about storing and saving their manioc reserves in a purely secular way. Family-based secular sago harvesting and storage may have been practiced by pre-mission Warao as well. But, under such individualistic economic conditions, the weak would have succumbed to food stress and starvation in larger numbers than under the system of cooperative solidarity enforced by the rain shaman.

It is precisely these organizational and conceptual differences, however, that identify the practice of sago storage in subtribal Warao temples with the establishment of food repositories in colonial mission villages. Provisioning the colonial storehouse, like supplying the temple store, was a communal responsibility. The political and organizational aspects of food procurement were practically identical in both the tribal and the mission contexts. Food production and storage in the mission was organized by the corrigidor, who appointed and scheduled the cuadrillas of workers. In tribal communities, similar work teams are selected and scheduled by the trumpet player for the foundation ritual of the *nahanamu* cycle. Adhering to the food depot in the mission was an eschatolgical component pertaining to deceased husbands and fathers. Similarly, the food reserves in the Warao temple provide for the living as well as for the ancestors of the group. The ritual adaptation of the procedure to its ancestor cult represents a specific spin Warao culture has given the technique in the course of the adaptive process.

The refinement of possibly precontact practices of harvesting and storage or the institutionalization of such procedures through adoption from Europeans became practical for the Warao because of the opportune convergence of need and event. Adopted were mainly the technical and organizational aspects of the practice and less so its ulterior religious purpose. Instead, the secular dimensions of the cultural borrowing served the Warao by reinforcing the ideational tenets of their autochthonous ancestor cult, so that implementation of more efficient winter provisioning by the central Warao and possibly other subtribal groups stabilized both their socioeconomic and their value systems. This improvement made their people less vulnerable to seasonal hunger and starvation and enabled them to become even more deeply entreched in the sanctuary of their homeland. It is my contention, therefore, that the adoption by the sacred trumpet player of the lay brother's technique of surplus food production and preservation, the transfer of the corregidor's power to the rain shaman, and the assimilation of the cabildo to the rain gods, have immeasurably contributed to the survival of preagricultural Warao society and culture. As a powerful external influence, these innovations have had a major impact on traditional climatic beliefs and, through a process of adaptive reformation, have recast Warao weather religion into a new syncretistic practice of high survival value.

Chapter Six

Mindful of Famine

The difficulties of human survival in the Orinoco Delta make it abundantly clear that Warao weather religion was designed to protect the Indians from seasonal hunger and recurrent famine. Climatic mythology, rain magic, and sago ritual all function to avert alimentary problems and to promote behavior conducive to attainment of this goal. The natural efficacy of religious climatology may, of course, be questioned, here as everywhere, but its cultural significance for Warao survival is indisputable (Berry et al. 1971).

As to the environmental adaptability of Warao culture, the Indians clearly understood that safety through geographic isolation necessitated the adoption of a self-sufficient life-style. Isolated in the Orinoco Delta, the Warao were obliged to inventory the area's finite potential and to relay this information across successive generations. While oral history enumerates the resources of deltaic microenvironments (Wilbert 1979, 139–44; Lévi-Strauss 1966, 184), a special oral literature, the earlier mentioned *namonina a re* ("transformation stories"), forms a separate genre of etiological cosmology (Lavandero 1971, 43). This genre, detailing certain features of the environment, may specify how a particular tree, for instance, has developed out of a prior form, why it grows here rather than elsewhere, why it looks the way it does, whether it is used for food or for raw material or both, and who are its "companions," that is, what plants, birds, animals, and spirits are found in its vicinity. Significantly, instead of a transcendent god who created the world by divine fiat, the *namonina* lore of the Warao reveals an immanent creative principle which operates through metamorphosis. Although mythology presents much of the manifest world as a given, large parts of its inventory are described as stemming from earlier forms. Warao transformation lore is thus ecological mythology, a blueprint of interrelationships between humans and their environment which reveals a treasure of adaptive wisdom and which is invaluable for the preservation of their way of life. Narrators, acclaimed for their knowledge of transformation myths, choose to relate samples of their repertoire at dawn or at dusk, when people tend to be at home in their open houses. The systematic practice of public storytelling exposes the society continuously to its existential knowledge, turning *namonina* narrating into an instrument of adaptation to a marginal biome.

Weather wisdom is also found in the domains of the priest-shaman (*wishiratu*), the light shaman (*bahanarotu*), and the dark shaman (*hoarotu*). The lore of these specialties relates strongly to issues of health and curing of endemic and exotic diseases, including weather-related pathologies purported to be mediated by rainmakers. To reinforce these coping mechanisms of narrative art and medical lore, the Warao developed a complex weather religion, as described in the volume at hand. Commensurate with the magnitude of their habitat's environmental challenge, it signals an unconditional imperative of survival: adaptation to the drenching downpours of a double rainy season in a sodden tidal swamp. Aggravating the hydraulic challenge were the botanical qualities of the moriche palm, the Warao's principal source of food. Its availability was shown to stand in an inverse relationship to precipitation: the more rain, the less sago. Heavy regional rains as well as local storms thus presented the daunting prospects of chronic affliction and endemic famine.

Hunger's Dragging Loincloth

To the Warao, hunger caused by seasonal shortages of food is no stranger. So familiar are they with its intermittent appearances that they picture Hunger, along with Anger and Death, as personified members of an apocalyptic trio. Hunger is a relentless stalker whose lurking presence is perceived through alimentary anxiety and the terror of starvation. The strength of his limbs and organs and the efficacy of his paraphernalia diminish in proportion to the energy acquired by people through nutrition. He thrives when humans starve and sickens when they eat. During the foundation ceremony of the harvest festival (*nahanamu*), when sago is abundant, defiant participants throw pieces of bread at Hunger to make him retreat from their camp (Osborn 1960, 80).

> According to a Warao story, the adults of a settlement who once went fishing, left their hungry offspring at home. While waiting for their parents to return with food, the children were visited by Hunger. He was like a man dressed in a dragging loincloth. When questioned, the children informed the visitor that their parents had gone to catch *morocoto* and *cachama* fish. Hunger laughed. "Ha, ha, ha! To me these fish are like the Criollos," he said, dragging his loincloth while dancing about. The children had no idea whence their visitor had come. When their father returned they told him about the stranger. He immediately suspected that the visitor was Hunger himself. "Tomorrow," he said, "I will go to gather manaca palm fruit and palm cabbage of manaca and moriche. Should Hunger return, make sure you cut off his loincloth. If he has his way, the loincloth will grow throughout the world and all people will starve."
>
> When Hunger did return the next day, the children told him where their father had gone. Again the visitor laughed and said, "Manaca fruits are actually my eyes. Heart of manaca makes me weak, heart of moriche is my pale arm, and the grubs of the moriche beetle are my curing rattle." He laughed again and once more danced about, trailing his loincloth behind him. Then he ran into the forest, and the loincloth shimmered and shone. He never returned.

Humans can see Hunger only when they are starving, for that is when he is likely to return. "We would lose our senses because of Hunger; when he appears as a man, we go out of our minds" (Osborn 1960, 73–74; see also Wilbert 1970, 166–67).

Natural Cause of Food Uncertainty

The natural cause of food uncertainty in the Orinoco Delta is meteorologically based on the translation back and forth of the intertropical convergence zone. Hunger makes his appearance during the rainy seasons when, in preagricultural times, the Warao ran out of food. During that period Warao economy was based on moriche sago, even though they and their prehistoric ancestors had been surrounded by Arawakan and Cariban horticulturalists for hundreds and possibly thousands of years, and despite the fact that many Warao groups had lived and farmed with representatives of these agricultural societies in the colonial missions. Unquestionably, therefore, they must have been familiar with cultivation. Yet the limitations imposed by the ecology of the delta and the unsuitability of available crops to the delta's swampy terrain inhibited them. Swidden agriculture, especially in the lower delta, became viable only after a tuber known as *ocumo chino,* or taro (*Colocasia antiquorum*), had been introduced around the turn of the century. Taro was well adapted to this superhumid land: it had no seasonal limitations, was easily planted, and required only a reasonable amount of care during cultivation (Heinen and Ruddle 1974, 119). As revealed by aerial photography, however, in the early 1930s cultivation was practiced only by the Warao living south of the Araguao River (map 1.2). The delta's central and western regions were then still inhabited by nonagricultural gatherers of moriche starch (Holker 1983). In any event, the natural cause of food uncertainty traditionally rested in the interrelationship (described earlier), between prevailing atmospheric conditions and the botanical cycle of sago production.

Anger and Fear

To keep Hunger at bay, the Warao cater to the wishes of the rain shaman and abide by his rules. Not only do they provide for him, they also encourage him to abstain from hard work to avoid injury and from going into the forest where he might be angered by bites and stings. In fact, anger as an emotional reaction to extreme discomfort lies at the root of Warao rain shamanism. It is recognized as a dangerously destabilizing factor which inevitably and with quasi-supernatural force seeks requital. Like Hunger, Anger is personified in Warao mythology as an uninvited guest, for in ancient times there was no anger (Wilbert 1970, 288–89). Anger came down from the sky, where frustrated shamans and other people had been left behind at the time when their fellowmen descended to earth. As a newcomer, he walked about until he reached the house of certain Warao, where he sat down in a hammock and stared at those present. His gaze infused them with so much anger that men began to beat their wives. Nowadays, anyone who becomes angry gives expression to Anger's nature by losing his or her temper in unreasonable irritability or revengeful rage. Feelings of anger can be pent up only for so long, and the Indians dread the moment when they erupt in fury and demand "payment" in compensation for corporal and mental suffering. Anger, especially of this kind, is precipitated by the environmental stresses of the rainy seasons, when husbands are prone to beat their wives for little reason, parents assail children with uncommon severity, and children break out in chronic crying.

Warao rain shamanism operates within this framework of anger. The rage of hungry people is the rage of the rain gods. The wrathful gods throw tantrums for hearing themselves accosted by the rain shaman. Succumbing to his goading by imagery of rejection, hatred, aggression, and violence, they retaliate with summary chastisement through similarly pain-causing rain. Rather than bestowing life-giving virtues from heaven, as in other parts of the world, rain in the delta drowns the land in darkness, spreading death and disease. Precipitation pertains to the night sky of the rain lords, the twilight of the western underworld, the chthonic darkness of the primeval ocean, and the depth of disease-bearing Orinoco floods. As such it is associated with dim-visioned necromancers and the pale underbelly of mental life. It deals with cannibal gods, devastating thunderers, man-snatchers, shapeshifters, and the bane of the alligator's pernicious fang. The hurt is reciprocal and deep-seated in gods, spirits, and humans alike. And rain is the vehicle for their resentment and vindictiveness.

In addition, there is the anger of the weak and disadvantaged: the anguish of raped rain maidens, the frustration of thwarted lovers, the insecurity of an uprooted rainbow husband, and the bereavement of women lamenting the death of their loved ones. Anguished symbolism permeates the water that falls to the earth as the urine, sweat, and tears of these embittered protagonists and is considered harmful to man. To get even for all the suffering sustained, it causes misery and havoc.

Within this complex of weather lore, the rain gods reveal themselves as expressions of the Warao's historic consciousness, infused with deep-seated anger and fueled by feelings of uncertainty and profound *Lebensangst*. As projections of the anxious mind, the rain lords join the assembly of directional gods around the world who owe their existence to food anxiety and existential fears, as well as to a host of other threats to survival that haunt the tribal memory. The gods reflect the assorted pre- and postcontact invaders (chapter 2), who posed serious challenges to Warao survival. Man-eating Carib neighbors, for instance, turned into denizens of the western underworld. Exotic pestilences were personified by directional gods (Wilbert 1983). Colonial slavers and soldiers were projected into the sky as armed enforcers of the northern and southern gods (*himabaka*), who keep humans in bondage and subtribal vassalage behind their respective priest-shamans. Terrorizing corregidors and *cabos* of the mission era found themselves transferred into the cloudy skies of the rain lords. In short, existential fear, which these powerful historical actors and their supernatural projections have provoked, has encumbered the Warao's existence throughout time, enabling them to recognize altruism as the most effective bulwark against such existential perils. Not surprisingly, Warao enculturation aims at suppressing egotistic tendencies and at instilling, instead, a modal attitude of magnanimity: not only does a society of generous people provide insurance for aging rainmakers and other vulnerable members (children, pregnant and nursing women, elderly commoners) of society; on a more general level, altruism supplants egotism, one of the known triggers of famine. To maintain low levels of rancorous deportment and a spirit of resource sharing, Warao culture developed a number of cathartic mechanisms that allow pent-up anger to be ventilated in institutionalized forms of aggression and in controlled outbursts of personal hostility.

Outbursts pertaining to Warao weather lore include, for instance, the dueling with rectangular shields between the heroes Earthquake and Armadillo at the beginning of time. However, their fight does not merely recall a mythological event that explains the origin of land and sea breezes. It is a current convention that permits two champions of opposing settlement groups (and any other man of either party who feels compelled to participate) to settle intergroup conflict in a nonlethal way. The men of each settlement confront one another with their shields and engage in paired shoving duels. The women on both sides execute verbal duels prior to and during the actual event, and they may even become entangled in brief outbursts of bodily aggression, such as hair pulling and fist blows. Only the two champions, however, have a really serious contest, in which the ego of the toppled fighter is bruised more hurtfully than his body. Nobody keeps score, and the overpowered opponent gets back on his feet to continue the fight until both men are physically exhausted and emotionally drained. Before separating in the late afternoon, and in emulation of the food-gift exchanges practiced by courting sun bitterns (i.e., thunderbirds), the opposing teams and their families often share a common meal. When the visitors depart with their battered shields, there have been no winners and no losers in this contest of ritualized aggression, just as there was no winner and no loser in the primordial shield fight between Huru, the earthquake (land breeze), and Oka, the armadillo (sea breeze), which ended in a draw between equals. Instead, friendships have been renewed and a cooperative attitude has been restored for the sacred trumpet player to rely on in the next season of ritual sago production.

Anticipatory Preventive

Long-range experience with hunger and starvation has thus taught the Warao that cooperative behavior constitutes an essential prerequisite in coping with the fear and the anxiety occasioned by periodic stresses. To institute and then to continue the annual foundation ceremony of the harvest festival as their most crucial hedge against critical food shortage, rainmakers, trumpet players, and other tribal leaders have relied, and in some local groups continue to rely, on the altruistic disposition of the members of their group. Every year during the primary dry season, when conspicuous consumption is the order of the day and environmental stress is at a minimum, they must sensitize their people to the transitory nature of plenty and make them perceive the dangers of a rainy season months down the road. I submit that the success story of postcontact Warao survival in the central delta, and possibly in other nonagricultural groups, has rested so far on the trumpet player's foundation ceremony, which he conducted in anticipation of the advent of a crisis of high or possibly extreme pressures. Rarely in lowland South America does one come across another example like this one, in which the long-range carry-over experience of recurring food shortages has introduced such an anticipatory component into a hunter-gatherer society's adaptive behavior, incorporating it into their biological regime (Bennett 1976a, 1976b; Braudel 1967, 38; Keys et al. 1950). Prior to the adoption of this crucial mechanism of famine prevention, food crises in the rainy seasons must have found communities so lacking in staples and so incapacitated by hunger and disease that mounting a collective effort beyond the household level to counteract the danger would have been impossible (Jelliffe and Jelliffe 1971). Instead, it has here been suggested that this technically, socially, and ritually sophisticated preventive strategy became institutionalized among the morichal-bound Warao as a result of the acculturative influence of colonial mission life (among Europeans, Criollos, and agricultural Indians) and because the modernizers recognized its advantage in mitigating the annual suffering and decimation precontact generations must have undergone. In addition to adopting the logistic and technical innovation of systematic procurement and storage of surplus food, however, the Warao needed to assimilate and perpetuate, through enculturation, the overwhelming existentialistic dread associated with the mission experience. In the absence of a strong traditional locus of political authority, this fear could serve as a powerful catalyst to rally the community behind their weather shamans and ritual trumpeters in support of a practice of surplus food procurement and extended storage. Furthermore, and in addition to this strategic innovation, the Warao adopted the custom of inviting to their sago-distribution feast the ranking members of neighboring subtribes and their families. The practice of maintaining extended friendships of this kind enhanced their atmospherically sensitive local food security by widening the safety net of social relationships (Minnis 1985, 8).

Repeated experiences have shown the Warao that, while the lack of sago may trigger a food crisis (with a high death toll) or a famine (with a catastrophic death toll), certain personal and social symptoms of famine are part and parcel of the famine syndrome and are equally dangerous. That is the reason why the weather shaman enforces cooperative behavior by instilling fear of personal symptoms like disease, loss of body weight, and malnutrition, and of the degradation of the consumption of emergency food like *temiche* sago, which is believed to be normally prepared by monkeys and inhabitants of the netherworld (Alamgir 1981, 20–21). Throughout the year, the weather shaman admonishes the people that these symptoms will be brought on and will be aggravated by selfish behavior. As an alternative, he champions a positive attitude toward resource sharing and redistribution and attempts to uphold altruism as a most important preventive of hunger and famine. The warning that selfish behavior will be punished by summoning the rain lords and by threatening to turn people into lightning rods is usually sufficient to effect compliance. If not, the rainmaker will identify the next storm as the one he conjured up as punishment for misconduct by destroying the sago or inflicting weather-connected discomfort and disease.

Disruption of cultural integrity as a social symptom of famine is repeatedly warned against in Warao weather lore. Young rainbow husbands who, living with their in-laws, become homesick are ridiculed by earth people. Young men are warned against the temptation of subtribal exogamy and the fatal consequences of a stranger's embrace. The invasion of the delta by people under Huru (Earthquake) presents the disquieting prospect of territorial war, in itself not an uncommon trigger or concomitant of famine in other parts of the world. Intergroup conflict is still settled, as noted, by shield fights, rather than by battle. The nonlethal matches thwart animosity, thereby preventing the breakdown of subtribal solidarity and the dissolution of family bonds, two major contributing factors to famine. Exogamous bands integrate endogamous subtribes and are encouraged to pledge increased sago quotas for the common good. Thus, Warao weather lore identifies the gamut of symptoms (environmental, health, personal, psychological, sociocultural) of the famine syndrome. Through oral art, rain shamanism, and sago ritual the Indians call upon a fund of related experiences to correct untoward attitudes and antisocial behavior. Meeting famine head-on in this fashion permits corrective monitoring of the famine symptoms on a continuous, incremental basis and the elimination of problems before they escalate into a major crisis. By overcoming natural food shortages through anticipatory action, neutralizing potential famine triggers by appropriate enculturation, and lessening food anxiety through ritual practices, Warao society has created a distinctive form of weather religion with institutionalized famine management that enables its rain shaman and its sacred trumpeter to ameliorate the consequences of periodic hunger and to forestall catastrophic starvation.

Warao weather religion evolved as a major adaptive institution designed to cope with an overpowering threat to personal and social survival (Wilbert 1975b, 1985). In responding to this challenge, the Indians marked egotism as quintessential transgressive behavior and placed selfishness into the moral sphere. Like many peoples the world over, they, thereby, accepted personal responsibility for altruistic behavior and for the consequences of failing to assume that responsibility (Pagels 1988, 145–47). This attitude provides a degree of causative order to seemingly random natural disasters and supernatural capriciousness. Thus, in times of sickness and widespread distress, when sufferers believe they are experiencing the injurious power of the ancestral gods, shamans make patients recognize their failings and transgressions. By way of ventriloquism or by human proxy the healer sits at his patient's side and dialogues with the sickness-causing spirit, using antiphonal chant. He asks the spirit why he is so angry that he wants to hurt or even kill the patient. And, since neither the afflicted nor any adult members of the community are permitted to sleep during the seance, the complaints of the spirit relating the patient's wrongdoing are enunciated for everybody to hear and to heed. In persuading the spirit to desist and leave the suffering person, the shaman promises reparation on behalf of the patient. Silently agreeing with the spirit's indictment and the shaman's pledge for amends, the patient aids in the cure and expedites the spirit's departure from the body (Barral 1964, 201–5). Suffering physically (by illness) and mentally (by guilt) because of selfish behavior may certainly cause acute pain, but it has given religious practitioners, including weather shamans and even the average lay person, a feeling of control over supernatural powers and divine punishment. Through the projection of terrors like cannibalism, slavery, expatriation, pestilence, mission strongmen, bad weather, and hunger into the supernatural world, these devastating powers were ritually domesticated as ancestral forebears or as kinfolk of the "father of rain," so that, through shamanic action, ritual, and personal comportment, they can be swayed to yield to human coercion and supplication.

Therefore, whereas the basic concept of Warao weather religion may represent no more than a religious orthodoxy of worldwide distribution, its idiosyncratic formulation and syncretic postcolonial reconstruction have enabled the Warao to mythologize a hostile landscape and transform it into a viable homeland for successive generations.

Appendix

The Mission of Cumaná

The Mission of Cumaná (1657–1810), ministered by the Capuchins of the province of Aragón (Spain), began to function in 1657. Its territory embraced the region between the Gulf of Paria and Cumaná and from there in a line leading south-southeast to the Orinoco River, to a point opposite the old town of San Félix. The mission also included, though not officially, the Orinoco Delta. In this region the missionaries founded fifty-six missions, forty-four of them still in existence at the end of missionary work in 1810 (Carrocera 1968, 1:xi–lx); see also map A.1).

Aboriginal groups in the Cumaná mission.—The mission's territory was inhabited by Arawak, Cariña (Carib), Chaima, Coaca (Cuaca), Paria (Pariagoto), and Warao Indians. Of these, the Arawak, who were the least numerous, lived dispersed among the Chaima.

Work in the Mission of Cumaná began with the padres placing the Carib-speaking Chaima, the most numerous people in the province, in various settlements along the coast between Cumaná and the Caripe River. More than half of the settlements thus were inhabited by either separate or mixed Chaima populations. The Chaima cooperated with the padres in their colonizing efforts, and Chaiman was the language best mastered by the missionaries.

All the early attempts of the padres to convert the Cariña living along the Guarapiche River failed. These people rebelled against mission rule and reportedly were at war with most of the other Indian groups in the region. In 1651, when Jesuit missionaries arrived on the Guarapiche River (in Capuchin territory), the Cariña accepted the French because they evangelized the Indians in their homes rather than in mission stations founded for that purpose. The Guarapiche mission, however, lasted less than three years, mainly because the Jesuits and a growing French presence alarmed the Spanish religious and political authorities. After an armed conflict between Spanish and French forces broke out, Capuchin missionaries agreed to pacify the Cariña. Between 1662 and 1669 they established three missions to serve these Indians, but all three were destroyed in a

French-supported Cariña rebellion during the period 1669–1673. Other missions that had been founded for Chaima Indians were also destroyed, as well as several ranches in the area and the village of San Carlos, founded precisely to protect the missions. Eventually, however, the Spanish forces prevailed; the French abandoned their plans for the Guarapiche, and the Cariña withdrew south to join their relatives on the Orinoco. Not until 1754, at Santa Bárbara de Tipirín, did the Capuchins finally succeed in settling Cariña for any length of time.

The Paria of Cariban affiliation, who were few in number, inhabited the peninsula and gulf of the same name. Five of the seven missions founded for Paria Indians were inhabited only by them; they shared the other two with Chaima Indians, whose language they spoke. The Saliva-speaking Coaca lived far from their primary distribution area along the middle Orinoco and the Meta rivers. Only a few of them inhabited the area of the Cumaná mission, and they suffered severely from Carib aggression. In four mission villages Coaca Indians lived alone, but one village they inhabited together with Chaima and Warao.

Finally, the Warao of the Orinoco Delta and adjacent regions northward to the Paria Peninsula were extremely reluctant to settle in mission areas outside their native land. Despite the missionaries' repeated forays into the delta to round up the Warao, no mission post was ever established in the Orinoco Delta in colonial times. The Warao, however, did leave their territory to trade with Indians living at the apex of the delta and on the southern coast of the Paria Peninsula, and many of them were persuaded, or forced, to settle in mission areas. As many as twenty Cumaná mission settlements were either entirely or partly populated by Warao (Carrocera 1968, 1:xxxvii–xl; see also tables A.1 and A.2 and map A.1).

TABLE A.1
Warao Only Missions (Cumaná)

1. Santa Isabel (1739–1752)
2. La Divina Pastora de Catacuao (1751–1754)
3. Nuestra Señora del Rosario de Yaguaraparo (1760–1769)
4. San Judas Tadeo de Maturín (1760)
5. Nuestra Señora de Guía de Uracoa (1784)
6. San Serafín de Tabasca (1784)
7. Divino (Buen) Pastor de Areo (or Guarapiche) (1786)
8. San Rafael de Barrancas (1790)
9. Guaritica (1791)
10. Simara (1784–1790)
11. Cojosanica (1784–1790)
12–16. Five missionaries whose names are unknown.

Appendix

MAP A.1
Colonial missions of Cumaná and Guayana.
(After Carrocera 1968[1]:404–5 and Nectario María 1924;
Drawing by Chase Langford)

Legend to Map A.1

Cumana Missions Inhabited by Warao

1. Santa Isabel (de Soro)
2. La Divina Pastora de Catacuao
3. Nuestra Señora del Rosario de Yaguaraparo
4. San Judas Tadeo de Maturín
5. Nustra Señora de Guía de Uracoa
6. San Serafín de Tabasca
7. Divino (Buen) Pastor de Areo (or Guarapiche)
8. San Rafael de Barrancas
9. Guaritica
10. Simara
11. Cojosanica
12. San Antonio de Padua de Capayacuar
13. Nuestra Señora Santa Ana de Sopocuar
14. La Purisima Concepción de Nuestra Señora de Cocuisas
15. Santa Cruz de Payacuar (or Cumaná)

Guayana Missions Inhabited by Warao

16. San Miguel de Unata
17. Santa Rosa de Maruanta
18. Payaraima
19. Santa Eulalia de Murucuri
20. Santa Cruz de Montecalvario
21. Santa Ana de Puga
22. San Buenaventura de Auguri (Guri)

Villages outside of Cumana and Guayana Missions Inhabited by Warao

23. San Juan Bautista de Buenavista
24. Borbón
25. Carolina
26. Santa Teresa de Orocopiche
27. Santa Rosa de Viterbo de Ocópi
28. Nuestra Señora de los Remedios (Mamo)

Plus five missions of unknown location in Cumaná mission territory.

1. *Santa Isabel* was founded in 1739 with an initial group of thirty Warao families which had originally been settled together with Chaima Indians in the Mission of Irapa on the south shore of the Paria Peninsula, in the hope that their numbers would increase. The mission was short-lived.

2. *La Divina Pastora de Catacuao*, founded in 1751, was given up in 1754 after two padres had been poisoned in two years.

3. *Nuestra Señora del Rosario de Yaguaraparo* was founded in 1760. The first settlers were a group of fifty families; by 1780 there were 360 persons in the mission. Frightened by an earthquake on 20 October 1766 and disturbed by the insufficient numbers of missionary personnel, most of the Indians escaped, although the founder missionary was later able to retrieve some of them. In 1768, however, after nine years of operation, the residents again fled the mission. When more missionaries arrived in 1770, an attempt was made to reopen the mission with five or six Warao families still in the area. Eventually they too ran away and the Capuchins permanently gave up on the mission.

4. *San Judas Tadeo de Maturín* was founded in 1760 and three years later had 151 residents. In 1789 the population of 244 was increased by a number of Chaima, who were brought in to stabilize fugacious Warao.

5. *Nuestra Señora de Guía de Uracoa*, founded in 1784 on the river Uracoa, had 265 residents by September 1789.

6. *San Serafín de Tabasca* was founded in 1784 by a missionary who claimed it had been extremely difficult to extricate the residents from the forests of the Orinoco Delta. But the mission grew rapidly; by 1795 the seventy-two resident families numbered about 288 individuals. The Indians in the mission were enterprising; as early as 1790 they had reportedly become self-sufficient by planting manioc, corn, and plantains, as well as other crops. They also worked in the Criollo villages in the neighborhood.

7. *Divino (Buen) Pastor de Areo* (or *Guarapiche*), founded in 1786, had a population of 283 by 1789.

8. *San Rafael de Barrancas* was founded in 1790. No demographic data are available.

9. *Guaritica* was founded in 1791. No demographic data are available.

10. *Simara* apparently was founded between 1784 and 1790. No demographic data are available.

11. *Cojosanica* was probably founded sometime during the period 1784–1790. No demographic data are available.

12–16. The five additional foundings reported in the mission records lack both names and demographic data. Like La Divina Pastora de Catacuao, they were probably short-lived.

TABLE A.2
Mixed Warao Missions (Cumaná)

1. San Antonio de Padua de Capayacuar (1713)
2. Nuestra Señora Santa Ana de Sopocuar (1714)
3. La Purisima Concepción de Nuestra Señora de Cocuisas (1728)
4. Santa Cruz de Payacuar (or Cumaná) (1716)

1. *San Antonio de Capayacuar*, founded in 1713 for Warao and Chaima Indians, had a population of 556 by 1780.

2. *Nuestra Señora Santa Ana de Sopocuar*, settled with thirty-two Warao families brought there in 1718, had been established in 1714 with seventy Chaima families. Also introduced were the remaining Indians (of unknown origin) of the mission San Miguel de Caripe, destroyed by Cariña in 1718. In 1789 Santa Ana had a population of 170.

3. *La Purisima Concepción de Nuestra Señora de Cocuisas*, founded in 1728 with Warao and Chaima, reported 288 residents in 1789.

4. *Santa Cruz de Payacuar* (or *Cumaná*), founded in 1717, was partly settled with Warao Indians; the non-Warao were of Chaima origin. Prior to 1716 the Warao had been assembled in another mission, Purísima Concepción, which was destroyed and abandoned by the Indians in 1707. The fugitives were recaptured and settled at the Santa Cruz mission, which by 1739 had a population of 112 families, or approximately 500 people. The church was built with alms given by residents of Veracruz, Mexico; the religious icons and paintings came from Veracruz and La Habana. By 1789 the population had dropped to 284.

Thus, as of 1713, the Warao, as residents of twenty settlements (sixteen segregated and four mixed) of the Cumaná mission, had had fairly intensive contact with representatives of several aboriginal groups (Cariña, Chaima, Paria, Saliva) and with Europeans over an approximately eighty-seven-year period.

The Warao had their closest contact with other groups in the Cumaná mission during the years 1760–1810. Excluding the five unknown missions (nos. 12–16), twelve of fifteen foundations including Warao still remained in 1810. Later, in the turbulence of the Venezuelan War of Independence, most of the Warao mission settlements vanished. Nevertheless, the twenty missions inhabited by Warao were about one-third (36 percent) of all fifty-six missions founded by the Aragonese Capuchins.

No statistics are available to gauge the Warao population in the mixed missions, and demographic figures for the settlements established between 1790 and 1810 are also unavailable. In 1780, however, there were forty-four mission pueblos in the Cumaná mission with a total population of

14,016 Indians (Carrocera 1968, 3:454). By 1810, when the Cumaná mission was closed, the total Indian population seems to have increased to about 15,000. During the years of its operation as many as 2,000 to 2,500 Warao may have resided for varying periods of time in the Cumaná mission.

The Mission of Guayana

The Mission of Guayana (1682–1817), ministered by Capuchins from Catalonia (Spain), was originally attached to Trinidad. During its twenty-seven years of effective operation (1687–1714), the Capuchins founded eight Indian missions, but the Warao seem to have been involved only as their occasional attackers (Noel 1972, 21).

In 1724, ten years after its separation from Trinidad, the Mission of Guayana, occasionally called the Mission of Caroní, began to operate on the mainland. Falling under its jurisdiction was a large part of eastern Greater Guiana, from the Atlantic along the right bank of the Orinoco to Angostura or New Guayana (Ciudad Bolívar) to the north, a line from there to the Amazon to the west, the left bank of the Amazon to the south, and the Atlantic coastline to the east. Although the eastern border of the mission province had not been clearly determined, it was really the western border of Dutch Guiana (Essequibo) and, later on, British Guiana (Guyana). Between 1724 and 1817 the Guayana mission founded fifty-two settlements, villages, and towns, some eighteen of them still in existence (Carrocera 1979, 1:xi–xxxii; see also map A.1).

Aboriginal groups in the Guayana mission:—Concentrating on the southeastern part of present-day Venezuela (Guayana), the Capuchins dealt with a variety of aboriginal groups, including Acawaio (Guaica), Cariña (Carib), Guayano, Locono (Arawak), Paria (Pariagoto), Saliva, Warao, and various smaller groups of Pemon origin.

The Carib-speaking Acawaio, a large population, inhabited the region between the Caroní and the confluence of the Cuyuni and the Yuruari rivers. With the Acawaio, the missionaries established five settlements, which endured until 1817. Three villages had mixed populations of Acawaio, Guayano, and Warao Indians.

The Cariña included refugees from the Guarapiche River region of the Cumaná mission who had escaped to the Orinoco after being attacked by the government in an offensive that lasted for three years (1718–1721). Some of the escapees settled south of the Orinoco near the estuaries of the Caroní and Aro rivers. A large number of Cariña lived in the regions of the rivers Cuyuni, Waini, and Aguire. With Cariña of the Sierra de Imataca region, the Capuchins were able to found several missions.

The Arawak-speaking Locono Indians lived along the southern bank of the Orinoco from the delta to the Caroní River. The padres settled Locono in three missions where Guayano and Warao Indians also lived.

The Guayano, a small group, inhabited an area along the southern shore of the Orinoco River, stretching from the delta to the vicinity of New Guayana, as well as parts of the tableland and savanna of Upata. They willingly cooperated with the missionaries.

Small numbers of Paria lived in five missions near Ciudad Guayana and along the banks of the Caroní and Paragua rivers, together with members of other local Carib-speaking groups. Most of these small populations were also represented in Barceloneta (La Paragua), a settlement of Spanish colonists.

The Saliva and several small, mostly Cariban-speaking local groups, were dispersed throughout the mission area.

The Warao were concentrated in missions along the lower Caroní and in villages on the Orinoco near Ciudad Guayana.

TABLE A.3
Warao Only Missions (Guayana)

1. San Miguel de Unata (1735)
2. Santa Rosa de Maruanta (1769)

1. *San Miguel de Unata*, founded in 1735 with 149 individuals, was destroyed soon thereafter by a Cariña raiding party. Later repopulated by Guayano and Locono, the mission had 751 inhabitants in 1816.

2. *Santa Rosa de Maruanta* was founded in 1769 with 150 people taken from the Orinoco Delta in a move sponsored by Governor Don Manuel Centurión Guerrero (1766–1776). In 1770 it had 286 residents, and by 1772 the number had increased to 385.

TABLE A.4
Mixed Warao Missions (Guayana)

3. Payaraima (1725–1740)
4. Santa Eulalia de Murucuri (1754)
5. Santa Cruz de Montecalvario (1760)
6. Santa Ana de Puga (1760)
7. San Buenaventura de Auguri (Guri) (1771)

3. *Payaraima*, founded sometime after 1724, had a population of 298 Arawak, Saliva, and Warao. It was destroyed in 1740 by a raiding party of hostile (Carib?) Indians.

4. *Santa Eulalia de Murucuri*, founded in 1754, was occupied by Cariña and Warao. In 1797 it had 609 Cariña and Warao inhabitants; by 1816 the number had grown to 730.

5. *Santa Cruz de Montecalvario* was founded in 1760 with Warao Indians. By 1761 its population had declined to forty-two because of food shortages. Seven years later, in 1768, its population was 290, including an unspecified number of Saliva. By 1772, 290 Warao and Saliva were residents, and in 1816 the number had grown to 517, including members of both tribes.

6. *Santa Ana de Puga*, founded in 1760 by orders of Governor Centurión, had 493 Arawak and Warao residents, who lived in two abandoned missions (San Juan Joaquín and San Félix). By 1770 its population had decreased to 446. For some time Saliva Indians seem to have joined the mission, but from 1797 on it was inhabited only by Arawak, Cariña, and Warao. In 1816 its population included 578 members of these three groups.

7. *San Buenaventura de Auguri (Guri)* was founded in 1771 for Cariña deserters from Santa Eulalia de Murucuri. The population was later augmented by Acawaio fugitives from other missions and by Warao who had escaped from Calvario. In 1775 San Buenaventura's population was 186, representing all three tribal groups. In 1816 there were 758 Akawaio and Cariña residents.

Warao settlements outside the Cumaná and Guayana missions:—In 1768 Governor Centurión, intent on breaking with the *reducciones* tradition of mission-ruled Indian settlements, sponsored several forays into the Orinoco Delta and regions to its west to extricate and relocate 1,170 Warao in five villages—Buenavista, Borbón, Carolina, Maruanta, and Orocopiche—near Ciudad Guayana (Archivo General de Indias, Leg. 20, fol. 3, V: 1779; Lodares 1930, 2: 241). The Warao population of Santa Rosa de Maruanta increased after the Centurión initiative (as noted above) and the increases at Santa Cruz de Montecalvario may probably be ascribed to the same cause. Two other villages also received Warao contingents as a result of the Centurión initiative, and still other incursions took place (Gómez Cañedo 1967).

Strictly speaking, six of these villages were located on territory assigned to the Mission of Píritu, west of the Cumaná and Guayana missions. For lack of secular clerics, the missions were administered by Observants and Franciscans from Píritu. Because of its geographical distance from and its incidental importance to the Warao, however, the Mission of Píritu in its entirety is not treated in a special section.

TABLE A.5
Warao Settlements outside the Cumaná and Guayana Missions

1. San Juan Bautista de Buenavista
2. Borbón
3. Carolina
4. Santa Teresa de Orocopiche
5. Santa Rosa de Viterbo de Ocópi
6. Nuestra Señora de los Remedios (Mamo)

1. *San Juan Bautista de Buenavista* was founded by Centurión in 1770, with Cariña and some two hundred of the Warao he ordered taken from their homes in the Orinoco Delta and its environs. In 1773 there were 284 Indians.

2. *Borbón*, originally established with thirty Spanish and Criollo families, by 1773 was populated by 239 Spaniards and about seventy-nine Warao.

3. *Carolina*, founded at Centurión's request, in 1773 had a population of fifty-eight Spaniards and about eighty Warao.

4. *Santa Teresa de Orocopiche*, founded in 1765 with one hundred Cariban-speaking Cumanagoto fugitives, in later years acquired more members of the same group as well as of other tribes. In 1770 Centurión assigned 172 Warao to the village, and an additional eighty-seven Warao were brought there in February 1755 after a certain Boroa Parracino had invaded the delta in the preceding December. In 1773, seventy-nine Spaniards and 312 Warao lived in the village of Orocopiche, but by 1774 thirty of the latter had fled. The remaining Warao, who had planned to follow the fugitives, could not do so because the plot was discovered and their leaders were incarcerated.

5. *Santa Rosa de Viterbo de Ocópi* was a Chaima foundation belonging to the Mission de Píritu. In 1732 a group of eighty to one hundred Warao, whom the Observants had captured near the Mamo lagoon, north of the Orinoco about halfway between the Caroní River and present-day Ciudad Bolivar, arrived at Santa Rosa de Viterbo. The Warao who lived there were engaged as an auxiliary force against the Cariña.

6. *Nuestra Señora de los Remedios (Mamo)* was founded in 1735 near the Mamo lagoon by fathers of the Píritu mission. The Warao population, living in the settlements near the lagoon, was increased by a number of Indians who had been taken from the Orinoco Delta by a Criollo named

Appendix 271

Juan Miguél, whom the missionaries had appointed as captain of the village. In September 1735 the newly founded mission was demolished by a raiding party of Cariña Indians.

Thus, during its ninety-three effective years of operation (1724–1817), the Mission of Guayana founded fifty-two missions, seven of them (21 percent) inhabited by Warao only or by populations of mixed tribal origins. The 1816 census of the Guayana mission accounts for twenty-seven missions with 19,164 Indian residents. Six villages in the present survey had a population of 1,300 and were under the jurisdiction of the Píritu mission. In all, there were thus thirty-three communities harboring 20,464 inhabitants.

Segregated statistics for Warao residents of the Guayana and Píritu missions are unavailable. But, in addition to the 1,170 Warao procured by Centurión, an estimated 750 had been in the area before the governor's incursions and approximately 800 were subsequently settled. Thus an estimated 2,720 Warao were involved in the seven Guayana missions and the six settlements of the Píritu mission. Adding these 2,720 Warao to the 2,000–2,500 estimated to have been involved in twenty Cumaná missions yields a total of thirty-three missions with an estimated total of 4,720 to 5,220 Warao involved for various lengths of time.

Glossary of Warao Words

ahaka	-	wind
ahaka arani	-	"wind mother," woman pregnant by unknown father
ahaka auka	-	"son of the wind," son by unknown father
ahaka aukatida	-	"daughter of the wind," daughter by unknown father
ahaka bari	-	changing winds
ahaka boto	-	soft wind, land or sea breezes
ahakaida	-	powerful coiling winds, hurricane, tornado, waterspout
ahakarima	-	Father of Wind, northern trade winds
ahaka taira	-	strong wind, northern trade winds
ahi simo	-	termite, *Nasutitermes corniger*
ahono	-	"tongue," lamella of sacred trumpet
aká	-	"leg," blowtube of sacred trumpet
akabamu	-	axman during sago ritual
akai	-	help!
amehokohi	-	soul
arani	-	mother
arawanera	-	melancholy
arokohi	-	"beard," decoration on sacred trumpet
arokoho	-	"opening of the neck," mouthpiece of sacred trumpet
aru arani	-	Mother of Sago
asebe	-	stingless bee, *Trigona capitata*
ateho	-	"body," resonance chamber of sacred trumpet
ayara	-	large hairy spider
ayari	-	poison, ill temper
bahahoro	-	graveyard
bahana	-	illness cured by light shaman
bahanarotu	-	light shaman
bisikari	-	Sp. *"fiscal,"* foreman
borisia	-	Sp. *"policía,"* police

daunona	-	sacred wooden image
daunona arani	-	Mother of Wooden Images
dausitore	-	valve device of sacred trumpet
diaba	-	sweet
diabaia	-	orgasm
diaru	-	cuajo tree, *Virola surinamensis*
dibatu aida	-	first speaker of local group
dibatu sanuka	-	second speaker of local group
domo (cf. *kuramo-komoko*)	-	"bird," Pleiades in mixed (male and female) company
duruduru	-	alligator, dwarf caiman
hahuba	-	Mother of Being, giant *uroboros* snake encircling the earth
hasebe (cf. *kuramo-komoko*)	-	Pleiades, in mixed (male and female) company
haukwaharu	-	male moriche palm
hearani	-	constellation of Cancer, Mother of Crabs
hebu	-	spirit, fever, illness
hebunaka arani	-	Mother without Illness, nickname of Mother of Sacred Trumpet
hia	-	striated heron, *Butorides striatus*, Master of Northern Trades
himabaka	-	caporal of directional gods
himaheru	-	wood with low flash point reserved for ritual purposes
hoa	-	spell of sorcerer
hoarotu	-	dark shaman
hoi	-	stingless bee, *Trigona hyalinata branneri*
hoida	-	flood, primary rainy season
hoidabaka	-	high tides
homanuka	-	low tides
horu	-	skin, bark
huba	-	snake
hubanasiko	-	"serpent with necklace," Rainbow
huru	-	earthquake
iboma	-	pubertal girl
inawaha	-	dry season
isimoi arani	-	Mother of Sacred Trumpet
isimoi arani ariawara	-	*Ur*-mother of Sacred Trumpet
isimoi arotu	-	player of sacred trumpet
kabitana	-	Sp. "*capitán*," captain, chief
kabo aderei	-	rain god of the southwest

Glossary of Warao Words

kabo arotutuma	-	Lords of Rain
kabo aukuashiwari	-	rain god of the northeast
kabo ayakeima	-	rain god of the west
kabo kwaihebere	-	rain god of the northwest
kabo kwaimare	-	rain god of the north
kabo yokoshewari	-	rain god of the south
kabo yokotari	-	rain god of the east
kabo yukawari	-	rain god of the southeast
kanamuno	-	Spirit of Whirlwinds
kanishawarao	-	denizens of the netherworld
kanobo	-	"Grandfather," ancestral supreme spirit
kanobo arima	-	"father of Grandfather-spirit," keeper of sacred rock
kanobo arimatuma	-	keepers of sacred rock
karoshimo	-	god at southern edge of the earth
kasisi	-	crab hawk, *Buteogallus aequinoctialis*, culture hero
kaunasa	-	Master of Coiling Winds
kobenahoro	-	Sp. "*gobernador*," governor
kobenahoro atida	-	governor's wife
kura hido	-	New Year's Day
kuramokomoko (cf. *hahesebe*)	-	Pleiades, among men
miana	-	magic spell of sorcerer and rain shaman
mutu	-	residual particles
nabarao	-	water spirits
nabarima	-	god at northern edge of the earth
nahakara	-	rectangular shield for ritual combat
nahanaka	-	primary rainy season
nahanamu	-	regional annual sago festival
nahanamu anamunaya	-	first phase of sago festival
naharani	-	"mother of rain," rain shamaness
naharima	-	"father of rain," rain shaman
naharutu	-	hoer during sago ritual
namomo	-	women who leach ritual sago
namonina	-	metamorphosis
namonina a re	-	transformation stories
noara	-	regional sago ritual
nohiabasi	-	Orion
obo monida	-	tuberculosis
obo sabana	-	bronchitis
ohiarao	-	female moriche palm

ohidu aru	-	moriche sago
oka	-	armadillo, *Dasypus novemcinctus*
shiborori	-	beautiful, handsome, mythical bird, *Agriocharis ocellata*
shimomu	-	adept honey seeker
tarita	-	thunder, Spirit of Thunder
tihidamo ayara	-	Spider Woman
tomonoho simo	-	wasp, *Stenopolybia fulvofasciata*
tuyuna	-	sun bittern, *Eurypyga helias helias*, thunderbird, Master of Southern Trades
uasí	-	expert craftsperson, professional
uhu kawahera	-	large open-weave basket
uhumutu	-	woman's densely meshed basket
ukokomoni	-	pneumonia
uraro	-	god at southern edge of the universe
ure	-	taro, *Colocasia esculenta*
wabahoro	-	coffin
waikuba	-	water containing thick liana
waiwari	-	butterfly announcing the rainy season
waraowitu	-	genuinely Warao
warowarao	-	god at northern edge of the universe
wirimusebe (cf. *kuramokomoko*)	-	Pleiades, in mixed (male and female) company
wishimo	-	*wishiratu*, pl., priest-shaman
wishiratu	-	priest-shaman

Bibliography

Aarne, Antti, and Stith Thompson
    1964   *The Types of the Folktale: A Classification and Bibliography.* Helsinki: Suomalainen Tiedeakatemia, Academia Scientiarum Fennica.

Abreu, João Capistrano de
    1914   *Rã-txa hu-ní-kuĩ , a lingua dos caxinauás do rio Ibuaçu, affluente do Maru (prefeitura de Tarauacá).* Rio de Janeiro.
    1938a   *Ensaios e estudos.* Sociedade Capistrano de Abreu. Rio de Janeiro: Livraria Briquiet.
    1938b   "Os Caxinauás." *Ensaios e estudos (critica e historia),* 3a Serie: 275–357. Rio de Janeiro.

Agostinho, Pedro
    1974   *Kwarìp: Mito e ritual no alto Xingu.* São Paulo: EPU, Editora da Universidade de São Paulo.

Aguiló, Federico
    1985   *El hombre del Chimborazo.* Quito: Ediciones Abya-Yala.

Ahlbrinck, W.
    1931   *Encyclopaedie der Karaïben: Behelzend taal, zeden en gewoonten dezer Indianen.* Amsterdam: Koninklijke Akademie van Wetenschappen.

Ahrens, C. Donald
    1985   *Meteorology Today: An Introduction to Weather, Climate, and Environment.* New York: West Publishing.

Alamgir, Mohiuddin
    1981   "An Approach toward a Theory of Famine." In John R. K. Robson, ed., *Famine: Its Causes, Effects and Management,* pp. 19–40. New York: Gordon and Breach Science Publishers.

Alarcón y Cañedo, José de, and Riccardo Pittini
    1924   *El Chaco paraguayo y sus tribus.* Turin: Sociedad Editora Internacional.

Albisetti, César, and Ângelo J. Venturelli
   1962–76   *Enciclopédia Bororo.* 3 vols. Campo Grande (Brazil): Museu Regional Dom Bosco.

Alvarado, Lisandro
   1953–58   *Glosario de voces indígenas de Venezuela,* vol. 1. Obras completas de Lisandro Alvarado. 8 vols. Caracas: Ministerio de Educación, Dirección de Cultura y Bellas Artes.

Alvarez, José
   1956   "Creencias y tradiciones de los Mashcos." *Misiones Dominicanas del Perú* (Lima) 38:3–6.

Anchieta, José (Joseph) de
   1812   *Epistola quamplurimarum rerum naturalium, quae S. Vincentii (nunc S. Pauli) provinciam incolunt, sistens descriptionem. Collecção de noticias para a historia e geografia das nações ultramarinas, que vivem nos dominios portuguezés, ou lhes são visinhas,* vol. 1. Lisbon.

Andree, Richard
   1887   *Die Anthropophagie.* Leipzig.

Appun, Karl Ferdinand
   1868   "Unter den Guaraúnos-Indianern." *Das Ausland* 41 (34, 38).

Arens, W.
   1979   *The Man-Eating Myth: Anthropology and Anthropophagy.* Oxford: Oxford University Press.

Aretz, Isabel
   1967   *Instrumentos musicales de Venezuela.* Colección La Heredad. Cumaná: Universidad de Oriente.

Armellada, Cesáreo de
   1957   "Bocas del Orinoco (Ahora Delta Amacuro)." *Venezuela Misionera* 19(225):301–4.
   1973   *Tauron panton II (Así dice el cuento).* Lenguas indígenas de Venezuela, 10. Caracas: Universidad Católica Andrés Bello, Instituto de Investigaciones Históricas, Centro de Lenguas Indígenas.

Armentia, Nicolas
   1905   *Descripción del territorio de las Misiones Franciscanas de Apolobamba por otro nombre Frontera de Caupolican.* La Paz: Tip. Arística.

Arp, Walter
1980   *Alas de mi tierra y de mi alma*. Fundación La Salle de Ciencias Naturales, Monografía, no. 29. Caracas.

Atkinson, B. W., and A. Gadd
1987   *Weather*. New York: Weidenfeld and Nicolson.

Aveni, Anthony F.
1972   "Astronomical Tables Intended for Use in Astroarchaeological Studies." *American Antiquity* 37(4):531–40.

Azara, Félix de
1923   *Viajes por la América Meridional*. Vol. 2. Calpe.

Baer, Gerhard
1969   "Ein besonderes Merkmal des südamerikanischen Schamanen." *Zeitschrift für Ethnologie* 94(2):284–92.
1984   *Die Religion der Matsigenka, Ost-Peru: Monographie zur Kultur und Religion eines Indianervolkes des oberen Amazonas*. Basel.

Barcelona, Bruno de, Félix de Villanueva, and Mariano de Sabadell
1979   "Puntos que, después de consultas con el P. Comisario general de Misiones, debían ser luego presentados al rey por los superiores de la misión de Guayana (1771)." In Buenaventura de Carrocera, *Misión de los Capuchinos en Guayana* 2:126–30. Biblioteca de la Academia Nacional de la Historia, Fuentes para la historia colonial de Venezuela, 140. Caracas.

Barral, Basilio María de
1947   "El incendio de la misión de Guayo." *Venezuela Misionera* 9(101):177–82.
1948   "Cantares Guaraúnos." *Venezuela Misionera* 10(116):264–66.
1949   "El Delta Amacuro o Bajo Orinoco." *Venezuela Misionera* 11(130–31):333–52.
1950a   "Cancionero Guaraúno: Wirinoko Arao." *Venezuela Misionera* 12(132–33):22–24.
1950b   "Mis excursiones por el Makareo y sus derivados afluentes." *Venezuela Misionera* 12(139):225–27.
1951a   "Piachería Guaraúna." *Venezuela Misonera* 13(146):82–85.
1951b   "Mis excursiones por el Bajo Orinoco." *Venezuela Misionera* 13(147):108–12.

1960   *Guarao Guarata. Lo que cuentan los indios Guaraos.* Caracas.
1964   *Los indios Guaraúnos y su cancionero.* Biblioteca "Missionalia Hispánica," vol. 15. Madrid.
1969   *Guarao a-ribu. (Literatura de los indios guaraos).* Lenguas indígenas de Venezuela, 1. Caracas: Universidad Católica Andrés Bello.
1972   *Mi batalla de dios: Reflejos de la vida y afanes de un misionera.* Burgos: Artes Gráficas Galica.
1979   *Diccionario Warao-Castellano, Castellano-Warao.* Caracas: El Políglota.

Barrett, Samuel Alfred
1925   *The Cayapa Indians of Ecuador.* 2 vols. Indian Notes and Monographs, 40. New York: Museum of the American Indian, Heye Foundation.

Barriales, Joaquin, and Adolfo Torralba
1970   *Los Mashcos hijos del Huanamei.* Lima: Santiago Valverde.

Beals, Ralph L.
1946   *Cherán: A Sierra Tarascan Village.* Smithsonian Institution, Institute of Social Anthropology, no. 2. Washington, D.C.: Government Printing Office.

Becher, Hans
1960   *Die Surára und Pakidái: Zwei Yanonámi-Stämme in Nordwestbrasilien.* Hamburg: Kommissionsverlag Cram, De Gruyter.
1974   *Pore/Perimbo.* Völkerkundliche Abhandlungen, 6. Publication series of the Völkerkunde-Abteilung des Niedersächsischen Landesmuseums und der Ethnologischen Gesellschaft Hannover. Hannover: Kommissionsverlag Münstermann-Druck.
1976   "Moon and Reincarnation: Anthropogenesis as Imagined by the Surára and Pakidái Indians of Northwestern Brazil." In Agehananda Bharati, ed., *The Realm of the Extra-Human: Ideas and Actions.* The Hague.

Bennet, John W.
1976a   "Anticipation, Adaptation, and the Concept of Culture in Anthropology." *Science* 192:847–53.
1976b   *The Ecological Transition.* New York: Pergamon.

Bernal Villa, S.
1954 "Medicina y magia entre los Paeces." *Revista Colombiana de Antropología* 2(2):219–64.

Bernand-Muñoz, Carmen
1977 *Les Ayoré du Chaco septentrional: Étude critique à partir des notes de Lucien Sebag.* Paris: Mouton.

Bernau, J. M.
1847 *Missionary Labours in British Guiana, with Remarks on the Manners, Customs, and Superstitious Rites of the Aborigines.* London: John Farquhar Shaw.

Berry, L., T. Hankins, R. W. Kates, L. Makil, and P. Porter
1971 *Human Adjustment to Agricultural Drought in Tanzania.* Bureau of Resource Assessment and Land Use Planning, University of Dar-es-Salaam, Research Paper 13. Dar-es-Salaam.

Berry, S. S.
1984 "The Food Crisis and Agrarian Change in Africa: A Review Essay." *African Studies Review* 27(2):59–112.

Bierhorst, John
1988 *The Mythology of South America.* New York: William Morrow.

Bolinder, Gustaf
1925 *Die Indianer der tropischen Schneegebirge: Forschungen im nördlichsten Südamerika.* Stuttgart.
1957 *Indians on Horseback.* London: Dennis Dobson.

Boomert, Arie
n.d. *The Arawak Indians of Trinidad and Coastal Guiana, ca. 1500–1650.* Trinidad: University of the West Indies.

Booth Mabilde, Pierre
1983 *Apontamentos sobre os indígenas selvagens da nação Coroados dos matos da província do Rio Grande do Sul (1836–1866).* Rio de Janeiro: Instituição Brasileira de Difusão Cultural.

Borde, Père de la
1886 "History of the Origin, Customs, Religion, Wars, and Travels of the Caribs, Savages of the Antilles in America." *Timehri* (Demarara) 5:224–54.

Bórmida, Marcelo and Mario Califano
1978 *Los indios Ayoreo del Chaco Boreal: Información básica*

acerca de su cultura. Buenos Aires: Fundación para la Educación, la Ciencia y la Cultura.

Braudel, Fernand
1967 *Capitalism and Material Life, 1400–1800.* New York: Harper and Row.

Breton, Raymond
1892 [1655] *Dictionaire caraibe-français, composé par le R. P. Raymond Borton, reimprimé par Jules Platzmann.* Ed. fascimilé. Leipzig: Jules Platzmann.

Brett, William H.
1852 *The Indian Tribes of Guiana. Their Condition and Habits.* New York.
1868 *The Indian Tribes of Guiana: Their Condition and Habits. With Researches into Their Past History, Superstitions, Legends, Antiquities, Languages. . . .* London: Bell and Daldy.
1880 *Legends and Myths of the Aboriginal Indians of British Guiana.* London.
1881 *Mission Work among the Indian Tribes in the Forests of Guiana.* New York: E. & J. B. Young.

Bridges, Thomas
1893 "La tierra del fuego y sus habitantes." *Revista del Museo de La Plata* 14:221–41.
n.d. Mémoire inédit.

Briggs, Charles L.
1988 "Disorderly Dialogues in Ritual Impositions of Order: The Role of Metapragmatics in Warao Dispute Mediation." *Anthropological Linguistics* 30(3/4):448–92.
1992 "'Since I Am a Woman, I Will Chastise My Relatives': Gender, Reported Speech, and the (Re)production of Social Relations in Warao Ritual Wailing." *American Ethnologist* 19(2):337–61.

British Guiana Boudary Case
1898 *Arbitration with the United States of Venezuela. Appendix to the Case on Behalf of the Government of Her Britannic Majesty.* 2 (1742–1763). London: Foreign Office.

Brown, C. B.
1877 *Canoe and Camp Life in British Guiana.* London.

Brown, Frank A.
1965 *Circadian Clocks*. Amsterdam: North Holland.
Budge, E. A. Wallis
1973 *Osiris and the Egyptian Resurrection*. 2 vols. New York: Dover Publications.
Bühlmann, Walbert
1976 *Wandlung zum Wesentlichen: Der Sinn der Evangelisierung*. Münzerschwarzach: Vier-Türme Verlag.
Bustamante, Crisóstomo M.
1946 *El siervo de Dios Padre Santos de Abelgas: Misionero en Bayamo (Cuba) y en el Caroní (Venezuela)*. Caracas: Editorial Venezuela.
Butt, Audrey J.
1956 "Ritual Blowing: Taling—A Causation and Cure of Illness among the Akawaio." *Man* 48:49–55.
1961 "Symbolism and Ritual among the Akawaio of British Guiana." *Nieuwe West-Indische Gids* 42(2):141–61.
1965 "The Guianas." *Bulletin of the International Committee on Urgent Anthropological and Ethnological Research* 7:69–90.
Butt Colson, Audrey J.
1971 "Comparative Studies of the Social Structure of Guiana Indians and the Problem of Acculturation." In Francisco M. Salzano, ed., *The Ongoing Evolution of Latin American Populations*. Springfield: Charles C. Thomas.
Butzer, K. W., ed.
1992 *The Americas before and after 1492: Current Geographical Research. Annals of the Association of American Geographers* 82(3).
Calazacón, Catalina, et al.
1985 *Ilusun: kuwenta layakajun pila (50 leyendas de los indios Colorado)*. Guayaquil: Museo Antropológico y Pinacoteca, Banco Central del Ecuador.
Califano, Mario
1982 *Etnografía de los Mashco de la Amazonia sud-occidental del Peru*. Buenos Aires: Fundación para la educasión, la ciencia y la cultura.
Campbell, Joseph
1968 *Historical Atlas of World Mythology*. Vol.1, part 1. New York: Harper and Row.

Cancella, Joseph
1956   *Jungle Call*. New York.
Carrocera, Cayetano (Buenaventura) de
1939   "Historia de un gran misionero, R. P. Santos de Abelgas. El Territorio Federal Delta-Amacuro." *Venezuela Misionera* 1(8):201–4.
1940   "Historia de un gran misionero, R. P. Santos de Abelgas. Otra Excursión a Mariusa." *Venezuela Misionera* 2(15): 398–400.
1941   *Cincuenta años de apostolado de los P. P. Franciscanos Capuchinos*. Caracas: Escuelas Gráficas Salesianas.
1949   "Araguaimujo, Primer Centro Misional." *Venezuela Misionera* 11(130–31):381–93.
1964   *Los primeros historiadores de las misiones Capuchinas de Venezuela*. Biblioteca de la Academia Nacional de la Historia, 69. Caracas.
1968   *Misión de los Capuchinos en Cumaná*. 3 vols. Biblioteca de la Academia Nacional de la Historia, 88, 89, 90. Caracas.
1979   *Misión de los Capuchinos en Guayana*. 3 vols. Biblioteca de la Academia Nacional de la Historia, 139, 140, 141. Caracas.
Carter, William E.
1965   *Aymara Communities and the Bolivian Agrarian Reform*. Gainsville: University of Florida Press.
Caspar, Franz
1956   *Tupari*. London: G. Bell and Sons
1975   *Die Tuparí: Ein Indianerstamm in Westbrasilien.* Monographien zur Völkerkunde 7. Hamburgisches Museum für Völkerkunde. Berlin: Walter de Gruyter.
Caulin, Antonio
1966   *Historia de la Nueva Andalucía*. 2 vols. Biblioteca de la Academia Nacional de la Historia, 81, 82. Caracas.
Ceñogal, Conrado de
1949   "Mi vida misionera." *Venezuela Misionera* 11(122): 78–79.
Censo Indígena de Venezuela
1985   *Nomenclador de Comunidades y Colectividades*. Caracas: Republica de Venezuela. Officina Central de Estadística e Informatica.

Centurión, Manuel
1979 "Carta del comandante general de Guyana D. Manuel Centurión al secretario del Consejo de Indias." In Buenaventura de Carrocera, *Misión de los Capuchinos en Guayana* 2:131–35. Biblioteca de la Academia Nacional de la Historia, Fuentes para la historia colonial de Venezuela, 140. Caracas.

Chagnon, Napoleon A.
1968 *Yanomamö, the Fierce People.* New York: Holt, Rinehart and Winston.

Chevalier, Jacques M.
1982 *Civilization and the Stolen Gift: Capital, Kin, and Cult in Eastern Peru.* Toronto: University of Toronto Press.

Chiara, Vilma
1961–62 "Folclore Krahó." *Revista do Museu Paulista* 13:333–75.

Cipoletti, María Susana
1988 *Aipë Koka: La palabra de los antiguos. Tradición oral Siona-Secoya.* Quito: Ediciones Abya-Yala.

Civrieux, Marc de
1974 *Religión y magia Kari'ña.* Lenguas indígenas de Venezuela, 13. Caracas: Universidad Católica Andrés Bello, Instituto de Investigaciones Históricas.
1976 "Los Caribes y la conquista de la Guayana Española (Etnohistoria Kari'ña)." *Montalbán* (Caracas) 5: 875–1021.
1980a "Los Cumanagoto y sus vecinos." In Walter Coppens and Bernarda Escalante, eds., *Los aborígenes de Venezuela,* vol. 1, *Etnología antigua,* ed. Audrey Butt Colson, pp. 27–239. Fundación La Salle de Ciencias Naturales, Instituto Caribe de Antropología y Sociología, 26. Caracas.
1980b *Watunna: An Orinoco Creation Cycle.* Ed. and trans. David M. Guss. San Francisco: North Point Press.

Clastres, Pierre
1992 *Mythologie des indiens Chulupi.* Ed. Michel Cartry and Hélène Clastres. Paris.

Cobo, Bernabé
1893 *Historia del Nuevo Mundo,* vol. 4. Seville.

Colbacchini, D. Antonio
    1929   *I Bororos Orientali "Orarimugudoge" del Matto Grosso.* Torino.

Colchester, Marcus
    1982   "The Cosmovision of the Venezuelan Sanema." *Antropológica* 58:97–174.

Coll, C. van
    1907–8   "Contes et légendes des Indiens de Surinam." *Anthropos* 2:682–89; 3:482–88.

Collier, John, and Aníbal Buitrón
    1949   *The Awakening Valley.* Chicago: University of Chicago Press.

Cook, S. F., and W. Borah
    1971   *Essays in Population History: Mexico and the Caribbean,* vol. 1. Berkeley and Los Angeles: University of California Press.

Coriat, Juan E.
    n.d.   *El hombre del Amazonas y ensayo monográfico de Loreto.* Lima.

Costello, Gerald M.
    1979   *Mission to Latin America: The Successes and Failures of a Twentieth-Century Crusade.* Maryknoll, N.Y.: Orbis Books.

Cotlow, Lewis
    1953   *Amazon Head-Hunters.* New York: Henry Holt.

Coudreau, Henri
    1897   *Viagem ao Tapajós.* São Paulo.

Crévaux, Jules Nicolas
    1883   *Voyages dans l'Amérique du Sud.* Paris: Librairie Hachette et Cie.

Crocker, Jon Christopher
    1985   *Vital Souls: Bororo Cosmology, Natural Symbolism, and Shamanism.* Tucson: University of Arizona Press.

Crosby, Alfred W., Jr.
    1972   *The Columbian Exchange: Biological and Cultural Consequences of 1492.* Contribution in American Studies, 2. Westport, Conn.: Greenwood Press.

Crow, John A.
    1992   *The Epic of Latin America.* Berkeley and Los Angeles: University of California Press.

Dalton, Henry G.
- 1855 *The History of British Guiana.* 2 vols. London.

Dance, Charles Daniel
- 1881 *Chapters from a Guianese Log-Book; or, The Folk-Lore and Scenes of Seacoast and River Life in British Guiana.* Georgetown, Demarara: Royal Gazette Establishment.

D'Ans, André-Marcel
- 1978 *Le dit des vrais hommes: Mythes, contes, légendes et traditions des indiens Cashinahua.* Paris.

de Garine, I., and G. A. Harrison, eds.
- 1988 *Coping with Uncertainty in Food Supply.* Oxford and New York: Oxford University Press.

de Goeje, Claudius Henrions de
- 1943 "Philosophy, Initiation and Myth of the Indians of Guiana and Adjacent Countries." *Archiv für Ethnographie* 44:129.
- 1967 "The Physical World, the World of Magic, and the Moral World of Guiana Indians." In Sol Tax, ed., *Indian Tribes of Aboriginal America,* pp. 266–70. Selected Papers of the 29th International Congress of Americanists, New York, 1949. New York: Cooper Square Publishers.

Denevan, William M.
- 1970a "The Aboriginal Population of Western Amazonia in Relation to Habitat and Subsistence." *Revista Geográfica* 72:61–86.
- 1970b "The Aboriginal Population of Tropical America: Problems and Methods of Estimation." In Paul Deprez, ed., *Population and Economics. Proceedings of Section V of the Fourth Congress of the International Economic History Association, 1968,* pp. 251–69. Winnipeg: University of Manitoba Press.
- 1976a "The Aboriginal Population of Amazonia." In William M. Denevan, ed., *The Native Population of the Americas in 1492,* pp. 205–34. Madison: University of Wisconsin Press.
- 1976b "Introduction: Estimating the Unknown." In William M. Denevan, ed., *The Native Population of the Americas in 1492,* pp. 1–12. Madison: University of Wisconsin Press.

Disselhoff, H. D.
1974 "Die Erben des Inkareiches." In H. D. Disselhoff and Otto Zerries, eds., *Die Erben des Inkareiches und die Indianer der Wälder*, pp. 15–78. Berlin: Safari Verlag.

Dobrizhoffer, Martin
1822 *An Account of the Abipones, an Equestrian People of Paraguay, in three volume*s, vol. 2. Trans. Sara Coleridge. London.

Dobyns, Henry F.
1966 "Estimating Aboriginal American Population: An Appraisal of Techniques with a New Hemispheric Estimate." *Current Anthropology* 7:395–416.
1989 "More Methodological Perspectives on Historical Demography." *Ethnohistory* 36:285–99.

D'Orbigny, Alside
1839 *L'Homme Americain*. 2 Vols. Paris.
1944 *El hombre americano*. Buenos Aires.

Drummond, L.
1977 "Structure and Process in the Interpretation of South American Myth: The Arawak Dog Spirit People." *American Anthropologist* 79(4):842–68.

Eder, Francisco Javier
1985 [1791] *Breve descripción de las reducciones de Mojos*. Cochabamba.

Edwards, Walter F., and Elizabeth Charette
1980 *A Short Dictionary of the Warau Language of Guyana*. Amerindian Languages Project. Georgetown: University of Guyana.

Ehrenreich, Paul
1891 "Beiträge zur Völkerkunde Brasiliens." *Veröffentlichungen aus dem königlichen Museum für Völkerkunde* 2(1-2). Berlin.
1905 *Die Mythen und Legenden der südamerikanischen Urvölker und ihre Beziehungen zu denen Nordamerikas und der alten Welt*. Berlin. Published as Supplement to *Zeitschrift für Ethnologie*, 37.
1948 "Contribuições para a etnologia do Brasil." *Revista do Museu Paulista* 2:7–136.

Escalante González, Bernarda, and Librado Moreleda
1992 *Narraciones Warao.* Caracas: Fundación La Salle, Instituto Caribe de Antropología y Sociología.

Evans, Clifford, and Betty J. Meggers
1960 *Archaeological Investigations in British Guiana.* Smithsonian Institution, Bureau of American Ethnology, Bulletin, no. 177. Washington, D.C.: Government Printing Office.

Fabian, Stephen Michael
1992 *Space-Time of the Bororo of Brazil.* Gainesville: University of Florida Press.

Farabee, William Curtis
1922 *Indian Tribes of Eastern Peru.* Papers of the Peabody Museum of American Archaeology and Ethnology, Harvard University, vol. 10. Cambridge, Mass.

1967 [1918] *The Central Arawak.* Anthropological Publications, Museum of the University of Pennsylvania, vol. 10. Oosterhout N. B. (The Netherlands).

Fejos, Paul
1943 *Ethnography of the Yagua.* Viking Fund Publications in Anthropology, 1. New York.

Ferguson R. B., and N. L. Whitehead
1992 "The Violent Edge of Europe." In R. Brian Ferguson and Neil L. Whitehead, eds., *War in the Tribal Zone: Expanding States and Indigenous Warfare.* Santa Fe: School of American Research Press.

Fernández, Patricio
1895 *Relación historial de las misiones de indios Chiquitos que en el Paraguay tienen los padres de la Compañía de Jesús.* Madrid: Librería de Victoriano Suárez.

Ferrero, Andres
1967 *Los Machiguengas: Tribu selvática del sur-oriente Peruano.* Puerto Maldonado: Instituto de Estudios Tropicales "Pio Aza."

Fiedler, Günther, and Lourdes Rivero
1979 "Sismología." *Atlas de Venezuela.* 2nd ed. Caracas: Republica de Venezuela. Ministerio del Ambiente y de los Recursos Naturales Renovables. Dirección de Cartografía Nacional.

Fitzhugh, William, ed.
 1985 *Cultures in Contact: The European Impact on Native Cultural Institutions in Eastern North America, A.D. 1000–1800*. Washington, D.C.: Smithsonian Institution Press.

Fock, Niels
 1963 *Waiwai: Religion and Society of an Amazonian Tribe*. With Appendices by Fridolin Weis Bentzon and Robert E. Hawkins. Nationalmuseets skrifter, Etnografisk raekke, 8. Cogenhagen: National Museum.

Foster, George M.
 1953a "Relationships between Spanish and Spanish-American Folk Medicine." *Journal of American Folklore* 66:201–17.
 1953b "Cofradía and Compadrazgo in Spain and Spanish America." *Southwestern Journal of Anthropology* 9(1):1–28.
 1972 "Aire." In Maria Leach, ed., *Standard Dictionary of Folklore, Mythology and Legend*, p. 31. New York: Funk and Wagnalls.

Furst, Peter F.
 1993 "Huichol Cosmogony: How the World was Destroyed by a Flood and a Dog-Woman Gave Birth to the Human Race." In Garry H. Gossen with Miguel Leon-Portilla, eds., *South and Meso-American Native Spirituality: From the Cult of the Feathered Serpent to the Theology of Liberation*, pp. 303–23. World Spirituality: An Encyclopaedic History of the Religious Quest, vol. 4. New York: Crossroad.

Gallardo, Carlos R.
 1910 *Los Onas*. Buenos Aires.

García, Argimiro
 1940 "Como un guarao joven cuidaba una raya que había escogido para mujer suya." *Venezuela Misionera* 18:517–18.
 1947 "Cuentos y tradiciones de los indios Guaraúnos." *Venezuela Misionera* 9(97):45–46.
 1971 *Cuentos y tradiciones de los indios Guraúnos*. Lenguas indígenas de Venezuela, 6. Caracas: Universidad Católica Andrés Bello, Seminario de Lenguas Indígenas.

Garcílaso de La Vega (El Inca)
    1723   *Primera parte de los commentarios.* 2nd ed. Madrid.

Garriga, Benito de la
    1898 [1758] "Letter of the Prefect of the Missions to the Commandant of Guiana." *British Guiana Boundary Case. Arbitration with the United States of Venezuela. Appendix of the Case on Behalf of the Government of Her Britannic Majesty* 2:145–49 (1724–1763). London.
    1979 [1769] "Informe del P. Prefecto Benito de La Garriga al rey, manifestándole la situación de la misión en relación sobre todo con los holandeses de Esequivo." (Altagracia, 6 julio 1769). In Buenaventura de Carrocera, *Misión de los Capuchinos en Guayana* 2:99–104. Biblioteca de la Academia Nacional de la Historia, Fuentes para la historia colonial de Venezuela, 140. Caracas.

Giaccaria, Bartolomeu, and Adalberto Heide
    1972   *Xavante.* São Paulo: Editorial Dom Bosco.
    1975   *Jerônimo Xavante conta: Mitos e lendas.* Campo Grande: [Casa da Cultura].

Gillin, John
    1936   *The Barama River Caribs of British Guiana.* Papers of the Peabody Museum of American Archaeology and Ethnology of Harvard University, vol. 14, no. 2. Cambridge, Mass.

Girard, Rafael
    1958   *Indios selváticos de la Amazonía Peruana.* Mexico City: Libro Mex.

Golden, Joseph Hilary
    1973   *The Life Cycle of the Florida Keys Waterspout as the Result of Five Interacting Scales of Motion.* Ann Arbor: University Microfilms (73-30, 281).

Goldman, Irving
    1963   *The Cubeo: Indians of the Northwest Amazon.* Urbana: University of Illinois Press.

Gómez Cañedo, Lino
    1967   *Las misiones de Píritu: Documentos para su historia.* 2 vols. Biblioteca de la Academia Nacional de la Historia, 83, 84. Caracas.

Gondim, Joaquim
1925 *A pacificação dos Parintintins.* Commissão Rondon. Publication 87.
1938 *Etnografía Indígena.* Ceara: Editora Fortaleza.

Gorski, John F.
1985 *El desarrollo historico de la misionología en America Latina: Orientaciones teológicas del Departamento de Misiones del CELAM (1966–1979).* La Paz: Talleres-Escuela de Artes Gráficas del Colegio Don Bosco.

Goslinga, Cornelius Ch.
1971 *The Dutch in the Caribbean and on the Wild Coast, 1580–1680.* Gainesville: University of Florida Press.

Goubaud, Carrera, A., J. de Dios Rosales, and S. Tax
1947 *Reconnaissance of Northern Guatemala, 1944.* Microfilm Collection of Manuscripts on Middle American Cultural Anthropology, 17. Chicago: University of Chicago Library.

Gregor, Thomas
1977 *Mehinaku: The Drama of Daily Life in a Brazilian Indian Village.* Chicago: University of Chicago Press.

Grimal, Pierre, ed.
1965 *Larousse World Mythology.* New York.

Grubb, W. Barbrook
1911 *An Unknown People in an Unknown Land: An Account of the Life and Customs of the Lengua Indians of the Paraguayan Chaco.* London: Seeley and Co.
1913 *An Unknown People in an Unknown Land: An Account of the Life and Customs of the Lengua Indians of the Paraguayan Chaco.* London.

Grzimek, Bernhard
1969 *Grzimeks Tierleben: Encyklopädie des Tierreichs*, vol. 8(2). Zürich: Kindler Verlag.

Gumilla, Joseph
1944 *El Orinoco ilustrado y defendido, historia natural, civil, y geografíca de este gran río, y de sus caudalosas vertientes.* 2 vols. Madrid. First edition, Madrid: Manuel Fernandez, 1745.
1963 *El Orinoco ilustrado y defendido.* Biblioteca de la Academia Nacional de la Historia, 68. Caracas.

Gusinde, Martin
1931   *Die Feuerland-Indianer.* Vol. 1, *Die Selk'nam: Vom Leben und Denken eines Jägervolkes auf der grossen Feuerlandinsel.* Mödling: Anthropos Verlag.
1937   *Die Feuerland-Indianer.* Vol. 2, *Die Yamana: Vom Leben und Denken der Wassernomaden am Kap Hoorn.* Mödling: Anthropos Verlag.

Hancock, James, and James Kushlan
1984   *The Herons Handbook.* London: Croom Helm.

Hanke, Wanda
1956   *Los indios Chacobo del Rio Benisito.* Trabajos y Conferencias, Seminario de Estudios Americanistas, 2(1). Madrid.

Harner, Michael
1962   "Jívaro Souls." *American Anthropologist* 64:258–72.
1973   *The Jívaro: People of the Sacred Waterfalls.* Garden City, N.Y.: Anchor Press, Doubleday.

Harris, M. P.
1973   "The Galapagos Avifauna." *Condor* 75:265–78.

Hartert, E.
1920   "Gattung Buturides, Blyth." In *Die Vögel der palaearktischen Fauna.* 2 vols. Berlin: Friedländer.

Havestadt, Bernard
1883   *Chilidúgu.* Leipzig: J. Platzmann. First ed., Monasterii Westphaliae, 1777.

Hawtrey, Seymour
1901   "The Lengua Indians of the Paraguayan Chaco." *Journal of the Anthropological Institute of Great Britain and Ireland* 31:280–99.

Heinen, H. Dieter
1988   "Los Warao." In Walter Coppens and Bernarda Escalante, eds., *Los aborígenes de Venezuela,* vol. 3, *Etnología contemporanea,* part 2, ed. Jacques Lizot, pp. 585–689. Fundación La Salle de Ciencias Naturales, Instituto Caribe de Antropología y Sociología, 35. Caracas.
1993   "Kosmologische Konzepte der Warao Indianer im religiösen und kulturellen Wandel." In Werner Krawietz, Leopold Pospišil, and Sabine Steinbrich, eds., *Sprache, Symbole und Symbolverwendungen in Ethnologie,*

Kulturanthropologie, Religion und Recht, pp. 171–201. Berlin: Duncker & Humblot.

Heinen, H. Dieter, and Hortensia Caballero Arias
1992 *Informe sobre los indígenas del estado Delta Amacuro.* Caracas: Instituto Venezolano de Investigaciones Científicas (IVIC).

Heinen, H. Dieter, José J. San José, Hortensia Caballero Arias, and Rubén Montes
1995 "Subsistence Activities of hte Warao Indians and Anthropogenic Changes in the Orinoco Delta Vegetation." *Scientia Guianai* 5:312–334. Caracas.

Heinen, H. Dieter, and Julio Lavandero
1973 "Computación del tiempo en dos subtribus Warao." *Antropológica* 35:3–24.

Heinen, H. Dieter and Kenneth Ruddle
1974 "Ecology, Ritual, and Economic Organization in the Distribution of Palm Starch among the Warao of the Orinoco Delta." *Journal of Anthropological Research* 30(2):116–38.

Henley, Paul
1982 *The Panare: Tradition and Change on the Amazonian Frontier.* New Haven: Yale University Press.

Henry, Jules
1941 *Jungle People, a Kaingáng Tribe of the Highlands of Brazil.* New York: J. J. Augustin.
1964 *Jungle People, a Kaingáng Tribe of the Highlands of Brazil.* New York: Vintage Books.

Hernández de Alba, Gregorio
1936 *Etnología guajira.* Bogotá.
1946 "The Highland Tribes of Southern Colombia." In Julian H. Steward, ed., *Handbook of South American Indians*, Vol. 2, *The Andean Civilizations*, pp. 915–60. Smithsonian Institution, Bureau of American Ethnology, Bulletin, no. 143. Washington, D.C.: Government Printing Office.
1948 "The Cultures of Northwest South America: Sub-Andean Tribes of the Cauca Valley." In Julian H. Steward, ed., *Handbook of South American Indians*, vol. 4, *The Circum-Caribbean Tribes,* pp. 297–327. Smithsonian

Institution, Bureau of American Ethnology, Bulletin, no. 143. Washington, D.C.: Government Printing Office.

Hilhouse, William

1898a   "Reconnaissance of the Post of Pomeroon, with the Adjacent Indian Settlements in the Morocco Creek and Its Vicinity [1823]." *British Guiana Boundary Case. Arbitration with the United States of Venezuela. Appendix of the Case on Behalf of the Government of Her Britannic Majesty* 6:23–24. London.

1898b   "Fragments of Report on Indians [1823]." *British Guiana Boundary Case. Arbitration with the United States of Venezuela. Appendix of the Case on Behalf of the Government of Her Britannic Majesty* 6:52–53. London.

1978 [1824]   *Indian Notices: or, Sketches of the Habits, Characters, Languages, Superstitions, Soil, and Climate of the Several Nations; with Remarks on their Capacity for Colonization, Present Government, and Suggestions for Future Improvement and Civilization. Also, the Icthyology of the Fresh Waters of the Interior* [1825]. New ed., with introduction and supplementary notes by M. N. Menezes. Georgetown: National Commission for Research Materials on Guyana.

Hill, Jonathan D.

1988   *Rethinking History and Myth: Indigenous South American Perspectives on the Past.* Urbana: University of Illinois Press.

Hissink, Karin, and Albert Hahn

1961   *Die Tacana.* Vol. 1, *Erzählungsgut.* Stuttgart: W. Kohlhammer.

Hoff, Berend Jacob

1968   *The Carib Language: Phonology, Morphonology, Morphology, Texts and Word Index.* s'-Gravenhage: Nederlandsche Boek- en Steendrukkerij, H. L. Smits.

Hohenthal, William D.

1954   "Notes on the Shucurú Indians of Serra de Araroba, Pernambuco, Brazil." *Revista do Museu Paulista* 8: 93–64.

Holker, Douglas Lee

1983   "Remote Sensing of the Orinoco Delta: The Forager-

Agriculturalist Transition of the Warao Indians." Master's thesis, University of California, Los Angeles.

Horcasitas, Fernando
1953   An Analysis of the Deluge Myth in Mesoamerica. Master's thesis, Centro de Estudios Universitarios, Mexico City College.

Hugh-Jones, Stephen
1979   *The Palm and the Pleiades: Initiation and Cosmology in Northwest Amazonia.* Cambridge: Cambridge University Press.
1987   "Yurupari." In Mircea Eliade, ed., *The Encyclopedia of Religion* 15:545–48. New York: Macmillan.
1988   "The Gun and the Bow: Myths of White Men and Indians." *L'Homme* 28(106–7):138–55.

Hultkrantz, Åke
1967   *The Religions of the American Indians.* Berkeley and Los Angeles: University of California Press.

Huschke, R. E., ed.
1959   *Glossary of Meteorology.* Boston: American Meteorological Society.

Huxley, Aldous
1978   *Plant and Planet.* Harmondsworth: Penguin Books.

Ibarra Grasso, Dick Edgar
1980   *Cosmogonía y mitología indígena americana.* Buenos Aires: Editorial Kier.

Im Thurn, Everard F.
1967 [1883]   *Among the Indians of Guiana.* London.

Izikowitz, K. G.
1935   *Musical and Other Sound Instruments of the South American Indians: A Comparative Ethnographical Study.* Göteborg.

Izaguirre, Bernardino
1922–29   *Historia de las misiones franciscanas y narración de los progresos de la geografía en el oriente del Perú: Relatos originales y producciones en lenguas indígenas de varios misioneros, por el padre fray Bernardino Izaguirre. . . 1619–1921.* 14 vols. Lima: Talleres Tipográficos de la Penitenciaría.

Jackson, Jean
1983   *The Fish People: Linguistic Exogamy and Tukanoan Identity in Northwest Amazonia.* Cambridge: Cambridge University Press.

Jackson, L. R.
1929   "The Tale of the Dog Husband: A Comparative Study of a North American Indian Folk Tale." Master's thesis, Indiana University.

Jeliffe, Derrick B., and E. F. F. Jeliffe
1971   "The Effects of Starvation on the Function of the Family and of Society." In G. Blix, ed., *Famine: A Symposium Dealing with Nutrition and Relief Operations in Times of Disaster,* pp. 54–62. Stockholm: Swedish Nutritional Foundation.

Kapfhammer, Wolfgang
1992   *Der Yurupari-Komplex in Nordwest-Amazonien.* Münchener Amerikanistik Beiträge, 28. Munich: Akademischer Verlag München.

Karsten, Rafael
1920   *Contributions to the Sociology of the Indian Tribes of Ecuador.* Acta Academiae Aboensis, Humaniora, 1(3). Åbo: Åbo Akademi.
1923   *The Toba Indians of the Bolivian Gran Chaco.* Acta Academiae Aboensis, Humaniora, 4(4). Åbo: Åbo Akademi.
1926   *The Civilization of the South American Indians.* New York: Alfred Knopf.
1932   *Indian Tribes of the Argentine and Bolivian Chaco: Ethnological Studies.* Societas Scientiarum Fennica, Commentationes Humanarum Litterarum, 4(1). Helsingfors: Akademische Buchhandlung.
1935   *The Head-Hunters of Western Amazonas. The Life and Culture of the Jibaro Indians of Eastern Ecuador and Peru.* Societas Scientiarum Fennica, Commentationes Humanarum Litterarum, 7(1). Helsinki-Helsingfors.
1954   *Some Critical Remarks on Ethnographical Field Research in South America.* Societas Scientiarum Fennica, Commentationes Humanarum Litterarum, 19(5). Helsingfors.

1955	"Los indios Shipibo del Río Ucayali." *Revista del Museo Nacional* (Lima):14:154–73.
1964	*Studies in the Religion of the South-American Indians East of the Andes.* Ed. Arne Runeberg and Michael Webster. Societas Scientiarum Fennica, Commentationes Humanarum Litterarum, 29(1). Helsinki-Helsingfors.

Keys, A., J. Brozek, A. Henschel, O. Michelson, and H. L. Taylor
   1950   *The Biology of Human Starvation.* Minneapolis: University of Minnesota Press.

Kirchhoff, Paul
   1948   "The Tribes North of the Orinoco River. In Julian H. Steward, ed., *Handbook of South American Indians,* Vol. 4, *The Circum-Caribbean Tribes*, pp. 481–93. Smithsonian Institution, Bureau of American Ethnology, Bulletin, no. 143. Washington, D.C.: Government Printing Office.

Kloos, Peter
   1971   *The Maroni River Caribs of Surinam.* Assen (The Netherlands): Van Gorcum and Co.
   1972   "Amerindians of Surinam." In Walter Dostal, ed., *The Situation of the Indian in South America*, pp. 348–57. Geneva: World Council of Churches.

Koch, Theodor
   1899   "Die Anthropophagie der südamerikanischen Indianer." *Internationales Archiv für Ethnographie* 12.

Koch-Grünberg, Theodor
   1916–28   *Vom Roroima zum Orinoco.* 5 vols. Stuttgart.
   1953   "Mitos e lendas dos índios Taulipáng e Arekuná." *Revista do Museu Paulista* 7:9–202.
   1967   *Zwei Jahre unter den Indianern: Reisen in Nordwest-Brasilien 1903–1905.* 2 vols. Graz: Akademische Druck- und Verlagsanstalt.

Koelewijn, Cees, with Peter Rivière
   1987   *Oral Literature of the Trio Indians of Surinam.* Caribbean Series, 6. Dordrecht: Koninklijk Institut voor Taal-, Land- en Volkenkunde.

Koppers, Wilhelm
   1930   *Der Hund in der Mythologie der zirkumpazifischen Völker.* Wiener Beiträge zur Kulturgeschichte und Linguistik, 1. Vienna.

Krause, Fritz
1911 *In den Wildnissen Brasiliens.* Leipzig.
Kretschmar, Freda
1938 *Hundestammvater und Kerberos.* Stuttgart: Strecker und Schröder.
Kruse, Albert
1951–52 "Karusakaybë, der Vater der Munduruкú." *Anthropos* 46:915–32, 47:992–1018.
La Barre, Weston
1948 *The Aymara Indians of the Lake Titicaca Plateau, Bolivia.* Menasha, Wis.: American Anthropological Association.
Landaburu, Jon, and Roberto Pineda
1984 *Tradiciones de la gente del hacha: Mitología de los indios Andoques del Amazonas.* Buenos Aires: Instituto Caro y Cuervo, Unesco.
Lane, Frank W.
1986 *The Violent Earth.* Topsfield: Salem House.
Lange, Algot
1914 *The Lower Amazon.* New York: Putnam's Sons.
Las Muñecas, Rodrigo de
1942 "Araguaimujo en fiestas de la 'carata'." *Venezuela Misionera* 4(44):215–18; 4(45):235–40.
1949 "Labor del Centro Misional de Araguaimujo en las rancherias." *Venezuela Misionera* 11(130–31):395–400.
Latocha, Hartwig
1982 *Die Rolle des Hundes bei südamerikanischen Indianern.* Münchner Beiträge zur Amerikanistik, 8. Hohenschäftlarn: Klaus Renner Verlag.
Lavandero, Pérez Julio
1971 "El mito de la paloma." *Venezuela Misionera* 33(382): 41–43.
1974 "Niaharabaka, el caiman." *Venezuela Misionera* 36(426): 308–16.
1975 "Jitoare y Jorane." *Venezuela Misionera* 37(430):56–63.
1980a "La formación de la selva." *Venezuela Misionera* 41 (485):22–24.
1980b "Murió el caiman feroz." *Venezuela Misionera* 42 (489):146–50.

1982   "La nube de las cuatro jovenes." *Venezuela Misionera* 43(508):56–58.
1991   *Ajotejana.* Vol. 2, *Mitos.* Caracas: Ediciones Paulinas.

Lavandero, Julio, and H. Dieter Heinen
1986   "Canciones y bailes del ritual de la Nouara." *Montalbán* (Caracas) 17:199–243.

Layrisse, Miguel, George Salas, and H. Dieter Heinen
1980   "Vital Statistics of Five Warao Subtribes." In Johannes Wilbert and Miguel Layrisse, eds., *Demographic and Biological Studies of the Warao Indians*, pp. 60–69. Los Angeles: University of California, Latin American Center Publications.

Leigue Castedo, Luis
1957   *El Iténez salvaje.* La Paz: Ministerio de Educación.

Léry, Jean de
1975 [1599]   *Histoire d'un voyage fait en la terre du Brésil, autrement dite Amérique.* Geneva.

Level, Andres
1898   "Visit to the Missions of Venezuela [1847]." *British Guiana Boundary Case. Arbitration with the United States of Venezuela. Appendix to the Case on Behalf of the Government of Her Britannic Majesty* 6:150–65 (1815–1892). London.

Lévi-Strauss, Claude
1969   *The Raw and the Cooked. Introduction to A Science of Mythology*, vol. 1. Trans. John and Doreen Weightman. New York: Harper and Row.
1973   *From Honey to Ashes. Introduction to A Science of Mythology*, vol. 2. Trans. John and Doreen Weightman. New York: Harper and Row.
1988   *The Jealous Potter.* Trans. Benedicte Chorier. Chicago: University of Chicago Press.

Lind, Ulf
1981   "Espiritos auxiliares dos xamãs Lengua no Paraguai." In *Contribuições à antropologia em homenagem ao Professor Egon Schaden*, pp. 129–34. Coleção Museu Paulista, Série Ensaios, vol. 4. São Paulo: Universidade de São Paulo. Fundo de Pesquisas do Musen Paulista.

Lizot, Jacques
1976 *Le cercle des feux.* Faits et dits des Indiens yanomami. Paris: Éditíons du Seuil.

Lodares, Baltasar de
1930 *Los Franciscanos Capuchinos en Venezuela.* 2 vols. Caracas: Empresa Gutenberg.

Lothrop, Samuel K.
1928 *The Indians of Tierra del Fuego.* Contributions from the Museum of the American Indian, Heye Foundation, vol. 10. New York.

Lovell, W. G.
1992 "Heavy Shadows and Black Night: Disease and Population in Colonial Spanish America." In K. W. Butzer, ed., *The Americas before and after 1492: Current Geographical Research,* pp. 426–43. *Annals of the Association of American Geographers* 82(3).

Lowie, Robert H.
1946 "The Cariri." In Julian H. Steward, ed., *Handbook of South American Indians,* Vol. 1, *The Marginal Tribes,* pp. 557–59. Smithsonian Institution, Bureau of American Ethnology, Bulletin, no. 143. Washington, D.C.: Government Printing Office.

Lublinski, Ida
1920–21 "Der Medizinmann bei den Naturvölkern Südamerikas." *Zeitschrift für Ethnologie* 52–53:234–63.

Lukesch, Anton
1962 "Beiträge zur Weltanschauung der Kayapó." *Akten des 34. Internationalen Amerikanistenkongresses, 1960.* Vienna.

1968 *Mythos und Leben der Kayapo.* Acta Ethnologica et Linguistica, Series Americana, 2. Vienna.

1976 *Mito e vida dos índios Caiapós.* Trans. from the German by Trude Arneitz von Laschan Solstein. São Paulo: Pioneira, Editora da Universidade de São Paulo.

Lund Skar, Sarah
1987 *Natives and Neighbors in South America.* Etnologiska Studier, 38. Göteborg: Ethnographical Museum Göteborg.

McCann, J.
1987 *From Poverty to Famine in Northeast Ethiopia: A Rural History, 1900–1935.* Philadelphia: University of Pennsylvania Press.

McCurrach, James C.
1960 *Palms of the World.* New York: Harper and Row.

McNeill, W. H.
1976 *Plagues and Peoples.* New York: Anchor Press.

Magaña, Edmundo
1987a "Astronomía shamanística tarëno." In *Contribuciones al estudio de la mitología y astronomía de los indios de las Guayanas,* pp. 167–214. Latin America Studies, 35. Amsterdam: Center for Latin American Research and Documentation.
1987b "Narrativas kaliña. Kaliña penatokonon aulanembo." In *Contribuciones al estudio de la mitología y astronomía de los indios de las Guayanas,* pp. 215–60. Latin America Studies, 35. Amsterdam: Center for Latin American Research and Documentation.
1988 "Reminiscencias personales de un indio tarëno." *Arbor* 131:177–218. Madrid.

Marino, Fray
1939 "Flores y espinas." *Venezuela Misionera* 2(15):395–97.

Mariscotti de Görlitz, Ana María
1973 "La posición del señor de los fenómenos meteorológicos en los panteones regionales de los Andes Centrales." *Historia y Cultura* (Lima) 6:207–15.

Maroni, Pablo
1988 [1738] *Noticias autenticas del famoso rio Marañon.* Iquitos: Instituto Nacional de Cultura.

Marrero, Levi
1964 *Venezuela y sus recursos.* Caracas: Cultura Venezolana.

Matteson, Esther
1965 *The Piro (Arawakan) Language.* Berkeley and Los Angeles: University of California Press.

Maxwell, Nicole
1961 *Witch Doctor's Apprentice.* Boston: Collier, Macmillan.

Métraux, Alfred
1928 *La religion des Tupinamba et ses rapports avec celle des*

autres tribus Tupí-Guaraní. Bibliothèque de l'École des Hautes Études, Sciences Religieuses, 45. Paris: Librairie Ernest Leroux.

1942 *The Native Tribes of Eastern Bolivia and Western Matto Grosso.* Smithsonian Institution, Bureau of American Ethnology, Bulletin, no. 134. Washington, D.C.: Government Printing Office.

1943 "The Social Organization and Religion of the Mojo and Manasi." *Primitive Man* 16(1–2):1–30.

1944a "Le chamanism chez les Indiens de l'Amérique du Sud tropicale." *Acta Americana* 2(4):320–41.

1944b "Estudios de etnografía Chaquense." *Anales del Instituto de Etnografía Americana* 5:263–314. Universidad Nacional del Cuyo.

1946a "Ethnography of the Gran Chaco." In Julian H. Steward, ed., *Handbook of South American Indians*, Vol. 1, *The Marginal Tribes,* pp. 197–370. Smithsonian Institution, Bureau of American Ethnology, Bulletin, no. 143. Washington, D.C.: Government Printing Office.

1946b "The Caingan." In Julian H. Steward, ed., *Handbook of South American Indians*, Vol. 1, *The Marginal Tribes,* pp. 445–75. Smithsonian Institution, Bureau of American Ethnology, Bulletin, no. 143. Washington, D.C.: Government Printing Office.

1946c *Myths of the Toba and Pilagá Indians of the Gran Chaco.* Memoirs of the American Folklore Society. New York.

1948 "Tribes of Eastern Bolivia and the Madeira Headwaters." In Julian H. Steward, ed., *Handbook of South American Indians*, Vol. 3, *The Tropical Forest Tribes*, pp. 381–454. Smithsonian Institution, Bureau of American Ethnology, Bulletin, no. 143. Washington, D.C.: Government Printing Office.

1949a "Religion and Shamanism." In Julian H. Steward, ed., *Handbook of South American Indians,* Vol. 5, *The Comparative Ethnology of South American Indians*, pp. 559–99. Smithsonian Institution, Bureau of American Ethnology, Bulletin, no. 143. Washington, D.C.: Government Printing Office.

1949b	"Warfare, Cannibalism, and Human Trophies." In Julian H. Steward, ed., *Handbook of South American Indians*, Vol. 5, *The Comparative Ethnology of South American Indians*, pp. 383–409. Smithsonian Institution, Bureau of American Ethnology, Bulletin, no. 143. Washington, D.C.: Government Printing Office.
1952	"Le magicien chez les indiens des Guyanes et du Brésil." *Cahiers du Sud* 39(316):380–96.
1966	"South American Thunderbirds." *Journal of American Folklore* 57.
1969	*Myths of the Toba and Pilagá Indians of the Gran Chaco.* Memoirs of the American Folklore Society. New York.

Meyer de Schauensee, Rodolphe, and William Phelps, Jr.
1978   *A Guide to the Birds of Venezuela.* Princeton: Princeton University Press.

Michelson, Truman
1930   *Contributions to Fox Ethnology*, vol. 2. Smithsonian Institution, Bureau of American Ethnology, Bulletin, no. 95. Washington, D.C.: Government Printing Office.

Miller, Elmer Schaffner
1980   *A Critical Annotated Bibliography of the Gran Chaco Toba.* New Haven: Human Relations Area Files.

Mindlin, Betty
1985   *Nós Paiter os Suruí de Rondônia.* Petropolis: Vozes.

Minnis, Paul E.
1985   *Social Adaptation to Food Stress.* Chicago: University of Chicago Press.

Molina, J. J.
1809   *The Geographical, Natural and Civil History of Chili.* London.

Monast, J. E.
1972   *Los indios Aimaraes.* Buenos Aires: Carlos Lohlé.

Morey, Nancy C., and Robert V. Morey
N.d.   "Post Contact Warfare Patterns in the Colombian and Venezuelan Llanos." Unpublished MS.

Morey, Robert V.
1979   "A Joyful Harvest of Souls: Disease and the Destruction of the Llanos Indians." *Antropológica* 52:77–108.

N.d. "The Effects of Carib Slaving in the Llanos of Colombia and Venezuela." Unpublished MS.

Müller, Jan
1956 "Report on a Botanical Reconnaissance in the Delta Amacuro." Unpublished MS.
1959 "Palynology of Recent Orinoco Delta and Shelf Sediments: Reports on the Orinoco Shelf Expedition." *Micropaleontology* 5(1):1–32.

Münzel, Mark
1973 *Erzählungen der Kamayurá*. Wiesbaden: Franz Steiner Verlag.

Murdock, George Peter
1980 *Theories of Illness*. Pittsburgh: University of Pittsburgh Press.

Murphy, Robert Francis
1958 *Mundurucú Religion*. Berkeley: University of California Press.

Mussolini, Gioconda
1979 *Ensaios de antropologia indígena e caiçara*. Rio de Janeiro: Paz e Terra.

Nectario María, Hermano
1924 *Mapa de las misiones católicas de Venezuela de 1652 hasta 1817*. Barquisimeto: Colegio La Salle.

Nimuendajú, Curt
1914 "Vokabular und Sagen der Cregêz-Indianer (Tajé)." *Zeitschrift für Ethnologie* 46:626–36.
1919–22 "Bruchstücke aus der Religion und Überlieferung der Šipáia-Indianer." *Anthropos* 14-15:1002–39, 16-17:367–406.
1924 "Os indios Parintintin do Rio Madeira." *Journal de la Société des Américanistes* 16:201–78.
1939 *The Apinayé*. Trans. Robert H. Lowie and John M. Cooper. Anthropological Series, 8. Washington, D.C.: Catholic University of America Press.
1952 *The Tukuna*. Trans. William D. Hohenthal. Berkeley: University of California Press.

Noel, Jesse A.
1972 *Trinidad, Provincia de Venezuela. Historia de la Administración Española de Trinidad*. Biblioteca de la Academia Nacional de la Historia, 109. Caracas.

Nordenskiöld, Erland
1912   *Indianerleben. El Gran Chaco (Südamerika).* Leipzig: Albert Bonnier.
1915   "Die religiösen Vorstellungen der Itonama-Indianer in Bolivia." *Zeitschrift für Ethnologie* 47(2-3):105–13.
1920   *The Changes in the Material Culture of Two Indian Tribes under the Influence of New Surroundings.* Göteborg.
1938   *An Historical and Ethnological Survey of the Cuna Indians.* Göteborg: Ethnographical Museum Göteborg.

Oberem, Udo
1980   *Los Quijos: Historia de la transculturación de un grupo indígena en el Oriente Ecuatoriano.* Otavalo: Instituto Otavaleño de Antropología.

Oberg, Kalervo
1949   *The Terena and the Caduveo of Southern Mato Grosso, Brazil.* Smithsonian Institution, Institute of Social Anthropology, 9. Washington, D.C.: Government Printing Office.
1953   *Indian Tribes of Northern Mato Grosso, Brazil.* Smithsonian Institution, Institute of Social Anthropology, 15. Washington, D.C.: Government Printing Office.

Oefner, Luis M.
1940-41   "Apuntes sobre una tribú salvaje que existe en el Oriente de Bolivia." *Anthropos* 35-36:100–108.

Ojer, Pablo
1966   *La formación del Oriente de Venezuela.* Vol. 1, *Creación de las gobernaciones.* Universidad Católica "Andrés Bello." Biblioteca de Estudios Universitarios, 6. Caracas.

Olsen, Dale A.
1975a   "Music-Induced Altered States of Consciousness among Warao Shamans." *Journal of Latin American Lore* 1:19–33.
1975b   "The Function of Naming in the Shamanistic Curing Songs of the Warao Indians of Venezuela." *Yearbook of Inter-American Musical Research,* 1974. Austin.

Orjuela, Héctor H.
1983   *Yurupary: Mito, leyenda y epopeya del Vaupés.* Con la traducción de la "Leggenda dell' Jurupary" del Conde

Ermanno Stradelli por Susana N. Salessi. Publicaciones del Instituto Caro y Cuervo, no. 64. Bogotá.

Ortiz, Fernando
1947 *El huracan, mitología y sus simbolos.* Mexico.

Ortner, Sherry
1984 "Theory in Anthropology since the 1960s." *Comparative Studies in Society and History* 26(1):126–66.

Osborn, Henry
1958 "Textos folklóricos en Guarao." *Boletín Indigenista Venezolano* 3–5:163–170; 6:157–73.
1960 "Textos folklóricos Guarao." *Antropológica* 9:21–38; 10:71–80.

Osgood, Cornelius
1946 *British Guiana Archaeology to 1945.* Yale University Publications in Anthropology, no. 36. New Haven.

Pagels, Elaine
1988 *Adam, Eve, and the Serpent.* New York: Random House.

Palha, Luiz
1942 *Indios curiosos: Lendas, constumes, lingua.* Rio de Janeiro.

Pauly, Antonio
1928 *Ensayo de etnografía americana: Viajes y exploraciones.* Buenos Aires: Talleres Casa Jacobo Preuser.

Payaguaje, Fernando
1990 *El bebedor de yaje.* Shushufindi (Rio Aguarico): Vicariato Apostólico de Aguarico.

Pelleprat, Pierre
1965 [1655] *Relato de las misiones de los padres de la Compañia de Jesús en las islas y en tierra firme de América Meridional.* Biblioteca de la Academia de la Historia, Fuentes para la historia colonial de Venezuela, 77. Caracas.

Perdue, Theda
1979 *Slavery and the Evolution of Cherokee Society, 1540–1866.* Knoxville: University of Tennessee Press.

Pérez Soto de Atencio, Sagrario
1971 "Clasificación y descripción." In Miguel G. Arroyo C., José María Cruxent, and Sagrario Pérez Soto de Atencio, eds., *Arte prehispanica de Venezuela.* Caracas: Fundación Eugenio Mendoza.

Perrier, J.
1948 "Religion d'une tribu d'Amérique du Sud: Les Carajàs." *Histoire générale des religions*. Paris: Librairie Aristide Quillet.

Perrin, Michel
1976 *Le chemin des indiens morts*. Paris: Payot.

Pfefferkorn, Hermann W., Karlfried Fuchs, and Christian Hecht
1988 "Recent Geology and Taphonomy of the Orinoco Delta: Overview and Field Observations." *Heidelberger Geowissenschaftliche Abhandlungen* 20:21–56.

Pineda Camacho, Roberto
1979 "El sendero del arco iris: notas sobre el simbolismo de los negocios en una comunidad Amazónica." *Revista Colombiana de Antropología* 22:29–58.

Pineda Giraldo, Roberto
1950 "Aspectos de la magia en La Guajira." *Revista del Instituto Etnológico Nacional* (Bogotá) 3(1):163.

Plassard, Louis
1868 "Los Guaraunos et le Delta de l'Orénoque." *Bulletin de la Société de Géographie* 15:568–92.

Polo de Ondegardo, Juan
1816[ca.1545] *Informaciones acerca de la región y gobierno de los Incas*. Lima.

Polykrates, Gottfried
1974 *Beiträge zur Religionsfrage der Yanonámi-Indianer*. Publications of the National Museum, Ethnographical Series, 14. Copenhagen: National Museum of Denmark.

Poma de Ayala, Felipe Guaman
1936 *El primer nueva corónica i buen gobierno*. Paris: Institut d'Ethnologie.

Posnansky, Arthur
1937 *Antropología y sociología de las razas interandinas y de las regiones adyacentes*. Instituto "Tihuanacu" de Antropología, Etnografía y Prehistoria. La Paz.

Pottier, J. P.
1986 "The Politics of Famine Prevention: Ecology, Regional Production and Food Complementarity in Western Rwanda." *African Affairs* 85:207–39.

Preuss, Konrad Theodor
1926 *Forschungsreise zu den Kágaba*. Vienna: Mechitharisten-Buchdruckerei.

Preuss, Mary H.
1986 "A Study of Jurakán of the *Popol Vuh*." In Edmundo Magaña and Peter Mason, eds., *Myth and the Imaginary in the New World*, Latin America Studies, 34:359–95. Amsterdam: Center for Latin American Research and Documentation.

Purdy, Barbara
1988 "American Indians after A.D. 1492." *American Anthropologist* 90:640–55.

Raleigh, Sir Walter
1970 [1596] *The Discovery of the Large, Rich and Beautiful Empire of Guiana with a Relation of the Great and Golden City of Manoa (which the Spaniards call Dorado), etc. Performed in the Year 1595.* Reprinted from the edition of 1596 with some Unpublished Documents Relative to that Country. Edited with Copious Explanatory Notes and a Bibliographical Memoir by Sir Robert H. Schomburgk, Ph.D. New York: Burt Franklin.

Ramenofsky, Ann
1987 *Vectors of Death: The Archaeology of European Contact*. Albuquerque: University of New Mexico Press.

Reichel-Dolmatoff, Gerardo
1951 *Los Kogi: Una tribu de la Sierra Nevada de Santa Marta, Colombia*. 2 vols. Bogotá.
1971 *Amazonian Cosmos: The Sexual and Religious Symbolism of the Tukano Indians*. Chicago: University of Chicago Press.
1975 *The Shaman and the Jaguar: A Study of Narcotic Drugs among the Indians of Colombia*. Philadelphia: Temple University Press.
1978 *Beyond the Milky Way: Hallucinatory Imagery of the Tukano Indians*. Los Angeles: UCLA Latin American Center Publications.
1985 *Los Kogi: Una tribu de la Sierra Nevada de Santa Marta, Colombia*. 2 vols. Bogotá: Procultura.

1986	"Algunos aspectos de geografía chamanística de los indios Desana de Colombia." In Edmundo Magaña and Peter Mason, eds., *Myth and the Imaginary in the New World,* Latin America Studies, 34:75–95. Amsterdam: Center for Latin American Research and Documentation.
1987	"The Great Mother and the Kogi Universe: A Concise Overview." *Journal of Latin American Lore* 13(1):73–113.
1989	"Biological and Social Aspects of the Yuruparí Complex of the Colombian Vaupés Territory." *Journal of Latin American Lore* 15(1):95–135.

Renard-Casevitz and O. Dollfus
1988   "Geografía de algunos mitos y creencias: espacios simbólicos y realidades geográficas de los Machiguenga del Alto-Urubamba." *Amazonia Peruana* 8(16):7–40.

Rey Fajardo, P. José del
1971   *Aportes jesuiticos a la filología colonial venezolana.* Lenguas indígenas de Venezuela, 4/5–6. 2 vols. Caracas: Universidad Católica Andrés Bello, Seminario de Lenguas Indígenas Históricas.

Ribeiro, Darcy
1950   *Religião e mitologia Kadiuéu.* Ministério da Agricultura, Conselho Nacional de Proteção aos Índios, 106. Rio de Janeiro: Serviço de Proteção aos Índios.
1974   *Uirá sai à procura de deus: Ensaios de etnologia e indigenismo.* Coleção Estudos Brasileiros, 2. Rio de Janeiro.
1980   *Kadiwéu: Ensaios etnológicos sobre o saber, o azar e a beleza.* Petrópolis: Vozes.

Riehl, Herbert
1954   *Tropical Meteorology.* New York: McGraw-Hill.

Rivière, Peter
1980   Review of *The Man-Eating Myth,* by W. Arens. *Man* 15(1):203–5.

Robiou-Lamarche, Sebastián
1986   "Ida y vuelta a Guanín, un ensayo sobre la cosmovisión taína." In Edmundo Magaña and Peter Mason, eds., *Myth and the Imaginary in the New World,* Latin America Studies, 34:459–98. Amsterdam: Center for Latin American Research and Documentation.

Robson, John R. K.
1981 *Famine: Its Causes, Effects and Management.* New York: Gordon and Breach Science Publishers.

Rochefort, C. de, and L. Poinci
1665 *Histoire naturelle et morale des iles Antilles de l'Amérique.* Rotterdam.

Roe, Peter G.
1982 *The Cosmic Zygote: Cosmology in the Amazon Basin.* New Brunswick: Rutgers University Press.

Roquette-Pinto, E.
1938 *Rondonia.* Brasiliane, 39. Biblioteca Pedagogica Brasileira. Rio de Janeiro: Companhia Editora Nacional.

Roth, Walter Edmund
1915 "An Inquiry into the Animism and Folk-Lore of the Guiana Indians." In *Thirtieth Annual Report of the Bureau of American Ethnology, 1908–1909*, pp. 103–386. Washington, D.C.: Government Printing Office.
1924 "An Introductory Study of the Arts, Crafts, and Customs of the Guiana Indians." In *Thirty-eighth Annual Report of the Bureau of American Ethnology, 1916–1917*, pp. 23–745. Washington, D.C.: Government Printing Office.

Rouse, Irving
1948 "The Carib." In Julian H. Steward, ed., *Handbook of South American Indians*, Vol. 4, *The Circum-Caribbean Tribes*, pp. 547–65. Smithsonian Institution, Bureau of American Ethnology, Bulletin, no. 143. Washington, D.C.: Government Printing Office.
1983 "Diffusion and Interaction in the Orinoco Valley and on the Coast." *Proceedings of the Ninth International Congress for the Study of Pre-Columbian Cultures of the Lesser Antilles, Santo Domingo, 2–8 August 1981.* Montreal.
1986 *Migrations in Prehistory: Inferring Population Movement from Cultural Remains.* New Haven: Yale University Press.

Rouse, Irving, and José M. Cruxent
1963 *Venezuelan Archaeology.* Caribbean Series, 6. New Haven: Yale University Press.

Royo y Gómez, José
    1960   "Pleistocene Vertebrates from the Muaco Deposit." *News Bulletin* 58:31–32. Society of Vertebrate Paleontology.

Ruddle, Kenneth, Dennis Johnson, Patricia K. Townsend, and John D. Rees
    1978   *Palm Sago: A Tropical Starch from Marginal Lands.* East-West Technology and Development Institute. Honolulu: University of Hawaii Press.

Ruis Blanco, Matías
    1965   *Conversión de Píritu. Estudio preliminar y notas del P. Ridel de Lejarza, O.F.M.* Biblioteca de la Academia Nacionale de la Historia, 78. Caracas.

Rumeu de Armas, Antonio
    1944   *Historia de la previsión social en España. Cofradías-gremios-hermandades-montepíos.* Madrid: Editorial Revista De Derecho Privado.

Rydén, Stig
    1933   "Throwing-Fork for Magical Use from the Toba Indians (El Gran Chaco)." *Man* 204–5:196.

Sabate, Luis
    1877   *Viaje de los padres misioneros del Convento del Cuzco a las tribus salvajes de los Campas, Piros, Cunibos y Sipibos en el año de 1847.* Lima.

Saint Clair, T. Staunton
    1834   *A Soldier's Recollection of the West Indies and America.* 2 vols. London.

Saint Cricq, M.
    1853   "Voyage du Pérou au Brésil par les fleuves Ucayali et Amazone." *Bulletin de Géographie.* Paris.

Salas, George, and H. Dieter Heinen
    1980   "Computerized Warao Demographic Listings." In Johannes Wilbert and Miguel Layrisse, eds., *Demographic and Biological Studies of the Warao Indians*, pp. 180–247. UCLA Latin American Studies, vol. 45. Los Angeles: University of California, Latin American Center Publications.

Salas, Juan
    1964   "Relación que hizo Juan de Salas, sobre la isla de
    [1520-70]   Margarita y sus terminos [1560–1570]." In Antonio A.

Moreno, ed., *Relaciones Geográficas de Venezuela*, pp. 51–56. Biblioteca de la Academia de la Historia, Fuentes para la historia colonial de Venezuela, 70. Caracas.

Sánchez Labrador, José
1910   *El Paraguay católico*. 2 vols. Buenos Aires.

Santos Ortiz de Villalba, Juan
1976   *Sacha Pacha: El mundo de la selva*. Quito: Colegio Tecnico "Don Bosco."

Savage-Landor, Henry
1913   *Across Unknown South America*. London.

Schmidt, Max
1905   *Indianerstudien in Zentralbrasilien*. Erlebnisse und ethnologische Ereignisse einer Reise in den Jahren 1900 bis 1901. Berlin: Dietrich Reimer (Ernst Vohsen).

Schomburgk, Moritz Richard
1847–48   *Reisen in Britisch-Guiana in den Jahren 1840–1844*. 3 vols. Leipzig: J. J. Weber.

Schomburgk, Robert H.
1840   *A Description of British Guiana*. London: Simpkin, Marshall, and Co.

Schuller, Rudolph
1922   "The Ethnological and Linguistic Position of the Tacana Indians of Bolivia." *American Anthropologist* 24:161–70.

Schultes, R. E., and R. F. Raffauf
1990   *The Healing Forest: Medicinal and Toxic Plants of the Northwest Amazonia*. Portland: Dioscorides Press.

Schultz, Harald
1961–62   "Informações etnográficas sôbre os Umutina." *Revista do Museu Paulista* 13:75–313.

Sebag, Lucien
1965   "Le chamanism Ayoréo." *L'Homme* (Paris) 5(1):5–32, 5(2):92–122.

Sekelj, Tibor
1950   *Durch Brasiliens Urwälder zu wilden Indianerstämmen*. Zürich: Orell Füssli Verlag.

Silverwood-Cope, Peter
1980   "Cosmología Maku." *Anuário Antropológico* 78:176–239. Rio de Janeiro.

Simson, Alfred
   1883   "Notes on the Napo Indians." *Journal of the Anthropological Institute of Great Britain and Ireland* 12: 21–27.

Skutch, A. F.
   1985   "Sunbittern." In Bruce Campbell and Elizabeth Lack, eds., *A Dictionary of Birds*. Vermillon, S.D.: Buteo Books for the British Ornithologists' Union.

Slud, Paul
   1964   "The Birds of Costa Rica: Distribution and Ecology." *Bulletin of the American Museum of Natural History*, 128.

Snethlage, Heinrich
   1937   *Atiko y: Meine Erlebnisse bei den Indianern des Guaporé*. Berlin: Klinkhardt & Biermann Verlag.

Snow, J. W.
   1976   "The Climate of Northern South America." In Werner Schwerdtfeger, ed., *Climates of Central and South America*, pp. 295–403. World Survey of Climatology, 12. New York: Elsevier Scientific Publishing Company.

Solarte, Benhur Cerón
   1986   *Los Awa-Kwaiker: Un grupo indígena de la selva pluvial del Pacífico Nariñense y el Nor-Occidente Ecuatoriano*. Quito: Abya-Yala.

Souza Brito, R. M., and A. A. Souza Brito
   1993   "Forty Years of Brazilian Medicinal Plant Research." *Journal of Ethnopharmacology* 39:53–67.

Stahl, Wilmar
   1982   *Escenario Indígena Chaqueño pasado y presente*. Filadelfia, Paraguay: Asociación de Servicios de Cooperación Indígena-Mennonita.

Stannard, David E.
   1992   *American Holocaust: Columbus and the Conquest of the New World*. Oxford: Oxford University Press.

Steinen, Karl von den
   1894   *Unter den Naturvölkern Zentral-Brasiliens*. Berlin: Dietrich Reimer.
   1897   *Unter den Naturvölkern Zentral-Brasiliens*. 2nd ed. Volksausgabe. Berlin: Dietrich Reimer.

Stirling, Metthew W.
1938   *Historical and Ethnographical Material on the Jivaro Indians*. Smithsonian Institution, Bureau of American Ethnology, Bulletin, no. 117. Washington, D.C.: Government Printing Office.

Suárez, María M.
1968   *Los Warao: Indígenas del Delta del Orinoco*. Caracas: Instituto Venezolano de Investigaciones Científicas.

Sullivan, Lawrence E.
1988   *Icanchu's Drum: An Orientation to Meaning in South American Religions*. New York: Macmillan.

Susnik, Branislava
1984-85   *Los aborígenes del Paraguay: Approximación a las creencias de los indígenas*. Asunción: Museo Etnográfico "Andrés Barbero," no. 6. Asunción.
1989   *Cultura religiosa*. Part 1, *Ambito americano*. Manuales del Museo Etnográfico "Andrés Barbero," no. 4. Asunción: Editorial Litocolor.

Sweet, David G.
1969   "The Population of the Upper Amazon Valley, 17th and 18th Centuries." Master's thesis, University of Wisconsin, Madison.
1974   "A Rich Realm of Nature Destroyed: The Middle Amazon Valley." Ph.D. diss., Madison: University of Wisconsin.

Tastevin, Constant
1923   "Les indiens Mura de la région de L'Autaz (Haut-Amazone)." *L'Anthropologie* 33:514–33.

Tauste, Francisco de
1680   *Arte y Bocabulario de la lengua de los Indios Chaymas, Cumanagotos, Cores, Parias, y otros diversos de la Provincia de Cumaná, o Nueva Andalucía, con un tratado a lo último de la doctrina christiana*. Madrid: Bernardo de Villa-Diego.

Taylor, Douglas
1946   "Notes on the Star Lore of the Caribbees." *American Anthropologist* 48:215–22.

Tello, Julio C.
1923   "El mito de los Amuesha." *Inca* (Lima) 1, no. 1: 128–30.

Thevet, André
    1944 [1557–58] *Les singularitez de la France Antarctique*. Paris.

Thompson, Stith
    1955–58   *Motif-Index of Folk-Literature. A Classification of Narrative Elements in Folktales, Ballades, Myths, Fables, Mediaeval Romances, Exempla, Fabliaux, Jest-Books and Local Legends*. 6 vols. Revised and enlarged edition. Bloomington: Indiana University Press.

Trimborn, Hermann
    1949   *Señorío y barbarie en el valle del Cauca. Estudio sobre la antigua civilización quimbaya y grupos afines del oeste de Colombia*. Madrid: Consejo Superior de Investigaciones Científicas. Instituto Gonzalo Fernández de Oviedo.

Trupp, Fritz
    1977   *Mythen der Makuna*. Acta Ethnologica et Linguistica, 40. Vienna.

Tschopic, Harry, Jr.
    1946   "The Aymara." In Julian H. Steward, ed., *Handbook of South American Indians*, Vol. 2, *The Andean Civilizations*, pp. 501–73. Smithsonian Institution, Bureau of American Ethnology, Bulletin, no. 143. Washington, D.C.: Printing Office.

Turrado Moreno, Angel
    1945   *Etnografía de los indios guaraúnos*. Caracas: Litografía y tipografía Vargas.

Utley, R., and W. Washburn
    1985   *Indian Wars*. New York: American Heritage.

Valdivia, Luis de
    1887   *Arte y gramatica general de la lengua que corre en todo el Reyno de Chile, con un vocabulario y confessionario*. Edición facsimilar. Leipzig. First ed., Lima, 1606.

van Andel, T.
    1956   "Note to Accompany a Provisional Sediment-Morphological Map of Delta Amacuro." Unpublished MS.
    1967   "The Orinoco Delta." *Journal of Sedimentary Petrology* 37:297–310.

van Andel, Tj. H., and Pl. L. Sachs
    1964   "Sedimentation in the Gulf of Paria during the Holocene

Transgression: A Subsurface Acoustic Reflection Study." *Sears Foundation: Journal of Marine Research* 22(1): 30–50.

Vaquero de Langayo, Antonio Enrique
1965 *Idioma Warao: Morfología, sintaxis, literatura.* Caracas: Editorial Sucre.
N.d. "Tradición oral del grupo Warao." Unpublished MS.

Vasco, Luis Guillermo
1985 *Jaibanás los verdaderos hombres.* Biblioteca Banco Popular, Textos Universitarios. Bogotá.

Vega, Augustín de
1974 "Noticia del principio y progresos del establecimiento de las misiones de gentiles en el río Orinoco, por la Compañía de Jesús, con la continuación, y oposiciónes que hicieron los Carives hasta el año de [1]744." In José del Rey Fajardo, ed., *Documentos jesuíticos relativos a la historia de la Compañía de Jesús en Venezuela,* vol. 3, pp. 3–149. Biblioteca de la Academia Nacional de la Historia, Fuentes para la historia colonia de Venezuela, 118. Caracas.

Venezuela, Ministerio del Ambiente y Recursos Naturales Renovables (MARNR)
1982 *Plan de manejo de las comunidades indígenas Warao.* Informe preliminar. Tucupita: Ministerio del Ambiente y Recursos Naturales Renovables, División de Administración del Ambiente. Zona Administrativa no. 12. Territorio Federal Delta Amacuro.

Verano, John W., and Douglas H. Ubelacker, eds.
1992 *Disease and Demography in the Americas.* Washington, D.C.: Smithsonian Institution Press.

Vila, Pablo, et al.
1960 "Geografía de Venezuela," In *El territorio nacional y su ambiente físico,* vol. 1. Caracas: Ministerio de Educación.

Villamarín, Juan A., and Judith E. Villamarín
1975 *Indian Labor in Mainland Colonial Spanish America.* Latin American Studies Program, Occasional Papers and Monographs, no. 1. Newark: University of Delaware.

Villarejo, Avencio
1943 *Asi es la selva. Estudio geográfico de la Provincia de*

Bajo Amazonas. Lima: Compañia de Impresiones y Publicidad.

Vliet, Kent A.
1989 "Social Displays of the American Alligator (*Aligator mississippiensis*)." *American Zoologist* 29:1019–31.

Volhard, Ewald
1939 *Kannibalismus*. Studien zur Kulturkunde, vol. 5. Stuttgart: Strecker and Schröder.

Voorde, P. K. J. van der
1962 "Soil Conditions of the Isla Macareo, Orinoco Delta, Venezuela." In *Mededelingen van de Stichting voor Bodemkartering. Boor en Spade*, 12:6–26. Wageningen: H. Veenman en Zonen.

Voorhies, Barbara, Erika Wagner, and Lilliam Arvelo
1981 "Mora: un yacimiento arqueológico en el Bajo Delta del Orinoco, Venezuela." *Antropológica* 55:31–50.

Wagley, Charles
1942 "O estado de éxtase do pagé Tupi." *Sociologia* 4(3):285–92. São Paulo.
1943 "Tapirapé Shamanism." *Boletim do Museu Nacional, Antropologia* (Rio de Janeiro) 3.
1977 *Welcome of Tears: The Tapirapé Indians of Central Brazil*. Oxford and New York: Oxford University Press.

Wagley, Charles, and Eduardo Galvão
1955 *Os índios Tenetehara: Uma cultura em transição*. Rio de Janeiro: Ministério de Educação e Cultura.

Wallace, Alfred Russel
1853 *Travels on the Amazon and Rio Negro. With an Account of the Native Tribes, and Observations on the Climate, Geology, and Natural History of the Amazon Valley*. London.
1889 *Travels on the Amazon and Rio Negro, with an Account of the Native Tribes, and Observations on the Climate, Geology, and Natural History of the Amazon Valley*. London: Ward, Lock and Co.
1934 *Narrative of Travels in the Amazon and the Rio Negro*. London.

Wassén, Henry
1934 "The Frog Motif in Indian Mythology and Imaginative World." *Anthropos* 29:319–70, 613–58.

Wavrin, Marquis de
- 1932   "Folk-lore du Haut-Amazone." *Journal de la Société des Américanistes* 24(1):121–78.
- 1937   *Moeurs et coutumes des indiens sauvages de L'Amérique du Sud.* Paris.

Weiss, Gerald
- 1969   *The Cosmology of the Campa Indians of Eastern Peru.* Ann Arbor: University Microfilms (69-18, 132).
- 1975   "Campa Cosmology. The World of a Forest Tribe in South America." *Anthropological Papers of the American Museum of Natural History* (New York) 52(5):217–588.

Werner, Dennis
- 1984   *Amazon Journey. An Anthropologist's Year among Brazil's Mekranoti Indians.* New York.

Whitehead, Neil L.
- 1984   "Carib Cannibalism: The Historic Evidence." *Journal de la Société des Américanistes* 70:69–88.
- 1988   *Lords of the Tiger Spirit: A History of the Caribs in Colonial Venezuela and Guyana.* Caribbean Series, 10. Dordrecht: Koninklijk Institut voor Taal-, Land- en Volkenkunde.
- 1992   "Tribes Make States and States Make Tribes: Warfare and the Creation of Colonial Tribes and States in Northeastern South America." In R. Brian Ferguson and Neil L. Whitehead, eds., *War in the Tribal Zone*, pp. 127–50. Santa Fe: School of American Research Press.

Wilbert, Johannes
- 1963   *Indios de la región Orinoco-Ventuari.* Fundación La Salle de Ciencias Naturales, Monografía, no. 8. Caracas: Instituto Caribe de Antropología y Sociología.
- 1969   *Textos folkloricos de los indios Warao.* Trans. Antonio Vaquero. Latin American Studies, vol. 12. Los Angeles: Latin American Center, University of California.
- 1972   *Survivors of Eldorado: Four Indian Cultures of South America.* New York: Praeger.
- 1975a   "The Metaphoric Snare: Analysis of a Warao Folktale." *Journal of Latin American Lore* 1:7–17.
- 1975b   "Eschatology in a Participatory Universe: Destinies of the Soul among the Warao Indians of Venezuela." In

Elizabeth P. Benson, ed., *Death and the Afterlife in Pre-Columbian America*, pp. 163–89. Washington, D.C.: Dumbarton Oaks Research Library and Collections.

1975c *Warao Basketry: Form and Function*. Los Angeles: University of California. Occasional Papers of the Museum of Cultural History, no. 3.

1975d "El violín en la cultura Warao: Un préstamo cultural complementario." *Montalbán* 4:189–215.

1976a "*Manicaria saccifera* and Its Cultural Significance among the Warao Indians of Venezuela." *Botanical Museum Leaflets* 24(10):275–335. Cambridge, Mass.: Harvard University.

1976b "La *Manicaria saccifera* y su significación cultural entre los indios Warao." *Memoria* 35(105):249–96.

1977a "To Become a Maker of Canoes. An Essay in Warao Enculturation." In Johannes Wilbert, ed., *Enculturation in Latin America: An Anthology*, pp. 308–58. UCLA Latin American Studies, vol. 37. Los Angeles: University of California, Latin American Center Publications.

1977b "Navigators of the Winter Sun." In Elizabeth P. Benson, ed., *The Sea in the Pre-Columbian World*, pp. 16–46. Washington, D.C.: Dumbarton Oaks Research Library and Collections.

1979 "Geography and Telluric Lore of the Orinoco Delta." *Journal of Latin American Lore* 5(1):129–50.

1980a "Genesis and Demography of a Warao Subtribe: The Winikina." In Johannes Wilbert and Miguel Layrisse, eds., *Demographic and Biological Studies of the Warao Indians*, pp. 13–47. UCLA Latin American Studies, vol. 45. Los Angeles: University of California, Latin American Center Publications.

1980b "The Temiche Cap." *Principes* 24(3):105–9.

1981 "The Warao Lords of Rain." In Giorgio Buccellati and Charles Speroni, eds., *The Shape of the Past. Studies in Honor of Franklin D. Murphy*, pp. 127–45. Los Angeles: Institute of Archaeology and Office of the Chancellor, University of California.

1983 "Warao Ethnopathology and Exotic Epidemic Disease." *Journal of Ethnopharmacology* 8:357–61.

1985	"The House of the Swallow-tailed Kite: Warao Myth and the Art of Thinking in Images." In Gary Urton, ed., *Animal Myths and Metaphors in South America*, pp. 145–82. Salt Lake City: University of Utah Press.
1987	*Tobacco and Shamanism in South America.* New Haven: Yale University Press.
1993	*Mystic Endowment: Religious Ethnography of the Warao Indians.* Religions of the World. Cambridge, Mass.: Harvard University Center for the Study of World Religions.
N.d.	"Warao Transformation Stories." Unpublished MS.

Wilbert, Johannes, ed.

1970	*Folk Literature of the Warao Indians: Narrative Material and Motif Content.* UCLA Latin American Studies, vol. 15. Los Angeles: UCLA Latin American Center, University of California.
1975	*Folk Literature of the Selknam Indians: Martin Gusinde's Collection of Selknam Narratives.* UCLA Latin American Studies, vol. 32. Los Angeles: UCLA Latin American Center Publications, University of California.
1977	*Folk Literature of the Yamana Indians: Martin Gusinde's Collection of Yamana Narratives.* Latin American Studies, vol. 40. Berkeley and Los Angeles: University of California Press.
1978	*Folk Literature of the Gê Indians,* vol. 1. UCLA Latin American Studies, vol. 44. Los Angeles: UCLA Latin American Center Publications, University of California.

Wilbert, Johannes, and Miguel Layrisse, eds.

1980	*Demographic and Biological Studies of the Warao Indians.* UCLA Latin American Sutides, vol. 45. Los Angeles: University of California, UCLA Latin American Center Publications.

Wilbert, Johannes, and Karin Simoneau, eds.

1982a	*Folk Literature of the Mataco Indians.* UCLA Latin American Studies, vol. 52. Los Angeles: UCLA Latin American Center Publications, University of California.
1982b	*Folk Literature of the Toba Indians,* vol. 1. UCLA Latin American Studies, vol. 54. Los Angeles: UCLA Latin American Center Publications, University of California.

1984	*Folk Literature of the Gê Indians*, vol. 2. UCLA Latin American Studies, vol. 58. Los Angeles: UCLA Latin American Center Publications, University of California.
1985	*Folk Literature of the Chorote Indians.* UCLA Latin American Studies, vol. 60. Los Angeles: UCLA Latin American Center Publications.
1987a	*Folk Literature of the Chamacoco Indians.* UCLA Latin American Studies, vol. 64. Los Angeles: UCLA Latin American Center Publications, University of California.
1987b	*Folk Literature of the Nivaklé Indians.* UCLA Latin American Studies, vol. 66. Los Angeles: UCLA Latin American Center Publications, University of California.
1988	*Folk Literature of the Mocoví Indians.* UCLA Latin American Studies, vol. 67. Los Angeles: UCLA Latin American Center Publications, University of California.
1989a	*Folk Literature of the Ayoreo Indians.* UCLA Latin American Studies, vol. 70. Los Angeles: UCLA Latin American Center Publications, University of California.
1989b	*Folk Literature of the Caduveo Indians.* UCLA Latin American Studies, vol. 71. Los Angeles: UCLA Latin American Center Publications, University of California.
1989c	*Folk Literature of the Toba Indians*, vol. 2. UCLA Latin American Studies, vol. 68. Los Angeles: UCLA Latin American Center Publications, University of California.
1992	*Folk Literature of the Sikuani Indians.* Latin American Studies, vol. 79. Los Angeles: UCLA Latin American Center Publications, University of California.
1992	*Folk Literature of South American Indians: General Index.* Latin Latin American Studies, vol. 80. Los Angeles: UCLA Latin American Center Publications, University of California.

Wilbert, Werner
  1986 "Warao Herbal Medicine: A Pneumatic Theory of Illness and Healing." Ph.D. diss., University of California, Los Angeles.
  1987 "The Pneumatic Theory of Female Warao Herbalists." *Social Science Medicine* 25(10):1139–46.

Yépez, Gerardo
  1979 "La Tigana." *Natura* 66:22–23. Caracas.

Zerries, Otto
- 1964 *Waika. Die kulturgeschichtliche Stellung der Waika-Indianer des oberen Orinoco im Rahmen der Völkerkunde Südamerikas.* Munich: K. Renner.
- 1979 "Indianer der Wälder und Savannen." In H. D. Disselhoff and Otto Zerries, eds., *Die Erben des Inkareiches und die Indianer der Wälder*, pp. 79–388. Berlin: Safari Verlag.

Zerries, Otto, and Meinhard Schuster
- 1974 *Mahekodotedi. Monographie eines Dorfes der Waika-Indianer (Yanoama) am oberen Orinoco (Venezuela).* Munich: K. Renner.

Index

Aboriginals
  destruction of, 39–40
  spread of diseases among, 40–45
  Warao contacts with other, 30
Abuse, of Indian laborers, 46
Acawaio Indians, in Guayana Mission, 267
Aerophone music, in homeopathic weather magic, 198, 199
Agriculture. *See also* Cacao production; Coffee production; Collective farming; Rice cropping; Rubber plantations; Sugar production
  anthropological studies and, 51
  educating Indians in, 232
  erosion of Warao society by, 69
  mission life and, 47–48
  among pre-Columbian tribes, 24
  sago festival and, 150–151
  of Warao Indians, 51–52, 245
Agriocharis ocellata, 91
Ahaka, 130
Ahaka arani, 136n
Ahaka aukatida, 136n
Ahaka auka, 136n
Ahakabari, 17, 82
Ahaka boto, 130
Ahakaida, 85
Ahakarima, 135
Ahaka taira, 135
Ahakatuma, 130

Ahi simo, 112n
Ahono, 149
Ahuéna, 207
Aká, 149
Akabamu, 151
Akai, 129
Akashibo, 235
Akawaio Indians, weather-blowing among, 169, 171
Alaka culture, 26
Alcaldes, 228
Alcoholic beverages, in homeopathic weather magic, 192–193
Alguacils, 228
Alligator bellowing, thunderstorms and, 190
Alligator imagery, in shamanism, 100–101
Alligator-sorcerers, 100–101, 122n
Alligator spirits, in Warao mythology, 216
Alligator teeth
  as amulets, 100
  in homeopathic weather magic, 190
Altruism, rainmaker and, xxi
Amblyopia, "darkened vision" and, 99
American Crocodile, 100n, 101
Amuesha Indians, rainbow mythology of, 219
Amulets, alligator teeth as, 100

Ana, 118, 120–121, 123–124
Anaconda
  in homeopathic weather magic, 196
  in rainbow mythology, 218*n*, 222
  in weather mythology, 216
Analgesia, from tobacco and nicotine, 167
Ancestor cult, 158
  brotherhoods and, 239–241
  derived features of, 244–245
Ancestral spirits, provisioning, 158–159
Anchieta, Father, 210
Andoque Indians, thunder and lightning demons of, 205
Anger, 250, 252–255
  of the Rain Lords, 110–114
  of thunder and lightning demons, 208–210
Angling, 53*illus.*
Angostura, tobacco trade with, 102
Anguiano, Mateo de, historical accounts of Spaniards and Indians by, 225–226
Animals. *See also* Alligator imagery; American Crocodile; Birds; Crabs; Frogs; Iguana; Insects; Lizards; Mammals; Snakes; Toads; Turtles
  as guises for rain deities, 213–214
  myths of unions between humans and, 32–34
Animistic causation of disease, 69
Annual temperatures, in Orinoco Delta, 8
Anserma Indians, weather-blowing among, 169
Anthurium flexuosum, 110*n*

Ants, 111
Apinaye Indians
  homeopathic weather magic of, 196
  thunder and lightning demons of, 203
Apprenticeship, of rain shamans, 97–98
Apytré-Mbyá Indians
  rain deities of, 214
  thunder and lightning demons of, 211
  wind demons of, 201
Araguaito, rainfall in, 10–13
Araguao River, 7
  tornado along, 86–87
Araona Indians
  weather-blowing among, 170–171
  wind demons of, 202
Araucanians
  homeopathic weather magic of, 199
  thunder and lightning demons of, 209
Arawabisi, xxv
Arawak Indians, 26
  myths derived from, 32–34
  occupation of Orinoco Delta by, 24
  seizure of slaves by, 27–29
  snake and rainbow mythology of, 218*n*
  Warao weather lore and, xxiii–xxiv
  weather-blowing among, 169
Arawanera, 135
Ardeidae, 82
Arecastrum, 137*n*
Arecastrum romanozoffianum, 137
Arekuna Indians
  rainbow mythology of, 222

snake and rainbow mythology of, 218*n*
Arenga, 137*n*
Armadillos, 254–255
　behavior of, 131–132n
　as water spirits, 216
　wind mythology and, 130–134, 198, 200
Arokohi, 149
Arokoho, 149
Arrows, 52. *See also* Bows and arrows
　lightning bolts as supernatural, 210
　in rituals against atmospheric spirits, 184–195
　in Tupí-Guaraní mythology, 212
Artisans, 238
Aru Arani, 159
　pollination of, 157
Aru Arani Ariawara, 158
Arukari, 48
Asáta piripiri, 170
Asebe, 112*n*
Asia, weather religion and, xxiii–xxiv
Asohsná, 213, 217
Asoojna, 175
Atalalá Indians, rain dances among, 177–178
Ateho, 149
Ateles belzebuth, 200
Atmospheric spirits, 199–222
　common features of, 222–224
　gesticulations and rituals dealing with, 180–189
　models for, 199
Autumnal equinox, in Orinoco Delta, 9
Average annual rainfall, 10*illus.*, 10–13, 11*illus.*, 12*illus.*
　availability of food staples and, 15*illus.*

moriche sago and, 14–15, 15*illus.*
Average temperatures, in Orinoco Delta, 8
Avoidance taboo, 59
Awaikoma Indians, weather chants among, 174
Awaikoma-Kaingang Indians
　homeopathic weather magic of, 193
　weather interpretations of, 165
Awa-Kwaiker Indians, rainbow mythology of, 221
Axes
　gathering palm sago with, 139–141
　in homeopathic weather magic, 198
Axmen, in sago harvest ritual, 151–152
Ayahuasco hallucinogen, 170*n*, 222
Ayara, 137
Ayari, 111, 113
Aymara Indians
　homeopathic weather magic of, 191, 192, 193, 194–195
　thunder and lightning demons of, 212
　weather-blowing among, 171
　wind demons of, 202
Ayoreo Indians
　homeopathic weather magic of, 191, 193
　rain deities of, 213, 215, 217
　rain shamans of, 166
　rituals against atmospheric spirits among, 185
　thunder and lightning demons of, 204, 210
　thunder mythology of, 208
　weather chants among, 175
　wind demons of, 201

Baba-buada, 202
Backwater swamps, 7–8
"Bad cough," 119
Bagre fisheries, 48
Bahana, 63, 112
Bahanarotu, 63, 87, 121
   wisdom of, 250
Bahana shaman, hawk as, 136
Bananas, 47, 51
Banisteriopsis caapi, 170*n*
Bará Indians
   homeopathic weather magic of, 192
   weather interpretations of, 165
Barasana Indians
   homeopathic weather magic of, 196–197
   rainbow mythology of, 222
   rain deities of, 213
Barbarism, 31
Barima,
   cannibalism among, 26–27
Barinés, 82, 85
Barineses, 17
   in Warao mythology, 79
Barrancas, 4–5
   slave trade out of, 28
Baskets, 57, 152–154, 245
   for carrying bones, 159*illus.*
Basket weavers, 238
Bathing, in palm sago, 158, 158*n*
Bebgorotí, 210
Beehive huts, 52
Beehives, experts at locating, 144
Bees, 110*n*, 112*n*
   honey production and, 144
   nests of, 111, 112
   rain shamanism and, 110–113
Belligerence, of weather supernaturals, 209–210
Bere, 89
Bestiality, 32, 33, 34

Big Dipper, in Inca mythology, 212
Birds. *See also* Calandra lark; Chickens; Cloud birds; Doves; Egret; Fork-tailed flycatchers; Geese; Green heron; Harpy eagles; Hawks; Herons; Jacamar; Mockingbird; Nightjars; Oscillated turkey; *Pauji* turkey; Pigeon; Rainbirds; Rheas; Rufous crab hawk; Stork; Stormbirds; Striated heron; Sun bittern; Thunderbird; Variegated tinamou
   origin of humanity as, 208
   thunderstorm imagery and, 205–206
   in Warao mythology, 146
   as weather deities, 217
   weather magic derived from eating, 166
Bisikari, 75
Biting insects, in Warao mythology, 79
Bitter manioc, 51
Blackwater streams, 5
Blanco, Matías Ruíz, on mission government, 228
Blood
   in homeopathic weather magic, 192–193, 195–196
   in Warao mythology, 79, 79*n*
Bloodsucking, by sorcerers, 128, 129
Bloodsucking insects, in Warao mythology, 79
Blowing against the wind, 167–174
Boarding schools, 47, 48
   elimination of, 49

Index 329

Boas
  in homeopathic weather magic, 196
  in rainbow mythology, 218, 218*n*
  in weather mythology, 216
Body painting, 57
Boils, 117
Bolívar state, Warao Indians in, 3
Bombyliidae, 79
Bone
  basket for carrying, 159*illus.*
  palm sago as, 158–159
Boquilla trifoliata, 199
Borbón settlement, 270
Borisia, 48, 75
Bororo Indians
  rain deities of, 214, 217
  snake and rainbow mythology of, 218*n*
  thunder and lightning demons of, 208
  weather-blowing among, 172, 173*illus.*
Botocudo Indians
  homeopathic weather magic of, 193
  rituals against atmospheric spirits among, 185
Bows and arrows, 52. *See also* Arrows
  lightning and, 210
  in rituals against atmospheric spirits, 184–185
Brachygalba spp., 200
Brackish water, in Orinoco Delta, 21, 143
Brandishing weapons, against atmospheric spirits, 180, 184–185
Breaking of vessels, in homeopathic weather magic, 193

Breath
  controlling weather with, 167–174
  in homeopathic weather magic, 198
Breezes, 16–17, 130. *See also* Land breezes; Sea breezes
Bronchitis, 119, 122*n*
Brooms, rain dances with, 177
Brotherhoods, ancestor cult and, 239–241
Brothers, rank and status of, 36
Brown water rivers, 7
Bucare forests, 7, 8
Buccal sores, remedies for, 110
Bull-roarers, in homeopathic weather magic, 192
Burial alive, 117
Buteogallus aequinoctialis, 136
Butorides striatus, 82, 135, 206
Butorides virescens, 135, 206

Cabildos, 75–76, 242
  organization of, 226–228
  of Warao deities, 235–236
Cabos, 242. *See also* Corregidors
  duties of, 228–231
  mismanagement of food depositories by, 231
  rain shamans as, 236–237
  Warao deities as, 235–236
Cacao production, 47
  forced labor in, 46
Cachama fish, 251
Cachicamo tree, 113*n*
  in Warao mythology, 72, 73
Caduveo Indians
  rain deities of, 217–218
  thunder and lightning demons of, 205
Calabashes, in homeopathic weather magic, 193
Calandra lark, as thunderbird, 207

Callinago Indians, weather-blowing among, 169
Camayura Indians
  homeopathic weather magic of, 192, 194, 196
  rain dances among, 177
Campa Indians
  homeopathic weather magic of, 193, 197
  rain deities of, 213, 214
  rituals against atmospheric spirits among, 186
  weather-blowing among, 170
  wind demons of, 202*n*
Camp structures, 52
Cancer (constellation), in Warao mythology, 81
Canelo Indians, weather-blowing among, 169
Canelos-Quichua Indians, rainbow mythology of, 219
Canine *Ur*-mother, 33
Cannibalism, 25–27
  ceremonial, 27
Canoe carpenters, 238
Canoes, 23, 57, 61*illus.*
  construction materials for, 72
Caños, 5
  of Orinoco Delta, 4*illus.*
Capitanías, 48
Capo, 236
Captain (of the Lords of the Rain), 75–77
Capuchin missionaries, xxiii, 29–30, 242
  cabildo organization and, 226–228
  chronicles of, 225–226
  cofradias and guilds of, 231–234
  Cumaná missions administered by, 261–267
  Guayana missions administered by, 267–269
  heroism of, 48
  in the 20th century, 46–50
  Warao population growth and, 50
  Warao resettlement efforts by, 44–45
Capuchin nuns, 47
  Western medicine provided by, 68–69
Capybaras, as water spirits, 216
Carajá Indians
  homeopathic weather magic of, 193–194
  rain deities of, 214
  rituals against atmospheric spirits among, 185, 189–190
  snake and rainbow mythology of, 218*n*
  weather-blowing among, 171
Caribbean islands, cannibal invaders from, 25
Caribs. *See also* Cariña Caribs
  cannibalism among, 26–27
  enslavement of, 27–28
  heron lore among, 135–136
  homeopathic weather magic of, 192–193
  massacre of Warao Indians by, 40
  origins of myths among, 33
  rain deities of, 215
  seizure of slaves by, 27–29
  thunder and lightning demons of, 209
  thunderbird of, 206
  trade network of, 37–39, 38*illus.*
  Warao weather lore and, xxiii–xxiv
  weather-blowing among, 169

Index 331

Carihona Indians, weather interpretations of, 165
Cariña Caribs
   cannibalism among, 27
   epidemics among, 41
   in Guayana Mission, 267–268
   homeopathic weather magic of, 199
   myths of creation of, 37
   origins of myths among, 33
   Spanish use of Warao against, 39–40
   thunder and lightning demons of, 211
   trade network of, 37–39
   as Warao enemy, 37
Carolina settlement, 270
Caroní, founding of apostolic vicariate at, 46
Caryocar butyrosum, 177
Caryota, 137*n*
Cashinaua Indians
   rainbow mythology of, 221
   rain deities of, 217
   thunder and lightning demons of, 208, 211
   wind demons of, 201, 202*n*
Catholicism, 49–50
Cayapa Indians
   thunder and lightning demons of, 203
   thunderbird of, 206
Cayapó Indians
   homeopathic weather magic of, 193
   rituals against atmospheric spirits among, 184, 185
   thunder and lightning demons of, 204, 210
Cedar smoke, in homeopathic weather magic, 196
CELAM (Consejo Episcopal Latinoamericano), 49
Central pole, 65*illus.*
Centurión, Manuel
   on effects of slave trade, 29
   militarization of corregidors by, 230–231
Ceramic period, 26
Ceremonial cannibalism, 27
CERIS (Centro de Estatística Religiosa e Investigações Sociaes), 49
Chacobo Indians, weather interpretations of, 165
Chaima Indians
   power contests with shamans of, 225–226
   rain deities of, 215
Chaima Mission of Santa Rosa de Ocópi, 39
Chamacoco Indians
   rain deities of, 215, 217
   thunder and lightning demons of, 203
   weather chants among, 175
   wind demons of, 201, 202*n*
Chandur, 171
Chané Indians
   homeopathic weather magic of, 193
   thunderbird of, 208
Chants
   of dark shamans, 99
   to Kabo Yokoshewari, 105–109
   of light shamans, 87–88
   of shamans, 166
   weather, 171–172, 174–176
Chapacura Indians, thunder and lightning demons of, 203–204
Charles V, 227
Chickens, 52
Chicuaco cuello gris, 82
Childbirth complications, 117

"Child of the Sky," 212
Children
  in Ayoreo weather mythology, 210
  homeopathic beatings of, 194
  in homeopathic weather magic, 191, 195
  at meals, 60*illus.*
  protection of, 90–92
  in rain dances, 178–180
  in rituals against atmospheric spirits, 185–186, 188–189
  separation from parents of, 45, 48
  weather-related diseases and deaths of, 90–91, 116–117, 118
Chiquitano Indians, rituals against atmospheric spirits among, 184
Chiquito-Manasi Indians
  rain deities of, 214
  thunder and lightning demons of, 211
Chiriguano Indians, snake and rainbow mythology of, 218n
Cholera, 41, 63
Chorote Indians
  homeopathic weather magic of, 192
  thunderbirds of, 207
  water spirits of, 216
  weather chants among, 175
  wind demons of, 202n
Church, the, modernization of, 49–50
Cigars, ritual preparation and smoking of, 114
Ciudad Bolívar
  hydraulic regimen at, 20*illus.*
  tobacco trade with, 102
Clapping, in homeopathic weather magic, 191–192
CLAR (Confederación Latinoamericano de Religiosos), 49
Clarinet, sacred trumpet as, 149, 240
Clay soils, in Orinoco Delta, 6–8
Climatological lore, xxiii
Clothing, 57, 232
Cloud birds, 217–218
  in Cashinaua mythology, 208
Cloud girls, 213
  maleficence of, 71
Cloud people, manifestations of, 71
Clouds, smoke as, 196–197
Clubs, in rituals against atmospheric spirits, 185–186
Cocama Indians, snake and rainbow mythology of, 218n
Coffee production, forced labor in, 46
Coffins, 127–129, 128*illus.*
Cofradias, 228, 242, 243
  purposes of, 231–234
  Warao priest-shamans and, 237–238
Cojosanica mission, 265
Collective farming, 47–48
Colocasia antiquorum, 252
Colocasia esculenta, 51
Colonial patterns, of Warao social organization, 241–243
Colophyllum lucidum, in Warao mythology, 72
Colorado Indians, rainbow mythology of, 219
Colors, in rainbow mythology, 218–219
Combat shields, 131*illus.*, 131–132
Commercialization, erosion of Warao society by, 69
Common Caiman, 100, 101
  Caiman crocodilus, 100

Index

Communal food repositories, 155, 231
  ancestor cult and, 239–241
  derived features of, 245
Communal sago repository, 155, 237
  ancestor cult and, 239–241
Compass, rain god directions and, 74*illus.*, 78, 235*n*
Conquistadors, 227
  demand for slaves by, 27
Constables, 228
Contagion, fear of, 41
Conversion, of Indians to Christianity, 227–228
Conversión, 227
Cooperation, rainmaker and, xxi
Cooperative behavior, in Warao culture, 255–259
Coroado Indians, rituals against atmospheric spirits among, 184
Corporal punishment, 46
Corregidors, 242
  duties of, 228–231
  militarization of, 230–231
  mismanagement of food depositories by, 231
  missions and, 227–228
  mistreatment of Indians by, 228, 229
  rain shamans as, 236–237
  Warao shamans as, 236–237
Corregimientos, 228
Corypha, 137*n*
Cotton, 232
Coughing, 90, 119, 122*n*
Cowardice, of Warao Indians, 35
Čōwhtóxen rain dance, 179–180
Crab nebula, 90
Crabs. *See also* Fiddler crabs
  collection of, 86
  as sacramental food, 137

Crab season, 90
  green heron and, 136
  ritual protection of children from disease during, 92
Craftsmen, 242
  among Spanish colonists, 232
  among Warao Indians, 238–239
Craho Indians, rainbow mythology of, 221
Creator-God, in Warao myths, 34–37
Crengez Indians, thunder and lightning demons of, 210
Cricket, 175
  weather mythology of, 215
Criollos, 29
  disease immunity of, 43
  as educators, 49
  myths of creation of, 34–37
  similarities of Warao rain gods to, 75
  Warao servitude imposed by, 46
Crocodile. *See* Alligator imagery, Common Caiman
Crocodylus acutus, 100*n*
Crocodylus intermedius, 100*n*
Crypturellus variegatus, 200
Crystal, sacred, 146
Cuadrillas, 232, 243
Cuajo tree, 106
  lightning and, 110, 112
Cuba, pre-Columbian occupation of, 24
Cumaná coast, slave trade along, 28
Cumanagoto Indians
  rain deities of, 215
  thunder and lightning demons of, 211
Cumaná Mission, 261–267
  aborigines residing in, 261–264
  establishment of, 228
  history of, 261–262

Cumaná Mission (*continued*)
  map of, 263*illus.*
  reopening, 46
Cumulonimbus clouds, 18
Cuna Indians
  rainbow mythology of, 220
  rituals against atmospheric spirits among, 185
  weather chants among, 176
Curiapo, rainfall in, 10–13
Curiapo parish, founding of, 47
Cushmas, 214, 220
Cuzco Indians, thunder and lightning demons of, 212
Cyclops, 215
Cyperaceae, 170*n*
Cyperus, hallucinogenic effects of, 170*n*

Dances, 153–154. *See also* Nahanamu dance ritual; Rain dances
  during sago distribution ritual, 156
Dariatuma, 25
"Darkened vision," 99
Dark shamans, 63
  accused of causing the death of Juan, 124–129
  as alligator alter egos, 100–101
  attempt to cure tuberculosis by, 122–123
  bloodsucking by, 129
  of the Mariusa subtribe, 98
  miana chants of, 99
  wisdom of, 250
Dasypus novemcinctus, 131*n*
Daunona Arani, 156
Daunona Arani Ariawari, 156
Daunona images, 156*illus.*, 156
Dausitore, 149
Death, 250
  rain associated with, 71, 115–130
  in rainbow mythology, 220–221, 222
  of a Warao boy (Juan), 118–130
Deer-bone flute, 152*illus.*
Delta Amacuro state, Warao Indians in, 3–4
Dema-ancestors, 210
Dema-deities, 175
Demons
  rain, 212–218
  rainbow, 218–222
  thunder and lightning, 203–212
  wind, 200–202
DESAL (Centro para el Desarrollo Económico y Social de America Latina), 49
Desana Indians, rainbow mythology of, 219
Dew, in Warao mythology, 71
Diaru, 110
Dibatu aida, 75
Dibatu sanuka, 75, 76
Diguyálo, 218
Dinínuwa, 196
Directional gods, 62–63
  childhood mortality and, 90
  wind demons as, 201
Diseases, 40–45
  bloodsucking insects and, 79
  cured by shamans, 57–69, 98–99
  rain associated with, 71–73, 104, 116
  in rainbow mythology, 220
  as supernatural punishment, 43–44
  in Warao mythology, 43–44
Diurnal temperature, in Orinoco Delta, 8
Divina Pastora de Araguaimujo mission, founding of, 46–47
Divino Pastor de Areo mission, 265

Index 335

Doctrina, 227
Dog-ancestor mythologem, 32*n*
Dogs
　in homeopathic weather magic, 194
　for hunting, 52
　myths of unions between humans and, 32–34
Dog-woman, in Warao myths, 33
Domesticated animals, 52
Dominican missionaries, 29–30
Domu, 80*n*
Double rainbows, in Warao mythology, 73
Doves, as weather deities, 217
Drainage canals, of Orinoco Delta, 4*illus.*
Drizzle, in Warao mythology, 71, 72–73
Drums, in homeopathic weather magic, 192
"Dry land," 137
Dry seasons. *See also* Long dry season
　availability of food during, 13, 14–15
　causes of, 8–9
　hydraulic regimen and, 20–21
　rain gods during, 74
　tides during, 21
Dry-weather piripiri, 170
Dueling combat shield, 131*illus.*
Dugout canoes, 57, 61*illus.*
　construction materials for, 72
Duruduru, 101
Dutch colonists
　in alliances with Indians against Spain, 39
　slave trade with, 28–29
Dutch Guiana. *See also* Surinam
　resettlement of Warao Indians in, 44–45

Dwarfs, in Sanemá-Yanomami mythology, 214
Dysentery, 63

Earth Mother, 202
Earthquakes, 254–255
　mythology of winds and, 130–134, 198, 200
　on Orinoco Delta, 134*n*
Eclipses, rituals to dispel, 184, 185
Education. *See* Boarding schools; Nationalized schools
Egret, as thunderbird, 206
Electric eel, weather mythology of, 172, 215
Electrophorus electricus, 215
Embera Indians, rainbow mythology of, 220
English colonists, alliances with Indians against Spain, 39
Entradas, 232
Epidemics, 40–45
　deaths of children during, 90
　as supernatural punishment, 43–44
Epidemiology, 63–68
Equatorial trough, Orinoco Delta seasons and, 8–9
Eremu chanting, 171–172, 176
Erythrina glauca, 7
Eta Orionis, times of visibility of, 80*n*
Etiology, of disease, 68
Eugeissona, 137*n*
Eunectus murinus, 196
Eunectus murinus gigas, 216
Europe, weather religion and, xxiii–xxiv
European colonists
　aboriginal aggression against, 29–30

European colonists (*continued*)
  demand for slaves by, 27–28
  disease immunity of, 43
  effects of diseases carried by, 40–45
  influence on Warao mythology of, 31–32, 34–37, 76–78
  Warao social conventions derived from, 246–247
Eurypyga helias, 82
Eurypyga helias helias, 206
Eurypygidae, 82
Euterpe sp., 7
  cigars made from, 114
Evangelization. *See also* Capuchin missionaries; Dominican missionaries; Franciscan missionaries; Missionaries; Missions
  following Vatican II, 49–50
  impact on Warao culture and religion of, 30–40
  prior to Vatican II, 47–48

Families
  in crisis, 118–130
  forced breakups of, 45, 48
Family quarrels, during wet season, 117–118
Family structure, of Warao Indians, 52–57, 59
Famine
  adverse weather conditions and, xxii–xxiii
  rainfall and, 13–15
  rainmaker and, xxi
  Warao adjustments to, xxiv–xxv
"Father of Rain," 96, 98
Father of Southern Trade Winds, 84*illus.*
"Father of the Ancestral Spirit," 146
  mythical origin of, 147–149

"Father of Wind," 134–137, 158, 202
Fear, 252–255
Febrile diseases, 63
Fecal odors, in homeopathic weather magic, 197
Female rain deities, 212–213
Ferdinand, cofradias legalized by, 233
Festivals. *See Nahanamu* festival; Religious festivals; Sago festival
Fiddler crabs, 87*n*
Fire, in homeopathic weather magic, 192, 196, 197
Firearms, in rituals against atmospheric spirits, 184
First constable (of the Lords of the Rain), 75–77
First speaker (of the Lords of the Rain), 75–77
Fiscalías, 48
Fiscals
  duties of, 232
  mistreatment of Indians by, 229
Fish demons, 203–204, 204*illus.*
Fisheries, 48
Fish gorge angling, 53*illus.*
Fishing, 51–52, 53*illus.*, 54*illus.*
  during palm sago preparation, 141
Fisicali, 75
Floodplains, 8
Floods, 20–21
  adverse agricultural effects of, 47
Food preparation, 52, 55*illus.*
Foods
  consumption of, 60*illus.*
  long dry season abundance of, 144–146
  of Warao Indians, 51–52

Food staples, xxi
  seasonal availability of, 13–14,
Food uncertainty
  causes of, 251–252
  preventing, 255–259
Foraging, 52
Forced labor, 45–46. *See also*
  Laborers
Forest Mother, 113*n*
  in Warao mythology, 72, 73
Forest spirits, 213
Fork-tailed flycatchers, in Maku
  mythology, 208
Franciscan missionaries, 29–30
French colonists, alliances with
  Indians against Spain, 39
Frogs
  in homeopathic weather magic,
    191, 194–195
  in Lake Titicaca, 191
Frontier life, impact on Warao
  culture of, xxiii
Fuegians
  homeopathic weather magic of,
    197, 198–199
  wind demons of, 201
Funerals, 127–130

"Gaseous emanations," 63
Gastrointenstinal disorders, 62–63
Gavilan de manglares, 136*n*
Geese, in weather mythology, 218
Geographic zones, of Orinoco
  Delta, 5–8
Gesticulations, against
  atmospheric spirits, 180–184
Giant armadillo, as wind demon,
  200
Gobernaciones, 48
God
  power contests between
    shamans and, 225–226
  Warao myths concerning, 34–37
Goddess of the Waters of the
  Manao, 213
God of Rain, 214
God of the east, 62–63
God of the noon sun, 158
God of the west, 63
Gods, 62–63
  offerings to, 144–146
  relationship of Warao to, 90–91
Golofa flies, in Warao mythology,
  79
Gos, 178
Governor (of the Lords of the
  Rain), 75–77
Governor's wife (of the Lords of
  the Rain), 75–77
Gran Chaco
  atmospheric deities of, 222
  homeopathic weather magic of,
    192
  rain dances of, 177–178
  rain deities of, 215
  rain shamans of, 166
  sago palms of, 137
  thunderbird motif of, 206–207,
    208
  weather-blowing rituals of, 171
  weather chants of, 175
Greater Antilles, Arawak
  occupation of, 24
Great Spirit, 208
Green heron, 135–136
  as thunderbird, 206
Green stone ax, in homeopathic
  weather magic, 198
Gremios, 233, 242
Guaicurú, 210
Guajiro Indians
  homeopathic weather magic of,
    192
  rain deities of, 215–216

Guajiro Indians (*continued*)
  rituals against atmospheric
    spirits among, 184
  weather chants among, 175
Guanahatabey, 24
Guaraní Indians, snake and
    rainbow mythology of, 218*n*
Guarayo Indians
  weather chants among, 175
  wind demons of, 201
Guardian-shaman, function of,
    146
Guardian spirits, 153
Guaritica mission, 265
Guató Indians, homeopathic
    weather magic of, 191
Guayakí Indians, rainbow
    mythology of, 222
Guayana Mission, 267–271
  map of, 263*illus.*
  regulation of *cabos* in, 230
  reopening of, 46
Guayano Indians, in Guayana
    Mission, 268
Guiana
  cannibal invaders from, 25
  origins of myths in, 33
  slave trade in, 28
Guiana coast, Arawak occupation
    of, 24
Guiana highlands, Carib trade
    routes and, 37
Guilds, 242, 243
  organization of, 238
  purposes of, 231–234
  among Warao Indians, 238–239
Güiria, wind rose of, 76–78,
    77*illus.*
Gulf of Paria, winds around, 76–
    78
Guyana
  rainfall in, 10–13
  seasons in, 8–9
  Warao Indians in, 3–4, 44–45
  Warao population of, 50*n*
Hadley cells, 18, 18*illus.*
Hahesebe, 80*n*
Hahuba, 88, 159
Hallucinogens
  in homeopathic weather magic,
    192
  piripiri as, 170*n*
  therapeutic effects of, 167–168
Halos. See Rainbow
Hammock makers, 238
Hammocks, 57
Hancornia speciosa, 177
Harpoon arrows, 52
Harpoons, 52, 54*illus.*
Harpy eagles, 209
Harvest baskets, 152–154
Hate, of thunder and lightning
    demons, 208–210
Haukwaharu, 137
Hawks
  in Sanemá-Yanomami
    mythology, 213
  as weather deities, 217
Headdresses, in Tapirapé weather
    ritual, 188–189
Hearani, 90
Heathenism, 31
Heaven, 236
Hebu, 63
Hebunaka arani, 147
Herbalism, 62, 68
Herbalists, 62, 63
  women as, 116–117
Hermandades, 233
Herons. See also Green heron;
    Striated heron; White heron
  as weather deities, 217
  weather mythology of, 136–137,
    146, 200

Index

Hia, 82, 146, 158
  in Warao mythology, 135–137
"High river," 20, 21
High tides, mythical origin of, 143
Hihíaiuné, 216
Himabaka, 153, 155, 237
Himaheru wood, 149
Hoa, 63, 123
Hoarani, 143
Hoarotu, 63, 79*n*, 101, 121, 122*n*
  attempt to cure tuberculosis by, 122–123
  wisdom of, 250
Hoers, in sago harvest ritual, 151–152
Hoes, 140*illus.*
  gathering palm sago with, 139–141
Hoho-hit, 240
Hoi, 111
Hoida, 81
Hoidabaka, 143
Homanuka, 143
Homeopathic weather magic, 190–199
Honey
  gathering of, 144
  intoxicating effects of, 110, 111
  surplus, 155
Horseflies, in Warao mythology, 79
House construction, 52. *See also* Pile dwellings; Stilt houses
Huari Huiracocha God, 194
Huarya-tata, 202
Huba, 72, 88
Hubanasiko, 71–72, 75
Human din, in homeopathic weather magic, 191
Human-dog unions, in myths, 32–34

Human emotions, weather phenomena as possessing, 161–164
Human origin myths, 33–34
Humiliation, *pegón* bee and, 111
Hunger, 250–251
  loincloth of, 251
  in missions, 229
  rage engendered by, 253
Hunger control, Warao weather religion as, xxiv, 250–251
Hunting, 51, 52
Hunting dogs, 52
Hurricanes, 19
  in Warao mythology, 85–89
  in weather mythology, 202
"Hurting lungs cough," 119
Huru, 255
  battle between Oka and, 131–134
Hydraulic regimen, 20*illus.*, 20–21

Iboma, 113*n*
Ibúma, 113*n*
Iguana
  as food, 141
  in weather mythology, 215
Immunity to diseases, of European colonists, 43
Immunization, Warao population growth and, 50
Improved health services, as contributing to Warao longevity, 96–97
Inawaha, 137
Incas
  homeopathic weather magic of, 194–195
  rainbow mythology of, 220
  rain ceremony of, 195*illus.*
  snake and rainbow mythology of, 218*n*

Incest taboo, 57
Incompetence, among rain shamans, 97–98
Indentured laborers, refugee Warao Indians and, xxiii
Indian tribes of South America, distribution map of, 162–164*illus.*
Induction fees, to become a rain shaman, 96–97, 98, 101, 103
Inferiority, of Warao culture, intelligence, and linguistic skills, 34–37
Infirmity, rain associated with, 71
Influenza, 42
Initiation, of rain shamans, 97–99, 101–104, 104–109, 114–115, 166
Inoculation, 42
Insects. *See also* Ants; Bees; Biting insects; Bloodsucking insects; Cricket; *Golofa* flies; Praying mantises; Termites; Wasps
  during long rainy season, 79
Intelligence, supposed aborigine inferiority in, 34–37
Intermediate zone, of Orinoco Delta, 7
Intertropical convergence zone
  Orinoco Delta seasons and, 8–9, 82
  uncertainty of Orinoco Delta food supply and, 251–252
Ioboura, 135
Ipurina Indians
  rainbow mythology of, 220
  snake and rainbow mythology of, 218*n*
Isabella, cofradias legalized by, 233
Ischnosiphon sp., 149

Isimoi, 146–152
  ancestor cult and, 240
  derived features of, 245
  described, 149–150
  learning to play, 153–154
  sacredness of, 151
Isimoi Arani, 239
  sons of, 156–157
Isimoi Arani Ariawara, 147
Isimoi arotu, 92, 146–152, 154
Isolation
  as a barrier to the spread of disease, 41
  Warao Indian society and, 3–4
Itiriti, 149

Jacamar, as wind demon, 200
Jacaranda trees, 215
Jaguars, 210
  in rainbow mythology, 222
  in sago rituals, 155
  in Warao mythology, 73
  as wind demons, 200
Jivaro Indians, 170*n*
  homeopathic weather magic of, 192
  rainbow mythology of, 221
  rituals against atmospheric spirits among, 185
  thunder and lightning demons of, 210
  weather-blowing among, 169–170
  weather interpretations of, 165
Joioana, *pegón* bee myths and, 111–112
Juan
  burial of, 127–129, 128*illus.*
  death from tuberculosis and burial of, 118–130
  mourning the death of, 125–130
Juracán complex, xxiii, 226

Juriquian, 226
Justices of the peace, 228
Juvenile mortality, Warao population growth and, 50

Kabitana, 75
Kabo, as a rain lord title, 235–236
Kabo Aderei, 76
Kabo arotutuma, 73
Kabo Aukuashiwari, 76, 115
Kabo Ayakeima, 76, 79, 85
Kabo Kwaihebere, 76, 89, 115
Kabo Kwaimare, 76
Kabo power, 115
Kaborai, 235
Kabo Yokoshewari, 76
  chant to, 105–109
  sun bittern (*tigana*) and, 83
Kabo Yokotari, 76, 85, 114
Kabo Yukawari, 76
Kalinago Indians, cannibalism among, 26–27
Kanamuno, 243
  appearance of, 88–89, 114–115
Kanawana, 186–187
Kanishawarao, 85
Kanobo, 237
Kanobo arima, 98, 146, 147, 237
Kanobo Yaukware, 158–159
Kapo, 236
Kapu, 236
Kasisi, 136–137
Kasum, 172
Kaunasa, 85–89
Kaunasa arani, 87
Kinship, among Warao Indians, 57
Kitchen houses, 60*illus.*
Kitchen middens, of Alaka culture, 26
Kloketen ceremony, 178–179
Knives, in rituals against atmospheric spirits, 186
Kobenahoro, 75

Kobenahoro atida, 75
Kogi Indians
  homeopathic weather magic of, 198
  rainbow mythology of, 219
  rain dances among, 177
  rain deities of, 213
  wind demons of, 202n
Kóteten weather dance, 178–179
Krishna, Kumar, 111n
Krupp, Edward C., 80n
Kumana Indians, rainbow mythology of, 221
Kura hida, 90
Kuramokomoko, 80n
Kwaríp ceremony, 194

Laborers, xxiii, 243. *See also* Forced labor
  under corregidors, 229
  honest wages paid to, 47
  Warao Indians as, 41–42, 232
La Divina Pastora de Catacuao mission, 78, 265
La Guajira peninsula, weather chants on, 175
Lake Titicaca
  frogs in, 191
  in weather mythology, 202
Lamentations, over death of a family member, 124–127
Lances, 52
  in rituals against atmospheric spirits, 185
Land breezes, 16*illus.*, 16–17
  mythological origins of, 130–131
La Purísima Concepción de Nuestra Señora de Cocuisas mission, 266
  mismanagement of food depository at, 231
Latex, 46

Laulau fisheries, 48
Law of Missions, 49
Lay brothers
  good works of, 232
  trumpet players as, 239
Lean-tos, 52
Lengua Indians
  homeopathic weather magic of, 196
  rainbow mythology of, 220
  rain deities of, 213
  rain shamans of, 166
  snake and rainbow mythology of, 218*n*
  thunderbird of, 206–207
  weather-blowing among, 171
Lesser Antilles, pre-Columbian invasions of, 23–24
Levees, 7–8
Liana juice, 143
Lifestyle
  of the Lords of the Rain, 74–75
  of Warao Indians, 51–69
Lightning, 110, 112
  demons of, 203–212
  in homeopathic weather magic, 192
  during rainmaker's initiation, 114–115
Lightning (as a deity), 203, 211
Light shaman, 63
  protective chant of, 87–88
  wisdom of, 250
Light shamanism, bees and tobacco and, 112–113
Lime powder, in homeopathic weather magic, 198
Linguistic skills, supposed aborigine lack of, 34–37
Lithic period, 26
Littoral zone, of Orinoco Delta, 5–7

Lizards. *See also* Iguana
  in homeopathic weather magic, 196
  in weather mythology, 216
  as wind demons, 201
Llanos
  crocodiles inhabiting, 100*n*
  local winds and, 17
  long rainy season and, 78
  slave trade from, 27–29
Loam, 7
Local councils, 75–76
Local winds, on Orinoco Delta, 17
Locono Indians, in Guayana Mission, 268
Loincloth, of Hunger, 251
Lokono Indians, homeopathic weather magic of, 196
Long dry season, 137–146. *See also* Dry seasons
  abundance of food during, 144–146
  rains during, 134–135
Longevity, of Warao Indians, 96–97
Long rainy season. *See also* Wet seasons
  arrival of blood-sucking insects during, 79
  disappearance of Orion and the Pleiades as initiating, 80–81
  Warao rain gods and, 78–81
Lords of the Rain, the, 73–78, 74*illus.*, 175–176. *See also* Warao rain-gods complex
  apparel of, 75
  appearance of, 89
  European features of, 243–244
  as expressions of Warao historic consciousness, 254
  as forming a cabildo, 235–236
  hierarchy of, 75–77

Index 343

invoking, 104–109
lifestyles of, 74–75
names, ranks, and locations of, 76
provoking, 110–114
rainmaker's mastery over, 110
relationship of wind conditions to ranks of, 77
sources of mythology of, 223–224
Lorenzano, Antonio, xxv, 105*n*
Low population density, as a barrier to the spread of disease, 41
"Low river," 20, 21
Low tides, mythical origin of, 143
Lumberjacks, Warao Indians as, 41–42

Macareo River, 7
Macaw tail feathers, in Tapirapé weather ritual, 188–189
Machetes
  in rituals against atmospheric spirits, 186
  in Tapirapé weather ritual, 187–188
Machiguenga Indians
  rainbow mythology of, 220–221, 221
  rain deities of, 214
Macuna Indians, rainbow mythology of, 221, 222
Maggots, myths of Cariña Caribs as, 37
Magical causation of disease, 69
Magistrates, missions and, 227–228
Maize, 47, 51
Maka Indians, rain deities of, 217
Maku Indians, cosmology of, 208
Makuna Indians, thunder and lightning demons of, 204
Mal aire, 68
Malaria, 42
Mammals. *See* Armadillos; Capybaras; Dogs; Giant armadillo; Jaguars; Nine-banded armadillo; Peccary; Pigs; Sheep; Spider monkey; Tapir; Weasels
Mamo araotuma, 40
Mamo lagoon, 39, 40
Mamo massacre, 39–40
Mamure, 110*n*
Manaca palms, 7, 8
Manaca stipule, cigars made from, 114
Manamo River, 4–5
Mangabeira, 177
Mangrove belts, 6–7
Manicaria, 137*n*
Manicaria saccifera, 7, 85, 137
Manihot dulcis, 51
Manihot esculenta, 51
Manioc, 51
  storage of, 245–246
Mapanare snakes, 117
Mapuche Indians
  homeopathic weather magic of, 199
  snake and rainbow mythology of, 218*n*
  thunder and lightning demons of, 209
Margarita, Carib trade routes and, 37
María, 121
Mario
  accused of causing the death of Juan, 124–129
  attempt to cure tuberculosis by, 121–122
  departure of, 129–130

Mariusa subtribe, xxv. *See also* Warao Indians
  shamans of, 98
Masato, 214
Mashco Indians
  rituals against atmospheric spirits among, 184
  thunder and lightning demons of, 209, 210
Master of Birds, 207
Master of Solstitial Rains, 84*illus.*
Master of Thunder and Lightning, 209
Master of Tobacco, 113
Master serpents, whirlwinds and, 88–89
Masters of Rain, 214, 215
"Masters of the Night Sky," 73
Mataco Indians
  homeopathic weather magic of, 192
  rain deities of, 215
Matrikin, 117*n*
Maturity, of shamans, 96
Mauritia, 137*n*, 139
Mauritia flexuosa, 7, 137, 138*illus.*
Mawari of the zenith, 63
Maya, Warao religion and, xxiii
Mbayá, 210
Mean annual rainfall. *See* Average annual rainfall
Mean monthly rainfall, availability of food staples and, 15*illus.*
Measles, 42, 90
Medicine
  access to Western, 68–69
  shamanism and, 57–69, 64*illus.*
  Warao population growth and, 50
Mehinaku Indians, wind demons of, 200

Melancholy, 135
Men
  as palm sago gatherers, 139–141, 151–155
  as practitioners of weather magic, 164–165
Méndez-Arocha, José Luis, 10*n*
Menstruating women, 134
  in homeopathic weather magic, 196
  mythology of, 213, 214, 216
  in rainbow mythology, 219, 221
Merrymaking, during sago ritual, 153–154
Metallurgy, 57
Metamorphosis
  creation of thunderbirds by, 207
  in Warao mythology, 249–250
Meteor ceremony, 172–174, 173*illus.*
Meteorological equator, 8–9
Metroxylon, 137*n*
Méyanow cannibals, 26
Miana magic, 79, 99
  invoking the Rain Lords with, 104
Middens. *See* Kitchen middens; Shell middens
Milky Way, in Inca mythology, 212
Mimus modulator, 207
Mimus orpheus, 207
Misión, 227
Missionaries, 29–30
  hazards of surrender to, 31
  the Lords of the Rain and, 75–76
  rejection of paternalistic attitudes by, 49
  in Warao creation myths, 36–37
Mission government, 34, 227–228
Mission militias, 39–40
Mission of Cumaná, 261–267, 263*illus.*

Mission of Guayana, 263*illus.*, 267–271
Mission of Píritu, 263*illus.*, 270–271
Mission of Santa Rosa de Ocópi, 39
Missions
 agriculture and, 47–48
 life for aborigines in, 31–32
 modernization of, 49–50
 postcolonial, 46–50
 spread of epidemics by, 42–43
 Western medicine provided by, 68–69
Mission settlements, establishment of, 227–228
Mission soldiering, 37–40
Mist
 rain shamans and, 104
 in Warao mythology, 71
Mistress of Rain, 175, 215
Mistress of the Forest, in Warao mythology, 72
Mockingbird, as thunderbird, 207
Mocoví Indians, rain deities of, 218
Modesty, 34
Mojo Indians, rainbow mythology of, 220, 224
Monagas state, Warao Indians in, 3
Monotonic chants, 175
Montaña
 atmospheric deities in, 222
 homeopathic weather magic in, 191
 rain shamans of, 166
 snake and rainbow mythology in, 218*n*
 weather-blowing in, 169–170
Moon, in Cuzco mythology, 212
Moriche palms, 7, 8, 137–139, 138*illus.*
 gathering and extracting sago from, 139–143, 140*illus.*, 142*illus.*
 mythical origin of, 136
 rainfall as triggering growth of, 13–14
 rainmaker's power over, 93
 Warao hunger and, 252
 as Warao staple food, 13, 51
Moriche sago. *See* Palm sago
Moriche sago hoe, 140*illus.*
Morocoto fish, 251
Morocoto fisheries, 48
Mosquitos, 63
 in Warao mythology, 79
Mother-in-law
 of Orion, 81
 respect for, 80*n*
"Mother of Being," 159
Mother of Crabs, 90
Mother of High River, 143
Mother of Low River, 143
"Mother of Rain," 96
"Mother of Sago," 159
 pollination of, 157, 158
Mother of the Forest, 113*n*, 220
 in Warao mythology, 72
Mother of the Sacred Trumpet, 147, 149, 158
 sons of, 156–157
"Mother of the Wooden Image," 156
Mother of Tides, 143
"Mother of Whirlwinds," 87
"Mother without Illness," 147
Mountains, as rain-god residences, 73–74
Mount Karoshimo, in Warao mythology, 147
Moyordomías, 237
Munduruku Indians
 rainbow mythology of, 219
 rituals against atmospheric spirits among, 184–185

Muscivora tyrannus monachus, 208
Music, 154. *See also* Rain dances
  dehiscence and, 158*n*
  in Indian education, 232
Musical instruments. *See* Aerophone music; Bullroarers; Deer-bone flute; Drums; *Isimoi*; *Isimoi arotu*; Rattles; Sacred trumpet
Music masters, 154, 240
Musimotuma, 25, 40
Myrcia sp., 171
Myths. *See also* Weather religion
  diseases and epidemics in, 43–44
  of inferior judgment, 34–37
  influence of European colonists on, 31–32
  of misbegotten origin, 32–34
  of unions between humans and animals, 32–34

Nabarao, 134
Nabarima, 147
Nabasanuka, xxv
Nadir goddess, 203
Nahakara, 132*n*
Nahanaka, 81
Nahanamu anamunaya, 151
Nahanamu dance ritual, 151
Nahanamu festival, 119, 120, 238, 239
  commencement of, 146, 150–151
  derived features of, 246
  distribution ritual of, 156–157
  European features of, 243
  Hunger and, 251
  ritual protection of children from disease at, 92
Nahanatakitani, 104

Naharani, 96
Naharima, 96, 226
Nambicuara Indians
  homeopathic weather magic of, 197
  rituals against atmospheric spirits among, 185, 190
Namomo, 151
Namonina a re, 99, 249
"Narrow historical passages," for Warao Indians, xxii
Nasi, 72
Nasutitermes corniger, 112*n*
National Census of 1960, 50*n*
Nationalized schools, 49
Natue, 159
Navigation
  as an Arawak skill, 24
  of Orinoco Delta, 5
Necromancy, 99, 100
New year, marking the arrival of, 90
Nicotiana rustica, 102
Nicotiana tabacum, 102
Nicotine. *See also* Tobacco; Tobacco smoke
  "darkened vision" and, 99
  effects on aspiring shamans, 103–104
  in Tapirapé weather ritual, 187, 188*illus.*
  therapeutic effects of, 167
Nightjars, 217
Nine-banded armadillo, 131–132*n*
Nivaklé Indians
  rain deities of, 217
  thunderbird of, 206–207, 208
Noara ritual, 150–151
  derived features of, 246
Nohihabasi, 80*n*
Noise, countering thunderstorms by making, 190–192

Nomadic lifestyle
  as a barrier to the spread of disease, 41
  of Warao Indians, 52–57
North America, weather religion and, xxiii–xxiv
North American Indians
  homeopathic weather magic of, 190–191
  thunderstorm imagery and, 205–206
Northern trade winds. *See also* Trade winds
  master of, 82, 136
North Wind, 201–202
Nudity, 34, 35, 57
Nuestra Señora de Guía de Uracoa mission, 265
Nuestra Señora de los Remedios mission, 270–271
  Mamo massacre at, 40
Nuestra Señora del Rosario de Yaguaraparo mission, 265
Nuestra Señora Santa Ana de Sopocuar mission, 266
Ñushamuanda, 171
Nyctibius grandis, 217

Object intrusion, disease and, 69
Oboe, sacred trumpet as, 154
Obo monida, 120–121
Ocean grandmother, 143
Ocumo chino, 252
Odors, in homeopathic weather magic, 197
Offerings to the gods, 144–146
Ogres, 153
Ohiarao, 136–137
Ohidu a muhu, 159
Ohidu aru, 245
Oka, 131–132*n*, 255
  battle between Huru and, 131–134

Oka nabarao, 132*n*
Oka sanuka, 132*n*
Old age, among Warao Indians, 97
Old World pestilences, 40–45
Olsen, Dale, 105*n*
Omaua, 176
One-Eye, 215
"Origin of the Sun," 80*n*
Orinoco-Apure line, 78
Orinoco Crocodile, 100*n*, 101
Orinoco Delta, 4*illus.*, 6*illus.*
  annual mean temperature of, 8
  cannibalism practiced on, 25–27
  Carib trade routes and, 37–39
  crocodiles inhabiting, 100*n*
  dangers of life and weather on, xxii–xxiii, xxiv
  data collection on, xxiv–xxv
  difficulties of survival in, 249–250
  earthquakes on, 134*n*
  European colonization of, 30
  geography of, 3–8
  hydraulic regimen of, 20–21
  land and sea breezes on, 16–17
  long rainy season in, 78–79
  mountains and *tepuis* near, 73–74
  navigation of, 5
  pre-Columbian invasions of, 23–24
  rainfall in, 10–13
  resettlement of Warao Indians outside, 44–45
  return of missionaries to, 46–50
  rubber plantations on, 45–46
  sago palms on, 137–139
  scarcity of tobacco on, 102–103
  slave trade on, 27–29
  tides affecting, 21
  uncertainty of food supply on, 251–252

Orinoco Delta (*continued*)
  visibility of Orion and the Pleiades from, 80*n*
  Warao childhood mortality statistics for, 90
  Warao distribution on, 4–8
  as Warao Indian home, xxi
  as a Warao refuge, 23
  waterway complex of, 5
  weather conditions on, 8–13
  winds affecting, 17–20, 76–78, 82
Orion, 206
  green heron and, 135–136
  times of visibility of, 80*n*
  in Warao mythology, 80*n*, 80–81, 90
Oscillated turkey, as protector of children from disease, 91–92
Otavalo-Quichua Indians, rainbow mythology of, 219
Outboard motors, as evil objects, 124, 124*n*
Oxbow lakes, 8

Pacha Mama, 202
Padres. *See also* Capuchin missionaries; Dominican missionaries; Franciscan missionaries; Missionaries
  agricultural efforts of, 47–48
  disease immunity of, 43
Paéz Indians
  rainbow mythology of, 221
  weather-blowing among, 171
Paint
  in homeopathic weather magic, 195, 198–199
  in rain dances, 178–179
Palm-borer larvae, as food, 141
Palm sago, 137–139, 199
  annual rainfall and, 14–15
  bathing in, 158, 158*n*
  container and temple for, 145*illus.*, 158
  gathering and extracting, 137–143, 137*n*, 140*illus.*, 142*illus.*
  mythical origin of, 137
  preparation of, 55*illus.*, 137–139
  propitiating gods with, 85
  rainmaker's power over, 93
  shortages of, 14
  storage of, 145*illus.*, 155, 158, 246
  as Warao staple food, xxi, 13, 51, 137–139
Palm sap, as drink, 141–143
Panare Indians, snake and rainbow mythology of, 218*n*
Paramanzillo trees, 7
Paria coast, slave trade along, 28
Paria Indians, in Guayana Mission, 268
Paria Peninsula
  earthquakes on, 134*n*
  winds around, 76–78
Parintintin Indians, weather-blowing among, 171
Parishes
  education in, 49
  founding of, 47
Pasain Indians, rain dances among, 177–178
Patagonian Plateau, rain dances of, 178
Pata toda leaves, in homeopathic weather magic, 197
Paternalism, rejection of, 49
Pauji turkey, 92
Paulo, 124
Payaguá Indians, rituals against atmospheric spirits among, 186

Index   349

Payaraima mission, 269
Pearl fisheries, 29
Peat, in Orinoco Delta, 6–8
Peccary, 214
Pedernales parish
  founding of, 47
  rainfall in, 10–13
Pegón bee, 111–113
Pelleprat, Pierre, on cannibalism, 27
Pemon Indians, snake and
  rainbow mythology of, 218n
Penicillin, 120
"People of Mamo," 40
Pestilence, 40–45
  as supernatural punishment, 43–44
"Pestilent exhalations," 63
Pigeon
  in Sanemá-Yanomami
    mythology, 213
  as thunderbird, 207
Pigs, 52
Pilagá Indians
  rainbow mythology of, 222
  thunder and lightning demons
    of, 203
  wind demons of, 201
Pile dwellings, 58*illus.*, 59*illus.*, 95*illus.*
  of the rain gods, 74–75
Piquí, 177
Piripiri, 169–170, 170n
Piritu Indians, rain deities of, 215
Píritu Mission, 271
  establishment of, 228
  map of, 263*illus.*
Piro Indians
  homeopathic weather magic of, 197
  rituals against atmospheric
    spirits among, 185, 186
  weather-blowing among, 170

Plant fertility, winds and, 136n
Plant leaves, in homeopathic
  weather magic, 197
Pleiades, 196
  times of visibility of, 80n
  in Warao mythology, 80n, 80–81, 90
Pneumatic rituals, 167. *See also*
  Blowing against the wind
Pneumatic theory of illness, 68
Pneumonia, 119, 122n
Point bars, 8
Police, 48
Political organization, of Warao
  Indians, 48, 225–247
Pollution, rain associated with, 71
Polygyny, 52, 61
Pomeroon coast, cannibalism
  along, 26
Pomeroon River Indians,
  homeopathic weather magic
  of, 190
Population growth, 50n
  erosion of Warao society by, 69
  of Warao Indians, 50
Postcolonial missions, 46–50
Postmenopausal women,
  protection of children by, 91–92
Pottery, 57
Praying mantises, 237
  as guardian spirits, 153
Precipitation. *See* Average annual
  rainfall; Rainfall;
  Thunderstorms
Pre-Columbian invasions, 23–24
  cannibalism and, 25–27
Pregnancy, winds and, 136n
Prejudices, against aboriginals, 31–32
Prelittoral zone, of Orinoco Delta, 7–8

Priests, power contests beween shamans and, 225–226
Priest-shaman, 62, 98, 122*n*
  attempt to cure tuberculosis by, 120–122
  cofradias and, 237–238
  Father of Wind as, 135
  functions of, 146
  in sago distribution ritual, 156–157
  wisdom of, 250
Priodontes, 200
Procurators, 228
Psychotropic plants, weather-blowing and, 170–171
Psychotropic snuff, in homeopathic weather magic, 191–192
Pterocarpus officinalis, 7, 110*n*
  blossoming of, 143–144
Pubic covers, 57
Pulmonary tuberculosis, 63
  death of a Warao boy from, 118–130
Punishments, meted out to Indians by corregidors, 228–229
Puntada epidemic, 43
Puruhá-Quichua Indians
  rainbow mythology of, 219
  rituals against atmospheric spirits among, 186
  wind demons of, 202
P'usarpayaña ritual, 171

Quechua Indians
  homeopathic weather magic of, 194–195, 197
  wind demons of, 202
Quichua Indians, thunder and lightning demons of, 203, 204–205

Rage, 113–114
Rain, 71–92. *See also* Atmospheric spirits
  alligators and, 101
  behavior of Warao during, 116
  demons of, 212–218
  diseases associated with, 71–73, 116
  dying in, 115–130
  the Lords of, 73–78, 89, 104–114
  mythologically deleterious effects of, 71
  rituals attempting to stop, 174–176
Rainbirds, 217–218
Rainbow, 75–77, 115*n*
  demons of, 218–222
  Snake of Being and, 88
  snakes in mythology of, 218, 218*n*, 222
  sources of mythology of, 224
  in Warao mythology, 71–73
Rain ceremony, of the Incas, 195*illus.*
Rain chants. *See* Chants
Rain dances, 176–180
  described, 176–177
  purposes of, 176
  sources of mythology of, 224
Rainfall, 10–13. *See also* Thunderstorms
  availability of food staples and, 15*illus.*
  charts of distribution of, 10*illus.*, 11*illus.*, 12*illus.*
  effects of slow-moving, 13–14
  famine and seasonal hunger and, 13–15
  moriche sago and, 15*illus.*
Rain gods. *See* Lords of the Rain, the; Warao rain-god complex

Rain magic devices, 189*illus.*, 189
Rainmaker, 93–115. *See also* Rain shaman; Windmaker
 cultural importance of, xxi
 decision to become, 97
 derived features of, 245
 empowerment of, 96–104
 humble appearance of, 93–94
 incantations of, 94–96, 104–109, 110–114
 initiation of, 97–99, 101–104, 104–109, 114–115
 initiation of female, 96*n*
 sun bittern (*tigana*) and, 82, 83
 types of, 63, 101
Rain Master, 215
Rain Mother, 220
Rain piripiri, 170
Rain shamans, xxi, 95*illus*. *See also* Rainmaker
 anger as supporting, 252–253
 as corregidors and *cabos*, 236–237
 derived features of, 244
 induction fees of, 96–97, 98, 101, 103
 initiation of, 97–109, 114–115, 166
 maturity of, 96
 method of curing disease employed by, 98–99
 powers of, 104
 present decline in numbers of, 97–98
 Rainbow myths and, 72–73
 sun bittern and, 84
 tobacco and, 102–104
 training of, 97–98
Rain spells, 94–96
Ramírez de Arrelano, Governor, 228
"Rattle of ruffled feathers," 66*illus*.

Rattles, 66*illus*.
 in homeopathic weather magic, 192, 198, 199
 in sago distribution ritual, 157
 storage of, 146
 in Tapirapé weather ritual, 187–188
 use of, 120–121
Red Faces, 25, 27, 40
Red mineral dye, in homeopathic weather magic, 195
Red paint, in rain dances, 178–179
Red stone ax, in homeopathic weather magic, 198
Refugee Warao Indians, indentured laborers and, xxiii
Religion. *See* Catholicism; Church, the; Evangelization; Missionaries; Universal Church; Vatican II Council; Weather religion
Religio-sociological institutes, 49
Religious brotherhoods, 233
Religious climatology, among Warao Indians, xxii–xxiii
Religious festivals, at Capuchin missions, 233–234
Revenge, as motive of weather supernaturals, 210–211
Rheas, in weather mythology, 218
Rice cropping, 47–48
Ridicule, of weather-blowing, 168–169
Río Bermejo, rain dances along, 177–178
Rio Grande, 4–5
 rubber plantations along, 46
Rituals
 to neutralize meteors, 172–174, 173*illus*.
 to protect children from disease, 91–92

Rituals (*continued*)
  shield fighting as, 132–134, 133*illus.*
  spread of disease and, 41
  among Warao Indians, xxii–xxiii
River fishing, 54*illus.*
Rock crystal, sacred, 146, 147–149
Rock spirit, 147–149
Romi Kuma, 213
Roystonea, 137*n*
Roystonea oleracea, 137
Rubber plantations, forced labor on, 45–46
Rubbing hands, in homeopathic weather magic, 196–197
Rufous crab hawk, 136*n*, 136–137

Sacred objects, 146. *See also* Rattles; Temples
Sacred rock crystal, 146
  mythical origin of, 147–149
Sacred trumpet, xxi, xxv, 65*illus.*, 66*illus.*, 148*illus.*, 150*illus.* *See also* Isimoi; *Isimoi arotu*
  ancestor cult and, 240
  derived features of, 244–245
  described, 149–150
  learning to play, 153–154
  playing during sago distribution ritual, 156–157
Sacred trumpet player, 94, 146–152, 238, 242–243
  ancestor cult and, 158
  initiation of, 147
  as lay brother, 239
  during sago distribution ritual, 156–157
  in sago harvest ritual, 151–152
  windmaker as, 146
Sacrilege, by shamans, 117
Sacupana River, 7

Sago. *See* Palm sago
Sago distribution ritual, 155–157
Sago festivals, 55*illus.*, 65*illus.*, 66*illus.*
  initiation of, 150
  marriages organized during, 57
  ritual protection of children from disease at, 92
Sago harvest ritual, 151–155
Sago hoe, 140*illus.*
Sago Mother, 136, 137, 139
Sago rituals, xxv, 151–157
Saliva Indians, in Guayana Mission, 268
Saltwater, in Orinoco Delta, 21
San Antonio de Capayacuar mission, 266
  founding of, 46–47
San Buenaventura de Auguri mission, 269
Sanemá-Yanomami Indians
  rainbow mythology of, 222
  rain deities of, 213, 216, 217
  snake and rainbow mythology of, 218*n*
  subterranean dwarfs in mythology of, 214
  thunder and lightning demons of, 203, 208, 211
San Francisco de Guyao mission, founding of, 47
Sangrito trees, 7, 110*n*
  blossoming of, 143–144
San José de Yaruara, rainfall and food availability in, 15*illus.*
San José mission, founding of, 46–47
San Juan Bautista de Buenavista settlement, 270
San Judas Tadeo de Maturín mission, 265
San Miguel de Unata mission, 268

Index

San Rafael de Barrancas mission, 265
San Serafín de Tabasca mission, 265
Santa Ana de Puga mission, 269
Santa Cruz de Montecalvario mission, 269
Santa Cruz de Payacuar mission, 266
Santa Eulalia de Murucuri mission, 269
Santa Isabel mission, 78, 265
Santa Rosa de Maruanta mission, 268
Santa Rosa de Viterbo de Ocópi settlement, 270
Santa Teresa de Orocopiche settlement, 270
Schultes, Richard Evans, 110*n*
Sea breezes, 16*illus.*, 16–17
　mythological origins of, 130–131
　water people and, 134
Sea serpents, rainbow mythology and, 218*n*
Seasonal hunger, rainfall and, 13–15
Seasonal temperatures, in Orinoco Delta, 8
Seasons, in Orinoco Delta, 8–9
Seclusion, Warao Indian society and, 3–4
Second constable (of the Lords of the Rain), 75–77
Second speaker (of the Lords of the Rain), 75–77
Second Vatican Council. *See* Vatican II Council
Selfless behavior, rain shaman's enforcement of, 93
Self-sufficiency, 249
　of missions, 47

Selknam Indians
　homeopathic weather magic of, 192, 196
　rain dances among, 178–180
　rituals against atmospheric spirits among, 185
　thunder and lightning demons of, 209
　weather ceremony of, 181*illus.*, 182*illus.*, 183*illus.*
　wind demons of, 201–202
Señorías, 228
Sensi Indians, rituals against atmospheric spirits among, 184
Sentient beings, weather phenomena as, 161–164
Serpents. *See also* Snakes
　whirlwinds as, 88–89
Servitude, 45–46. *See also* Slavery
Sexual frustration, *pegón* bee and, 111
Sexuality
　in rainbow mythology, 219
　during sago distribution ritual, 157
"Shaman chanters," 166
Shamanism
　alligator imagery and, 100–101
　canoe construction and, 61
　medicine and, 57–69
　rainmaker and, 93–115
　storytelling and, 99–100
　tobacco and, 99, 102–104
　transformation stories and, 99–100
　weather magic and, 165–166
Shamans, 64*illus. See also* Dark shaman; Light shaman; Priest-shaman; Rain shaman; Weather shamans

Shamans (*continued*)
    attempt to cure tuberculosis by, 120–122
    burials of, 67*illus.*
    claims of supernatural powers by, 225–226
    power contests beween Christian priests and, 225–226
    as practitioners of weather magic, 164–166
    sacrilege by, 117
    in Warao mythology, 44
Sharanahua Indians, 170*n*
Sharpa Indians
    homeopathic weather magic of, 191, 196
    rainbow mythology of, 220, 222
    rain deities of, 216
    snake and rainbow mythology of, 218*n*
    weather-blowing among, 169
Shavante Indians
    snake and rainbow mythology of, 218*n*
    wind demons of, 202*n*
Sheep, homeopathic sacrifices of, 194
Shell middens, 26
Shiborori, as protector of children from disease, 91–92
Shield fighting, 132*n*, 133*illus.*
Shimomu, 144
Shipaya Indians
    fish demon of, 204*illus.*
    lightning spirits of, 208
    rituals against atmospheric spirits among, 180–184
Shipibo Indians
    origin myths of, 208
    rainbow mythology of, 220, 221, 222
    snake and rainbow mythology of, 218*n*

thunder and lightning demons of, 211
weather-blowing among, 170
Shipwrights, Warao Indians as, 41–42
Shoving contests, 132, 132*n*
Shucurú Indians, weather chants among, 174
Siawani, 25
Sikuani Indians, homeopathic weather magic of, 193
Silence, in homeopathic weather magic, 191
Simara mission, 265
Singing, 152
Siona-Secoya Indians
    thunder and lightning demons of, 205
    wind demons of, 200
Sky, 236
Sky people, 204
Sky woman, 213
Slave raiders, 27–29
Slavery, xxiii, 27–29. *See also* Servitude
    epidemics resulting from, 40–41
Smallpox, 42
Smoke, as clouds, 196–197
Smoking, 235. *See also* Tobacco; Tobacco smoke
Snake of Being, 88
Snakes. *See also* Anaconda; Boas; Mapanare snakes
    in rainbow mythology, 218, 218*n*, 222
    in weather mythology, 216
Snelling, Roy R., 111*n*
Sodomy, 34
Soft rain
    rain shamans and, 104
    in Warao mythology, 71
Son of Rain, 175

Sorcery
  alligator imagery in, 100–101
  dread of, 41, 97
  public, 99
Soto, Cesáreo, xxv, 105*n*
Sound, dehiscence and, 158*n*
South America
  Carib trade routes in, 38*illus.*
  comparative weather lore map of, 162–164*illus.*
  homeopathic weather magic in, 190
  modern missionary work in, 49
  mythology of, 32
  thunderbird motif in, 205–208
  weather religion and, xxiii–xxiv, 161–224
Southern Cross
  as protector of children from disease, 91
  in Warao mythology, 81
Southern trade winds. *See also* Trade winds
  master of, 82
  Tuyuna and, 83
South Wind, 201–202
Spain
  European-Indian alliances against, 39
  influence on Warao of, xxiv
  liberation of Venezuela from, 44–45
Spanish colonists
  slave trade with, 28–29
  Warao social organization and, 225–247
Spears, in rituals against atmospheric spirits, 185
Spider monkey, as wind demon, 200
Spider Woman, 137, 158–159
Spirit aggression, disease and, 69

Spit-blowing, 170
Starch, in palm sago, 139–141
Starvation diets, 46
Stenopolybia fulvofasciata, 112*n*, 113
Stiff-Bearded One, 201
Stilt houses, 52, 58*illus.*
Stones, in homeopathic weather magic, 198
Stork, as thunderbird, 207
Stormbirds, as wind demons, 201
Storytelling, 99–100
Strength, of the armadillo, 132*n*
Striated heron, 82, 136*n*
  Father of Wind as, 135–136
  as thunderbird, 206
Subtribal groups, loss of cohesion among, 69
Sucre state, Warao Indians in, 3
Suffering
  during long rainy season, 90
  rain associated with, 71, 118
Sugarcane, 47, 51
Sugar production, forced labor in, 46
Suicide, 130
Summer solstice, in Orinoco Delta, 9
Sun
  in Cuzco mythology, 212
  mythological origin of, 80*n*, 81
Sun bittern, 84*illus.*, 255
  as thunderbird, 206
  in Warao mythology, 82–85, 146, 200
Sunshowers
  diseases from, 104
  in Warao mythology, 73
Supay, 202
Superiority, of Criollo culture, intelligence, and linguistic skills, 34–37

Surinam. *See also* Dutch Guiana
  pre-Columbian invasions of, 23–24
  Warao Indians in, 3–4, 50*n*
Surui Indians, weather chants among, 176
Survival rate. *See* Longevity
Swallower of initiates, 88–89, 114–115
Swamp forest, 6–7
Swamps, 5–8
  Warao Indians protected by, 5
Swans, myths concerning, 32*n*
Sweet manioc, 51
Swidden agriculture, 252
Symphonia globulifera, 7
Syncretistic renewal, of European social conventions, 243–247

Tacana Indians, wind demons of, 202
Taling ritual, 171
Tamanaco Indians, rain deities of, 215
Tamoi, 175
Tapir, 210
Tapirapé Indians
  ritual against atmospheric spirits among, 186–189, 188*illus.*
  thunder and lightning demons of, 203
  weather-blowing among, 171
Tariano Indians, weather-blowing among, 168, 169
Tarita, 115, 243
  appearance of, 88–89
Taro, 47, 51, 122, 252
  preparation of, 56*illus.*
Tatusiso, 214
Taurepan Indians
  rainbow mythology of, 222
  snake and rainbow mythology

of, 218*n*
Tauste, Francisco de, 225
Tears, in homeopathic weather magic, 192–193, 193–194
Temiche palms, 7, 85, 139
  drinking "milk" of, 143
Temperature, in Orinoco Delta, 8
Temples
  for holding sacred objects, 145*illus.*, 146
  for palm sago storage, 155, 239–241
Tepuis, 73–74
Tereno Indians
  rain deities of, 216
  weather chants among, 174
Termite nests, in homeopathic weather magic, 196
Termites, 111*n*, 112, 112*n*, 214
"Terrible cough," 119, 120–121
Thatched roofs, 52
Therapeutic blowing, 167
Thorbjarnavson, John, 101
Thunder
  demons of, 203–212
  during rainmaker's initiation, 114–115
Thunder (as a deity), 203, 211, 212, 215
  in Maku cosmology, 208
  in Tapirapé weather ritual, 188*illus.*, 189
Thunderbird, 82–85, 84*illus.*, 205–208, 217, 255
Thunder ceremony, of the Tapirapé Indians, 186*n*, 186–189, 188*illus.*
Thunderer, the, 88–89, 115
Thunderstorms. *See also* Atmospheric spirits
  alligators and, 101
  barineses and, 17

Index

behavior of Surui during, 176
behavior of Warao during, 116
conjuring up, 110–114
demons of, 203–212
long rainy season and, 78–79
making noise to counter, 190–192
rainmakers' incantations against, 94–96, 95*illus.*
rain shamans and, 104
during wet seasons, 13–14, 83–85
Tidal action, intermediate zone and, 7
Tidal shifts, of Orinoco Delta, 5
Tides, 20–21
origin myths of, 143
Tierra del Fuego, rain dances of, 178–180
Tigana, 82–83, 106
Tihidamo ayara, 158–159
Tillet, Steven, 110*n*
Toads
in homeopathic weather magic, 191
in weather mythology, 215
Tobacco. *See also* Nicotine
inducing trances with, 114
pegón bee and, 112–113
shamanism and, 99, 102–104
Tobacco juice blowing, 170
Tobacco smoke
Bororo Indians' use of, 172–174
Jivaro Indians' use of, 170
in rain shaman's incantations, 96
in rituals against atmospheric spirits, 185
in sago distribution ritual, 157
in Tapirapé weather ritual, 187
therapeutic effects of, 167–168
weather-blowing and, 171

Yagua Indians' use of, 169
Tobagua, Carib trade routes and, 37
Toba Indians
homeopathic weather magic of, 192
rainbow mythology of, 222
rain deities of, 215, 217
rituals against atmospheric spirits among, 190
thunder and lightning demons of, 203
thunderbird of, 207
weather chants among, 175, 176
wind demons of, 201
Toba-Pilagá Indians, rainbow mythology of, 219
Tomonoho simo, 112*n*, 113
Toothache, remedies for, 110
Topü-spirits, 187
Tornadoes, 19
eyewitness accounts of, 86–87
in Warao mythology, 85–89
Toromona Indians, wind demons of, 202
Torture, by biting and bloodsucking insects, 79
Trade, 37–39
as a source of epidemic disease, 41–42
Trade winds, 17–18, 130
long dry season and, 134–135
long rainy season and, 78
in Orinoco Delta, 8–9
in Warao mythology, 82
Tradition, xxiii
Traditional Indian ways, eradication of, 48
Trances, tobacco-induced, 114
Transformation stories, 99–100, 249–250
"Tree of Life." *See* Moriche palm

Tree trunks, in homeopathic weather magic, 192
Tree women, in Warao mythology, 73
Tribal zones, 39
Tribute, 227
    inability to pay, 230–231
    paid to corregidors, 228–229
Trigona capitata, 112*n*
Trigona hyalinata branneri, 110*n*, 111
Trinidad
    Arawak occupation of, 24
    Carib trade routes and, 37–39
    slave trade in, 28
    tobacco trade with, 102
Trumpeting, in homeopathic weather magic, 192
Tuberculosis, 122*n*
    death of a Warao boy from, 118–130
Tucupita
    founding of apostolic vicariate at, 46
    tobacco trade with, 102
Tukano Indians, snake and rainbow mythology of, 218*n*
Tuminkar, 172
Tupâ, 211–212
Tupan, 201, 205
    in Tupí-Guaraní mythology, 208, 211–212
Tupari Indians
    homeopathic weather magic of, 191–192
    rainbow mythology of, 222
    thunder and lightning demons of, 205
Tupí-Guaraní Indians, thunder and lightning demons of, 205, 208, 211–212
Tupí Indians, thunder and lightning demons of, 211

Tupinamba Indians, thunder and lightning demons of, 205, 210–211, 211
Tupuiranca, 203–204
Turrado Moreno, Angel, rain spell recorded by, 94
Turtles, as food, 141
Tuyuna, 82–85, 146

Umutina Indians
    thunder and lightning demons of, 204
    weather chants among, 174
Underworld, 79*n*
    denizens of, 99
Universal Church, missionary work for, 49–50
Uraro, 118, 147
Ure, 245
Urine
    in homeopathic weather magic, 192–193, 196, 197
    in rainbow mythology, 221–222
Uroboros, 88
Urubu-Kaapor, 210
Utoaztecan Indians, homeopathic weather magic of, 190–191
Uxorilocal families, 52, 59*illus.*
Uxorilocal residence rule, 117*n*

Vaapuka, 184
Vaccines, 42
Variegated tinamou, as wind demon, 200
Vatican II Council
    evangelization practices after, 49–50
    evangelization practices before, 47–48
Vaupés-Caquetá region, weather-blowing in, 169
Vaupés River, thunder and lightning demons along, 209

Venezuela
  appearance of cabildos in, 227
  Carib trade routes and, 37–39
  the Church in, 49
  earthquakes in, 134n
  pre-Columbian invasions of, 23–24
  reopening of missions in, 46–50
  slave trade in, 27–29
  Warao isolation in, xxiv, 3–8
  Warao population of, 50n
  War of Independence of, 44–45
  wind data for, 76–78, 77*illus.*
Vernal equinox
  behavior of striated heron during, 135
  gathering palm sago after, 139–143, 140*illus.*, 142*illus.*
  long rainy season and, 78
  in Orinoco Delta, 9
Vicariate Apostolic of Caroní, founding of, 46
Vicariate Apostolic of Tucupita, founding of, 46
Vilela Indians
  rain dances among, 177–178
  snake and rainbow mythology of, 218n
Village councils, 242
  organization of, 226–228
Villages, 58*illus.*
Vindictiveness, of thunder and lightning demons, 208–210
Violence, 113–114
Virilocal residence, 117n
Virola surinamensis, 110, 110n
Vociferation, in homeopathic weather magic, 198
Voropí, 216

Wabai, 125
Wadoriwä, 176

Wafting-in-the-Air Bearded One, 201
Wagley, Charles, 186n
Waikuba, 143
Waiwai Indians
  thunder and lightning demons of, 205, 209
  weather-blowing among, 171–172
  weather chants among, 176
Waiwari butterflies, 81
Wanülü, 216
Wapishana Indians
  rain deities of, 215
  thunderbird of, 206
  weather-blowing among, 172
Waramuri Indians, shell middens of, 26
Warao culture
  adaptability of, 249
  cooperative behavior in, 255–259
  derived features of, 254
  supposed inferiority of, 34–37
Warao Indians. *See also* Mariusa subtribe; Winikina subtribe
  agriculture among, 51–52
  ancestor myths of, 158–159
  ancestors of, 23–24
  anger and fear among, 252–255
  anthropological studies of, 51
  archaeology and history of, 23–69
  cannibalism and, 25–27
  Capuchin efforts to resettle, 44–45
  childhood mortality statistics for, 90
  colonial analogues to European social organization among, 241–247
  communal food repositories of, 237

Warao Indians (*continued*)
  contemporary, 50–69
  creation myths of, 34–37
  at Cumaná Mission, 262–264
  death among, 115–130
  deplorable conditions of, 45
  diseases spread among, 40–45
  education of, 49
  effects of adverse weather conditions on, xxii–xxiii
  effects of evangelization attempts on, 30–40
  escape from slave trade by, 29
  exploitation of, 230–231
  family structure of, 52–57
  female rain deities of, 212–213
  food preparation among, 52
  as forced labor on rubber plantations, 45–46
  geographical distribution of, 3–8
  at Guayana Mission, 264, 268–270
  homeopathic weather magic of, 190, 192, 193, 196, 197, 198, 199
  house construction among, 52
  hydraulic regimen affecting, 20–21
  influence of land and sea breezes on, 16–17
  isolation of, 3–4
  longevity of, 96–97
  militia enslavement and training of, 39–40
  mythological origin of, 81
  myths of, 32–37
  old age among, 97
  origin myths of, 33–34, 208
  outside Cumaná and Guayana Missions, 264, 269–271
  palm sago and, xxi
  political organization of, 48, 225–247
  population growth of, 50
  prejudices against, 31–32
  rainbow mythology of, 219, 220, 221, 222
  rain deities of, 216
  rainfall experienced by, 10–13
  rain mythology of, 71–130
  rain shamanism among, 93–115, 168–169
  relationship of gods to, 90–91
  sago ritual of, 151–157
  seasons experienced by, 8–9
  settlement distribution of, 6*illus.*
  shamanism among, 57, 57–69
  sources of mythology of, 222–224
  Spanish influences on social organization of, 235–241, 241–243
  stormbirds as wind demons of, 201
  supposed lack of intelligence of, 34–37
  survival strategies of, 3
  threat of slavery and, 27–29
  thunder and lightning demons of, 203, 204, 208–209
  thunderbird of, 206
  tides affecting, 21
  tobacco and, 99, 102–104
  weather-blowing among, 168–169
  weather chants among, 175–176
  weather interpretations of, 165–166
  weather religion of, xxi
  Western technology and, 36–37
  whirlwinds affecting, 19–20
  wind demons of, 200, 202*n*
  wind mythology of, 130–151

Index 361

winds affecting, 17–20
Warao rain-gods complex, 73–78.
  See also Lords of the Rain, the
  European features of, 243–244
  origins of, xxiii–xxiv
Warao society, 225–247
  political organization of, 226
Warao songs, cannibal invasions
  described in, 25
Waraowitu, 116
Warfare
  among pre-Columbian tribes, 24
  between Warao and cannibals,
  25–27
Warowaro, 147
Warriors, 25
Wasps, 112*n*
  honey production and, 144
  rain shamanism and, 112–114
Watauinewa, 175
Water
  in homeopathic weather magic,
  192–193
  in rainbow mythology, 222
Water people, 134
Water spirits, 134
Waterspouts, 19–20
  eyewitness accounts of, 85–86
  in Warao mythology, 85–89
"Wave women," 213
Weasels, as water spirits, 216
Weather-blowing, 167–174
Weather conditions, on Orinoco
  Delta, xxii–xxiii, 8–13
Weather dancing. *See* Rain dances
Weather deities. *See* Atmospheric
  spirits
Weather lore, 71–159, 161–224,
  254–255
  breath and, 167–174
  combating atmospheric spirits
  in, 180–190

homeopathic magic in, 190–199
practitioners of weather magic
  and, 161–166
rain chants in, 171–172, 174–176
rain dancing in, 176–180
relationships of Warao weather
  lore to that of other South
  American Indians, 222–224
weather gods and demons in,
  199–222
Weather magic, 161–166
Weather religion. *See also* Myths
  as based in mystical retribution,
  43
  bitterness of, 113*n*
  European elements in, 243–247
  foreign elements in, xxiii–xxiv
  origins of, xxiii–xxiv, 15
  power contests between
  Christianity and, 225–226
  "Tree of Life" of, 138*illus.*
  of Warao Indians, xxi, xxii–
  xxiii, 249
Weather rituals
  among Selknam Indians,
  181*illus.*, 182*illus.*, 183*illus.*
  among Warao Indians, xxii–xxiii
Weather shamans, 165–166. *See
  also* Rainmaker; Rain
  shamans; Windmaker
  common features of, 222–223
  derived features of, 244
Weaving, 57
Were-jaguars, Cariña Caribs as, 37
Western medicine, Warao access
  to, 68–69
Western technology, Warao
  feelings toward, 36–37
Wet seasons. *See also* Long rainy
  season
  availability of food during, 14–
  15

Wet seasons (*continued*)
  causes of, 8–9
  diseases associated with, 104
  hydraulic regimen and, 20–21
  rain gods during, 74, 75
  scarcity of food during, 13–14
  tides during, 21
Whirlwinds, 19–20, 130, 200–201
  master serpents and, 88–89
  in Warao mythology, 85–89
White heron, as weather deity, 217
Whooping cough, 90
Wicunda palm, in homeopathic weather magic, 196
Wilbert, Werner, 68, 86*n*
"Wild Coast," slave trade along, 28
Wind
  demons of, 200–202
  rituals to control, 198
Wind demons, common features of, 223
Windmaker, 146–151. *See also* Rainmaker
  cultural importance of, xxi
  derived features of, 245
  ritual protection of children from disease and, 92
  as sacred trumpeter, 146
"Wind mother," 136*n*
Wind pollination, 136*n*
Wind roses, 77*illus.*
  hierarchy of the Lords of the Rain and, 76–78
Winds, 17–20, 130–159. *See also* Local winds; Trade winds; Whirlwinds
  ancestral spirits and, 158–159
  armadillo mythology and, 130–134
  blowing against, 167–174
  earthquakes and, 130–134
  epidemics and, 63–68
  the Father of, 134–137
  long dry season and, 137–146
  mythological origins of, 130–134
  sago rituals and, 151–157
  windmaker and, 146–151
Wind spirits, 130, 200–202
Winikina, xxv
  rainfall and food availability in, 14–15, 115–116
  rainfall in, 10–13
Winikina subtribe. *See also* Warao Indians
  anthropological studies of, 51
  childhood mortality statistics for, 90
  death in, 115–130
  longevity of members of, 96–97
  rain shamanism among, 94–96
Winter (as a deity), 186
Winter rituals, 186
Winter solstice, in Orinoco Delta, 9
Wirimusebe, 80*n*
Wishimo, 121
Wishiratu, 63, 94, 101, 121, 122*n*, 237
  wisdom of, 250
Wishiratu-shaman, 116
Witoto Indians
  rainbow mythology of, 221–222
  weather interpretations of, 165
Women. *See also* Family structure; Menstruating women; Uxorilocal families
  as herbalists, 116–117
  at meals, 60*illus.*
  menstruating, 134
  as palm sago gatherers, 141–143, 142*illus.*, 151–153, 154–155
  Pleiades and, 80n, 80–81, 90

Index 363

postmenopausal, 91–92
as practitioners of weather
   magic, 164–165
in Warao guilds, 238–239
water spirits and, 134
Work teams, 232
World
   destruction of, 85
   Snake of Being encircling, 88
Writing, 232

Xexeu, 208
Xingú River, rain dances along, 177
Xingú-Tocantins region, rituals against atmospheric spirits in, 180–184

Yábura, 135
Yacuma, 171
Yagua Indians
   homeopathic weather magic of, 196
   weather-blowing among, 169
Yakúdenánsu plant, in homeopathic weather magic, 197
Yamana Indians
   homeopathic weather magic of, 191
   rituals against atmospheric spirits among, 185–186
   weather chants among, 175
Yanōmami Indians
   homeopathic weather magic of, 195–196
   origin myth of, 195–196
   rain deities of, 214
   thunder and lightning demons of, 211
   weather chants among, 176
   wind demons of, 200–201
Yekuana Indians, thunder and lightning demons of, 209, 211
Yoriquian, 226
Yúmi piripiri, 170
Yuracaré Indians
   rain deities of, 214
   rituals against atmospheric spirits among, 184
   thunder and lightning demons of, 204
Yurema root, 206
Yurupari, 150
Yurupary, 209

Zaparo Indians, weather-blowing among, 169
Zapata, Jaime, xxv
Zaragoza, Lorenzo de
   mission festivities described by, 233–234
Zones, of Orinoco Delta, 5–8